As a Reincarnated ARISTOCRAT, I'll Use My Appraisal Skill to Rise in the World

3

[Story] **Miraijin A**
[Art] **Natsumi Inoue**
[Character Design] **jimmy**

☆☆☆☆☆

CONTENTS

Chapter 18: A Storm Is Brewing!

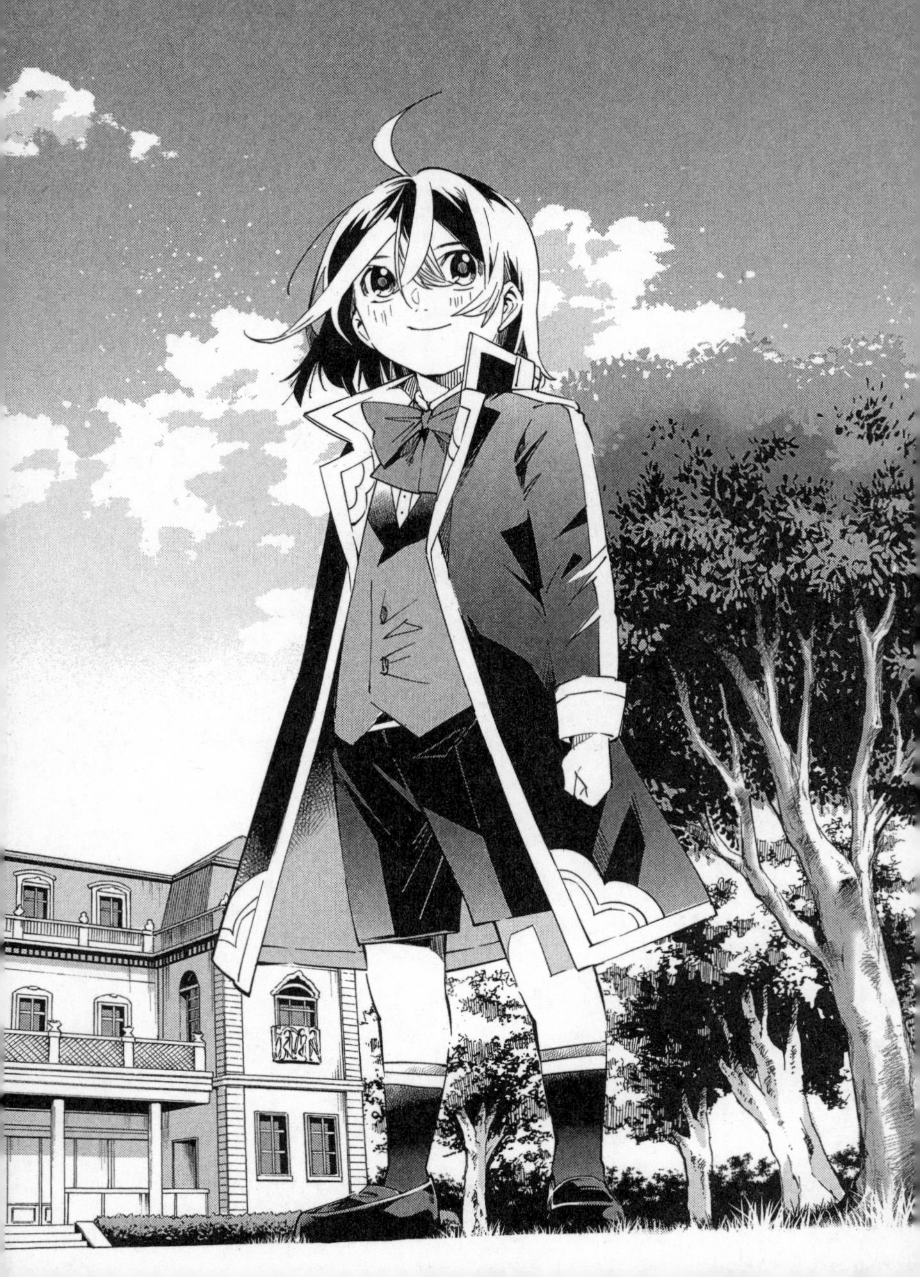

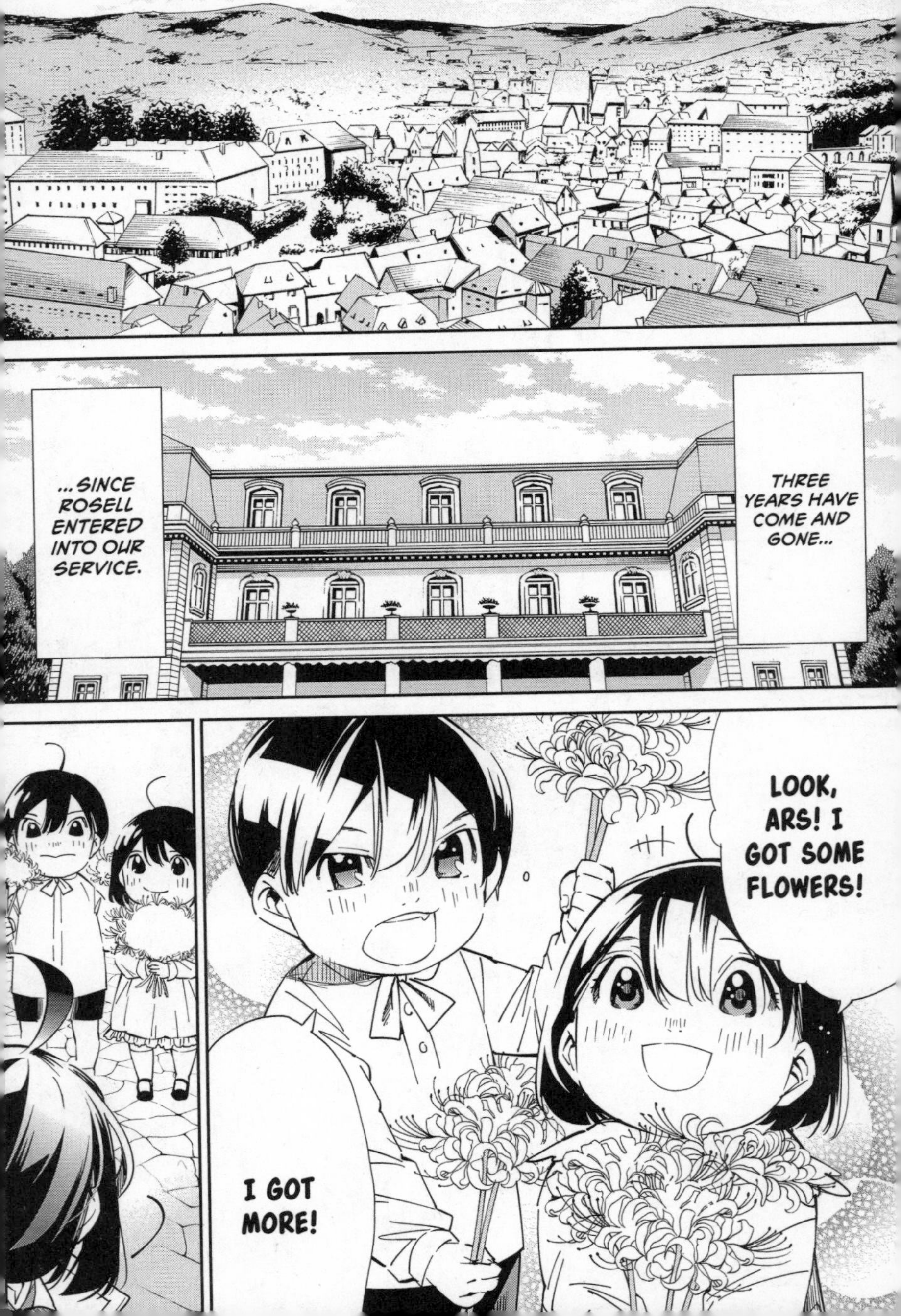
THREE YEARS HAVE COME AND GONE...
...SINCE ROSELL ENTERED INTO OUR SERVICE.
LOOK, ARS! I GOT SOME FLOWERS!
I GOT MORE!

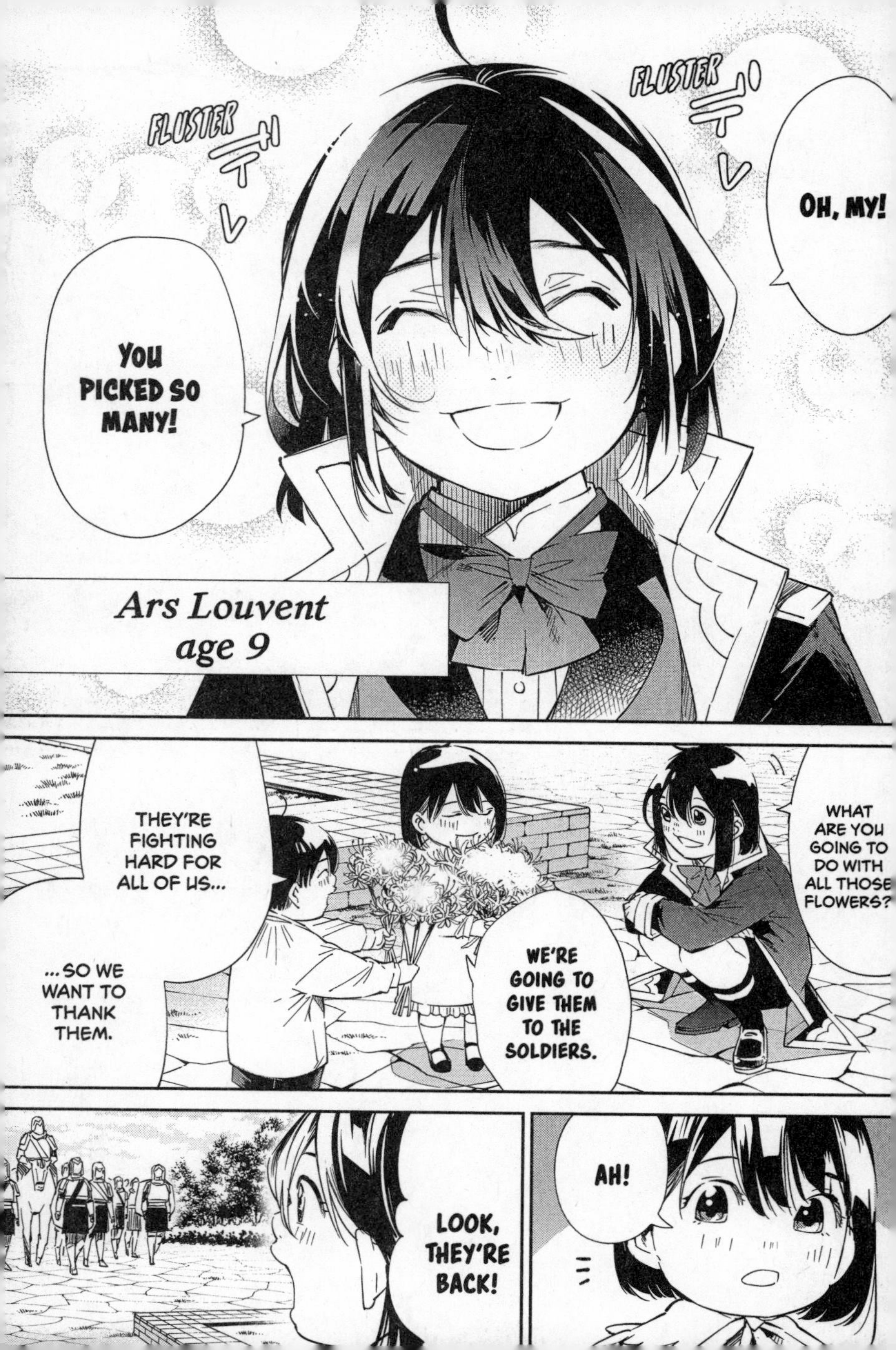
FLUSTER
OH, MY!
FLUSTER
YOU PICKED SO MANY!
Ars Louvent age 9
WHAT ARE YOU GOING TO DO WITH ALL THOSE FLOWERS?
WE'RE GOING TO GIVE THEM TO THE SOLDIERS.
THEY'RE FIGHTING HARD FOR ALL OF US...
...SO WE WANT TO THANK THEM.
AH!
LOOK, THEY'RE BACK!

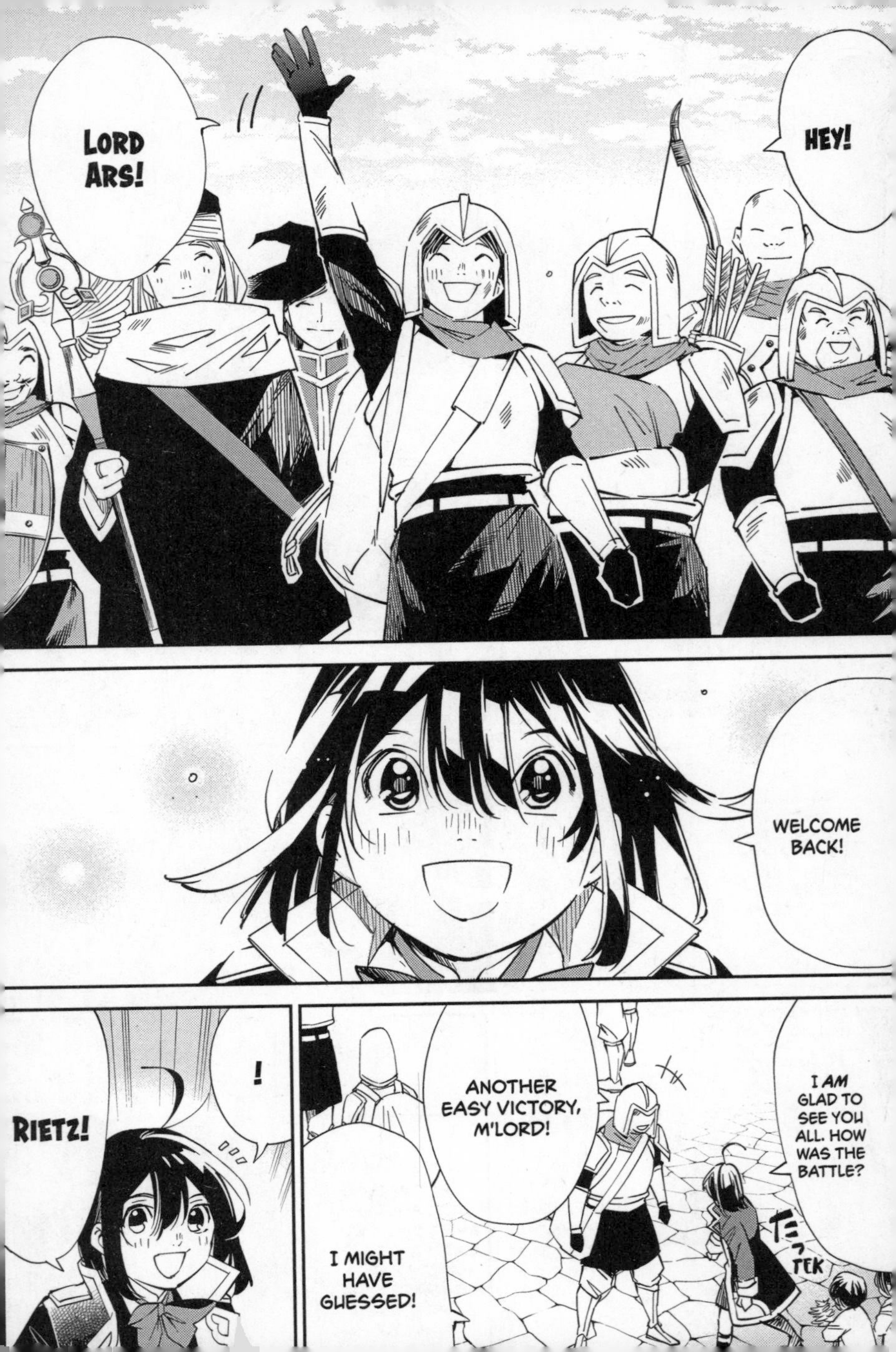
HEY!
LORD ARS!
WELCOME BACK!
I AM GLAD TO SEE YOU ALL. HOW WAS THE BATTLE?
TEK
ANOTHER EASY VICTORY, M'LORD!
I MIGHT HAVE GUESSED!
!
RIETZ!

★★★★★
Rietz Muses - Age 20 ♂

Stats	CURRENT	MAX
Command	9 5	9 9
Prowess	8 9	9 0
Intellect	9 5	9 9
Diplomacy	9 0	1 0 0
Ambition		2 1

Aptitude

Fighter	A	Cavalier	S	Archer	A
Mage	C	Engineer	S	Armorer	A
Mariner	D	Pilot	C	Tactician	S

MY LORD!

IT'S GOOD TO BE HOME.

THANKS TO HIM, WE'VE ENJOYED ONE VICTORY AFTER ANOTHER.

ALL THAT FIGHTING HAS SENT HIS PROWESS SOARING. HE'S GOTTEN STRONGER ALL AROUND!

OVER THE PAST THREE YEARS, RIETZ HAS STARTED GOING INTO BATTLE REGULARLY.

NO NEED, MY LORD.

IT IS AN HONOR TO FIGHT FOR YOU.

BETWEEN TUTORING ME AND GOING INTO BATTLE, YOU'VE HARDLY HAD A MOMENT'S REST. I CAN'T THANK YOU ENOUGH.

I'M SURE YOU MUST BE TIRED!

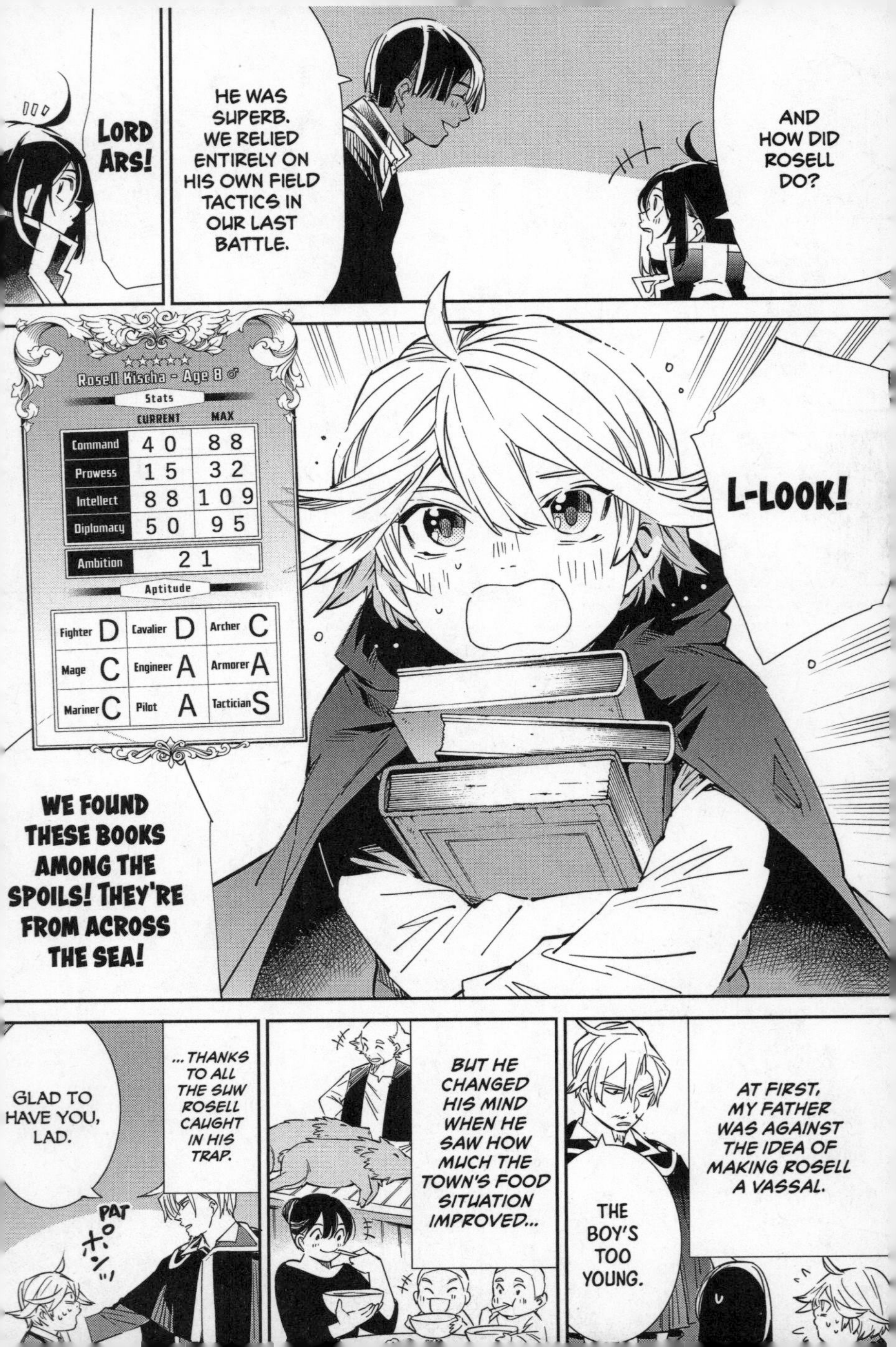
AND HOW DID ROSELL DO?
HE WAS SUPERB. WE RELIED ENTIRELY ON HIS OWN FIELD TACTICS IN OUR LAST BATTLE.
LORD ARS!
L-LOOK!
★★★★★
Rosell Kischa - Age 8 ♂
Stats
CURRENT MAX
Command 40 88
Prowess 15 32
Intellect 88 109
Diplomacy 50 95
Ambition 21
Aptitude
Fighter D Cavalier D Archer C
Mage C Engineer A Armorer A
Mariner C Pilot A Tactician S
WE FOUND THESE BOOKS AMONG THE SPOILS! THEY'RE FROM ACROSS THE SEA!
AT FIRST, MY FATHER WAS AGAINST THE IDEA OF MAKING ROSELL A VASSAL.
THE BOY'S TOO YOUNG.
BUT HE CHANGED HIS MIND WHEN HE SAW HOW MUCH THE TOWN'S FOOD SITUATION IMPROVED...
...THANKS TO ALL THE SUW ROSELL CAUGHT IN HIS TRAP.
GLAD TO HAVE YOU, LAD.
PAT

WHAT'S MORE, HIS BROTHERS HAVE TURNED OUT TO BE A FEARSOME PAIR ON THE BATTLEFIELD.

EEEK!

ROSELL HAS BEEN TAGGING ALONG WITH THE ARMY SO HE CAN GET FIRST-HAND STRATEGY LESSONS FROM RIETZ.

ROSELL'S STATS HAVE GONE UP STEADILY, TOO. I'M ESPECIALLY IMPRESSED BY HIS GROWTH AS A TACTICIAN.

HE'S STILL LEARNING, BUT HE'S ALREADY USING THAT QUICK MIND OF HIS TO COME UP WITH ALL SORTS OF NEW AND CLEVER IDEAS. EVEN RIETZ CAN'T HELP BEING AMAZED.

UP YOU GO! YOU LIKE THAT?

Charlotte Lace - Age 17 ♀

Stats

	CURRENT	MAX
Command	78	92
Prowess	103	116
Intellect	44	45
Diplomacy	36	40
Ambition	1	

Aptitude

Fighter	D	Cavalier	D	Archer	D
Mage	S	Engineer	D	Armorer	D
Mariner	D	Pilot	D	Tactician	D

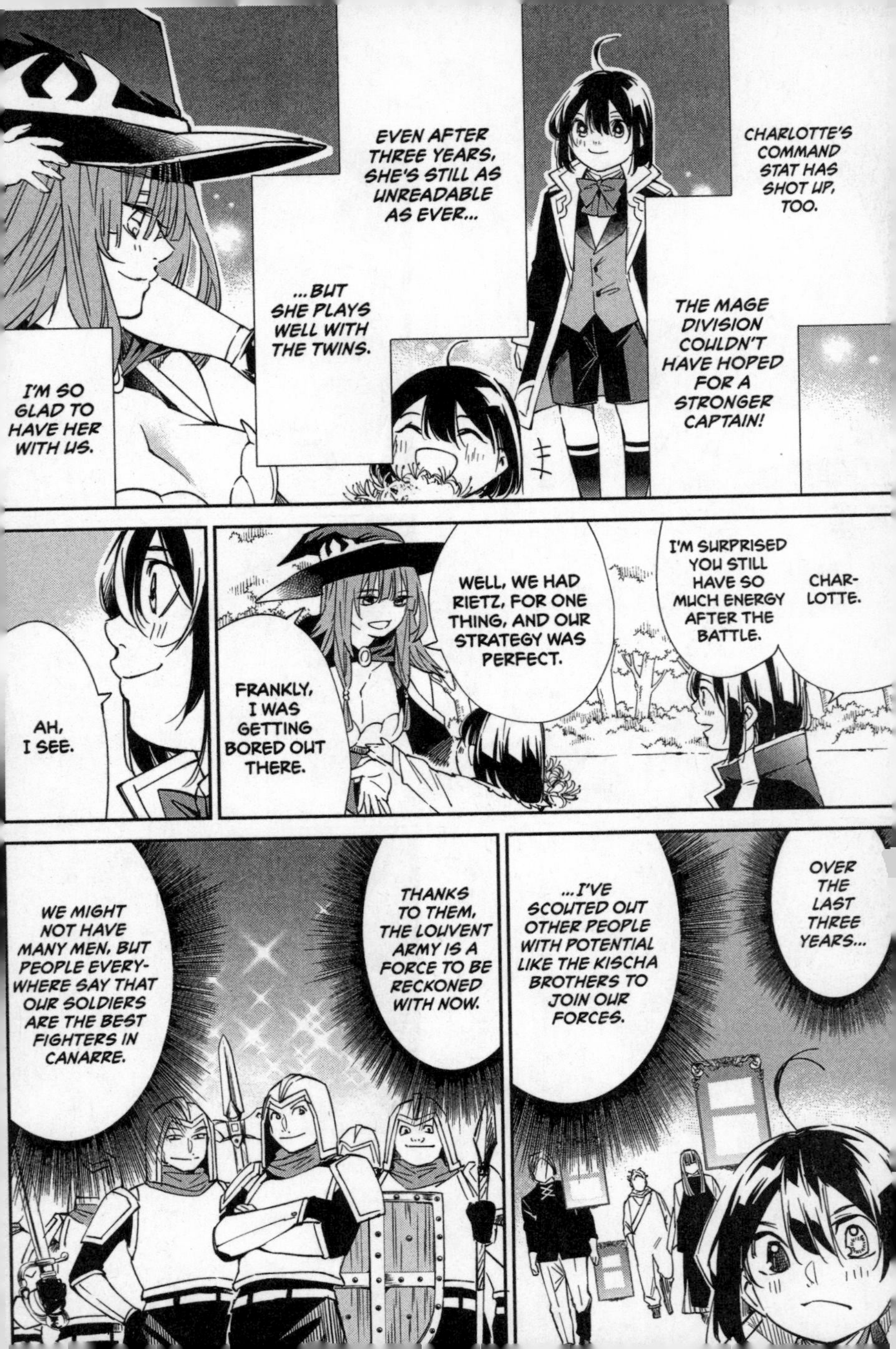
CHARLOTTE'S COMMAND STAT HAS SHOT UP, TOO.
THE MAGE DIVISION COULDN'T HAVE HOPED FOR A STRONGER CAPTAIN!
EVEN AFTER THREE YEARS, SHE'S STILL AS UNREADABLE AS EVER...
...BUT SHE PLAYS WELL WITH THE TWINS.
I'M SO GLAD TO HAVE HER WITH US.
CHAR-LOTTE.
I'M SURPRISED YOU STILL HAVE SO MUCH ENERGY AFTER THE BATTLE.
WELL, WE HAD RIETZ, FOR ONE THING, AND OUR STRATEGY WAS PERFECT.
FRANKLY, I WAS GETTING BORED OUT THERE.
AH, I SEE.
OVER THE LAST THREE YEARS...
...I'VE SCOUTED OUT OTHER PEOPLE WITH POTENTIAL LIKE THE KISCHA BROTHERS TO JOIN OUR FORCES.
THANKS TO THEM, THE LOUVENT ARMY IS A FORCE TO BE RECKONED WITH NOW.
WE MIGHT NOT HAVE MANY MEN, BUT PEOPLE EVERY-WHERE SAY THAT OUR SOLDIERS ARE THE BEST FIGHTERS IN CANARRE.

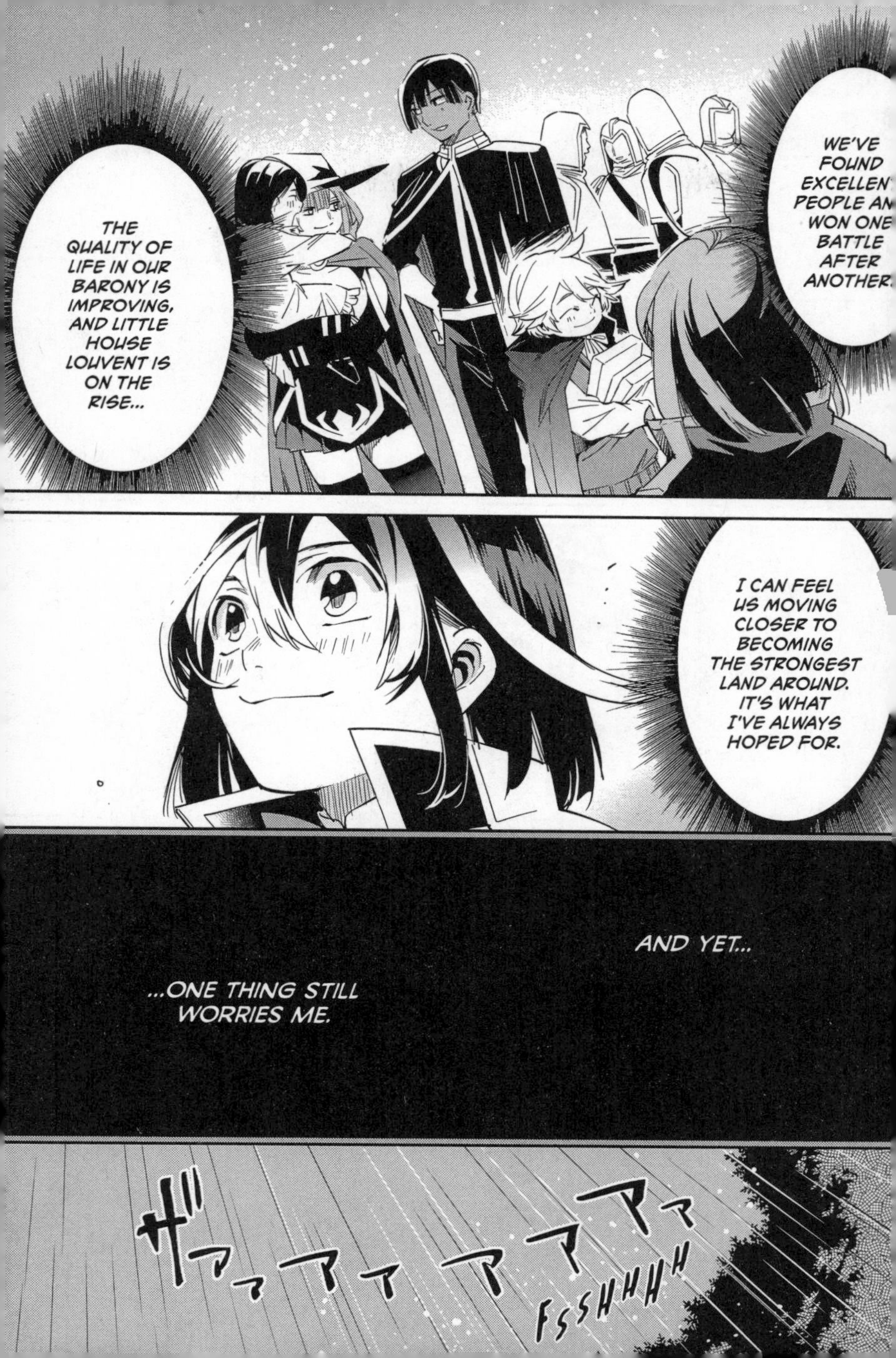
WE'VE FOUND EXCELLEN PEOPLE AN WON ONE BATTLE AFTER ANOTHER.
THE QUALITY OF LIFE IN OUR BARONY IS IMPROVING, AND LITTLE HOUSE LOUVENT IS ON THE RISE...
I CAN FEEL US MOVING CLOSER TO BECOMING THE STRONGEST LAND AROUND. IT'S WHAT I'VE ALWAYS HOPED FOR.
AND YET...
...ONE THING STILL WORRIES ME.
FSSHHHH

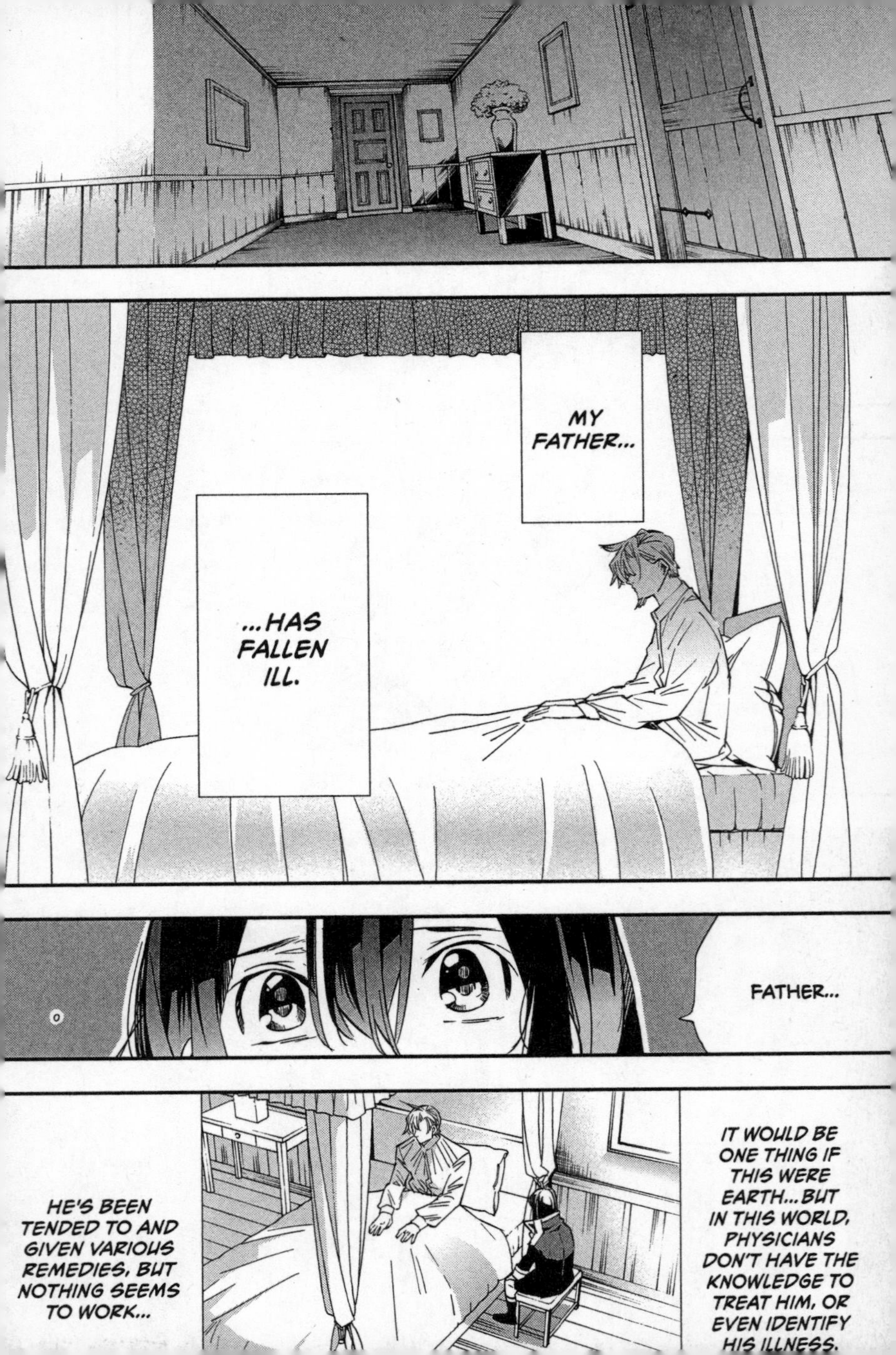
MY FATHER...
...HAS FALLEN ILL.
FATHER...
IT WOULD BE ONE THING IF THIS WERE EARTH... BUT IN THIS WORLD, PHYSICIANS DON'T HAVE THE KNOWLEDGE TO TREAT HIM, OR EVEN IDENTIFY HIS ILLNESS.
HE'S BEEN TENDED TO AND GIVEN VARIOUS REMEDIES, BUT NOTHING SEEMS TO WORK...

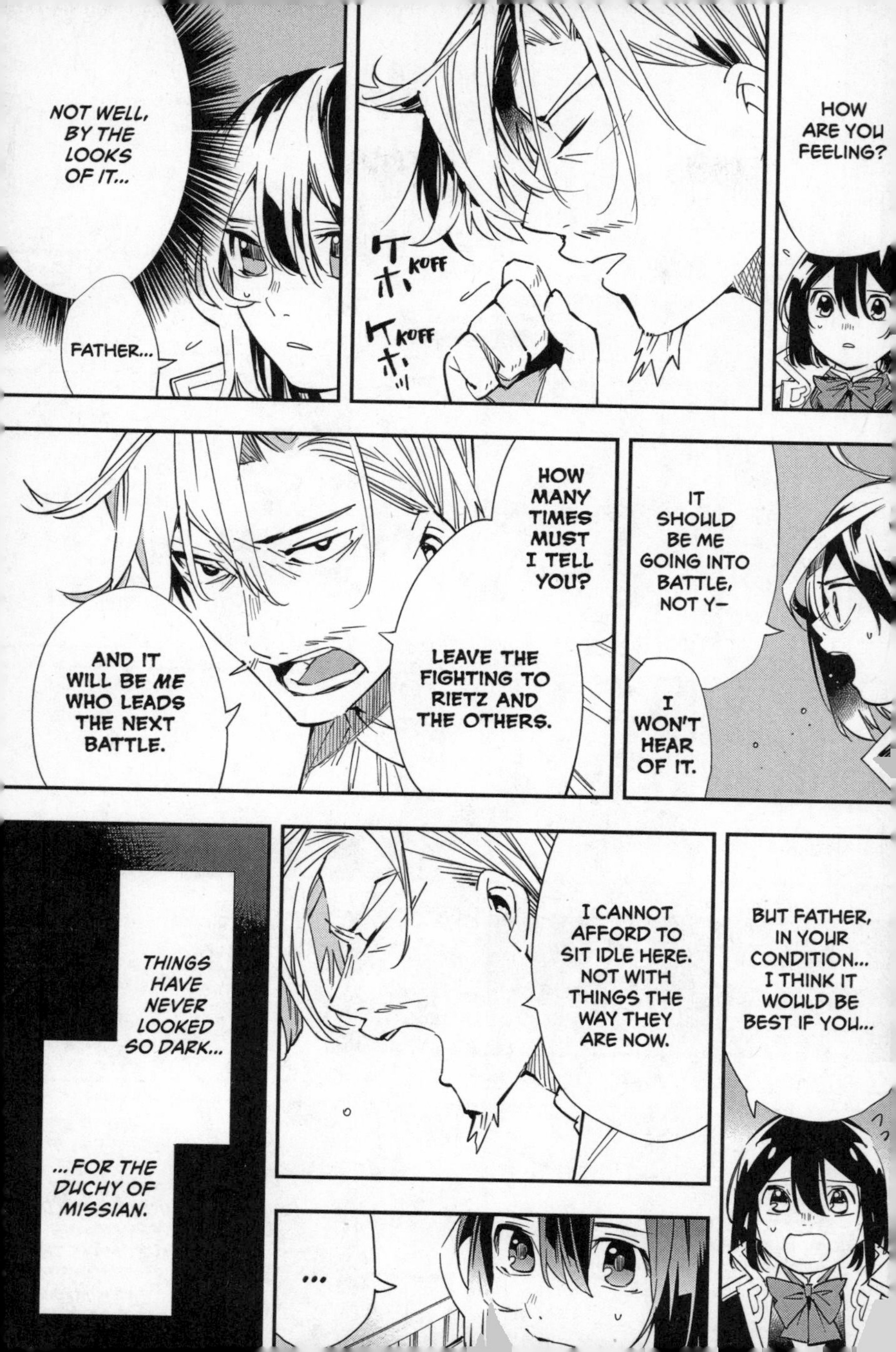
HOW ARE YOU FEELING?
KOFF
KOFF
NOT WELL, BY THE LOOKS OF IT...
FATHER...
IT SHOULD BE ME GOING INTO BATTLE, NOT Y—
I WON'T HEAR OF IT.
HOW MANY TIMES MUST I TELL YOU?
LEAVE THE FIGHTING TO RIETZ AND THE OTHERS.
AND IT WILL BE *ME* WHO LEADS THE NEXT BATTLE.
BUT FATHER, IN YOUR CONDITION... I THINK IT WOULD BE BEST IF YOU...
I CANNOT AFFORD TO SIT IDLE HERE. NOT WITH THINGS THE WAY THEY ARE NOW.
...
THINGS HAVE NEVER LOOKED SO DARK...
...FOR THE DUCHY OF MISSIAN.

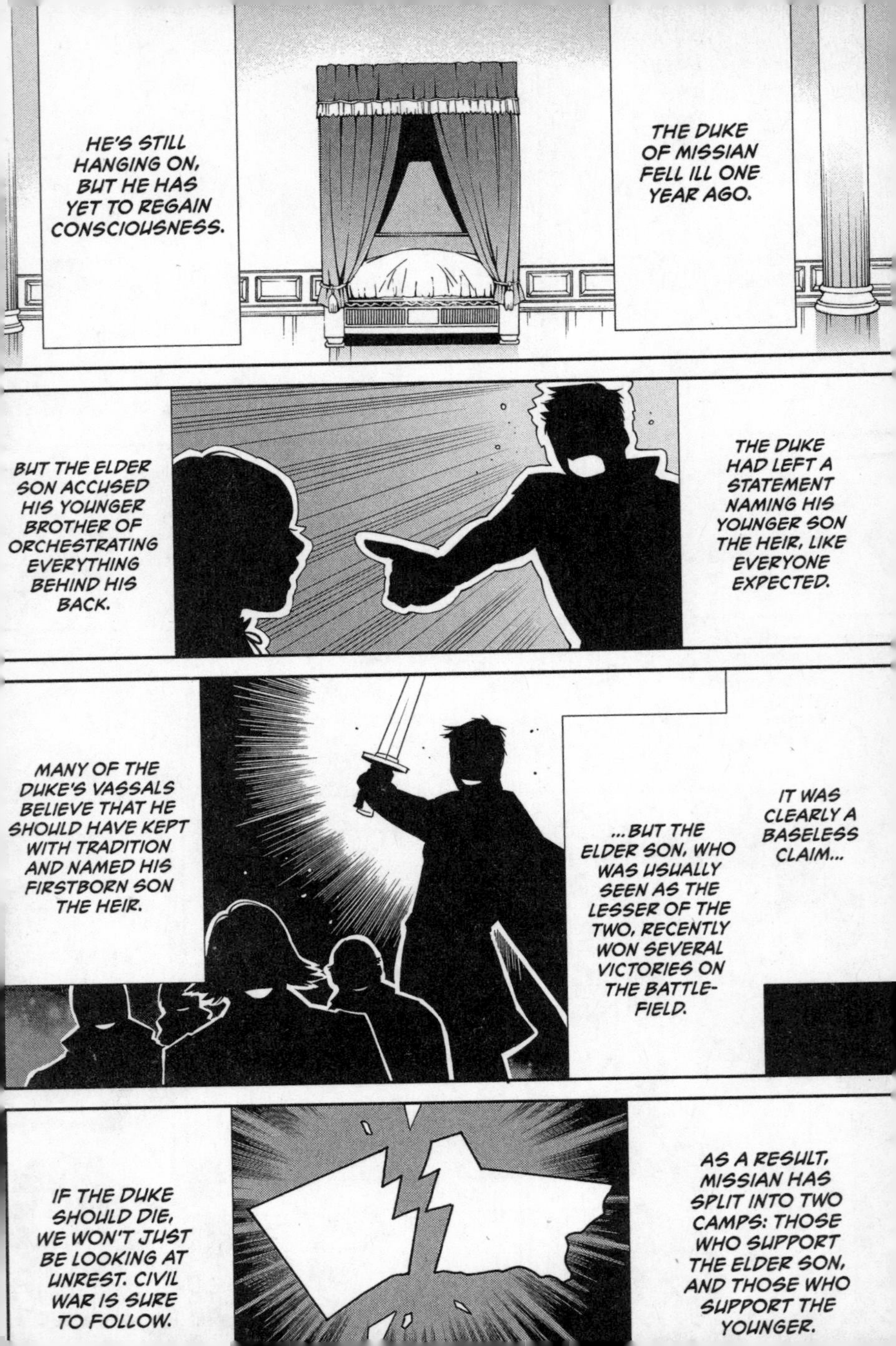
THE DUKE OF MISSIAN FELL ILL ONE YEAR AGO.
HE'S STILL HANGING ON, BUT HE HAS YET TO REGAIN CONSCIOUSNESS.
THE DUKE HAD LEFT A STATEMENT NAMING HIS YOUNGER SON THE HEIR, LIKE EVERYONE EXPECTED.
BUT THE ELDER SON ACCUSED HIS YOUNGER BROTHER OF ORCHESTRATING EVERYTHING BEHIND HIS BACK.
IT WAS CLEARLY A BASELESS CLAIM...
...BUT THE ELDER SON, WHO WAS USUALLY SEEN AS THE LESSER OF THE TWO, RECENTLY WON SEVERAL VICTORIES ON THE BATTLE-FIELD.
MANY OF THE DUKE'S VASSALS BELIEVE THAT HE SHOULD HAVE KEPT WITH TRADITION AND NAMED HIS FIRSTBORN SON THE HEIR.
AS A RESULT, MISSIAN HAS SPLIT INTO TWO CAMPS: THOSE WHO SUPPORT THE ELDER SON, AND THOSE WHO SUPPORT THE YOUNGER.
IF THE DUKE SHOULD DIE, WE WON'T JUST BE LOOKING AT UNREST. CIVIL WAR IS SURE TO FOLLOW.

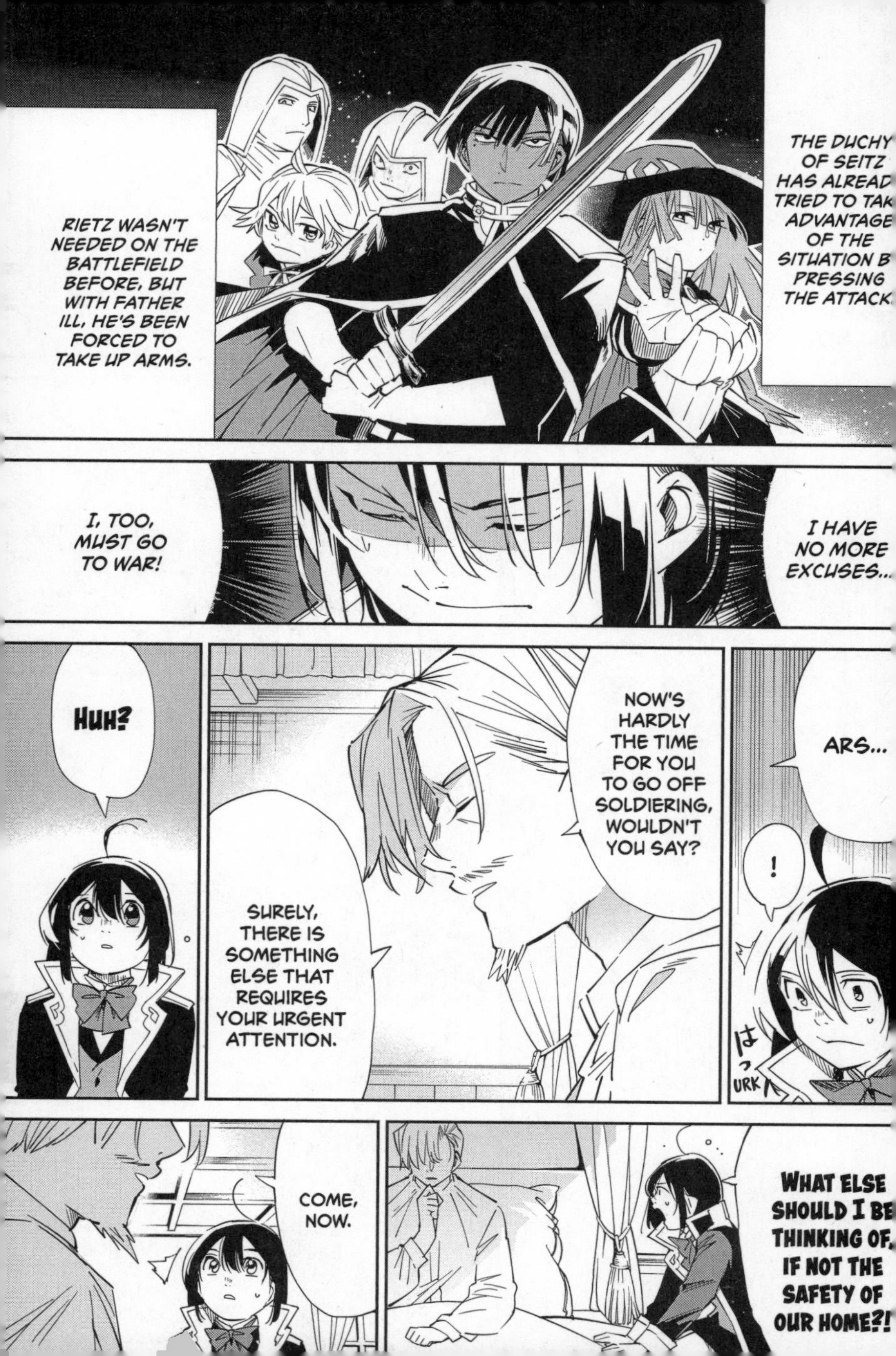
THE DUCHY OF SEITZ HAS ALREAD TRIED TO TAK ADVANTAGE OF THE SITUATION B PRESSING THE ATTACK.
RIETZ WASN'T NEEDED ON THE BATTLEFIELD BEFORE, BUT WITH FATHER ILL, HE'S BEEN FORCED TO TAKE UP ARMS.
I HAVE NO MORE EXCUSES...
I, TOO, MUST GO TO WAR!
ARS...
!
はっ
URK
NOW'S HARDLY THE TIME FOR YOU TO GO OFF SOLDIERING, WOULDN'T YOU SAY?
SURELY, THERE IS SOMETHING ELSE THAT REQUIRES YOUR URGENT ATTENTION.
HUH?
...
WHAT ELSE SHOULD I BE THINKING OF, IF NOT THE SAFETY OF OUR HOME?!
COME, NOW.

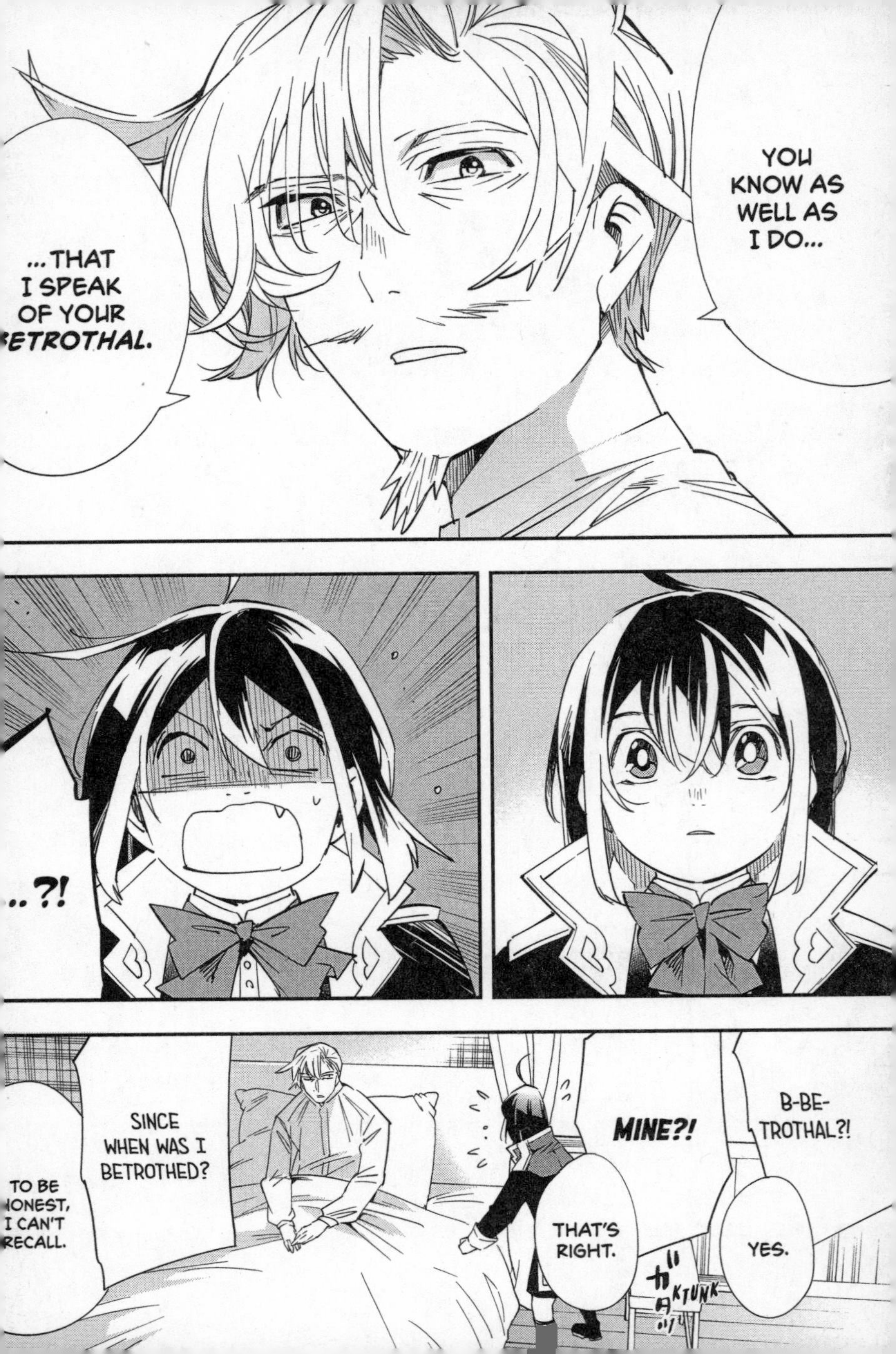
YOU KNOW AS WELL AS I DO...
...THAT I SPEAK OF YOUR ETROTHAL.
..?!
B-BE-TROTHAL?!
YES.
MINE?!
THAT'S RIGHT.
KTUNK
SINCE WHEN WAS I BETROTHED?
TO BE IONEST, I CAN'T RECALL.

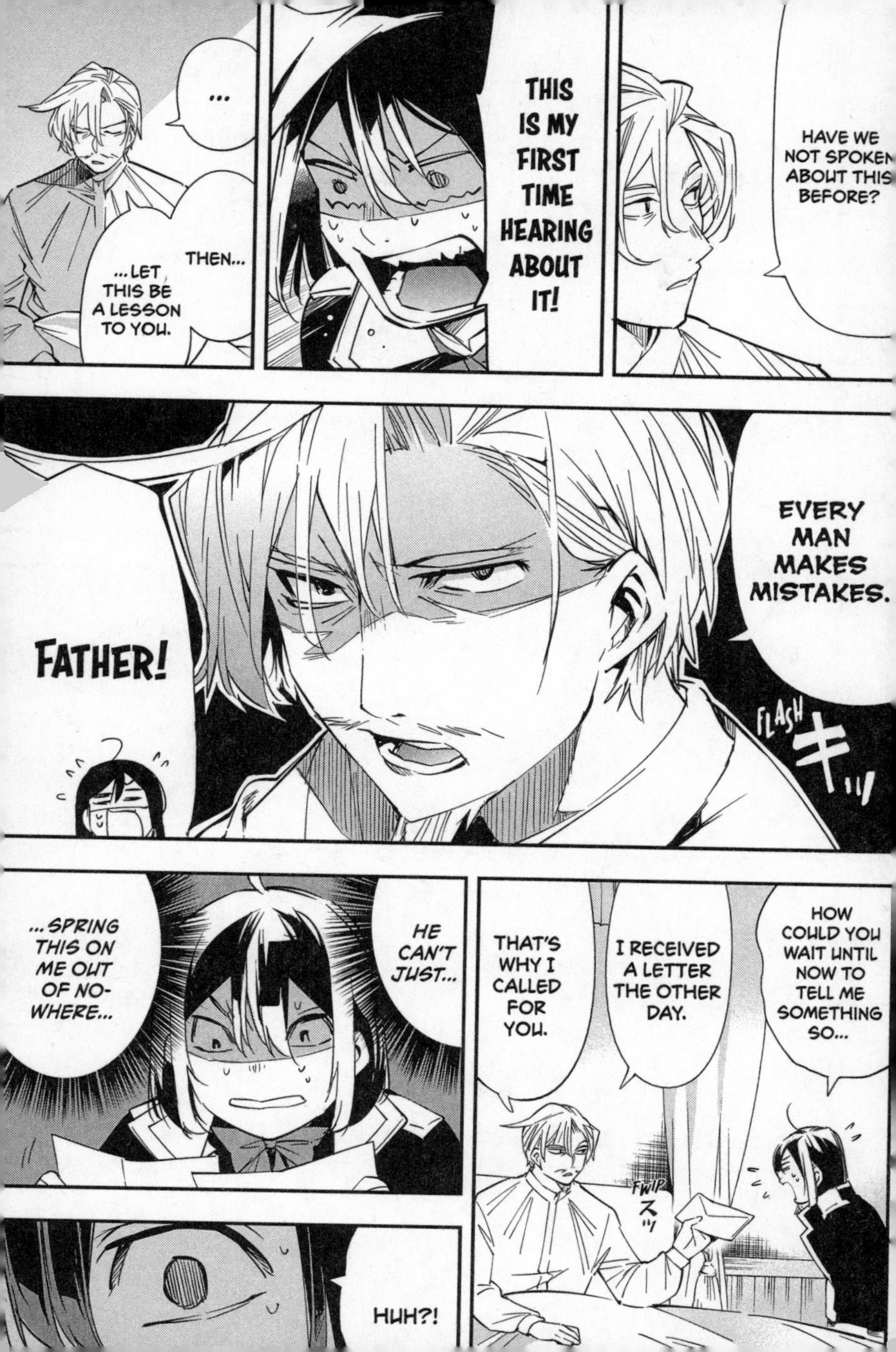
HAVE WE NOT SPOKEN ABOUT THIS BEFORE?
THIS IS MY FIRST TIME HEARING ABOUT IT!
...
THEN...
...LET THIS BE A LESSON TO YOU.
EVERY MAN MAKES MISTAKES.
FLASH
FATHER!
HOW COULD YOU WAIT UNTIL NOW TO TELL ME SOMETHING SO...
I RECEIVED A LETTER THE OTHER DAY.
THAT'S WHY I CALLED FOR YOU.
FWIP
HE CAN'T JUST...
...SPRING THIS ON ME OUT OF NO-WHERE...
HUH?!

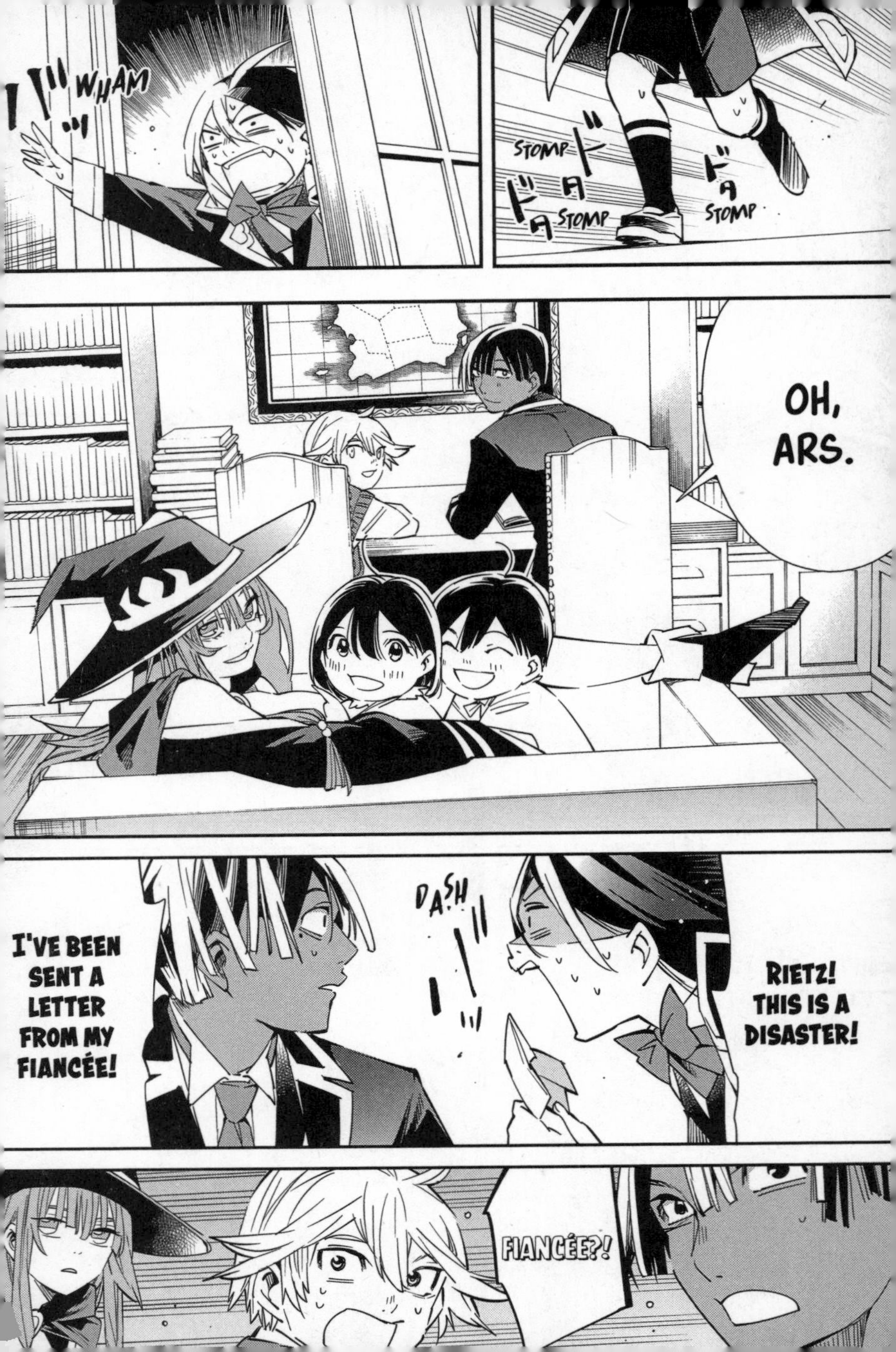
STOMP ドタ
ドタ STOMP
ドタ STOMP
WHAM
OH, ARS.
RIETZ! THIS IS A DISASTER!
DASH
I'VE BEEN SENT A LETTER FROM MY FIANCÉE!
FIANCÉE?!

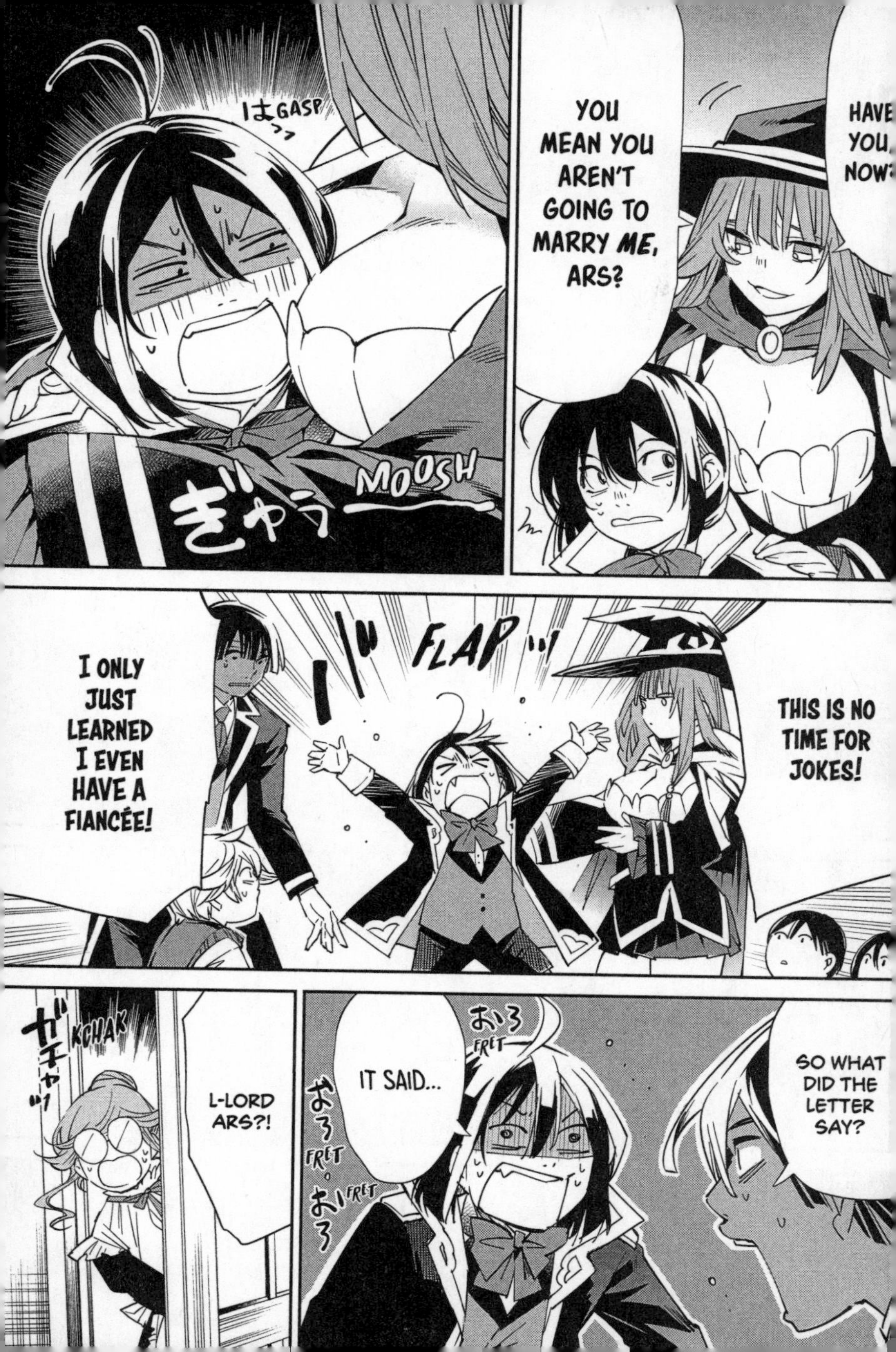
HAVE YOU, NOW
YOU MEAN YOU AREN'T GOING TO MARRY *ME*, ARS?
は GASP
ぎゅう MOOSH
THIS IS NO TIME FOR JOKES!
FLAP
I ONLY JUST LEARNED I EVEN HAVE A FIANCÉE!
SO WHAT DID THE LETTER SAY?
おろ FRET
IT SAID...
おろ FRET
おろ FRET
L-LORD ARS?!
ガチャ KCHAK

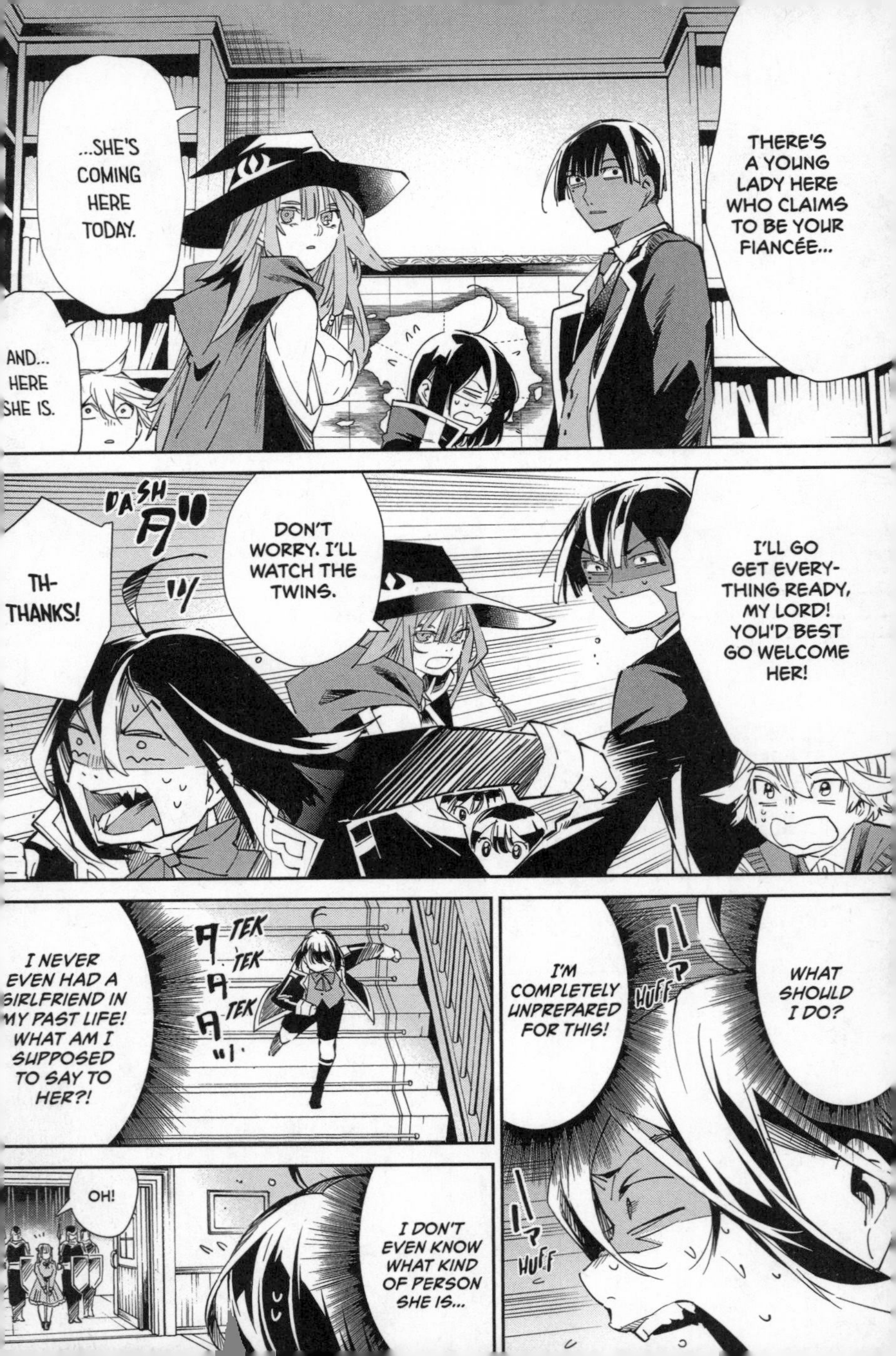
THERE'S A YOUNG LADY HERE WHO CLAIMS TO BE YOUR FIANCÉE...
...SHE'S COMING HERE TODAY.
AND... HERE SHE IS.
I'LL GO GET EVERY-THING READY, MY LORD! YOU'D BEST GO WELCOME HER!
DON'T WORRY. I'LL WATCH THE TWINS.
DASH
TH-THANKS!
WHAT SHOULD I DO?
HUFF
I'M COMPLETELY UNPREPARED FOR THIS!
HUFF
TEK TEK TEK
I NEVER EVEN HAD A GIRLFRIEND IN MY PAST LIFE! WHAT AM I SUPPOSED TO SAY TO HER?!
I DON'T EVEN KNOW WHAT KIND OF PERSON SHE IS...
OH!

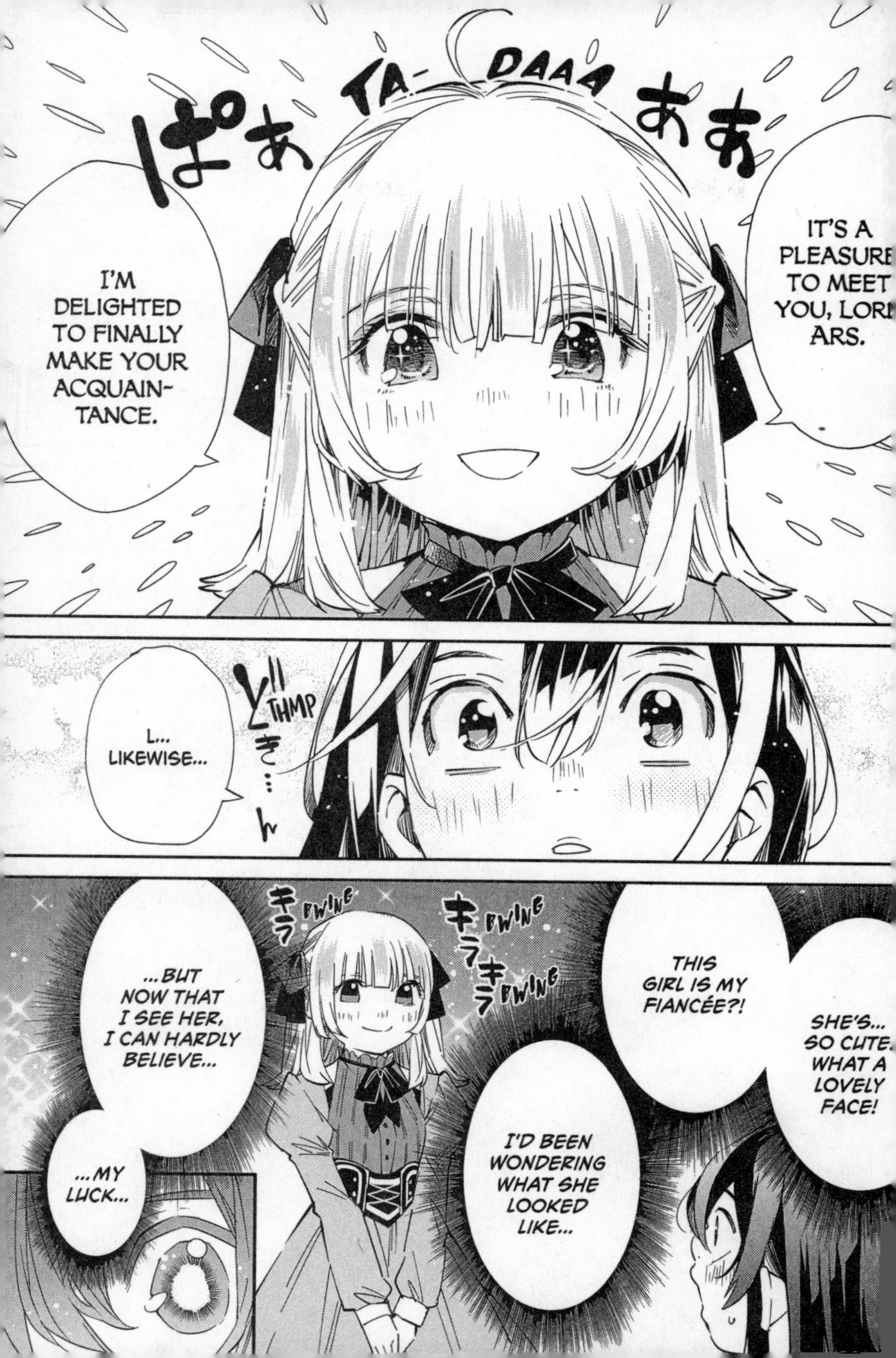
ぱぁああ
TA-DAAA
IT'S A PLEASURE TO MEET YOU, LORD ARS.
I'M DELIGHTED TO FINALLY MAKE YOUR ACQUAIN-TANCE.
どきん THMP
L... LIKEWISE...
SHE'S... SO CUTE. WHAT A LOVELY FACE!
THIS GIRL IS MY FIANCÉE?!
キラキラ BWING BWING
キラ BWING
I'D BEEN WONDERING WHAT SHE LOOKED LIKE...
...BUT NOW THAT I SEE HER, I CAN HARDLY BELIEVE...
...MY LUCK...

BEAM

★★★★★
Licia Pleide – Age 10 ♀

Stats

	CURRENT	MAX
Command	5	10
Prowess	5	10
Intellect	45	73
Diplomacy	77	100
Ambition	80	

Aptitude

Fighter	D	Cavalier	D	Archer	D
Mage	D	Engineer	D	Armorer	D
Mariner	D	Pilot	D	Tactician	B

...HUH?

DIPLOMACY, 100?!

AMBITION, 80...

KRAK

?

...IS ABSOLUTELY TERRIFYING!

IS SOMETHING WRONG?

THIS GIRL...

Chapter 19: The Promised Licia Pleide

☆☆☆☆☆
Licia Pleide - Age 10 ♀

Stats

	CURRENT	MAX
Command	5	10
Prowess	5	10
Intellect	45	73
Diplomacy	77	100

Ambition	80

Aptitude

Fighter	D	Cavalier	D	Archer	D
Mage	D	Engineer	D	Armorer	D
Mariner	D	Pilot	D	Tactician	B

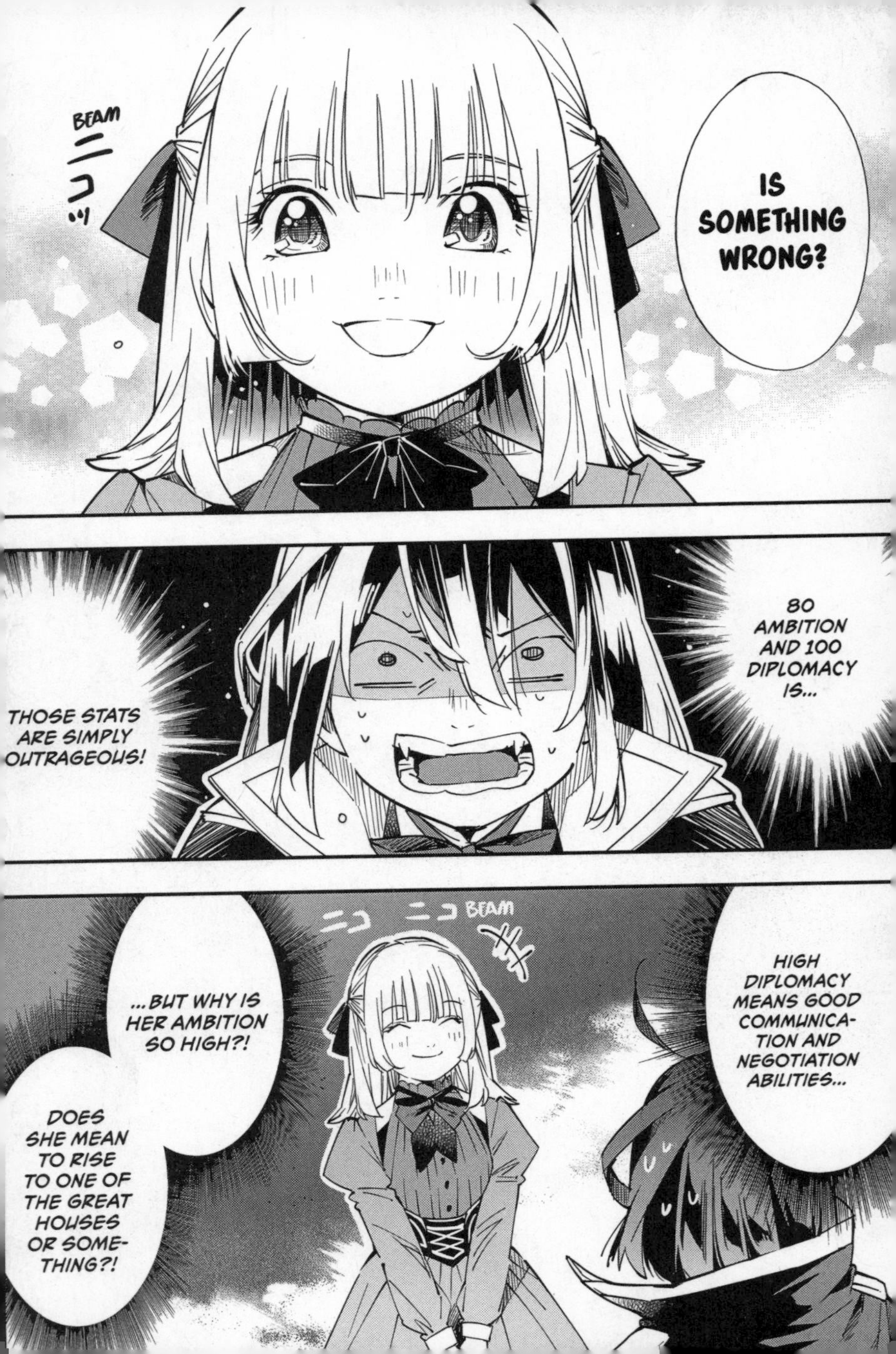
IS SOMETHING WRONG?
ニコッ
BEAM
80 AMBITION AND 100 DIPLOMACY IS...
THOSE STATS ARE SIMPLY OUTRAGEOUS!
HIGH DIPLOMACY MEANS GOOD COMMUNICA-TION AND NEGOTIATION ABILITIES...
ニコ ニコ
BEAM
...BUT WHY IS HER AMBITION SO HIGH?!
DOES SHE MEAN TO RISE TO ONE OF THE GREAT HOUSES OR SOME-THING?!

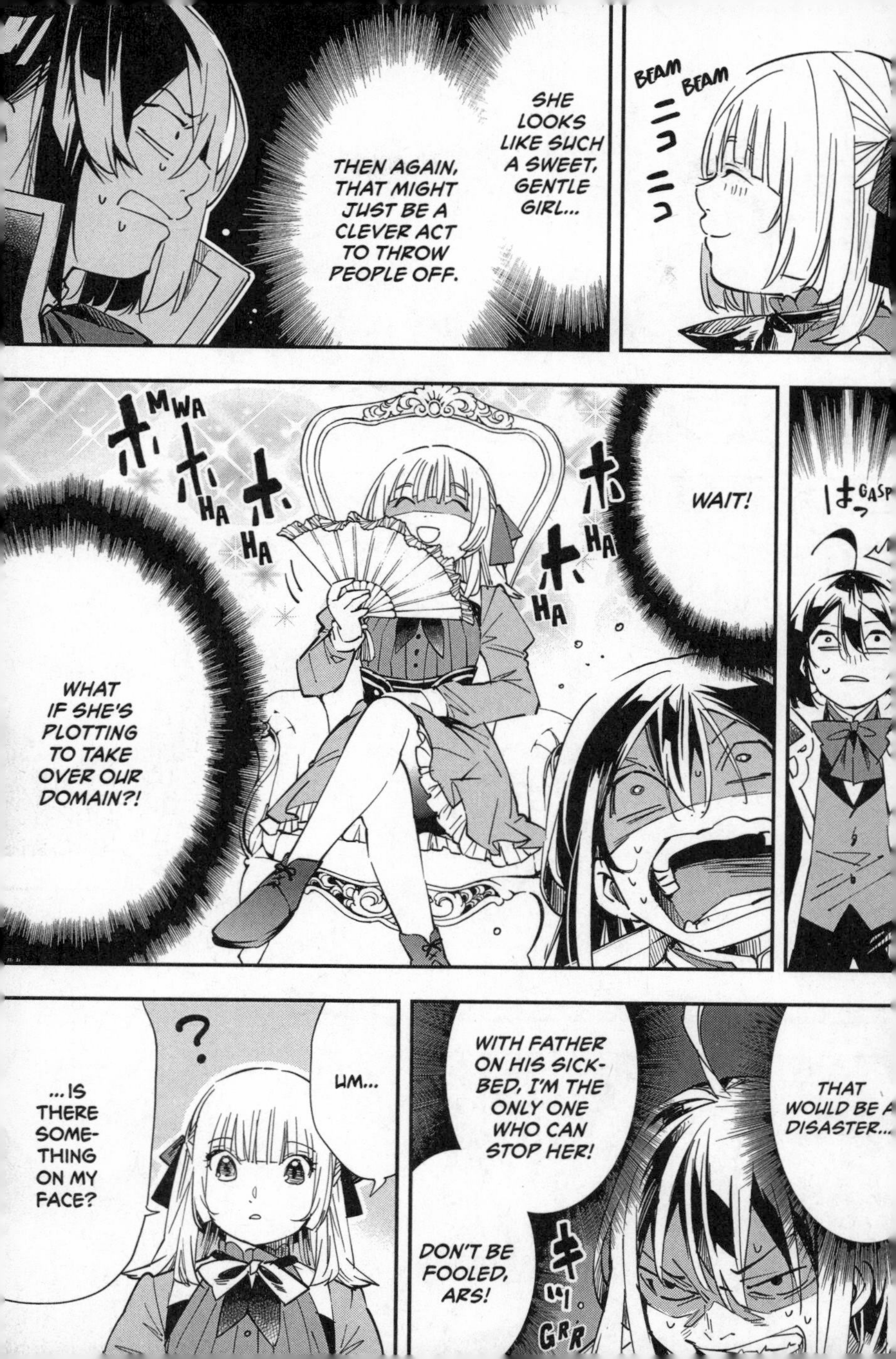
BEAM BEAM
SHE LOOKS LIKE SUCH A SWEET, GENTLE GIRL...
THEN AGAIN, THAT MIGHT JUST BE A CLEVER ACT TO THROW PEOPLE OFF.
GASP
WAIT!
HA HA
MWA HA HA HA
WHAT IF SHE'S PLOTTING TO TAKE OVER OUR DOMAIN?!
THAT WOULD BE A DISASTER...
WITH FATHER ON HIS SICK-BED, I'M THE ONLY ONE WHO CAN STOP HER!
DON'T BE FOOLED, ARS!
GRR
UM...
?
...IS THERE SOME-THING ON MY FACE?

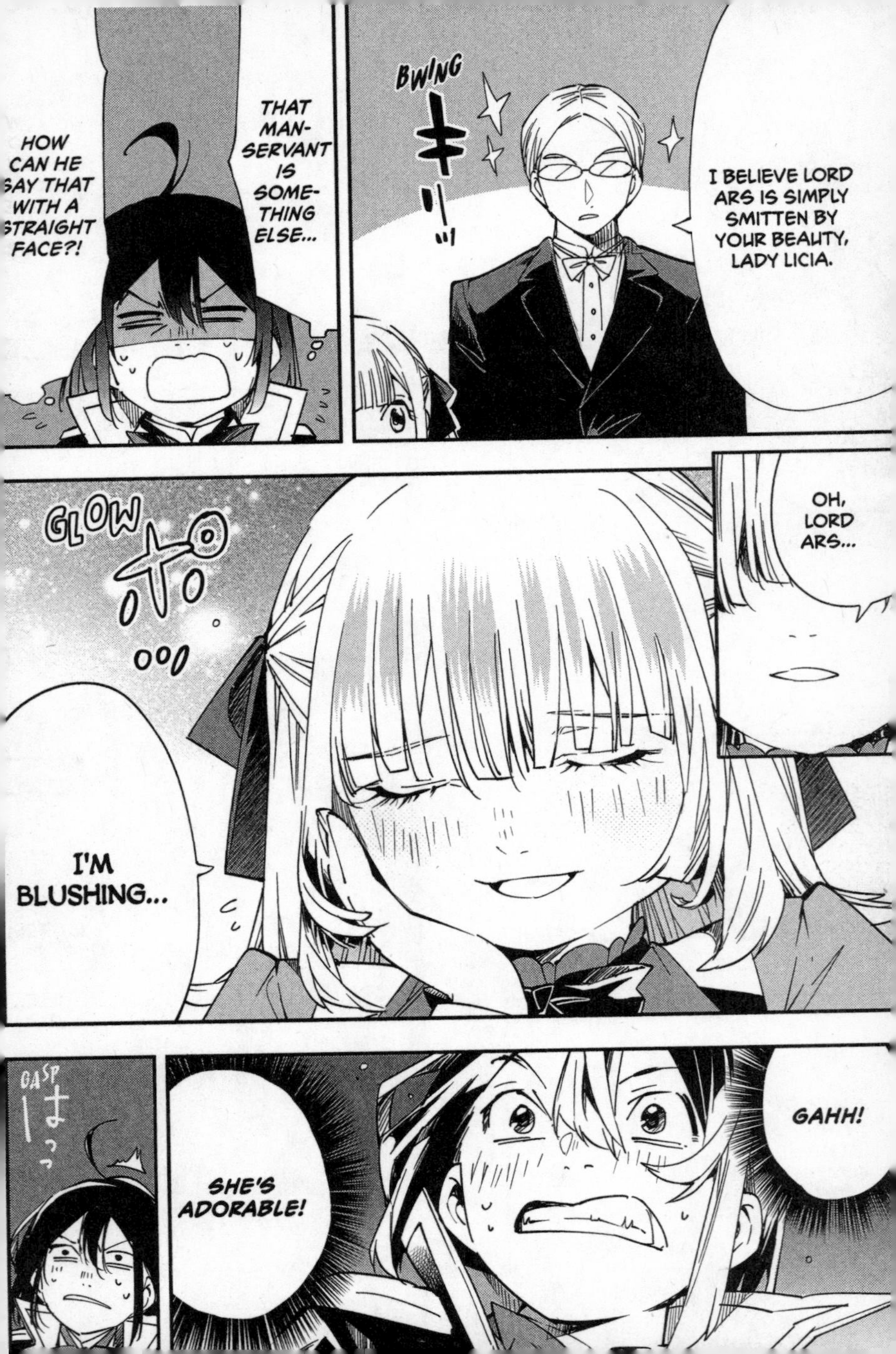
I BELIEVE LORD ARS IS SIMPLY SMITTEN BY YOUR BEAUTY, LADY LICIA.
BWING
THAT MAN-SERVANT IS SOME-THING ELSE...
HOW CAN HE SAY THAT WITH A STRAIGHT FACE?!
OH, LORD ARS...
GLOW
I'M BLUSHING...
GAHH!
SHE'S ADORABLE!
GASP

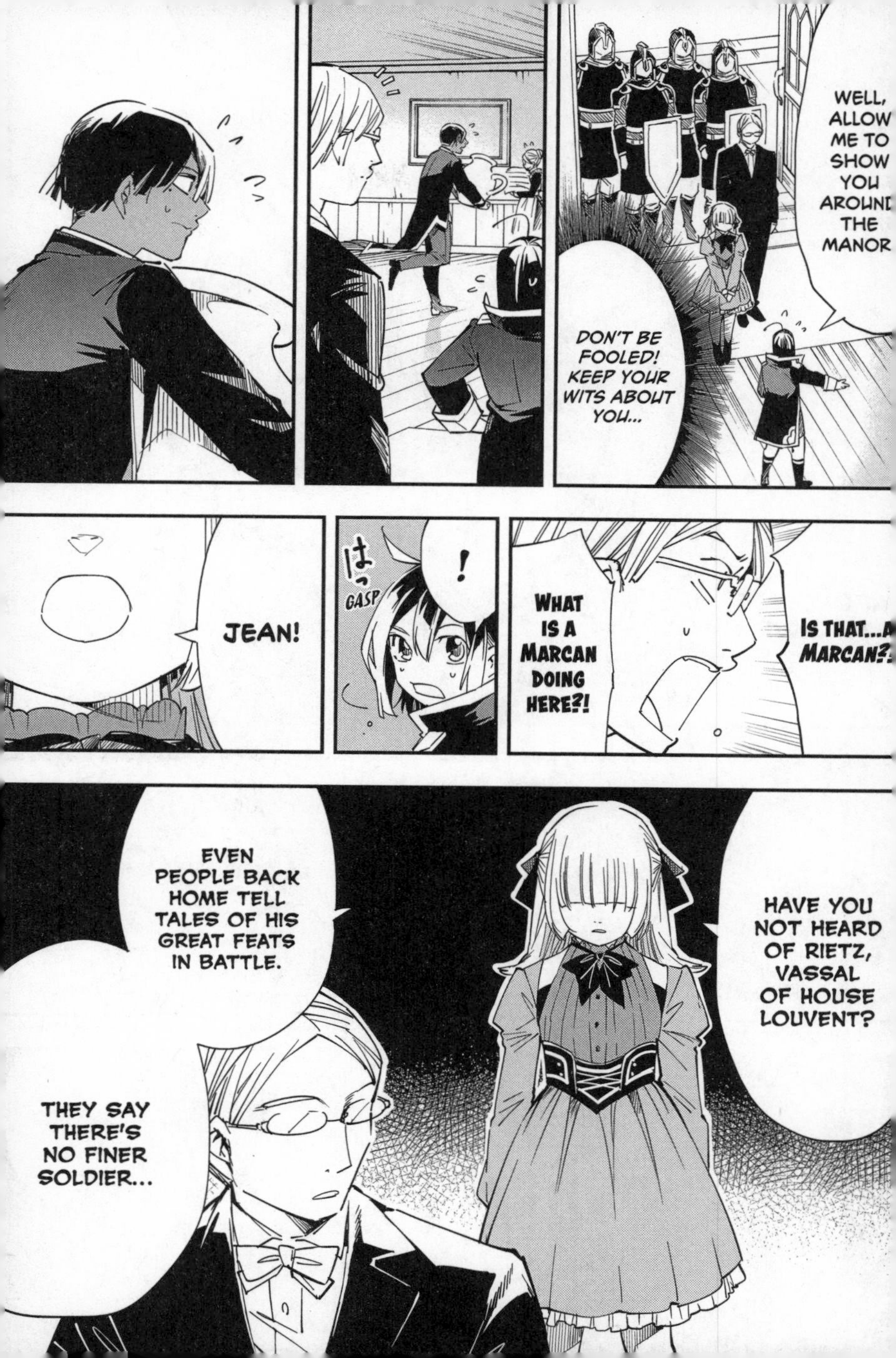

WELL, ALLOW ME TO SHOW YOU AROUND THE MANOR
DON'T BE FOOLED! KEEP YOUR WITS ABOUT YOU...
IS THAT...A MARCAN?!
WHAT IS A MARCAN DOING HERE?!
!
はっ
GASP
JEAN!
HAVE YOU NOT HEARD OF RIETZ, VASSAL OF HOUSE LOUVENT?
EVEN PEOPLE BACK HOME TELL TALES OF HIS GREAT FEATS IN BATTLE.
THEY SAY THERE'S NO FINER SOLDIER...

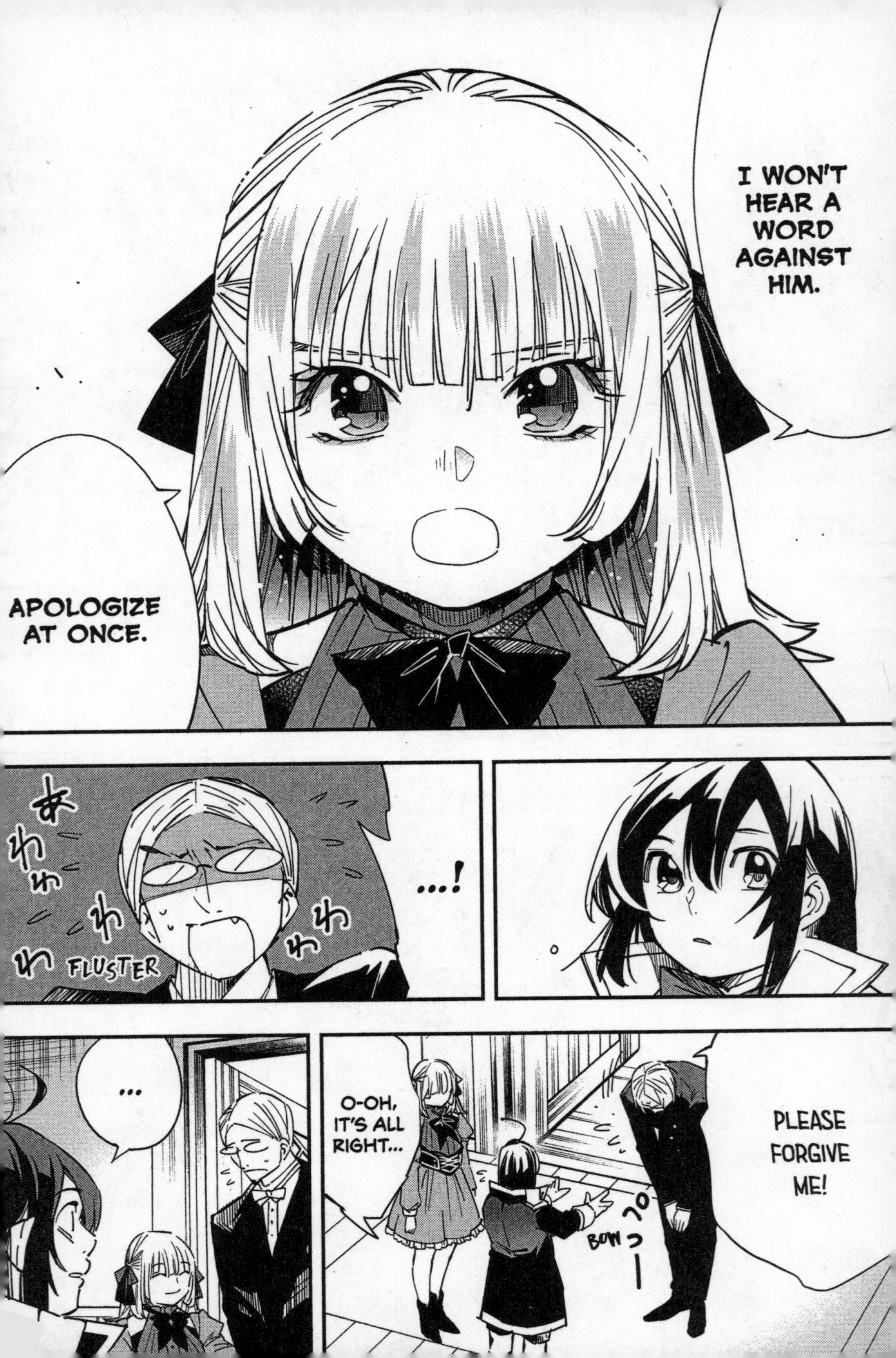
I WON'T HEAR A WORD AGAINST HIM.
APOLOGIZE AT ONCE.
...!
あわわわわわわ
FLUSTER
PLEASE FORGIVE ME!
BOW
O-OH, IT'S ALL RIGHT...
...

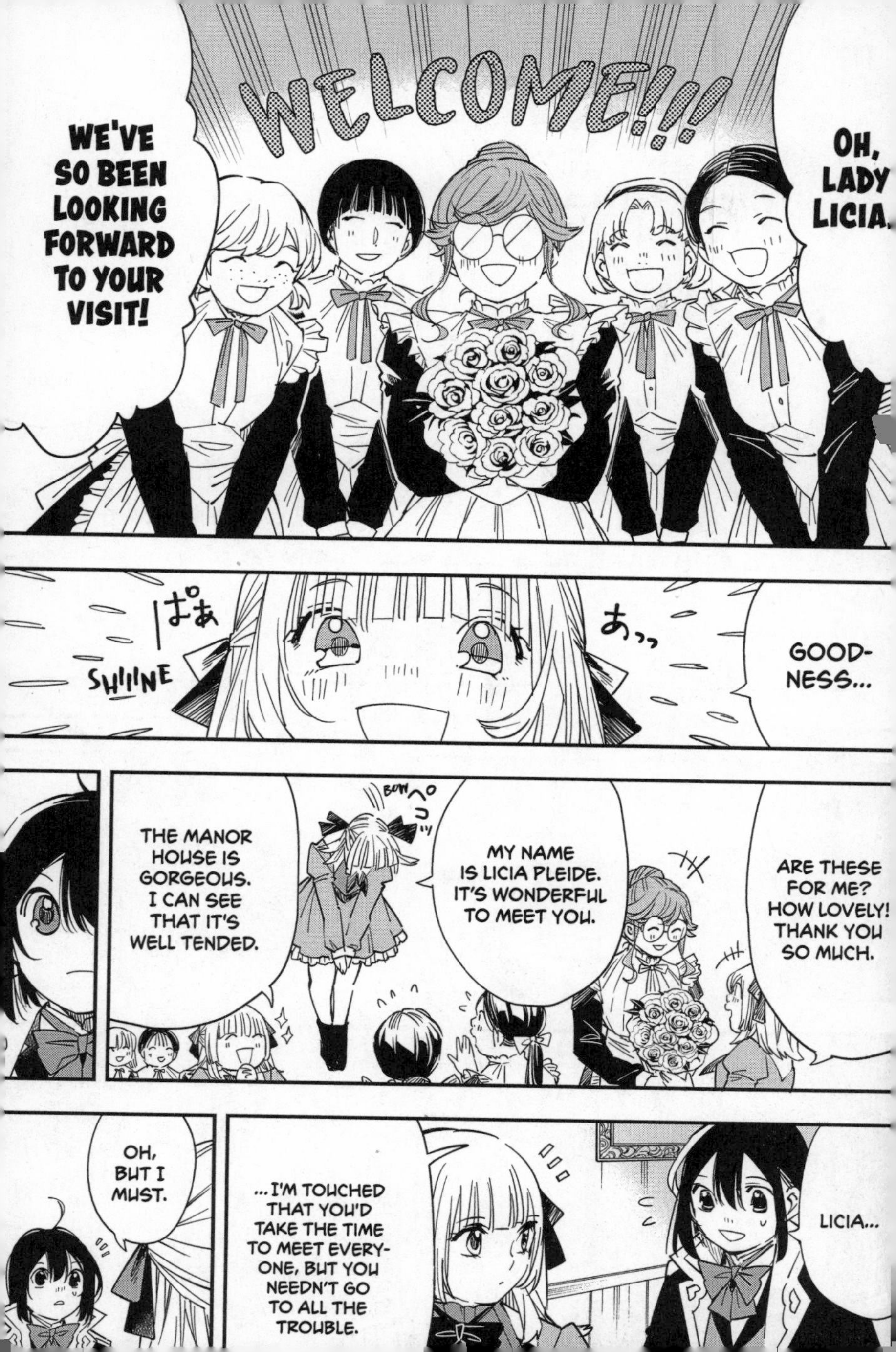
WELCOME!!!
OH, LADY LICIA.
WE'VE SO BEEN LOOKING FORWARD TO YOUR VISIT!
GOOD-NESS...
あっっ
ぱぁ
SHIIINE
ARE THESE FOR ME? HOW LOVELY! THANK YOU SO MUCH.
MY NAME IS LICIA PLEIDE. IT'S WONDERFUL TO MEET YOU.
BOW
ぺこっ
THE MANOR HOUSE IS GORGEOUS. I CAN SEE THAT IT'S WELL TENDED.
LICIA...
...I'M TOUCHED THAT YOU'D TAKE THE TIME TO MEET EVERY-ONE, BUT YOU NEEDN'T GO TO ALL THE TROUBLE.
OH, BUT I MUST.

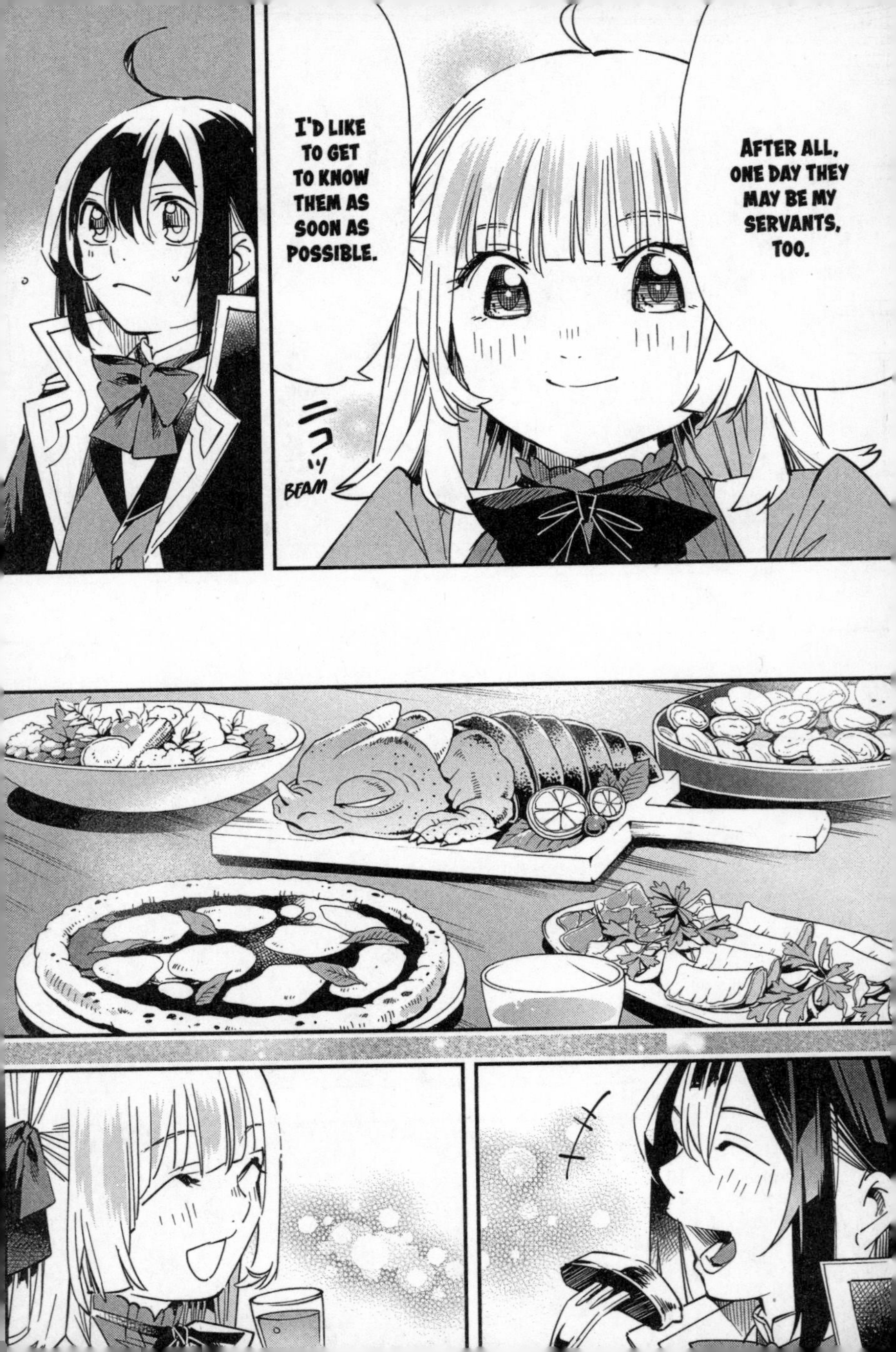
AFTER ALL, ONE DAY THEY MAY BE MY SERVANTS, TOO.
I'D LIKE TO GET TO KNOW THEM AS SOON AS POSSIBLE.
ニコッ
BEAM

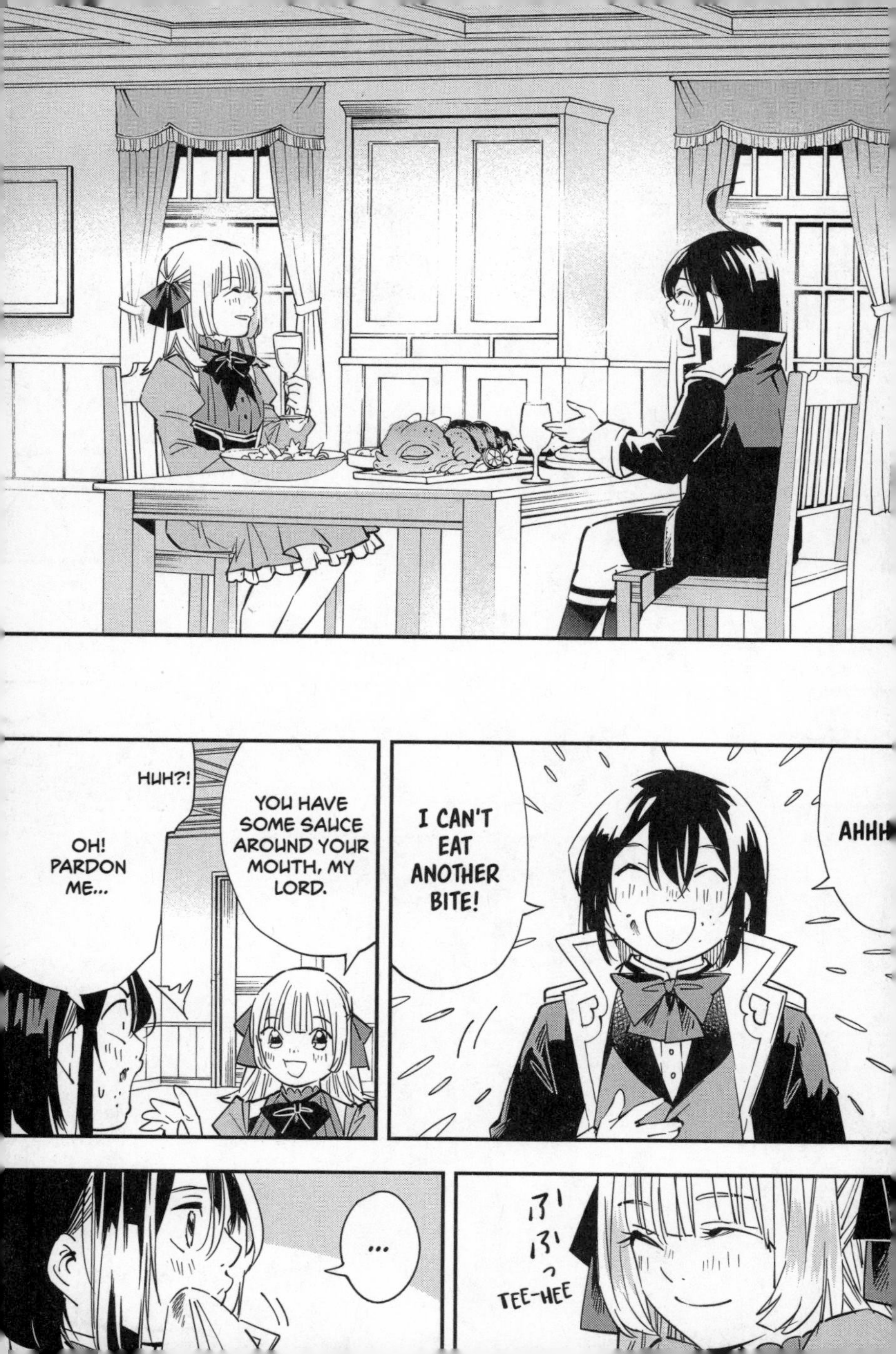
AHHH
I CAN'T EAT ANOTHER BITE!
YOU HAVE SOME SAUCE AROUND YOUR MOUTH, MY LORD.
HUH?!
OH! PARDON ME...
ふふっ
TEE-HEE
...

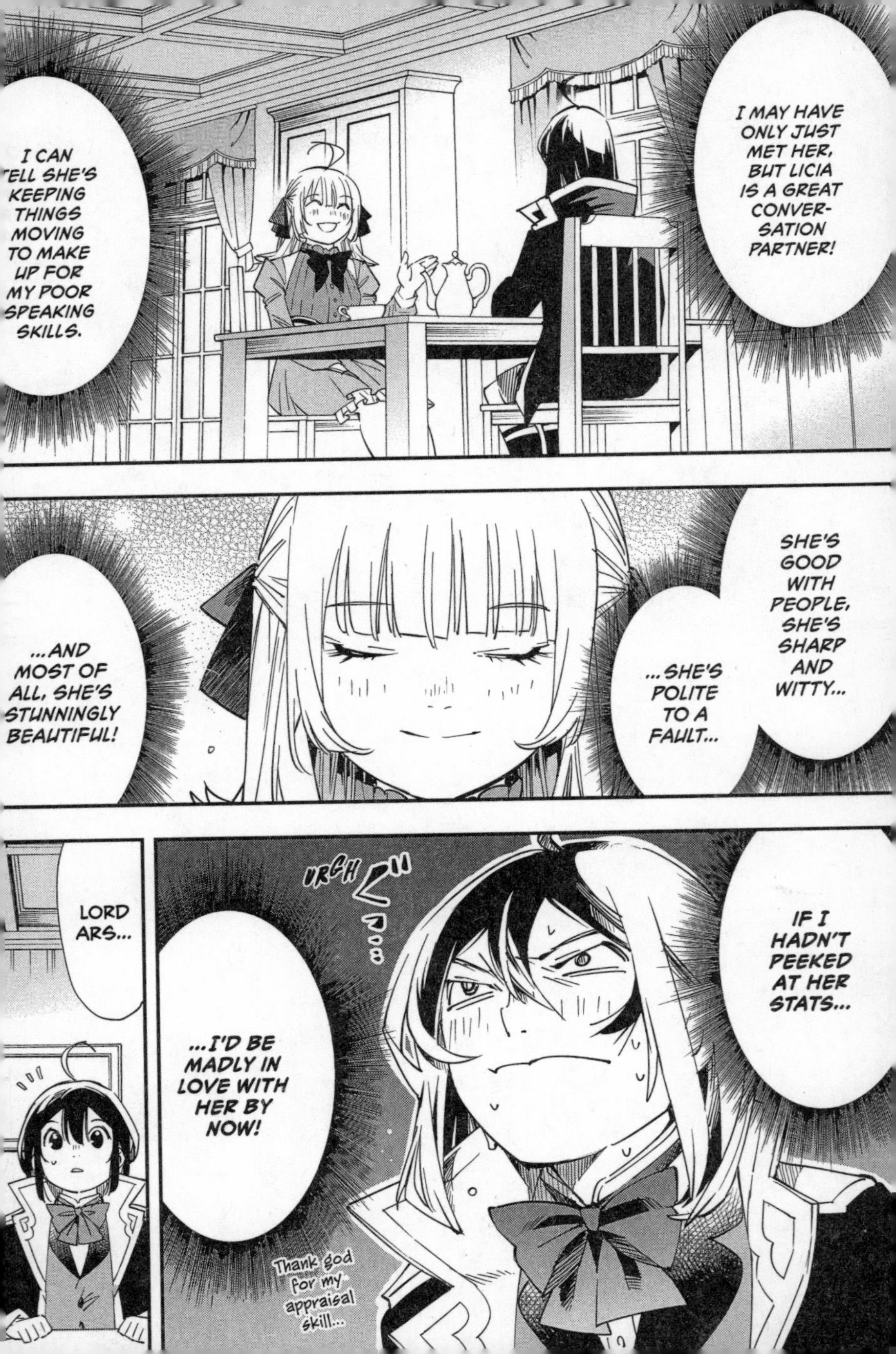
I MAY HAVE ONLY JUST MET HER, BUT LICIA IS A GREAT CONVER-SATION PARTNER!
I CAN TELL SHE'S KEEPING THINGS MOVING TO MAKE UP FOR MY POOR SPEAKING SKILLS.
SHE'S GOOD WITH PEOPLE, SHE'S SHARP AND WITTY...
...SHE'S POLITE TO A FAULT...
...AND MOST OF ALL, SHE'S STUNNINGLY BEAUTIFUL!
IF I HADN'T PEEKED AT HER STATS...
URGH
...I'D BE MADLY IN LOVE WITH HER BY NOW!
Thank god for my appraisal skill...
LORD ARS...

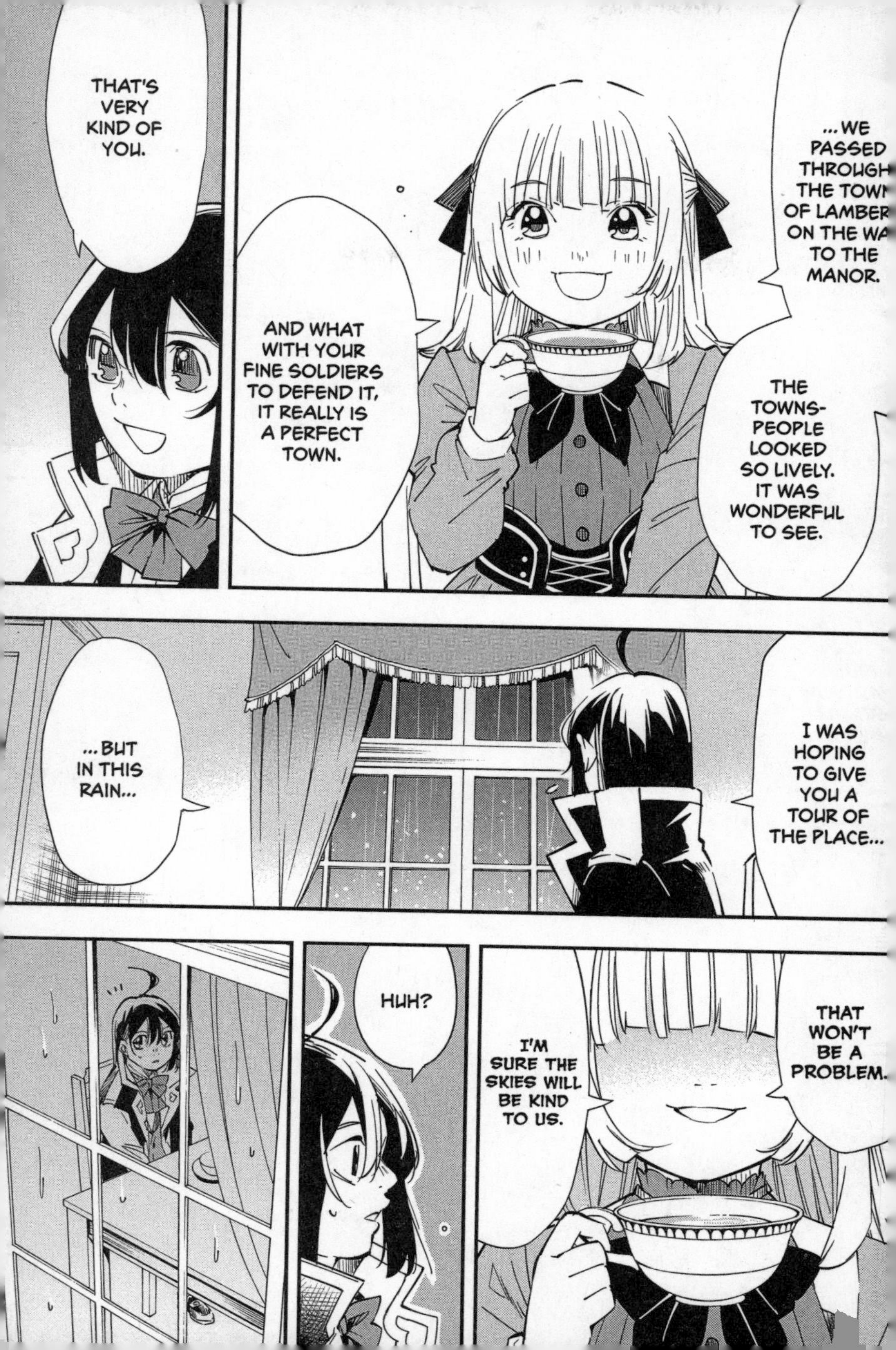
...WE PASSED THROUGH THE TOWN OF LAMBER ON THE WA TO THE MANOR.
THE TOWNS-PEOPLE LOOKED SO LIVELY. IT WAS WONDERFUL TO SEE.
AND WHAT WITH YOUR FINE SOLDIERS TO DEFEND IT, IT REALLY IS A PERFECT TOWN.
THAT'S VERY KIND OF YOU.
I WAS HOPING TO GIVE YOU A TOUR OF THE PLACE...
...BUT IN THIS RAIN...
THAT WON'T BE A PROBLEM.
I'M SURE THE SKIES WILL BE KIND TO US.
HUH?

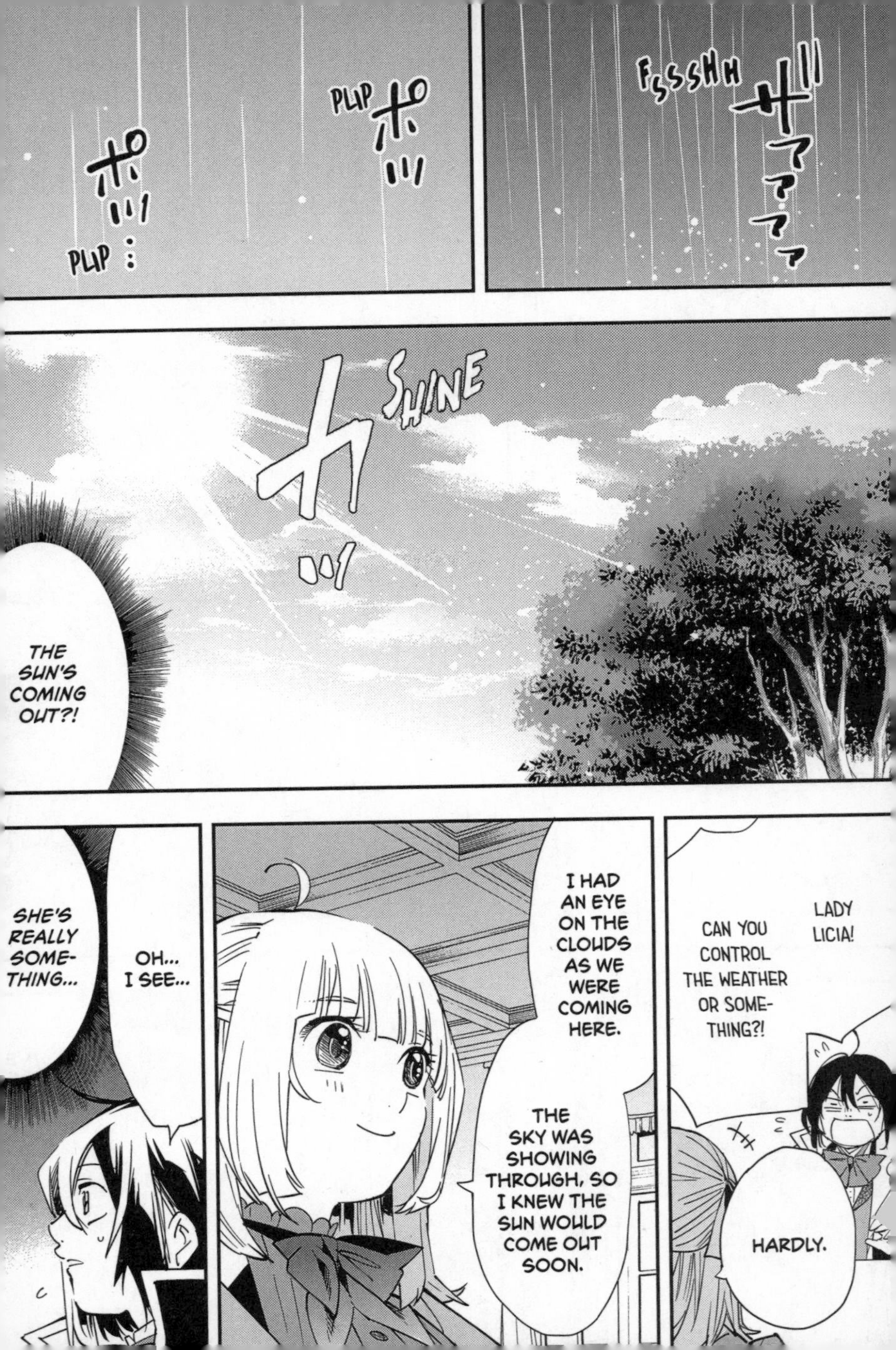
FSSSHH
PLIP
PLIP...
SHINE
THE SUN'S COMING OUT?!
LADY LICIA!
CAN YOU CONTROL THE WEATHER OR SOME-THING?!
HARDLY.
I HAD AN EYE ON THE CLOUDS AS WE WERE COMING HERE.
THE SKY WAS SHOWING THROUGH, SO I KNEW THE SUN WOULD COME OUT SOON.
OH... I SEE...
SHE'S REALLY SOME-THING...

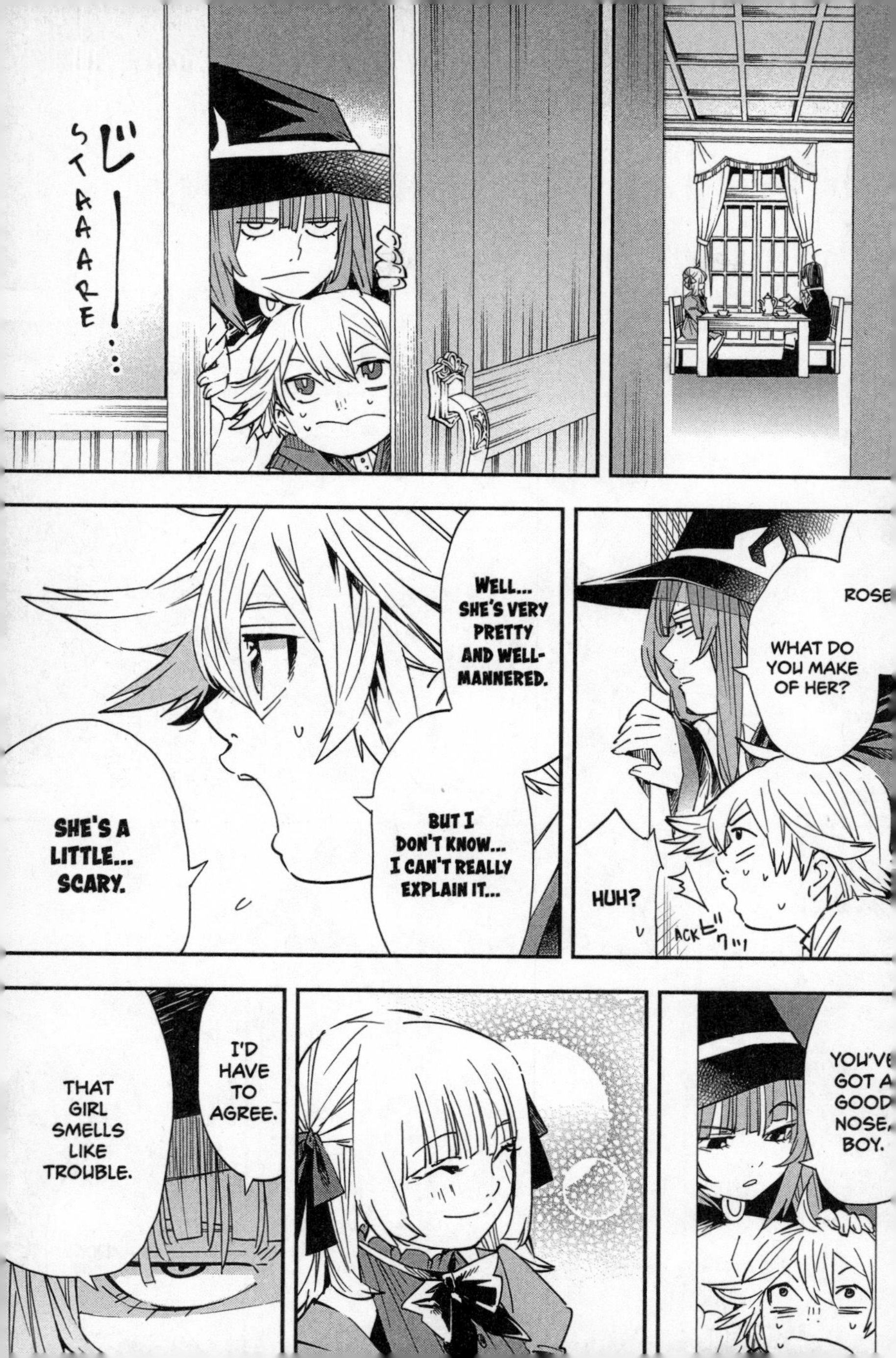
ジー…
STAAARE
ROSE
WHAT DO YOU MAKE OF HER?
HUH?
ACK ビクッ
WELL... SHE'S VERY PRETTY AND WELL-MANNERED.
BUT I DON'T KNOW... I CAN'T REALLY EXPLAIN IT...
SHE'S A LITTLE... SCARY.
YOU'VE GOT A GOOD NOSE, BOY.
I'D HAVE TO AGREE.
THAT GIRL SMELLS LIKE TROUBLE.

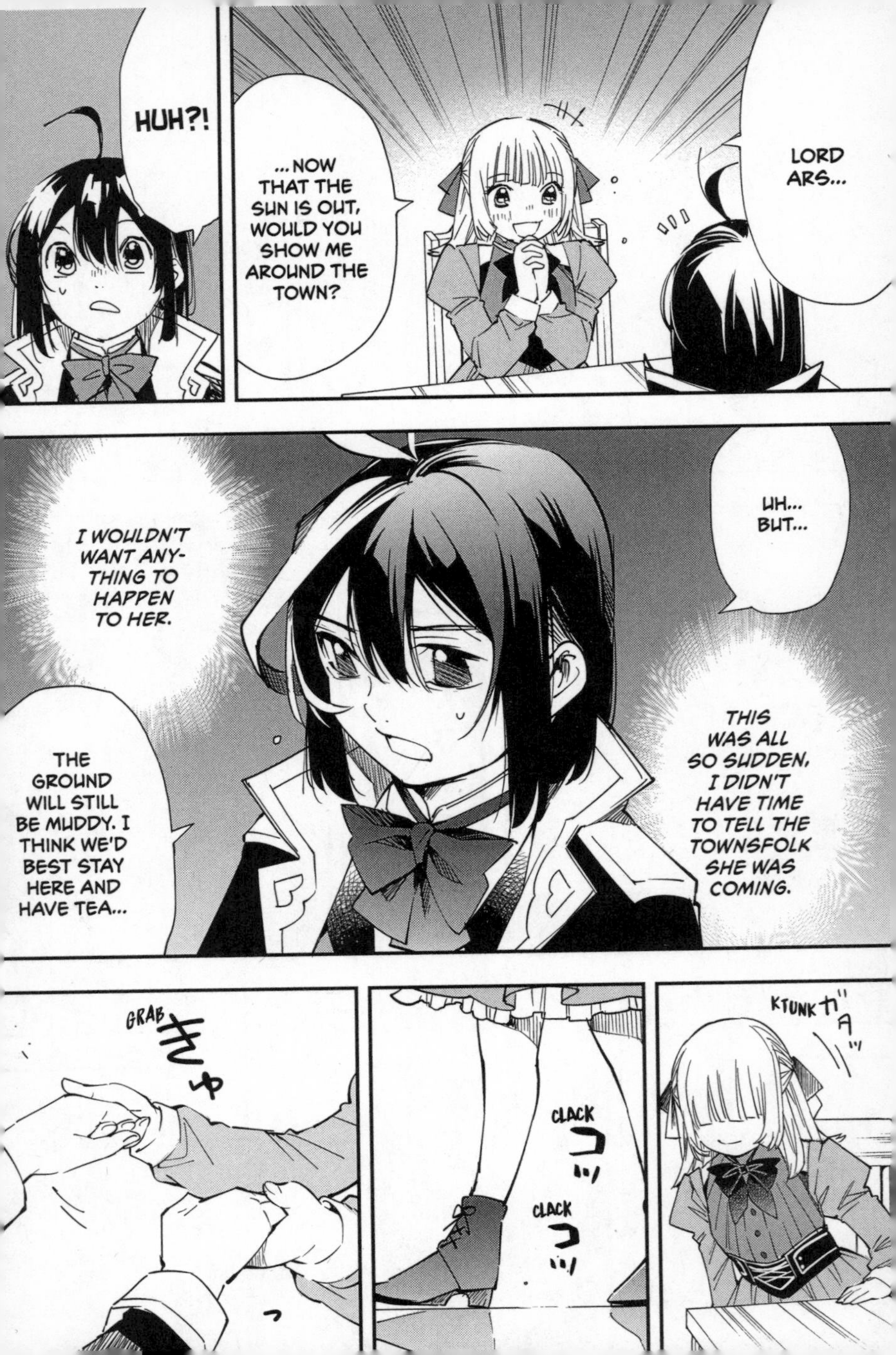
LORD ARS...
...NOW THAT THE SUN IS OUT, WOULD YOU SHOW ME AROUND THE TOWN?
HUH?!
UH... BUT...
THIS WAS ALL SO SUDDEN, I DIDN'T HAVE TIME TO TELL THE TOWNSFOLK SHE WAS COMING.
I WOULDN'T WANT ANYTHING TO HAPPEN TO HER.
THE GROUND WILL STILL BE MUDDY. I THINK WE'D BEST STAY HERE AND HAVE TEA...
KTUNK
CLACK
CLACK
GRAB

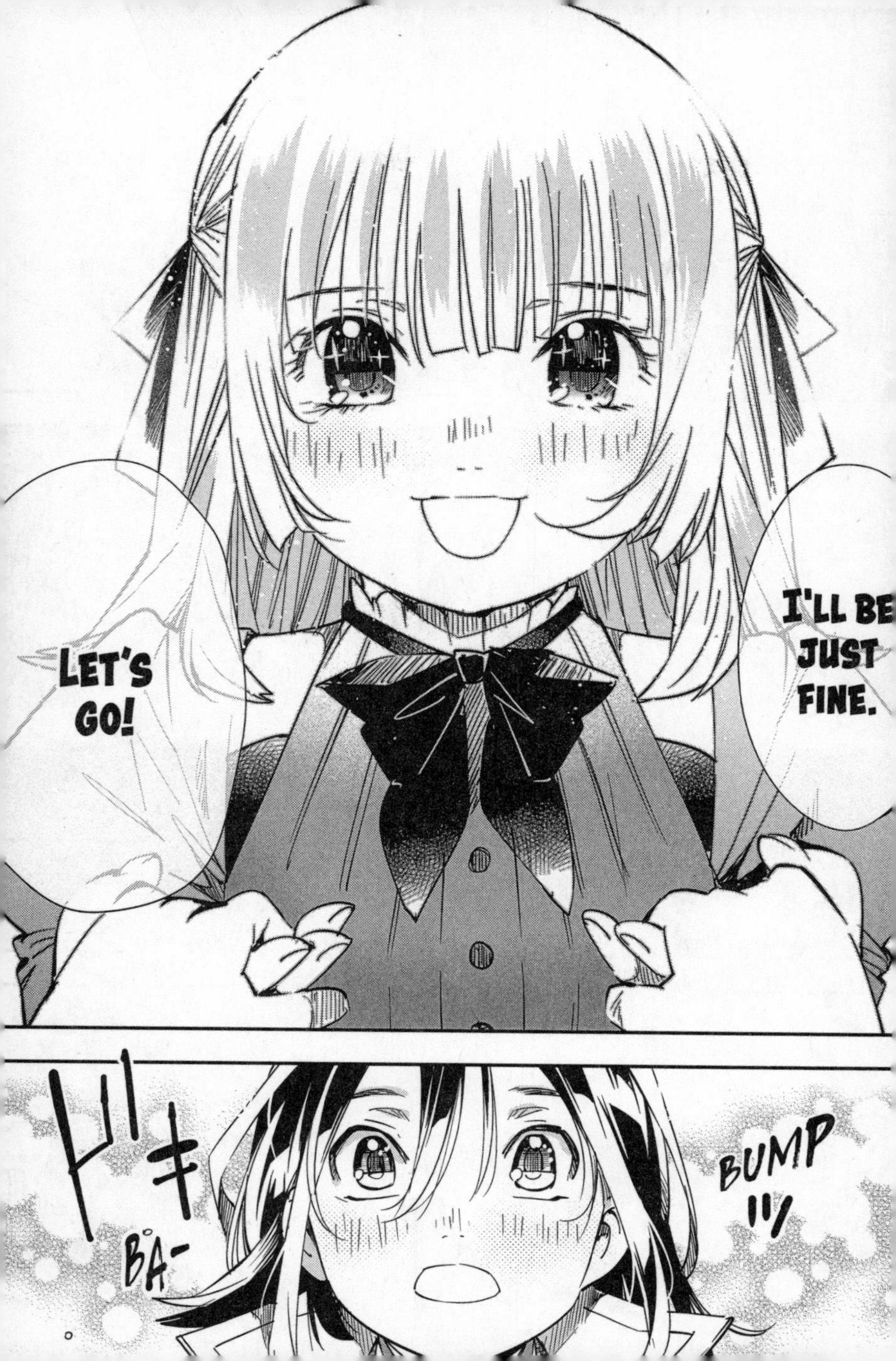
I'LL BE JUST FINE.
LET'S GO!
ドキ
BA-
BUMP

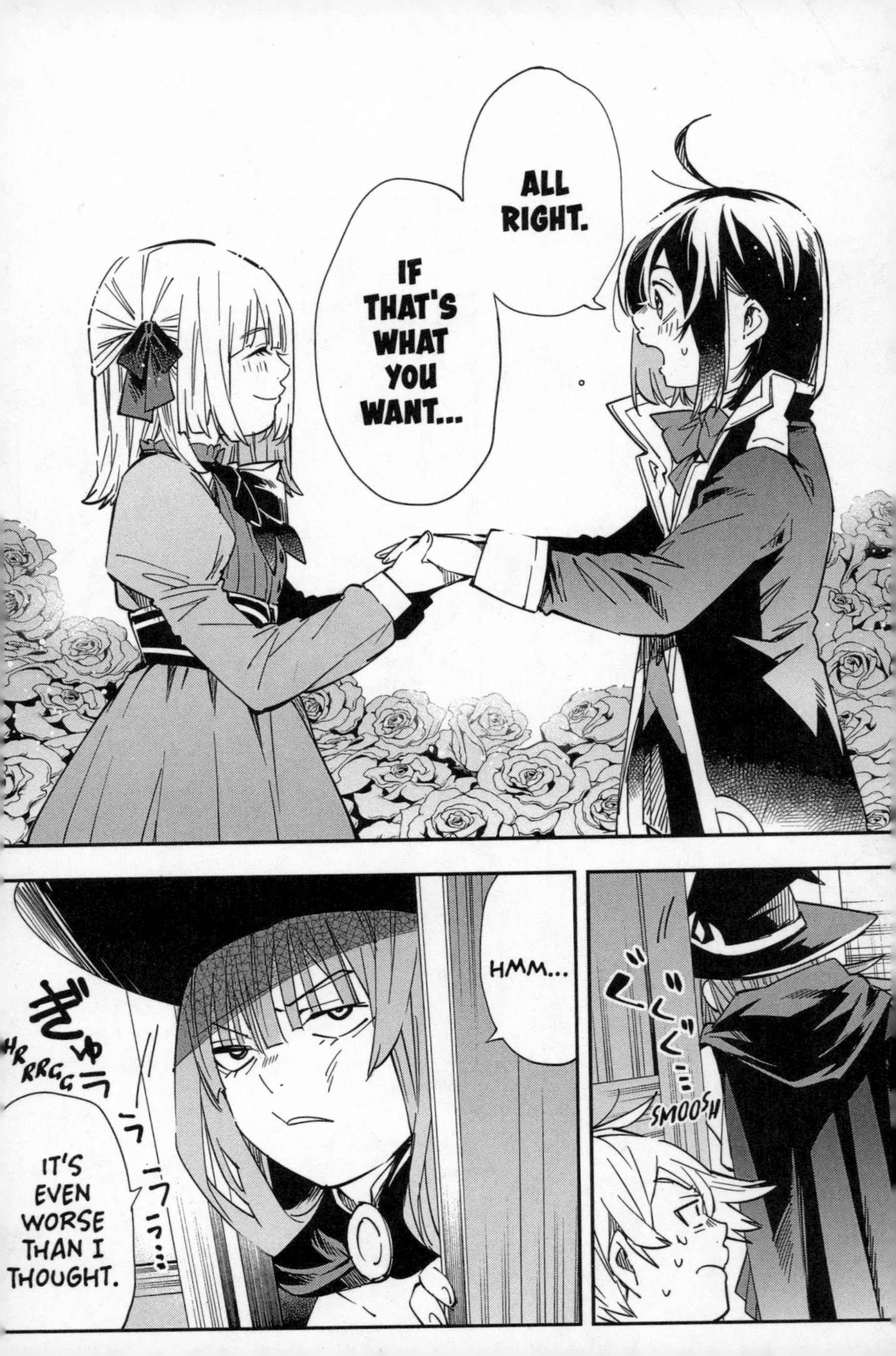
ALL RIGHT.
IF THAT'S WHAT YOU WANT...
SMOOSH
HMM...
HRRRGG
IT'S EVEN WORSE THAN I THOUGHT.

Chapter 20: A Fiancée's Request

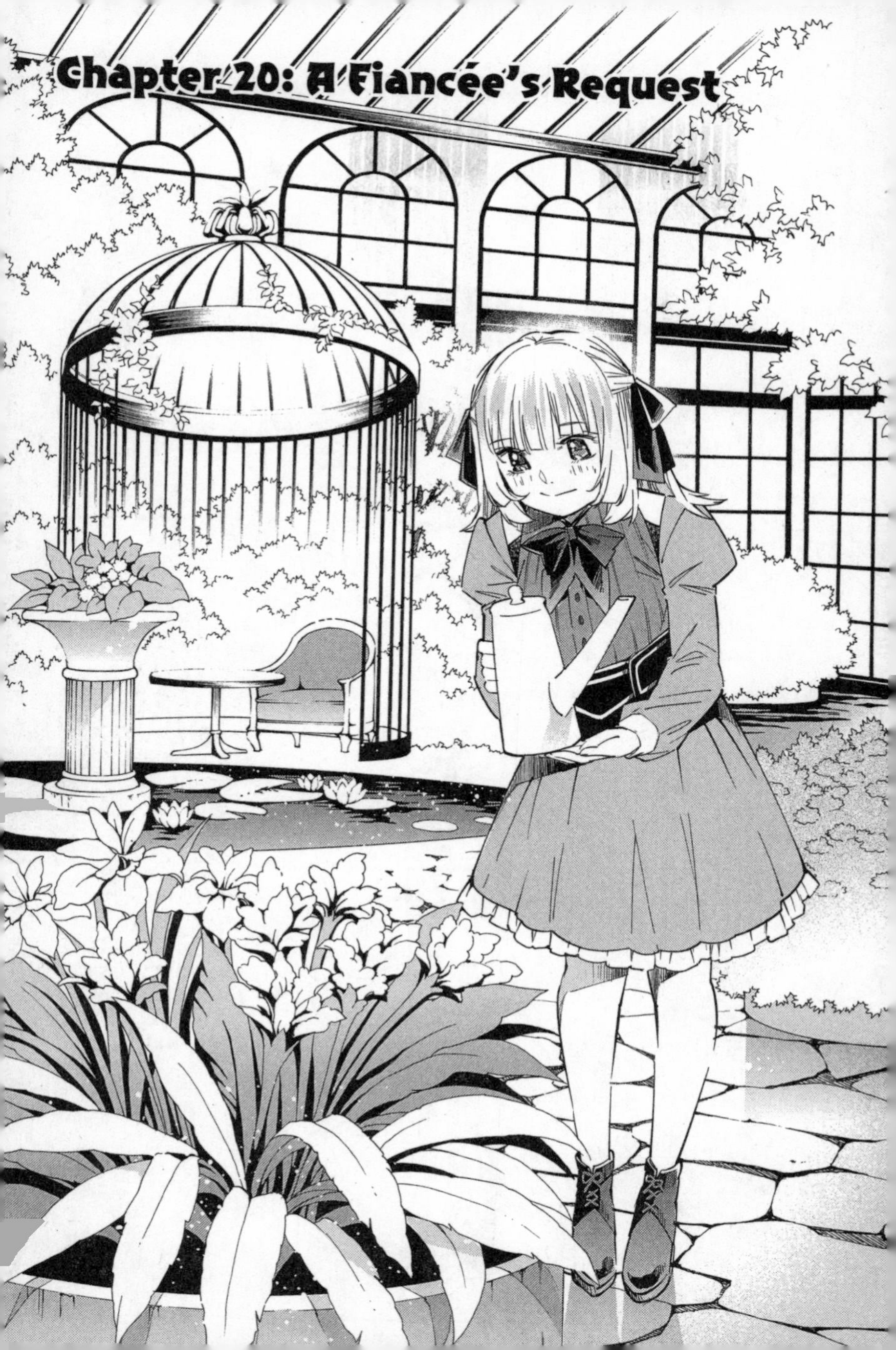

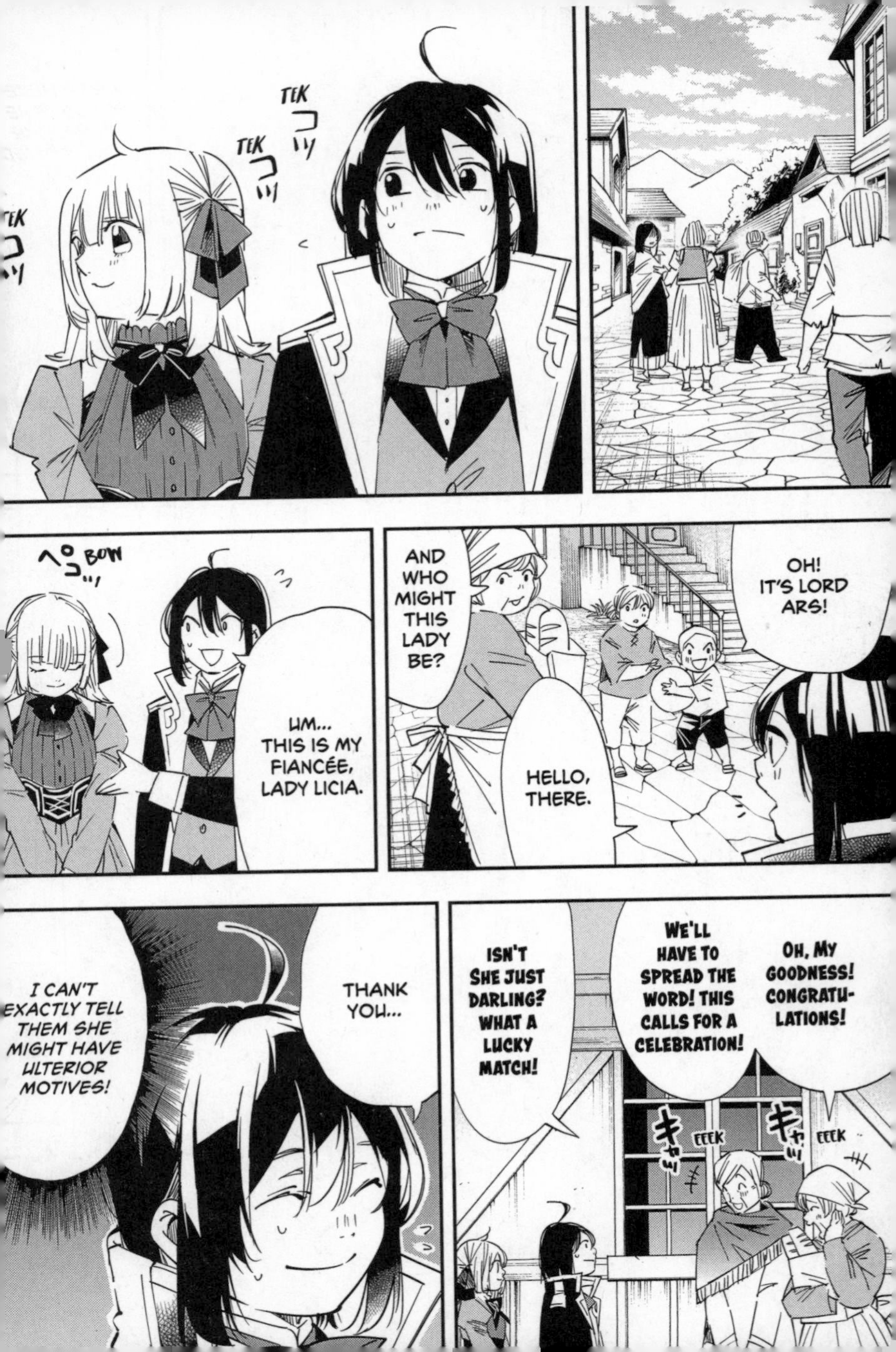
TEK
TEK
TEK
OH! IT'S LORD ARS!
AND WHO MIGHT THIS LADY BE?
HELLO, THERE.
BOW
UM... THIS IS MY FIANCÉE, LADY LICIA.
OH, MY GOODNESS! CONGRATU-LATIONS!
WE'LL HAVE TO SPREAD THE WORD! THIS CALLS FOR A CELEBRATION!
ISN'T SHE JUST DARLING? WHAT A LUCKY MATCH!
EEEK
EEEK
THANK YOU...
I CAN'T EXACTLY TELL THEM SHE MIGHT HAVE ULTERIOR MOTIVES!

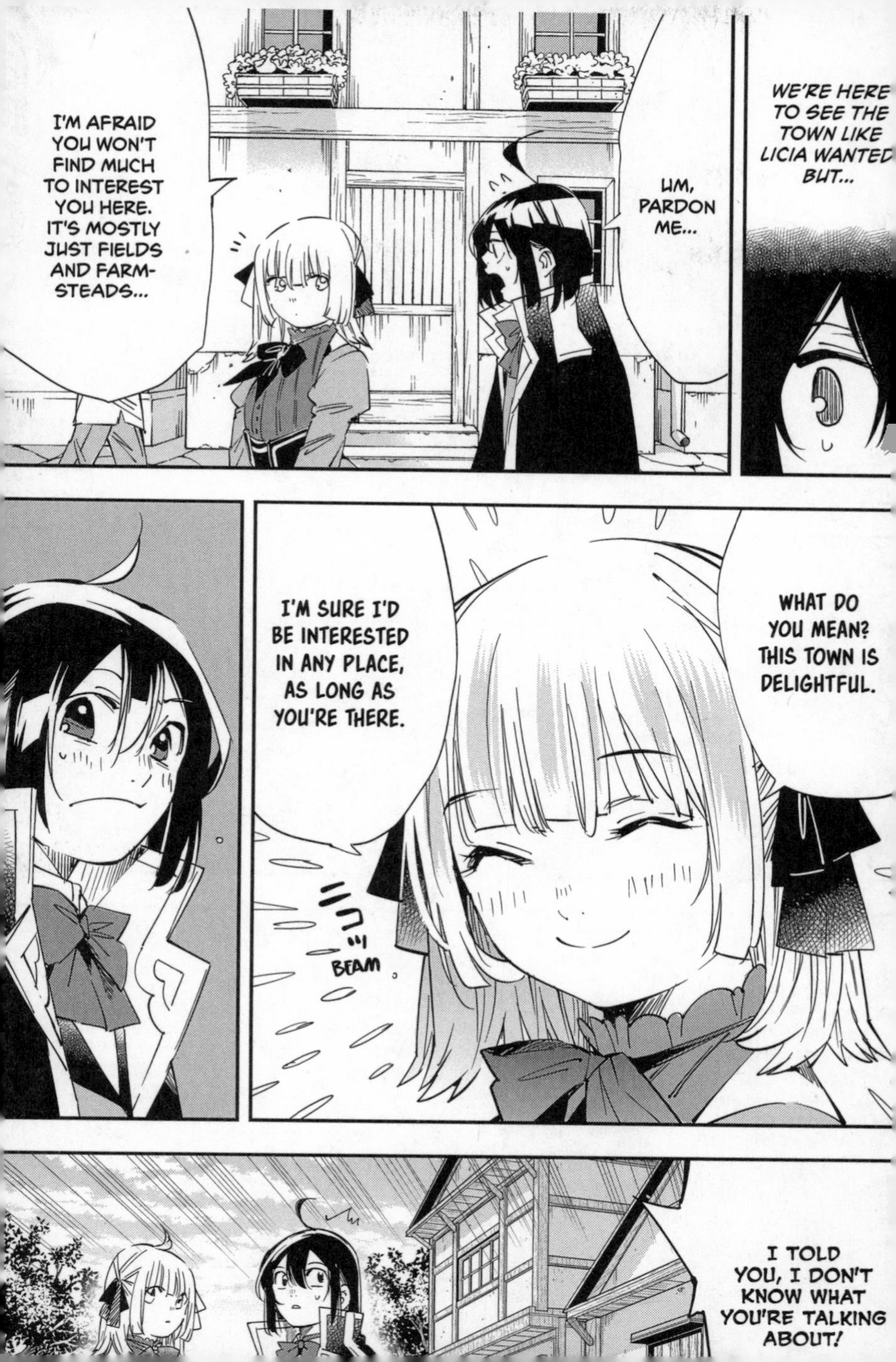
WE'RE HERE TO SEE THE TOWN LIKE LICIA WANTED BUT...
UM, PARDON ME...
I'M AFRAID YOU WON'T FIND MUCH TO INTEREST YOU HERE. IT'S MOSTLY JUST FIELDS AND FARM-STEADS...
WHAT DO YOU MEAN? THIS TOWN IS DELIGHTFUL.
I'M SURE I'D BE INTERESTED IN ANY PLACE, AS LONG AS YOU'RE THERE.
BEAM
I TOLD YOU, I DON'T KNOW WHAT YOU'RE TALKING ABOUT!

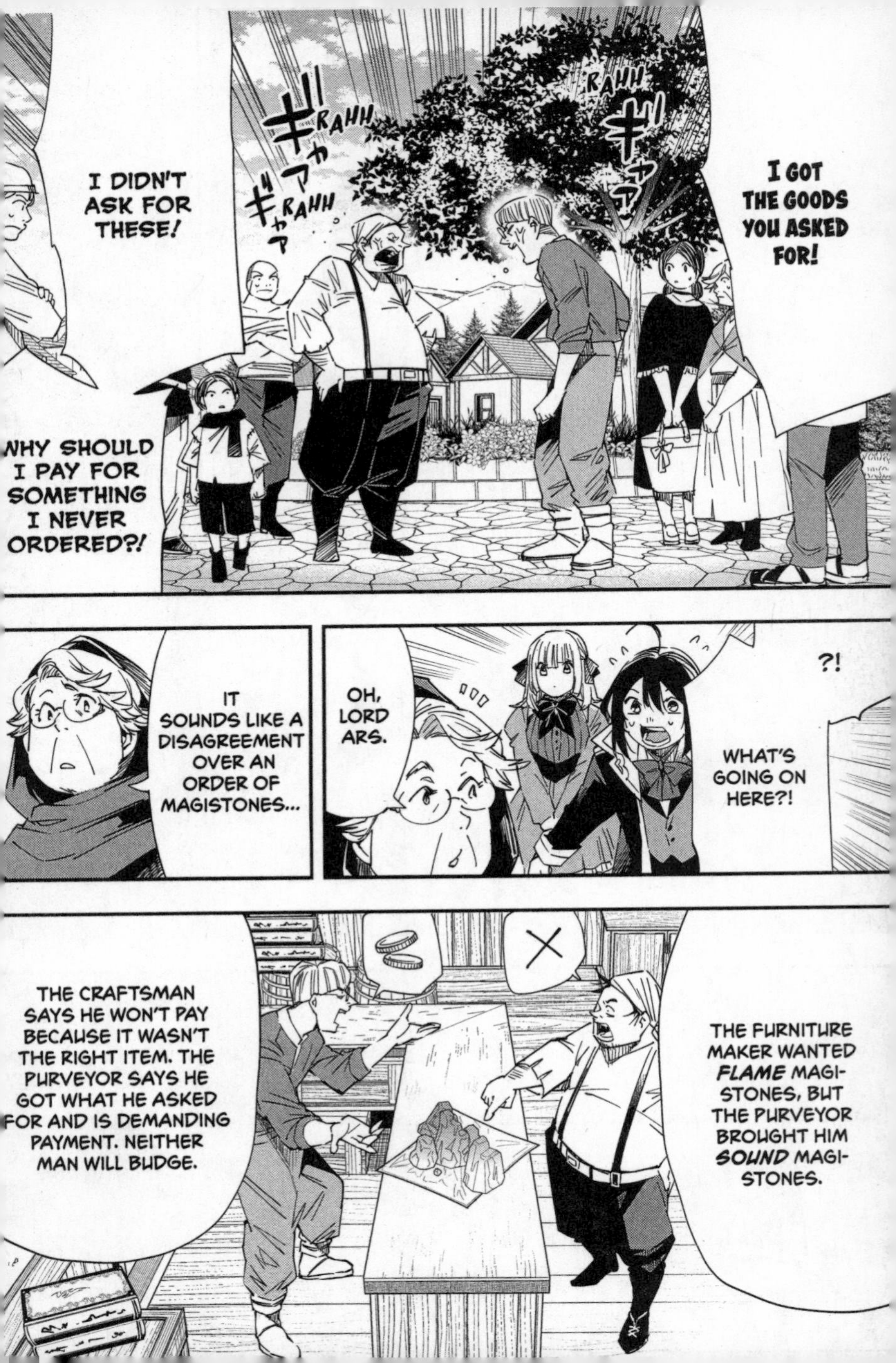
I GOT THE GOODS YOU ASKED FOR!
RAHH
RAHH
RAHH
I DIDN'T ASK FOR THESE!
WHY SHOULD I PAY FOR SOMETHING I NEVER ORDERED?!
?!
WHAT'S GOING ON HERE?!
OH, LORD ARS.
IT SOUNDS LIKE A DISAGREEMENT OVER AN ORDER OF MAGISTONES...
THE FURNITURE MAKER WANTED *FLAME* MAGI-STONES, BUT THE PURVEYOR BROUGHT HIM *SOUND* MAGI-STONES.
THE CRAFTSMAN SAYS HE WON'T PAY BECAUSE IT WASN'T THE RIGHT ITEM. THE PURVEYOR SAYS HE GOT WHAT HE ASKED FOR AND IS DEMANDING PAYMENT. NEITHER MAN WILL BUDGE.

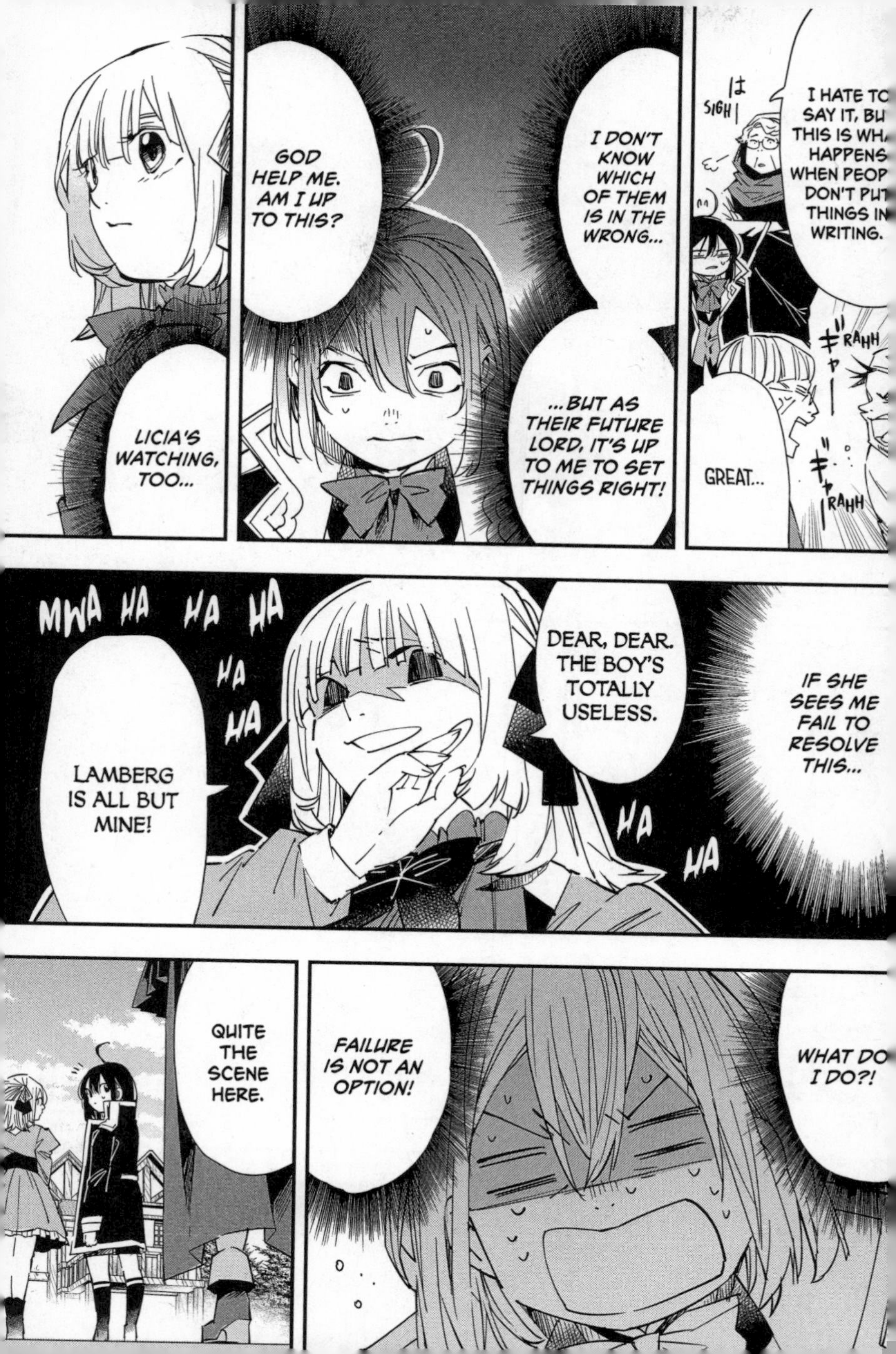
I HATE TO SAY IT, BU THIS IS WH HAPPENS WHEN PEOP DON'T PUT THINGS IN WRITING.
は SIGH
ギャー RAHH
ギャ RAHH
GREAT...
I DON'T KNOW WHICH OF THEM IS IN THE WRONG...
...BUT AS THEIR FUTURE LORD, IT'S UP TO ME TO SET THINGS RIGHT!
GOD HELP ME. AM I UP TO THIS?
LICIA'S WATCHING, TOO...
IF SHE SEES ME FAIL TO RESOLVE THIS...
DEAR, DEAR. THE BOY'S TOTALLY USELESS.
MWA HA HA HA HA HA HA HA
LAMBERG IS ALL BUT MINE!
WHAT DO I DO?!
FAILURE IS NOT AN OPTION!
QUITE THE SCENE HERE.

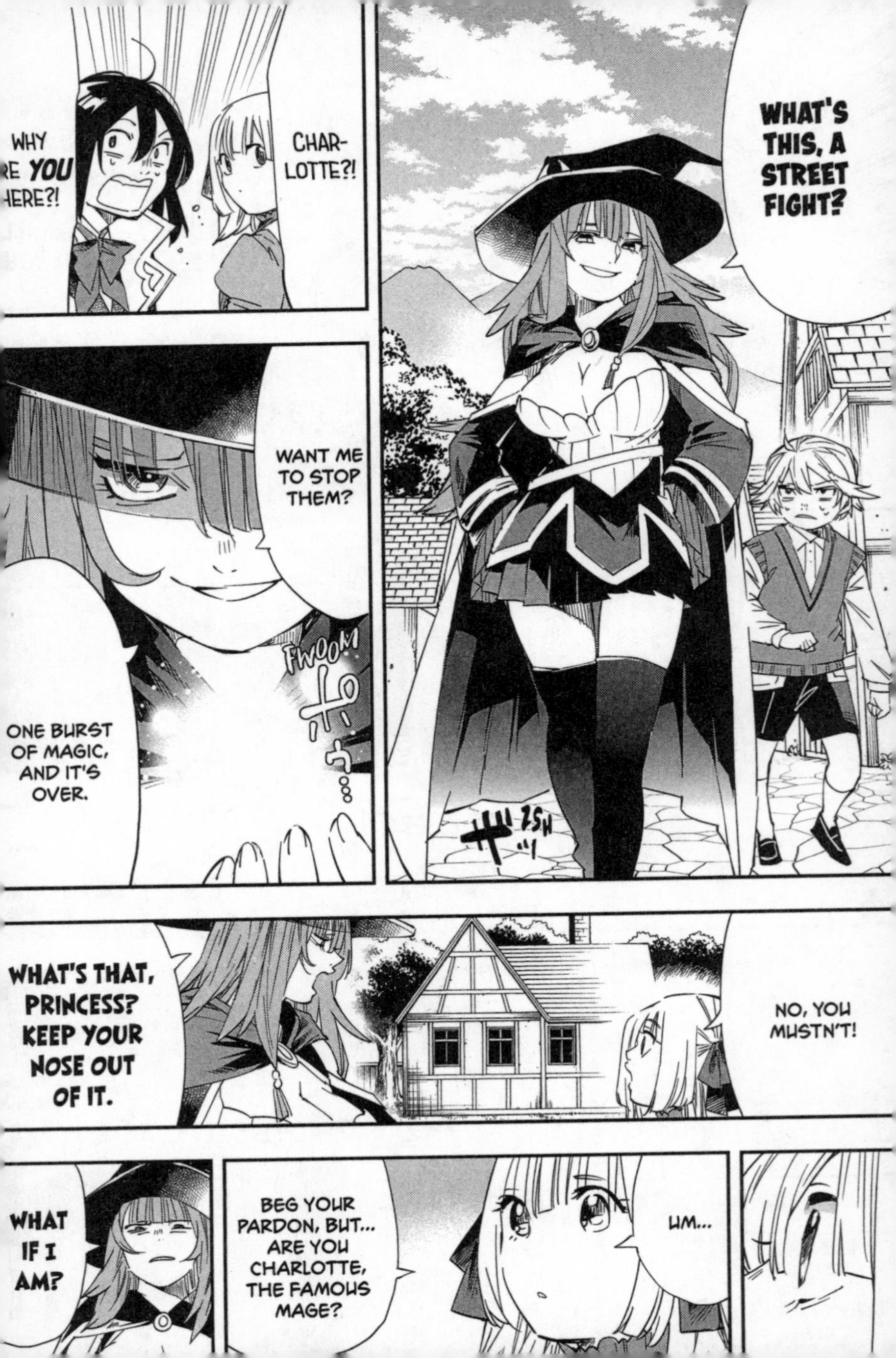
WHAT'S THIS, A STREET FIGHT?
ZSH
CHAR-LOTTE?!
WHY RE YOU HERE?!
WANT ME TO STOP THEM?
FWOOM
ONE BURST OF MAGIC, AND IT'S OVER.
NO, YOU MUSTN'T!
WHAT'S THAT, PRINCESS? KEEP YOUR NOSE OUT OF IT.
UM...
BEG YOUR PARDON, BUT... ARE YOU CHARLOTTE, THE FAMOUS MAGE?
WHAT IF I AM?

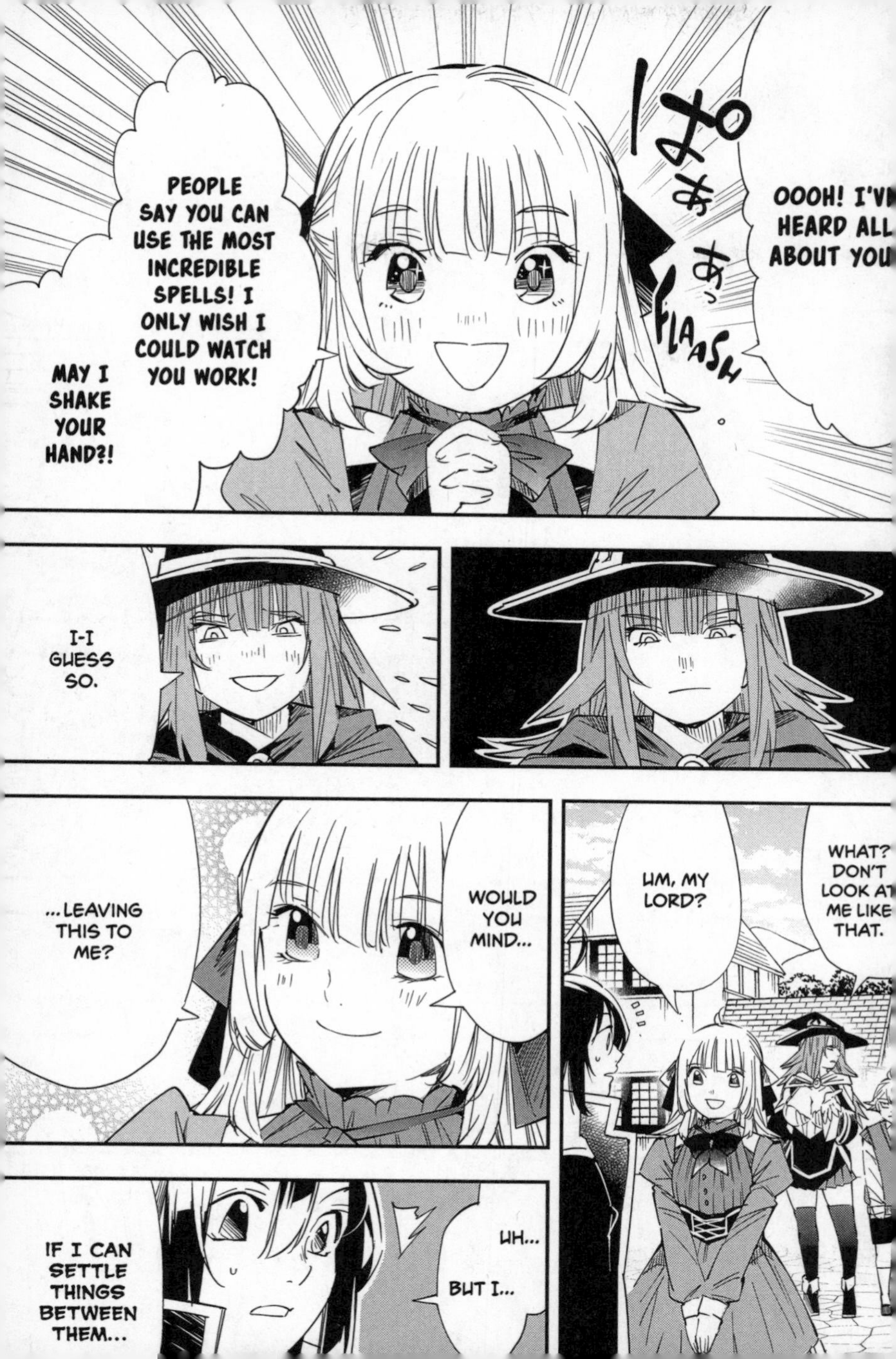
OOOH! I'VE HEARD ALL ABOUT YOU
ぱぁぁっ
FLAASH
PEOPLE SAY YOU CAN USE THE MOST INCREDIBLE SPELLS! I ONLY WISH I COULD WATCH YOU WORK!
MAY I SHAKE YOUR HAND?!
I-I GUESS SO.
WHAT? DON'T LOOK AT ME LIKE THAT.
UM, MY LORD?
WOULD YOU MIND...
...LEAVING THIS TO ME?
UH...
BUT I...
IF I CAN SETTLE THINGS BETWEEN THEM...

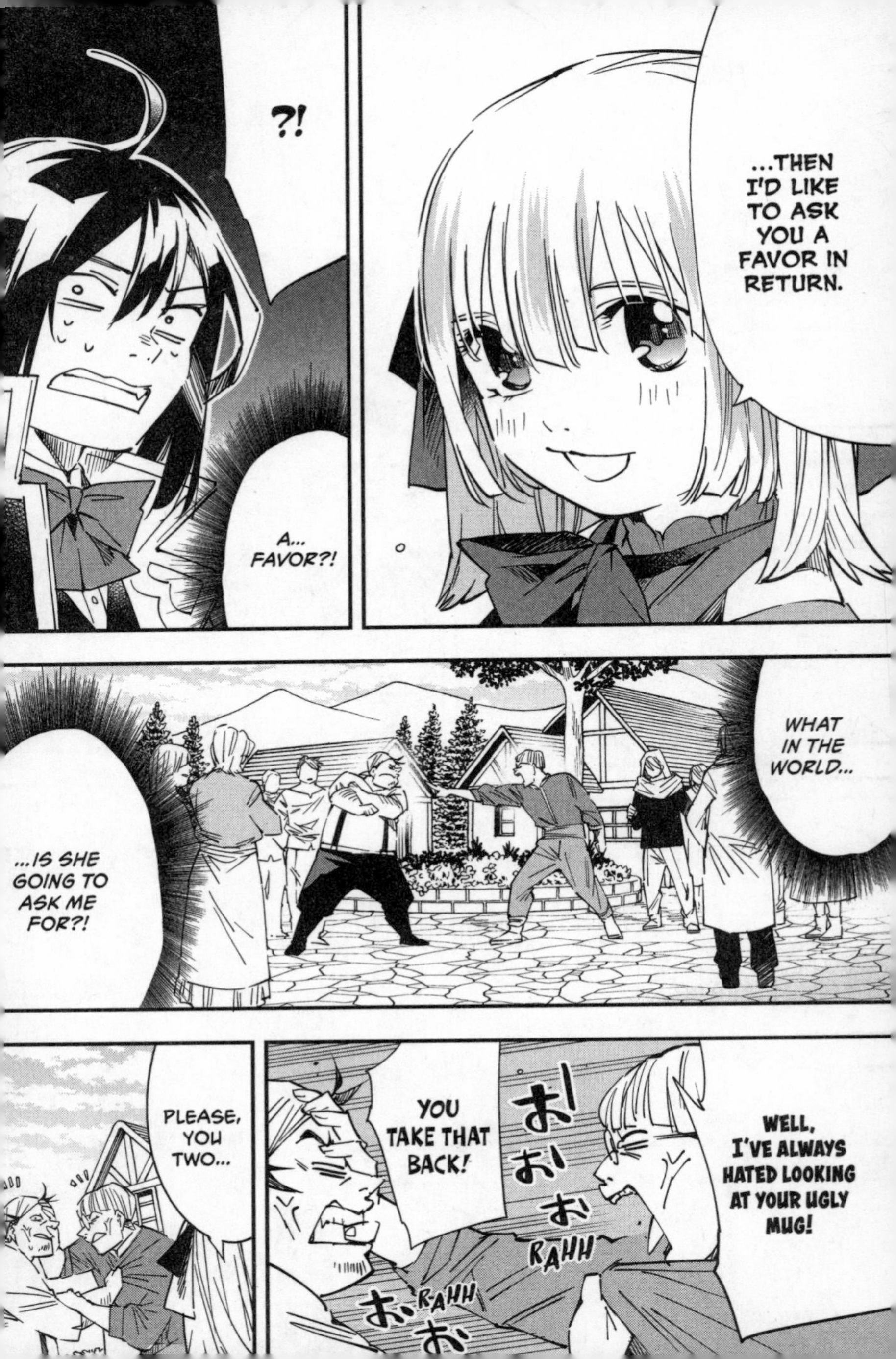
...THEN I'D LIKE TO ASK YOU A FAVOR IN RETURN.
?!
A... FAVOR?!
WHAT IN THE WORLD...
...IS SHE GOING TO ASK ME FOR?!
WELL, I'VE ALWAYS HATED LOOKING AT YOUR UGLY MUG!
YOU TAKE THAT BACK!
おおお
RAHH
おお
RAHH
PLEASE, YOU TWO...

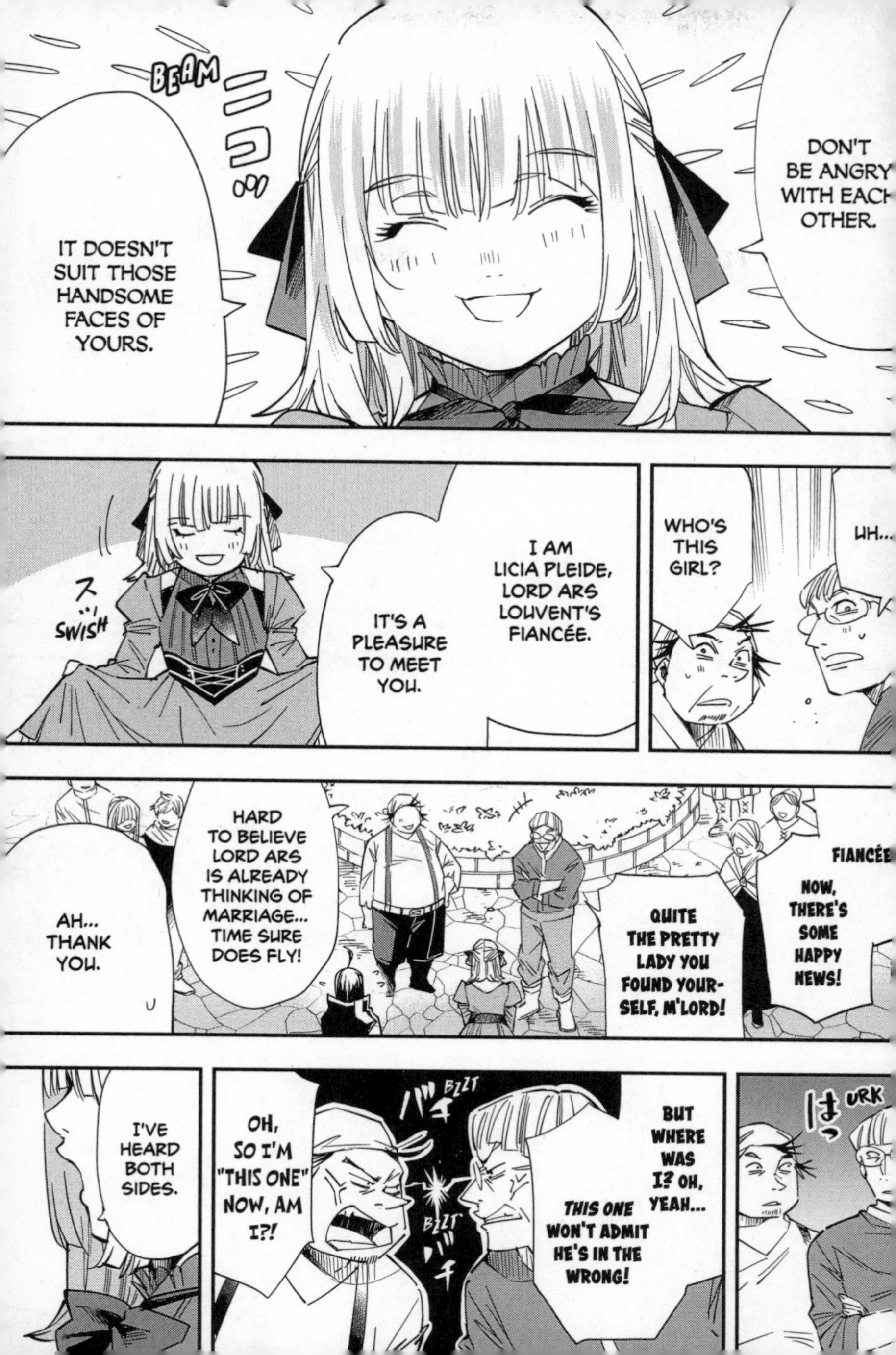
DON'T BE ANGRY WITH EACH OTHER.
BEAM
IT DOESN'T SUIT THOSE HANDSOME FACES OF YOURS.
UH...
WHO'S THIS GIRL?
I AM LICIA PLEIDE, LORD ARS LOUVENT'S FIANCÉE.
IT'S A PLEASURE TO MEET YOU.
SWISH
FIANCÉE
NOW, THERE'S SOME HAPPY NEWS!
QUITE THE PRETTY LADY YOU FOUND YOUR-SELF, M'LORD!
HARD TO BELIEVE LORD ARS IS ALREADY THINKING OF MARRIAGE... TIME SURE DOES FLY!
AH... THANK YOU.
URK
BUT WHERE WAS I? OH, YEAH...
THIS ONE WON'T ADMIT HE'S IN THE WRONG!
BZZT
BZZT
OH, SO I'M "THIS ONE" NOW, AM I?!
I'VE HEARD BOTH SIDES.

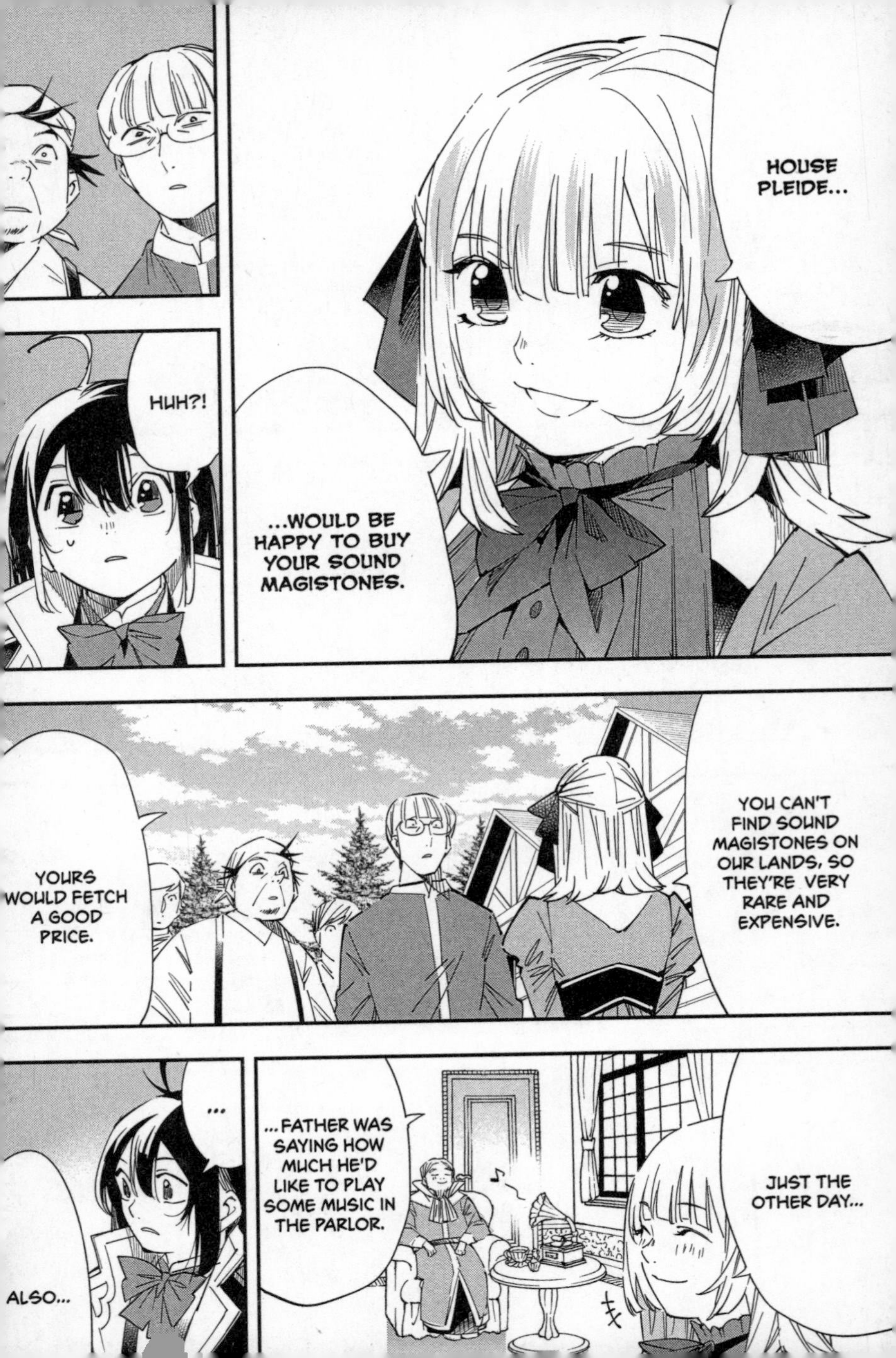
HOUSE PLEIDE...
...WOULD BE HAPPY TO BUY YOUR SOUND MAGISTONES.
HUH?!
YOU CAN'T FIND SOUND MAGISTONES ON OUR LANDS, SO THEY'RE VERY RARE AND EXPENSIVE.
YOURS WOULD FETCH A GOOD PRICE.
JUST THE OTHER DAY...
...FATHER WAS SAYING HOW MUCH HE'D LIKE TO PLAY SOME MUSIC IN THE PARLOR.
...
ALSO...

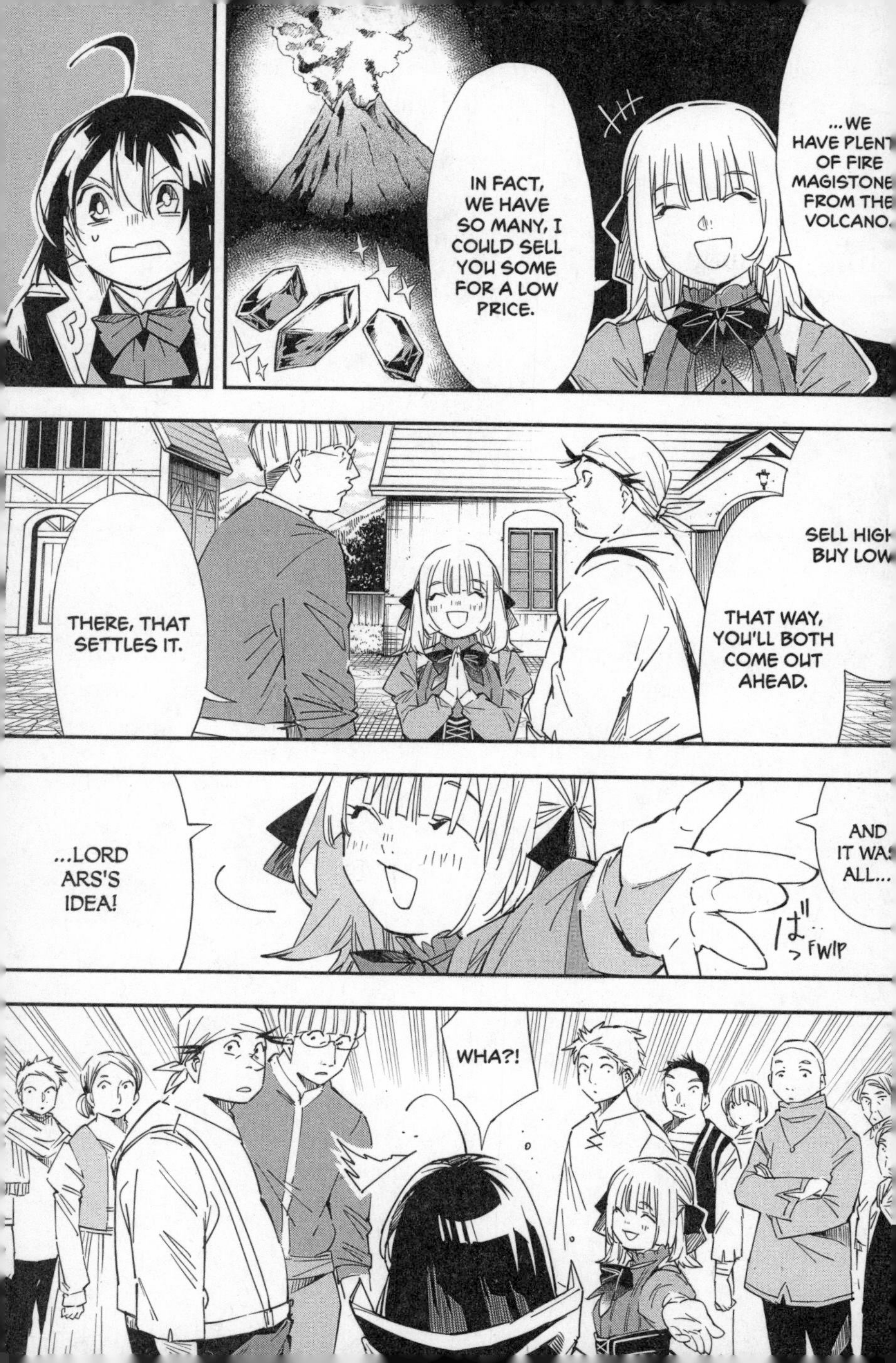
...WE HAVE PLENTY OF FIRE MAGISTONES FROM THE VOLCANO.
IN FACT, WE HAVE SO MANY, I COULD SELL YOU SOME FOR A LOW PRICE.
SELL HIGH BUY LOW
THAT WAY, YOU'LL BOTH COME OUT AHEAD.
THERE, THAT SETTLES IT.
AND IT WAS ALL...
ぱ… FWIP
...LORD ARS'S IDEA!
WHA?!

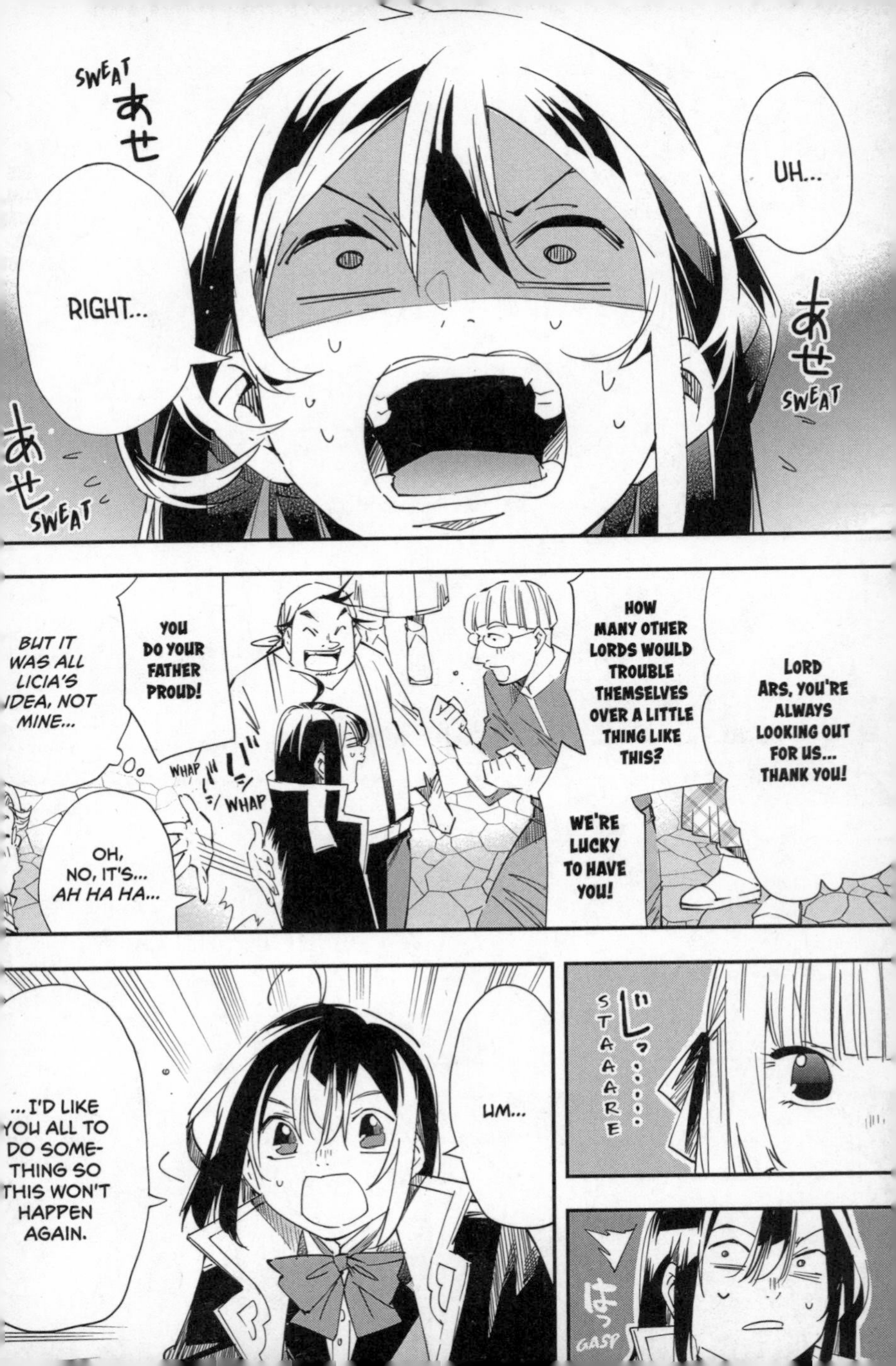

UH...
あせ SWEAT
SWEAT あせ
RIGHT...
あせ SWEAT
LORD ARS, YOU'RE ALWAYS LOOKING OUT FOR US... THANK YOU!
HOW MANY OTHER LORDS WOULD TROUBLE THEMSELVES OVER A LITTLE THING LIKE THIS?
WE'RE LUCKY TO HAVE YOU!
YOU DO YOUR FATHER PROUD!
BUT IT WAS ALL LICIA'S IDEA, NOT MINE...
WHAP WHAP
OH, NO, IT'S... AH HA HA...
じーっ...... STAARE
はっ GASP
UM...
...I'D LIKE YOU ALL TO DO SOMETHING SO THIS WON'T HAPPEN AGAIN.

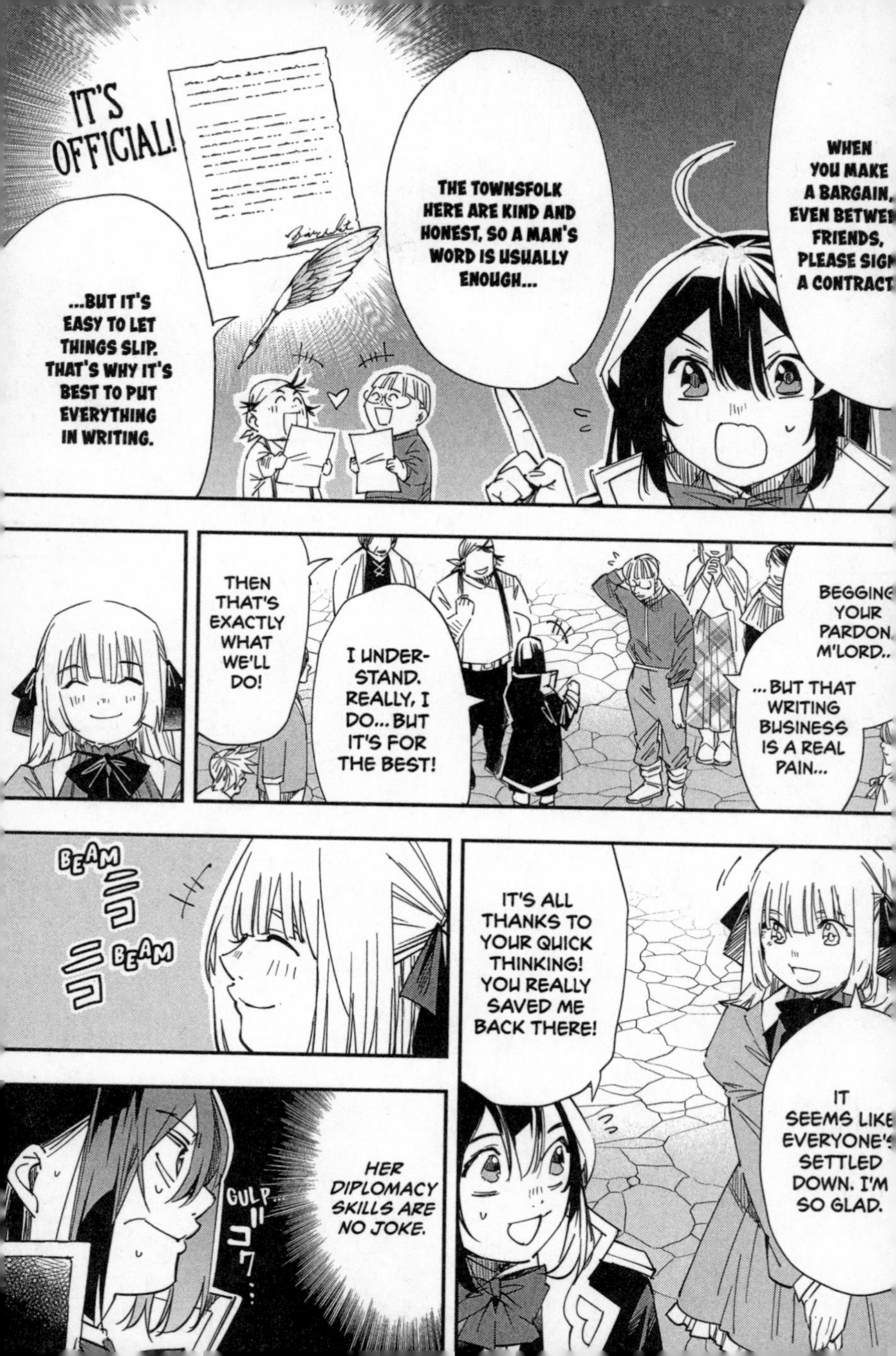
WHEN YOU MAKE A BARGAIN, EVEN BETWE FRIENDS, PLEASE SIG A CONTRACT
THE TOWNSFOLK HERE ARE KIND AND HONEST, SO A MAN'S WORD IS USUALLY ENOUGH...
IT'S OFFICIAL!
...BUT IT'S EASY TO LET THINGS SLIP. THAT'S WHY IT'S BEST TO PUT EVERYTHING IN WRITING.
BEGGING YOUR PARDON, M'LORD..
...BUT THAT WRITING BUSINESS IS A REAL PAIN...
I UNDER-STAND. REALLY, I DO... BUT IT'S FOR THE BEST!
THEN THAT'S EXACTLY WHAT WE'LL DO!
IT'S ALL THANKS TO YOUR QUICK THINKING! YOU REALLY SAVED ME BACK THERE!
IT SEEMS LIKE EVERYONE'S SETTLED DOWN. I'M SO GLAD.
BEAM ニコ
ニコ BEAM
HER DIPLOMACY SKILLS ARE NO JOKE.
GULP... ゴク...

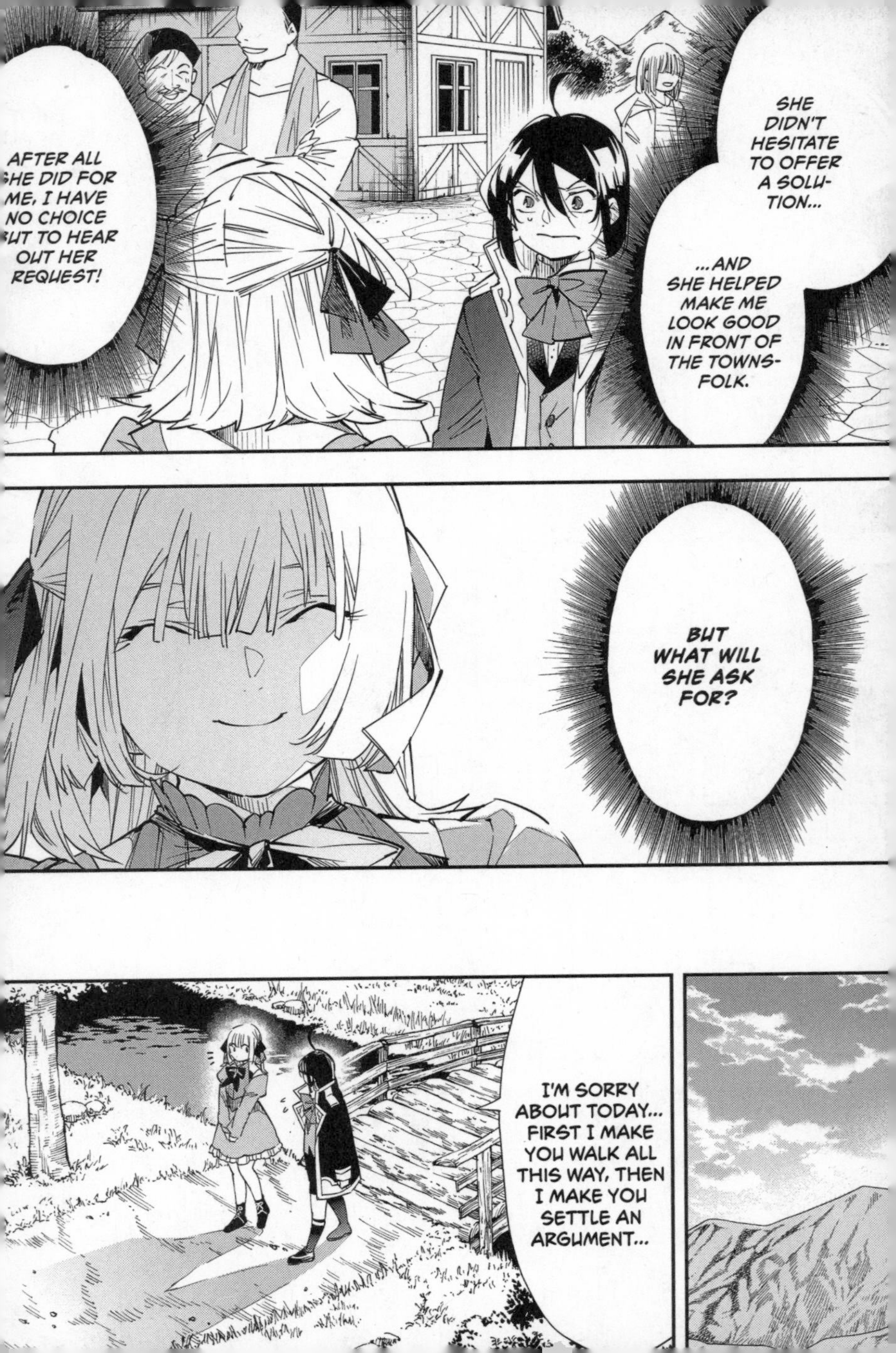
SHE DIDN'T HESITATE TO OFFER A SOLUTION...
...AND SHE HELPED MAKE ME LOOK GOOD IN FRONT OF THE TOWNSFOLK.
AFTER ALL SHE DID FOR ME, I HAVE NO CHOICE BUT TO HEAR OUT HER REQUEST!
BUT WHAT WILL SHE ASK FOR?
I'M SORRY ABOUT TODAY... FIRST I MAKE YOU WALK ALL THIS WAY, THEN I MAKE YOU SETTLE AN ARGUMENT...

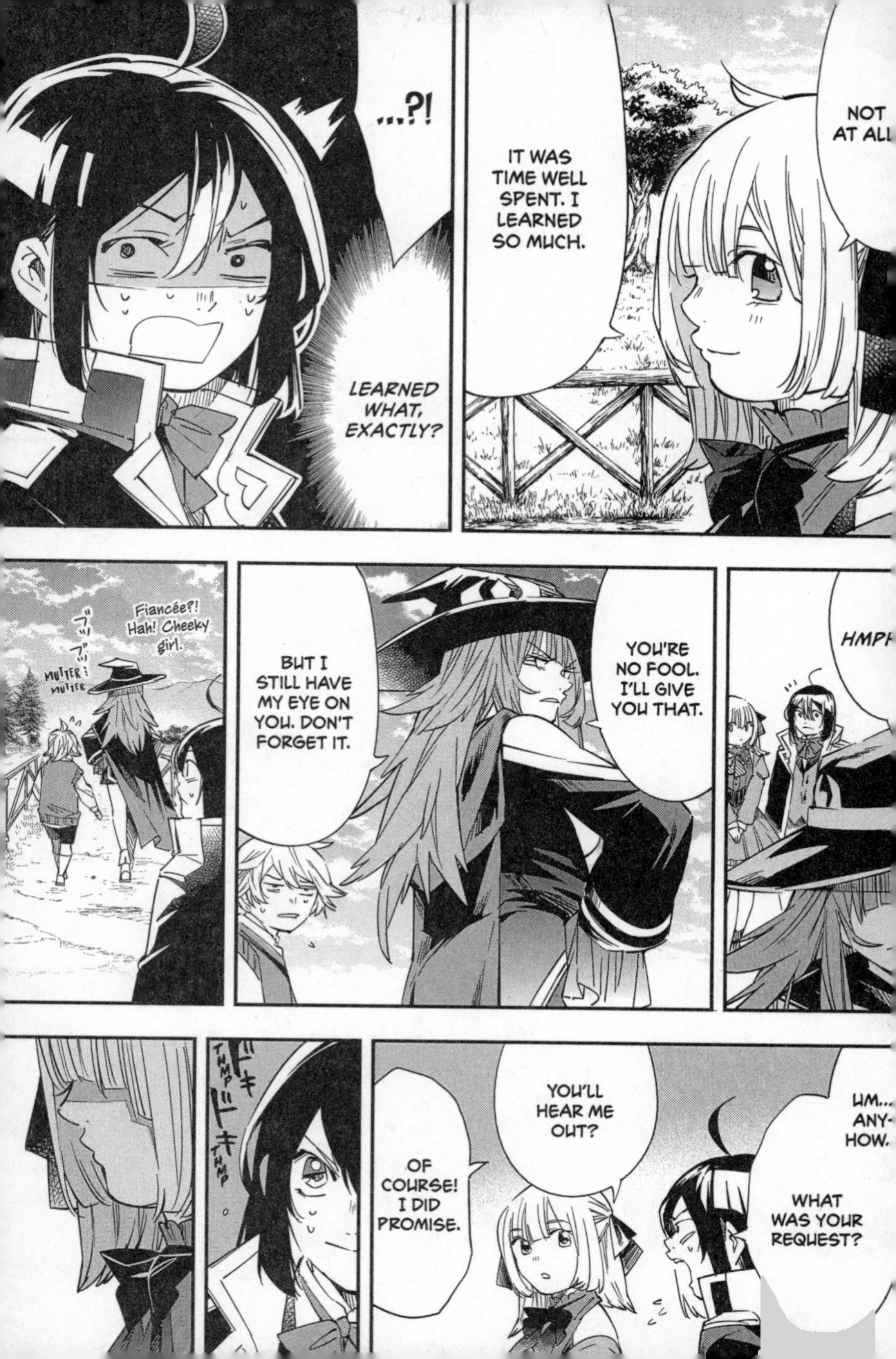

NOT AT ALL
IT WAS TIME WELL SPENT. I LEARNED SO MUCH.
...?!
LEARNED WHAT, EXACTLY?
HMPH
YOU'RE NO FOOL. I'LL GIVE YOU THAT.
BUT I STILL HAVE MY EYE ON YOU. DON'T FORGET IT.
Fiancée?! Hah! Cheeky girl.
ブツブツ
MUTTER MUTTER
UM... ANY-HOW.
WHAT WAS YOUR REQUEST?
YOU'LL HEAR ME OUT?
OF COURSE! I DID PROMISE.
ドキドキ
THMP THMP

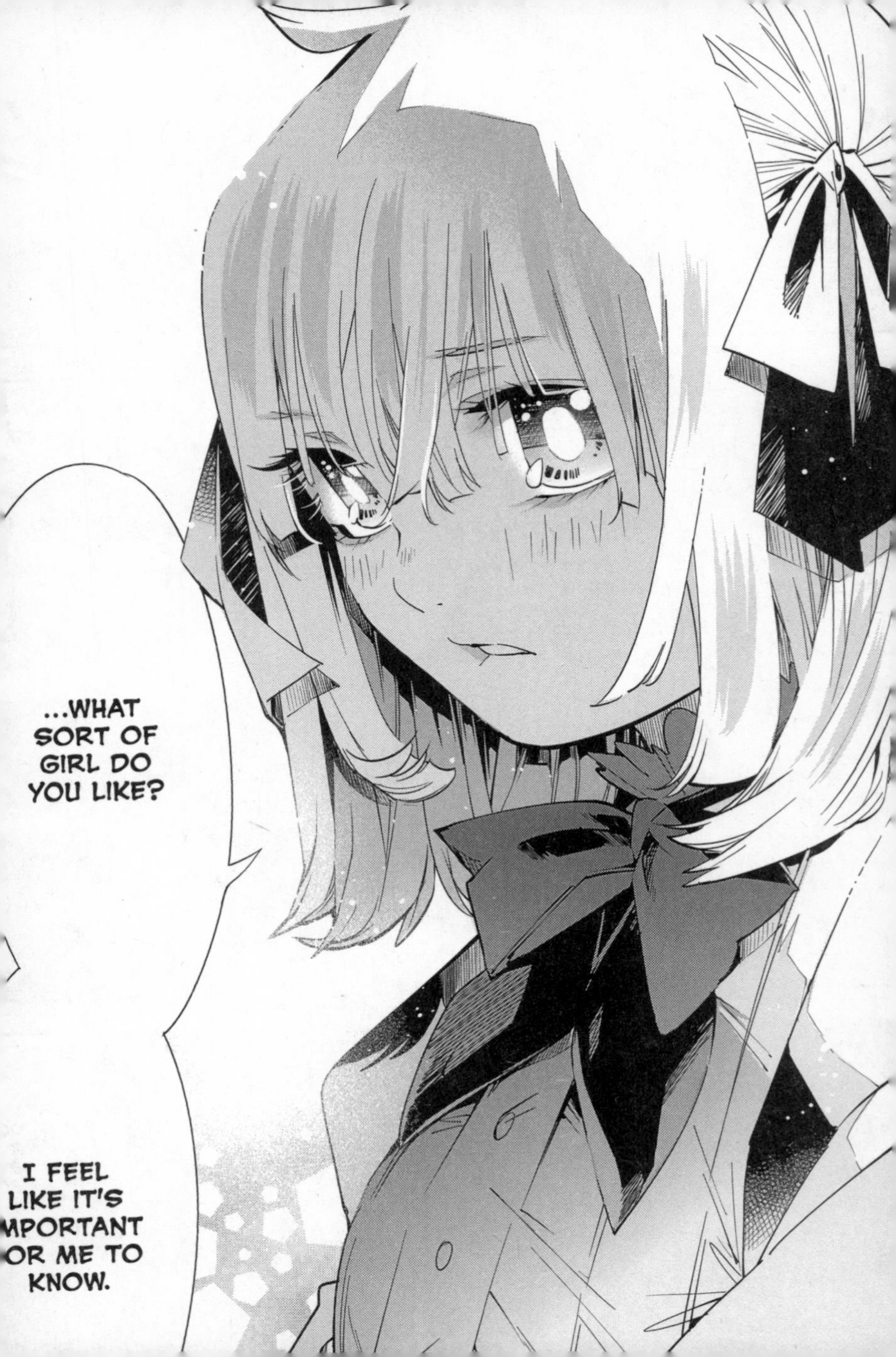
...WHAT SORT OF GIRL DO YOU LIKE?
I FEEL LIKE IT'S MPORTANT OR ME TO KNOW.

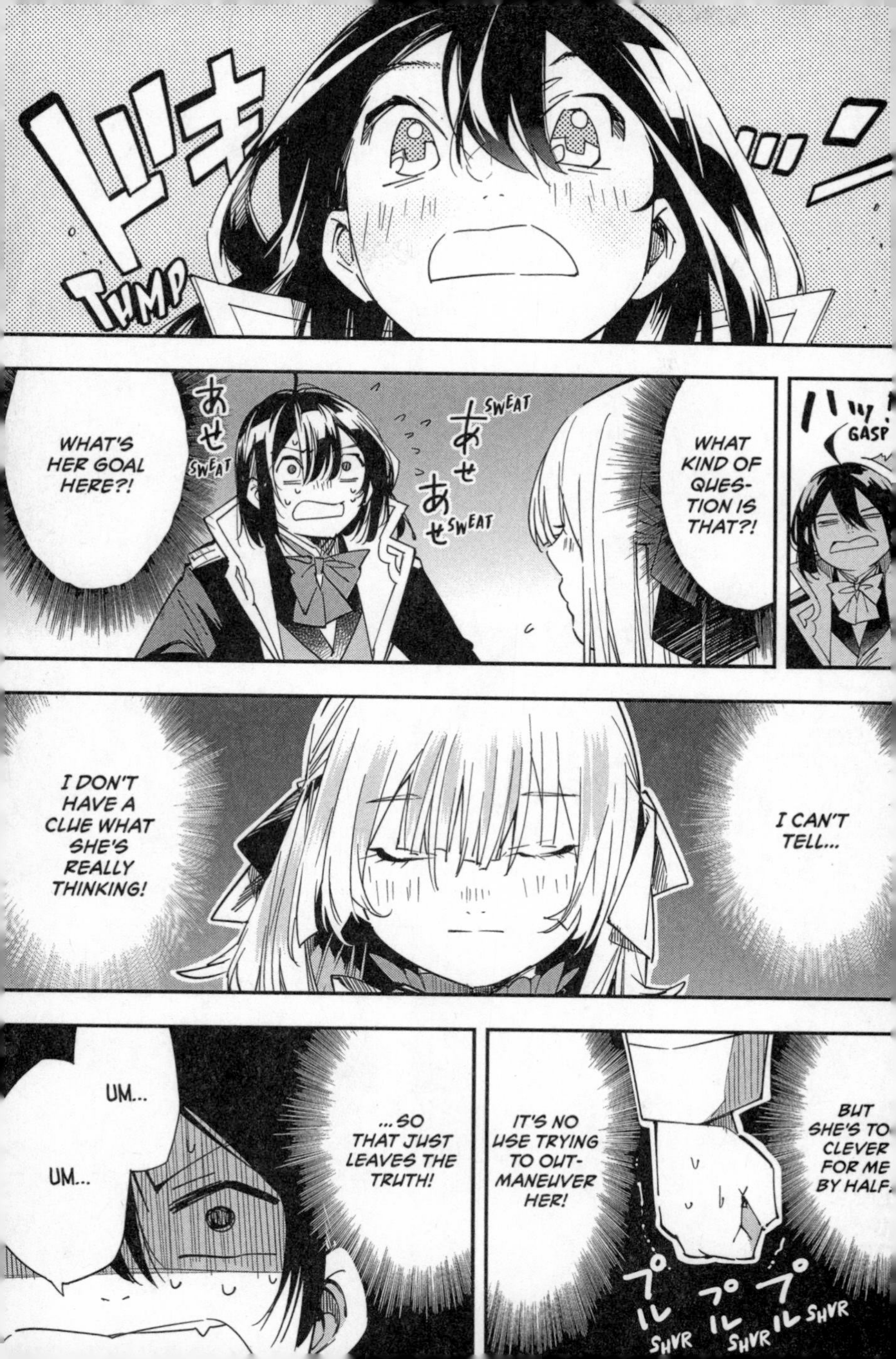
ドキッン
THMP
ハッ!
GASP
WHAT KIND OF QUES-TION IS THAT?!
あせ SWEAT
あせ SWEAT
あせ SWEAT
WHAT'S HER GOAL HERE?!
I CAN'T TELL...
I DON'T HAVE A CLUE WHAT SHE'S REALLY THINKING!
BUT SHE'S TO CLEVER FOR ME BY HALF.
IT'S NO USE TRYING TO OUT-MANEUVER HER!
プル SHVR
プル SHVR
プル SHVR
...SO THAT JUST LEAVES THE TRUTH!
UM...
UM...

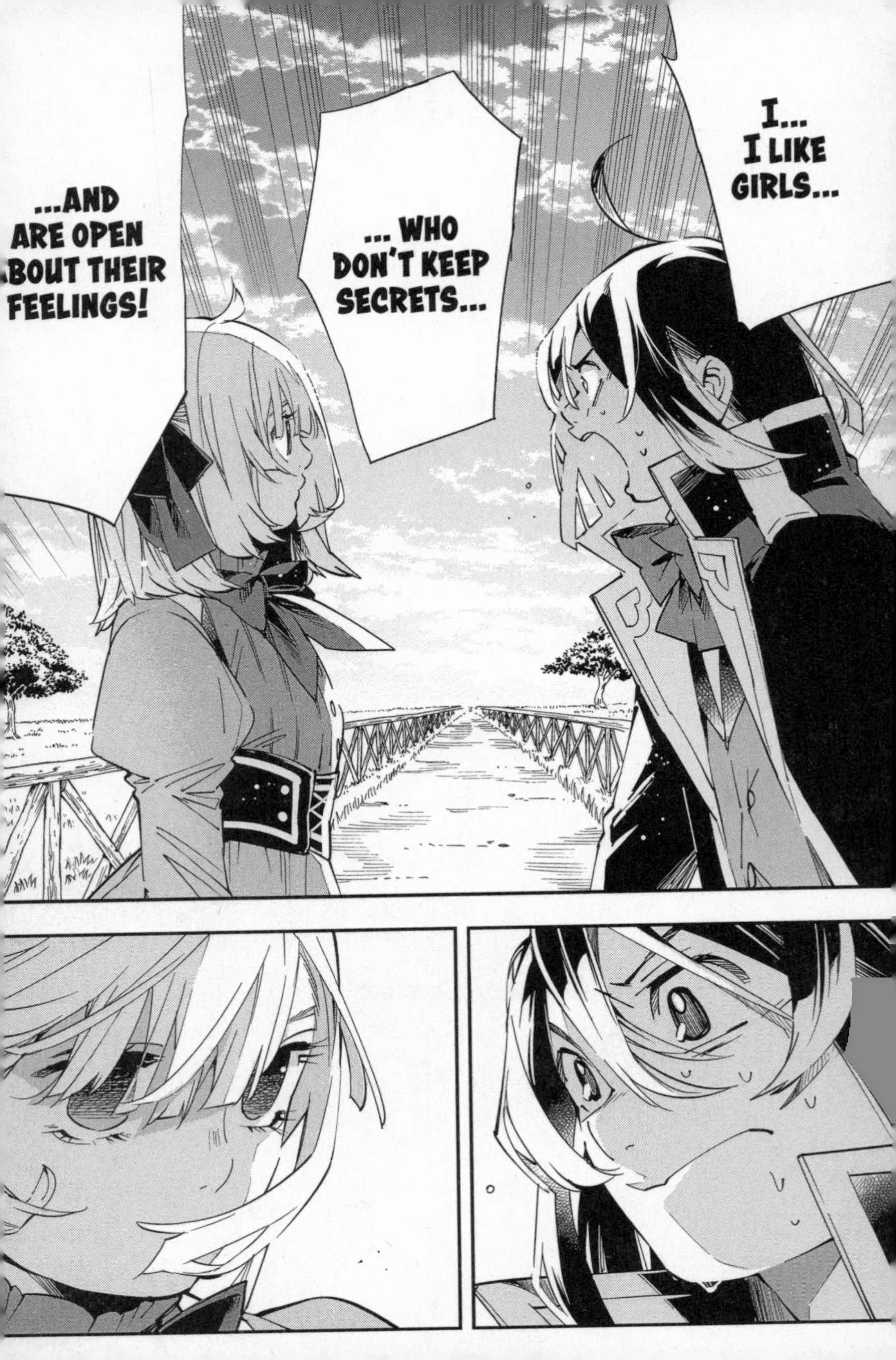
I... I LIKE GIRLS...
... WHO DON'T KEEP SECRETS...
...AND ARE OPEN BOUT THEIR FEELINGS!

Chapter 21: Truth and Honesty

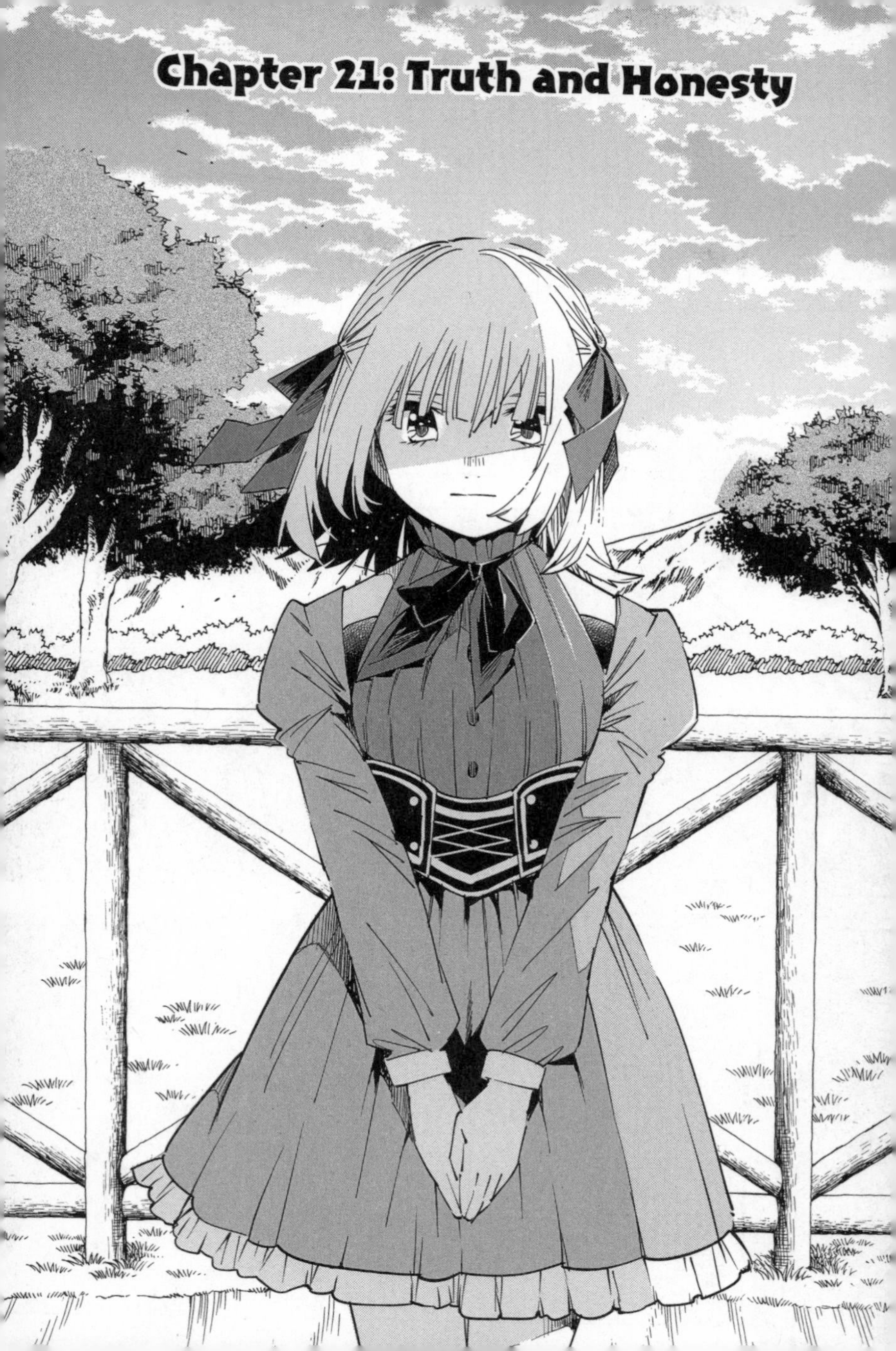

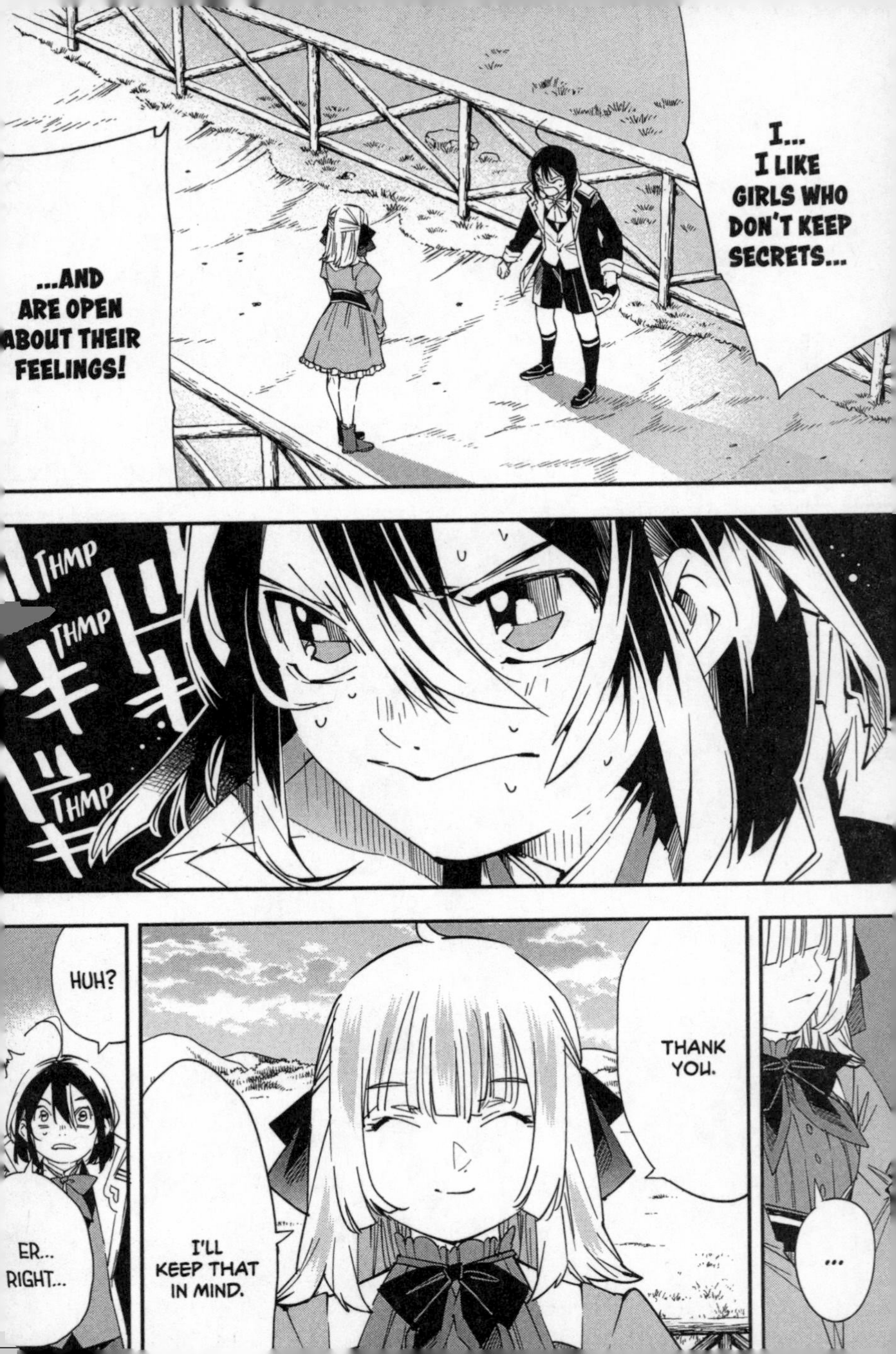
I...
I LIKE GIRLS WHO DON'T KEEP SECRETS...
...AND ARE OPEN ABOUT THEIR FEELINGS!
THMP
THMP
THMP
...
THANK YOU.
I'LL KEEP THAT IN MIND.
HUH?
ER... RIGHT...

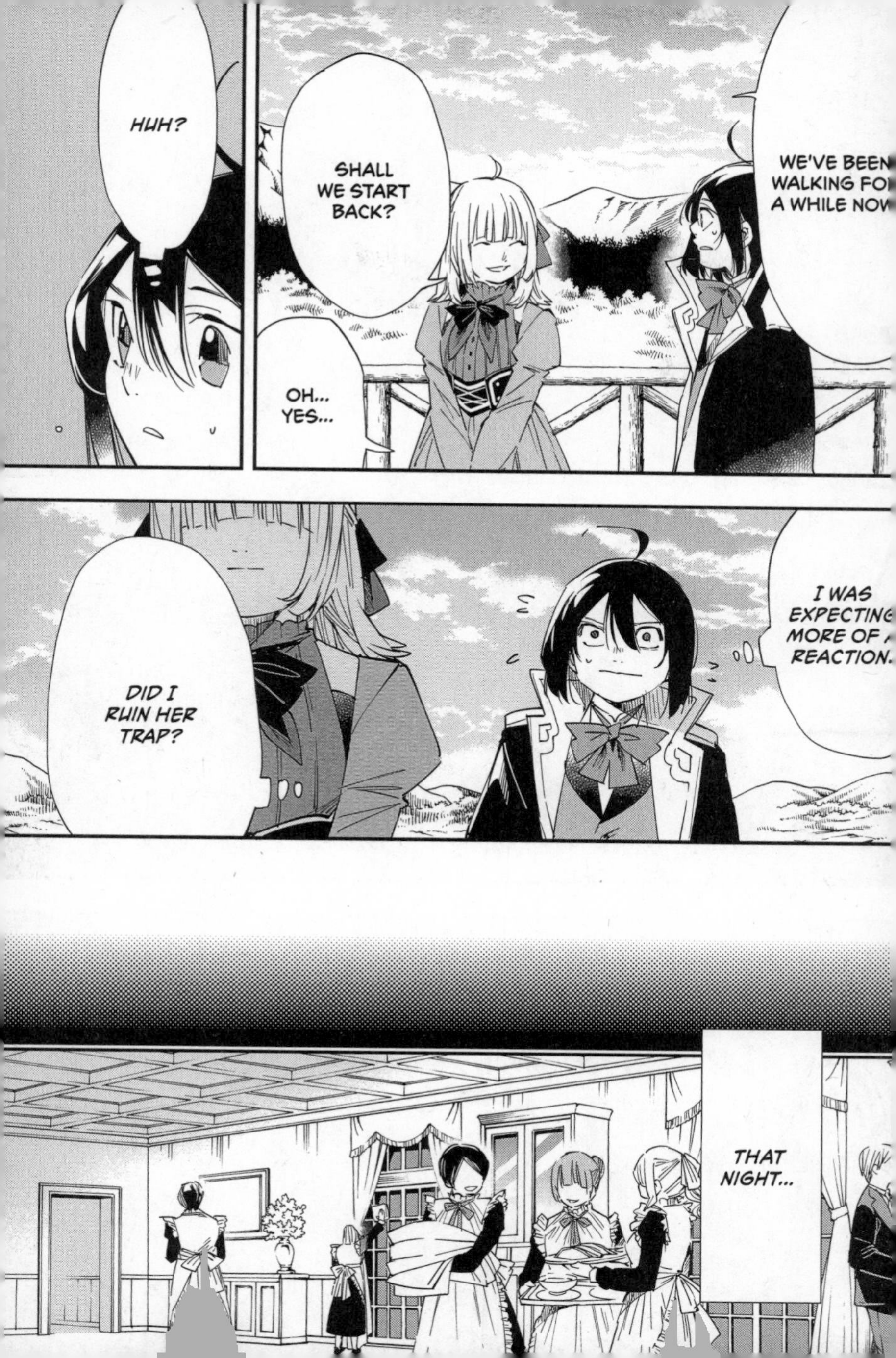
WE'VE BEEN WALKING FO A WHILE NOW
SHALL WE START BACK?
OH... YES...
HUH?
I WAS EXPECTING MORE OF REACTION.
DID I RUIN HER TRAP?
THAT NIGHT...

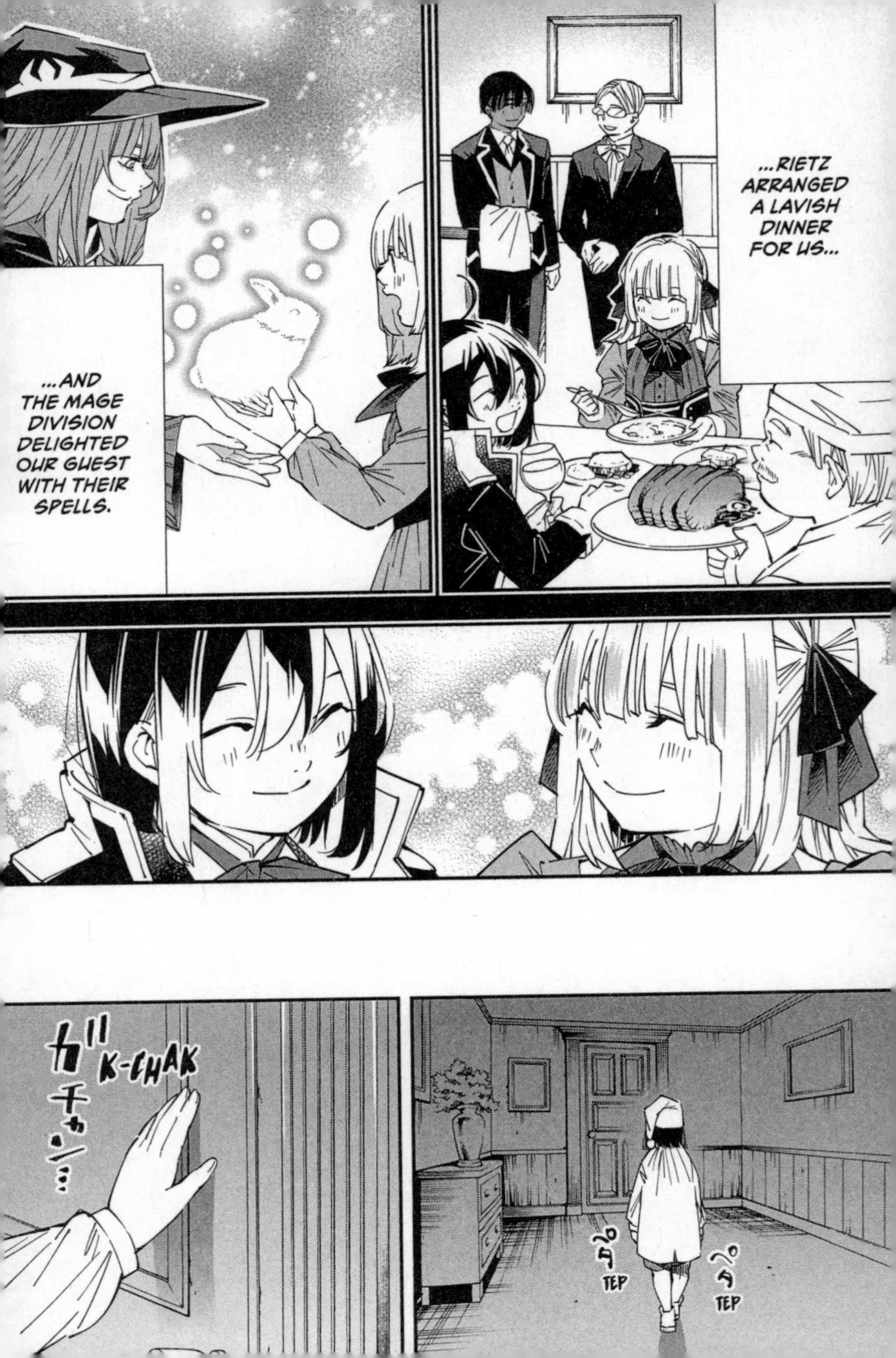
...RIETZ ARRANGED A LAVISH DINNER FOR US...
...AND THE MAGE DIVISION DELIGHTED OUR GUEST WITH THEIR SPELLS.
TEP
TEP
K-CHAK

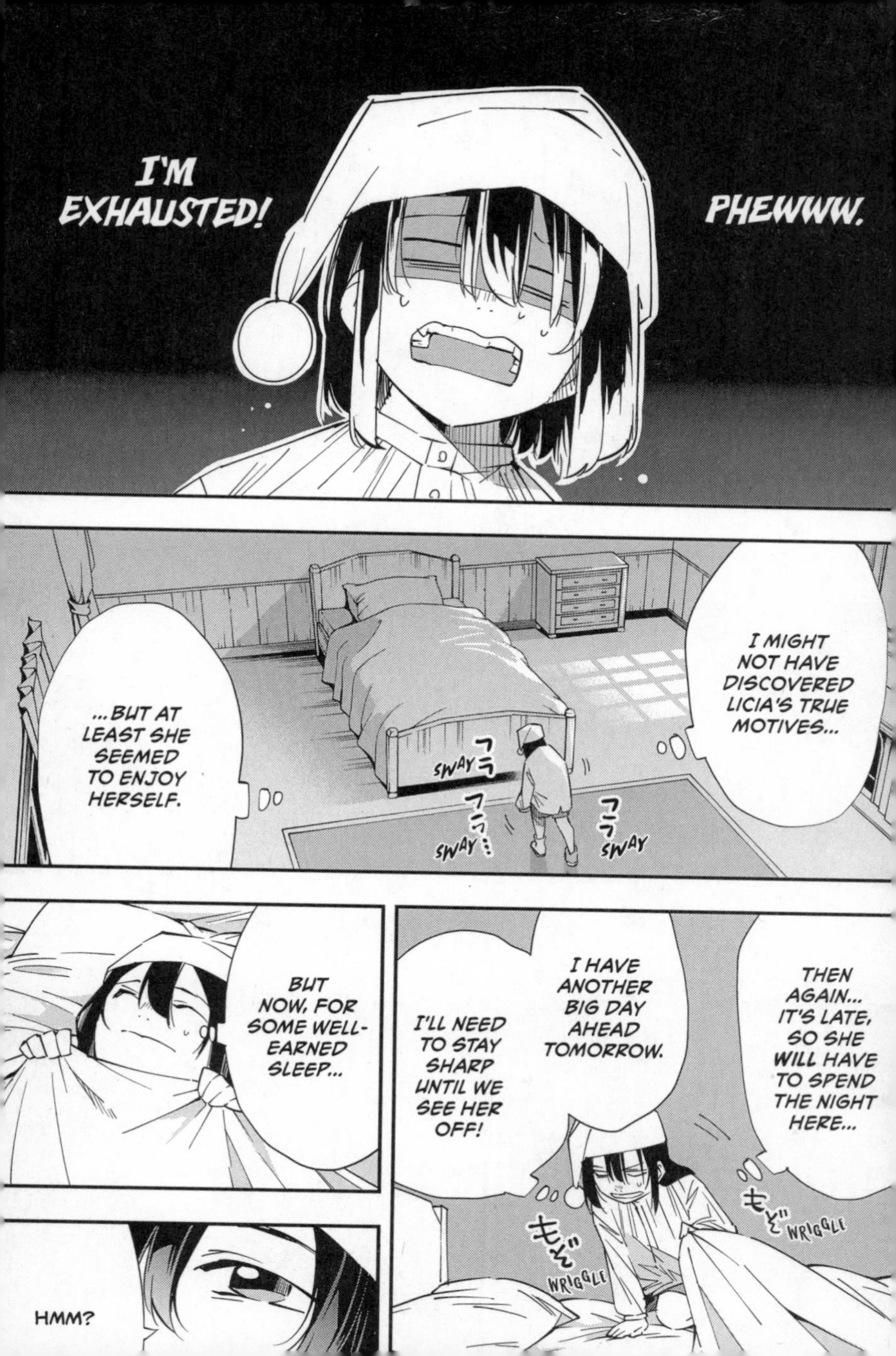
PHEWWW.
I'M EXHAUSTED!
I MIGHT NOT HAVE DISCOVERED LICIA'S TRUE MOTIVES...
フラ SWAY
フラ SWAY
フラ... SWAY...
...BUT AT LEAST SHE SEEMED TO ENJOY HERSELF.
THEN AGAIN... IT'S LATE, SO SHE WILL HAVE TO SPEND THE NIGHT HERE...
I HAVE ANOTHER BIG DAY AHEAD TOMORROW.
I'LL NEED TO STAY SHARP UNTIL WE SEE HER OFF!
もぞ WRIGGLE
もぞ WRIGGLE
BUT NOW, FOR SOME WELL-EARNED SLEEP...
HMM?

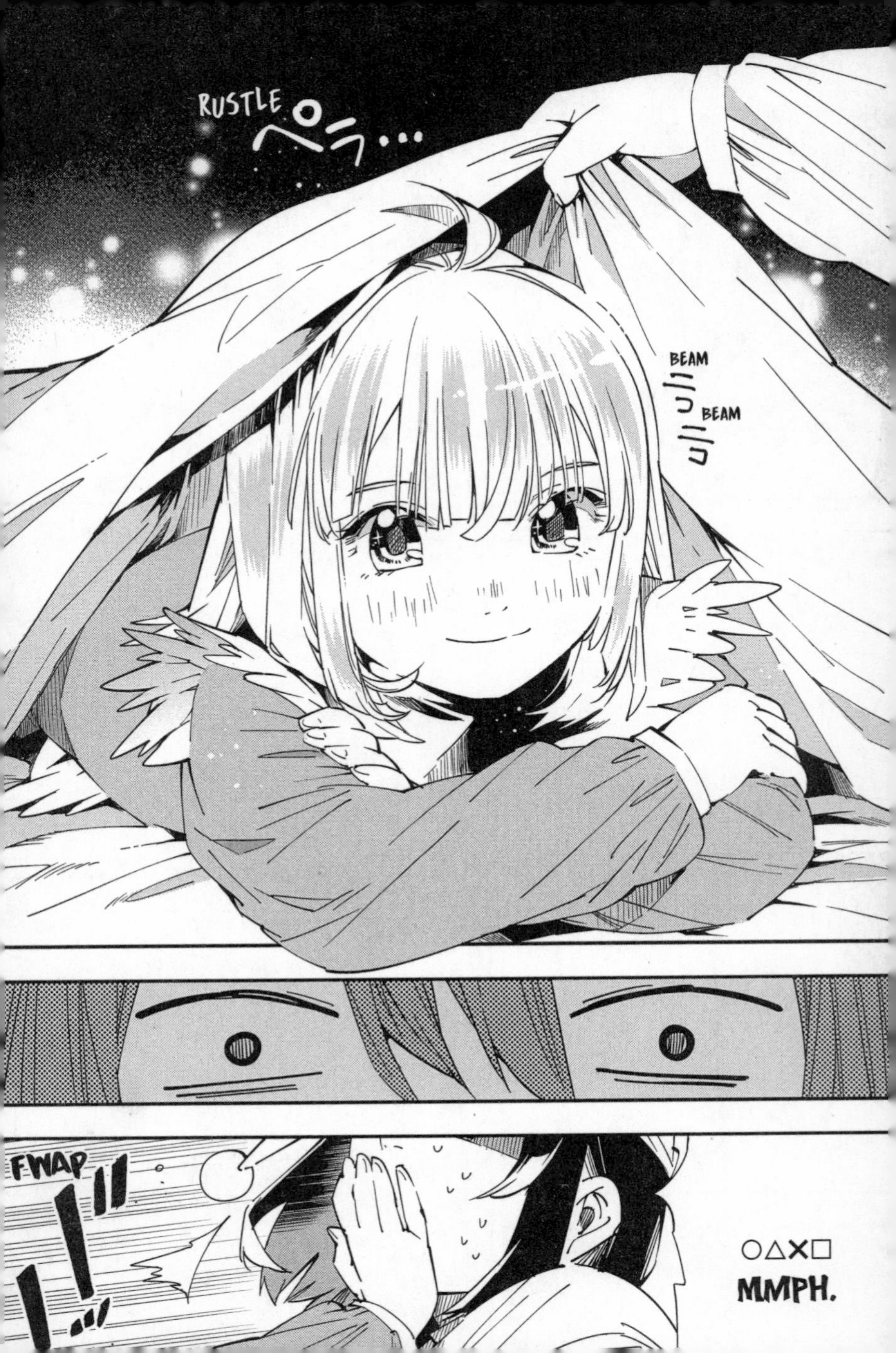
RUSTLE
ペラ…
BEAM
ニコ
BEAM
ニコ
○△×□
MMPH.
FWAP
!!

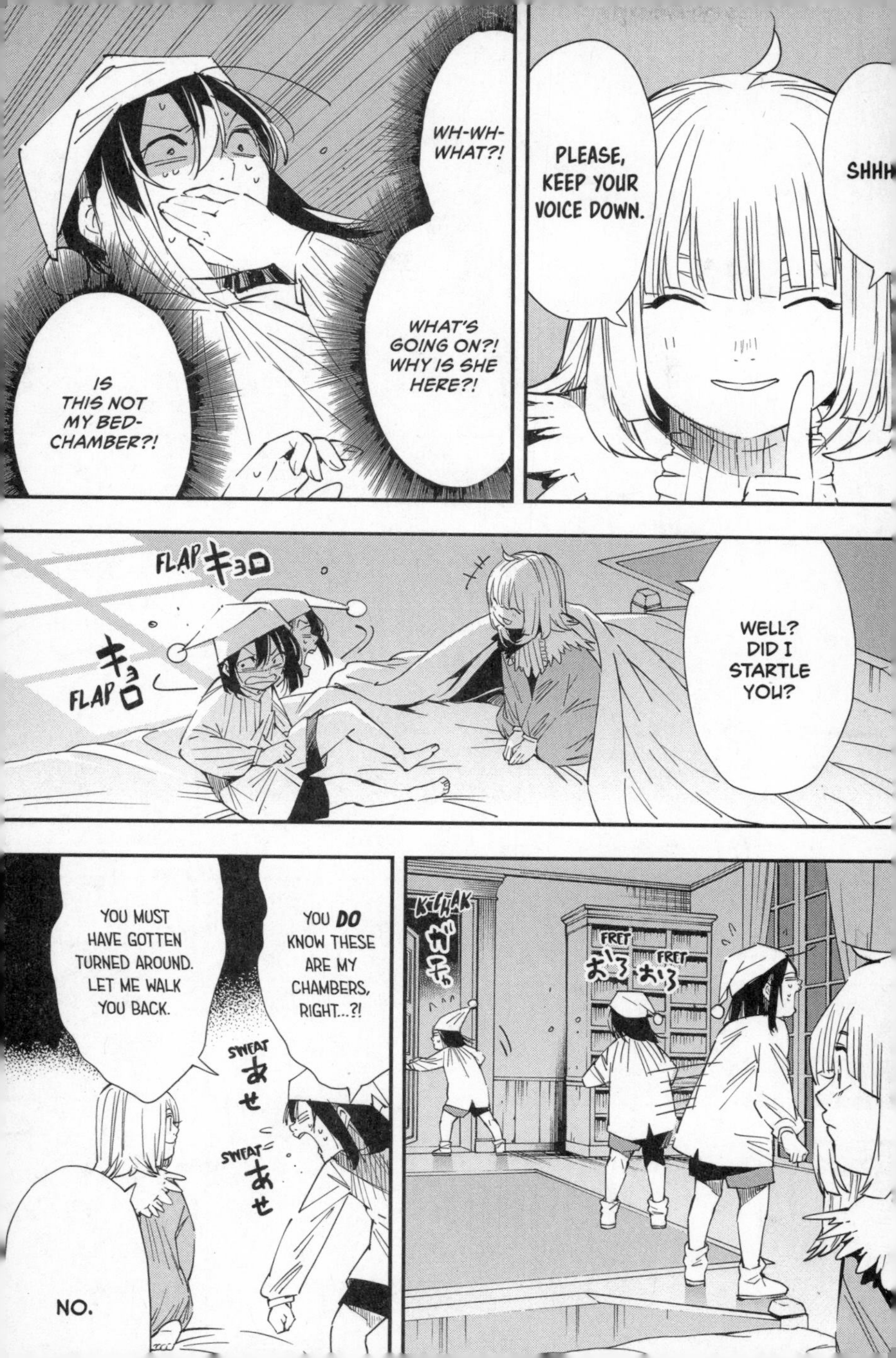
SHHH
PLEASE, KEEP YOUR VOICE DOWN.
WH-WH-WHAT?!
WHAT'S GOING ON?! WHY IS SHE HERE?!
IS THIS NOT MY BED-CHAMBER?!
WELL? DID I STARTLE YOU?
FLAP キョロ
キョロ FLAP
K-CHAK ガチャ
FRET おろ
FRET おろ
YOU **DO** KNOW THESE ARE MY CHAMBERS, RIGHT...?!
YOU MUST HAVE GOTTEN TURNED AROUND. LET ME WALK YOU BACK.
SWEAT あせ
SWEAT あせ
NO.

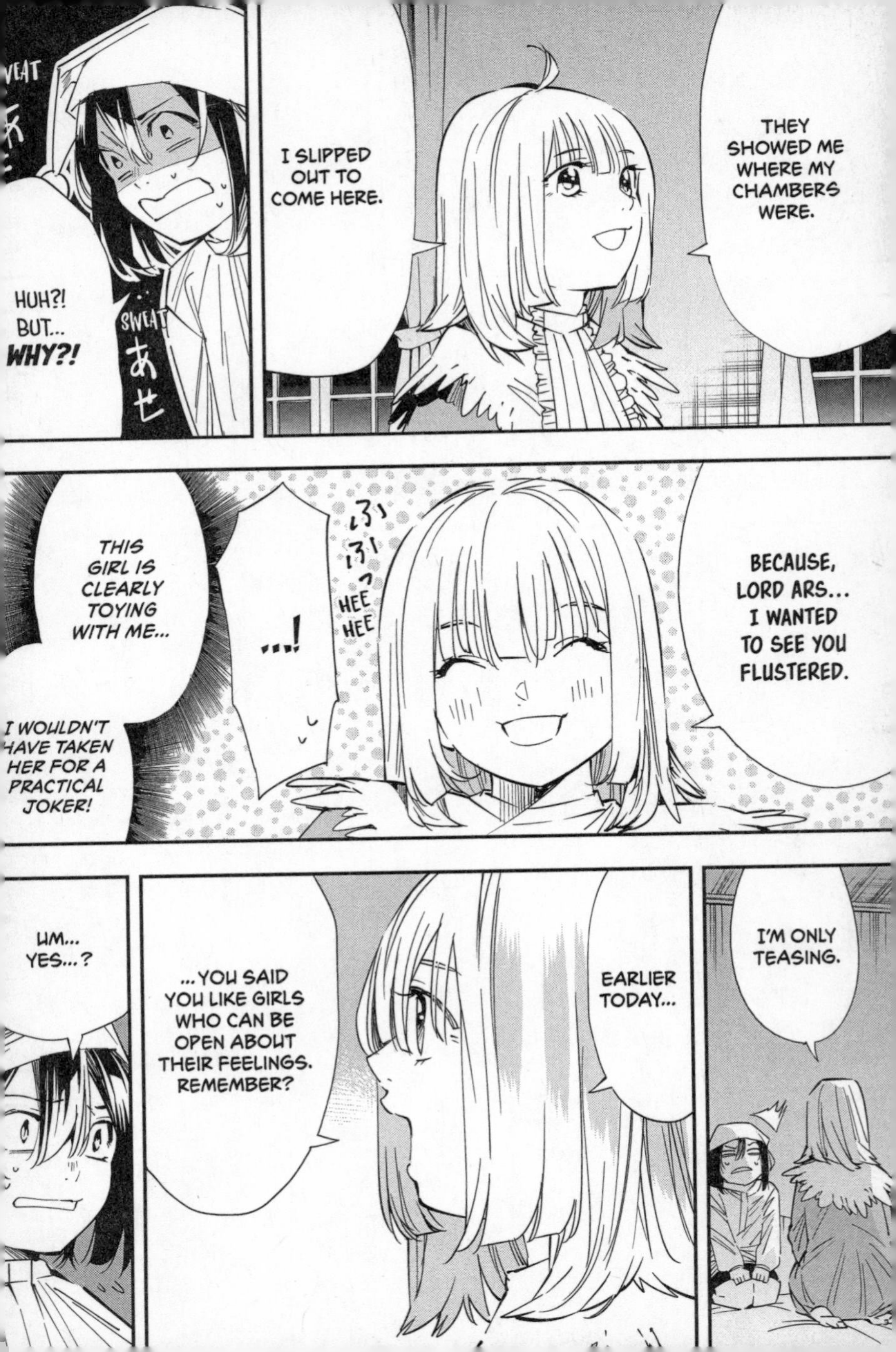
THEY SHOWED ME WHERE MY CHAMBERS WERE.
I SLIPPED OUT TO COME HERE.
HUH?! BUT... **WHY?!**
SWEAT あせ
BECAUSE, LORD ARS... I WANTED TO SEE YOU FLUSTERED.
ふふっ HEE HEE
...!
THIS GIRL IS CLEARLY TOYING WITH ME...
I WOULDN'T HAVE TAKEN HER FOR A PRACTICAL JOKER!
I'M ONLY TEASING.
EARLIER TODAY...
...YOU SAID YOU LIKE GIRLS WHO CAN BE OPEN ABOUT THEIR FEELINGS. REMEMBER?
UM... YES...?

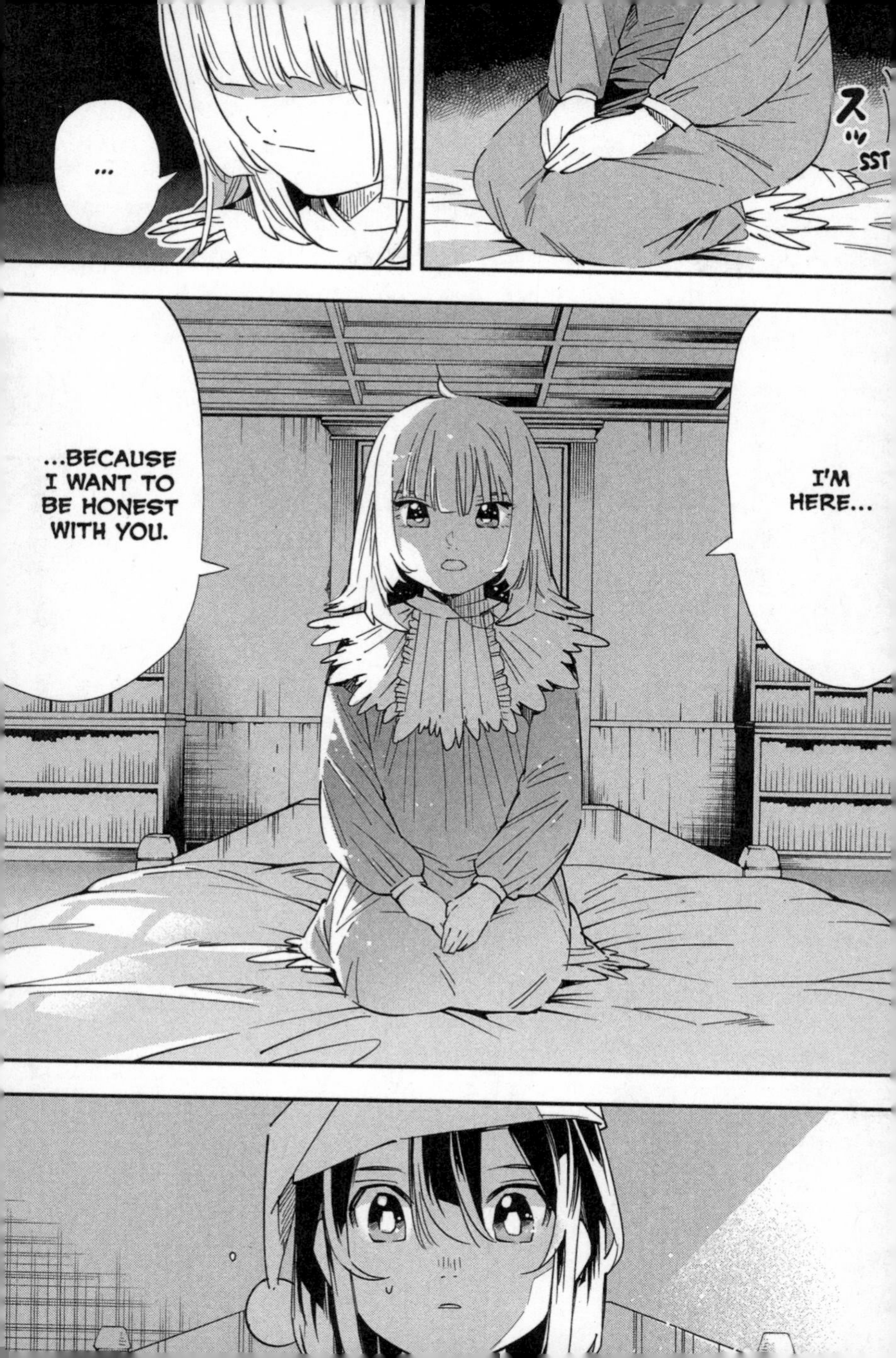
スッ
SST
...
I'M HERE...
...BECAUSE I WANT TO BE HONEST WITH YOU.

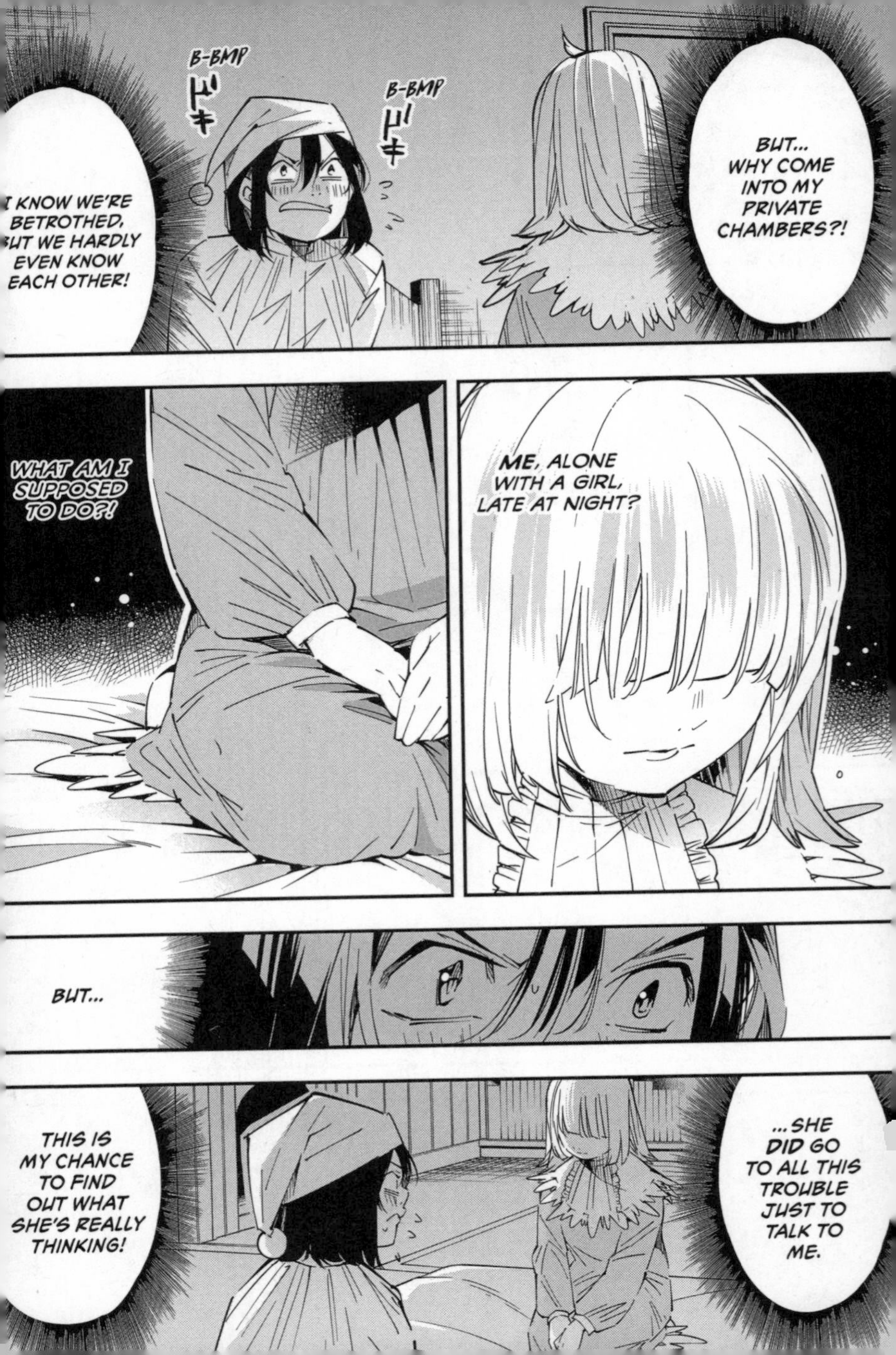
BUT... WHY COME INTO MY PRIVATE CHAMBERS?!
B-BMP ドキ
B-BMP ドキ
I KNOW WE'RE BETROTHED, BUT WE HARDLY EVEN KNOW EACH OTHER!
ME, ALONE WITH A GIRL, LATE AT NIGHT?
WHAT AM I SUPPOSED TO DO?!
BUT...
...SHE DID GO TO ALL THIS TROUBLE JUST TO TALK TO ME.
THIS IS MY CHANCE TO FIND OUT WHAT SHE'S REALLY THINKING!

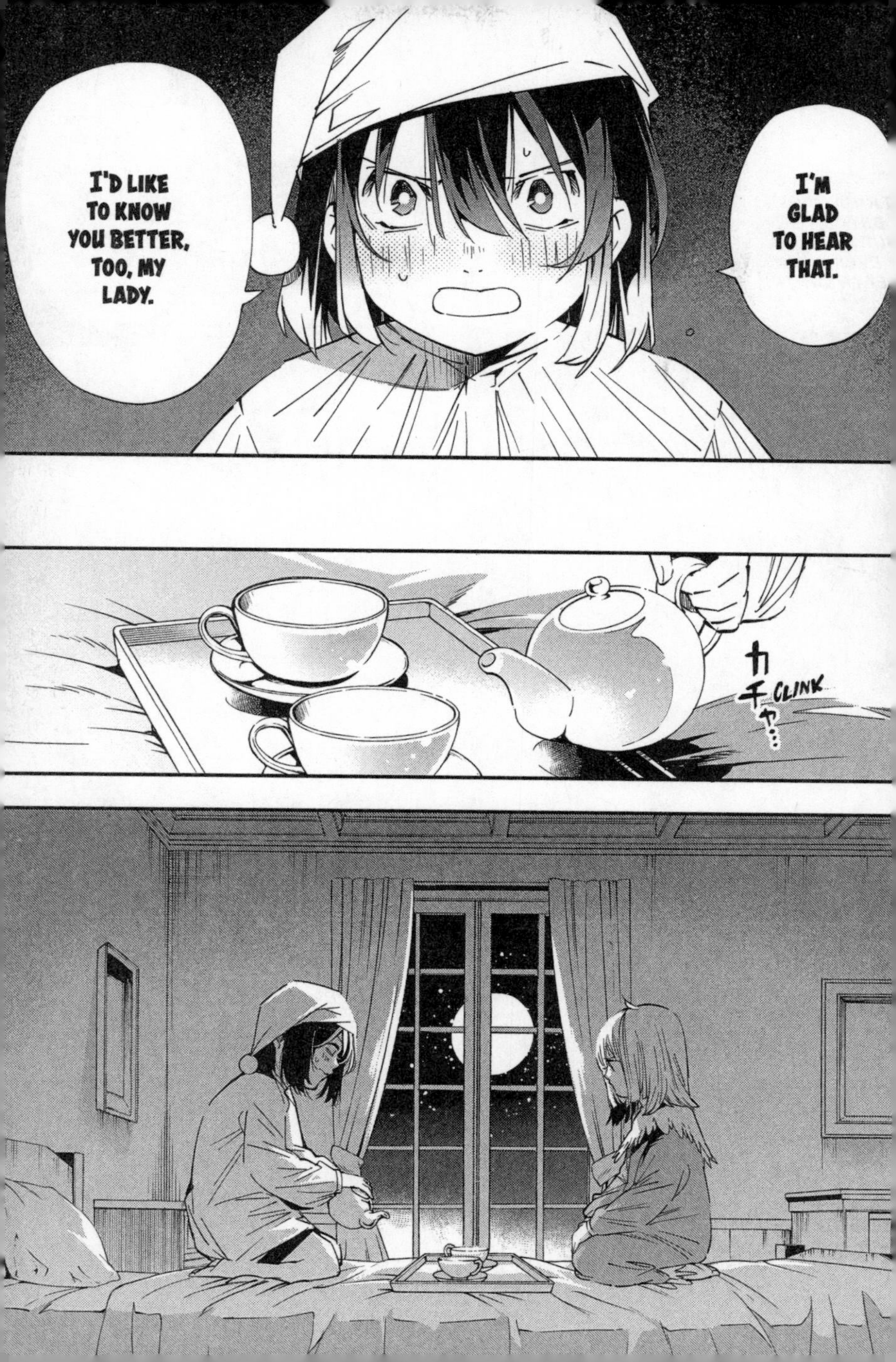
I'M GLAD TO HEAR THAT.
I'D LIKE TO KNOW YOU BETTER, TOO, MY LADY.
カチャ…
CLINK

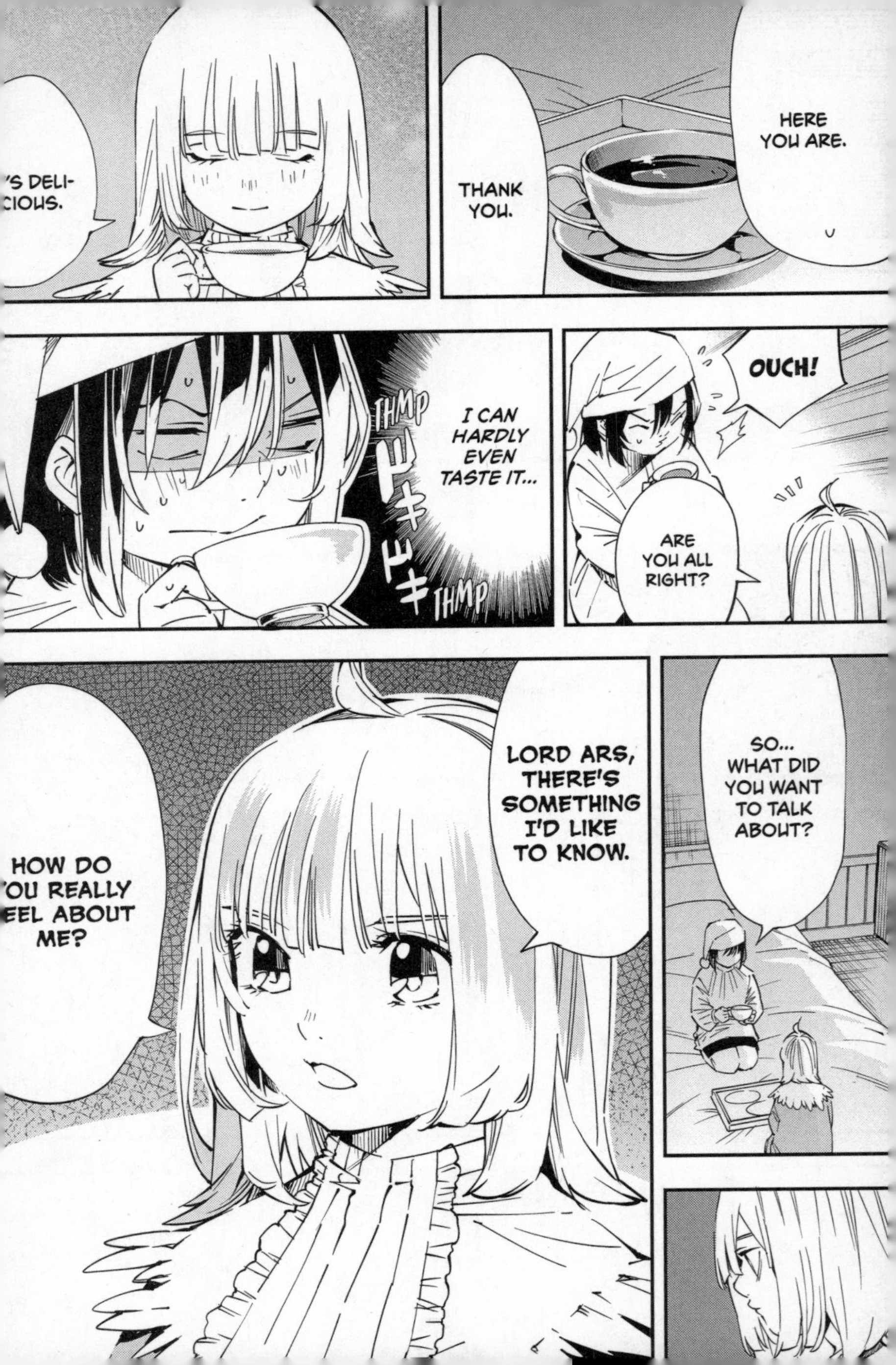
HERE YOU ARE.
THANK YOU.
'S DELI-CIOUS.
OUCH!
ARE YOU ALL RIGHT?
I CAN HARDLY EVEN TASTE IT...
THMP
THMP
SO... WHAT DID YOU WANT TO TALK ABOUT?
LORD ARS, THERE'S SOMETHING I'D LIKE TO KNOW.
HOW DO 'OU REALLY EEL ABOUT ME?

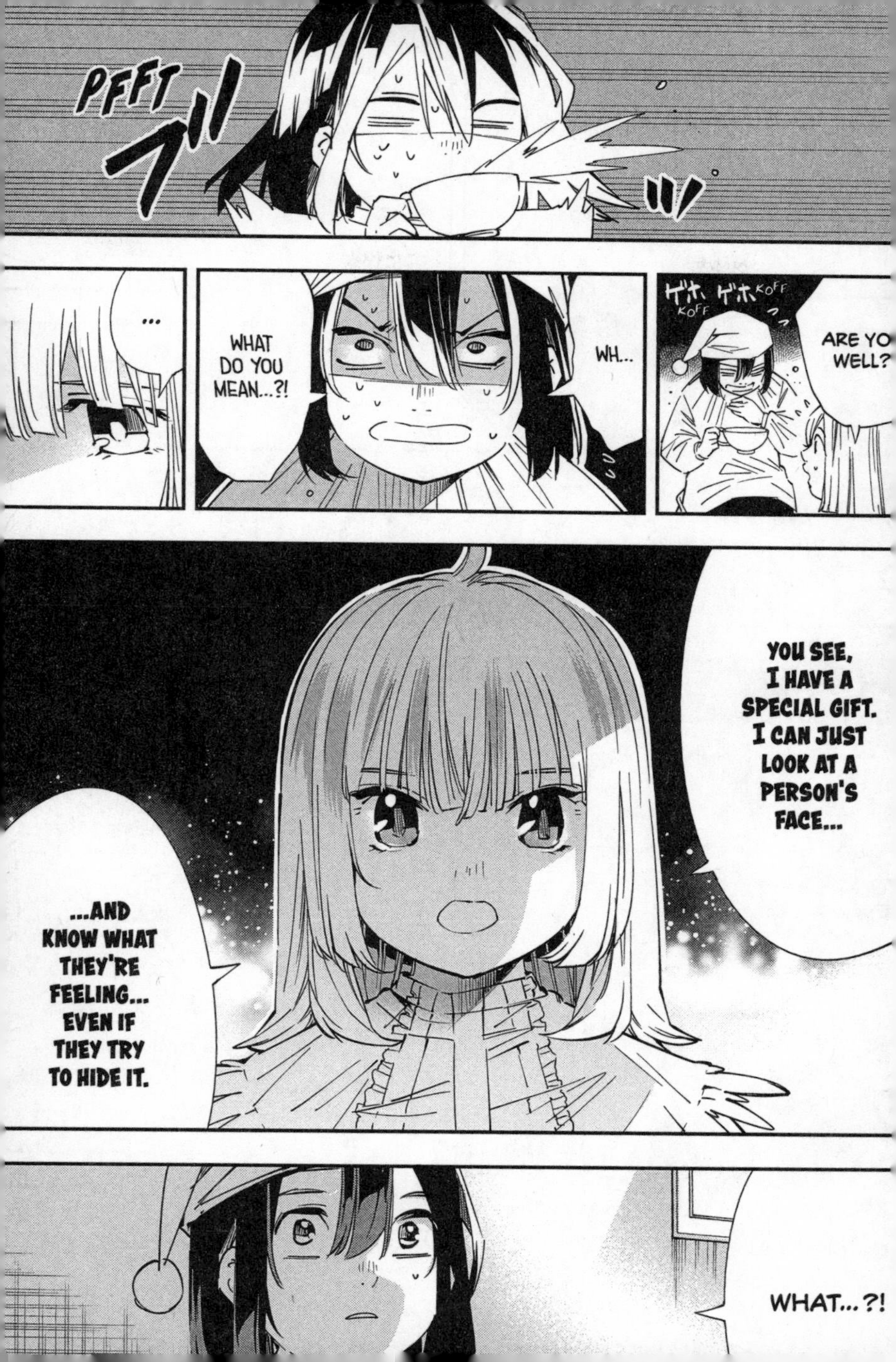
PFFT
ブッ
ゲホ ゲホ
KOFF KOFF
ARE YO WELL?
WH...
WHAT DO YOU MEAN...?!
...
YOU SEE, I HAVE A SPECIAL GIFT. I CAN JUST LOOK AT A PERSON'S FACE...
...AND KNOW WHAT THEY'RE FEELING... EVEN IF THEY TRY TO HIDE IT.
WHAT...?!

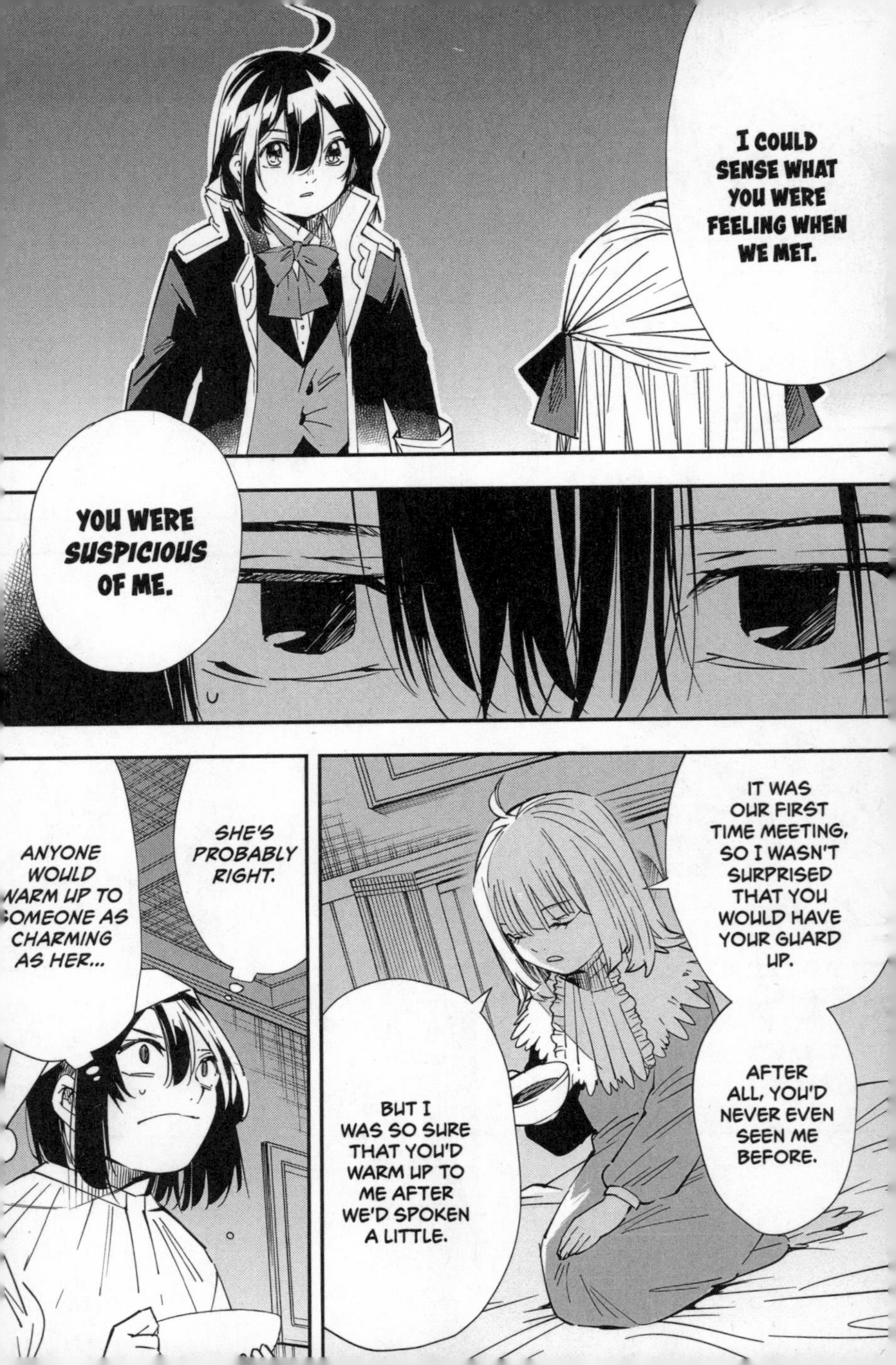

I COULD SENSE WHAT YOU WERE FEELING WHEN WE MET.
YOU WERE SUSPICIOUS OF ME.
IT WAS OUR FIRST TIME MEETING, SO I WASN'T SURPRISED THAT YOU WOULD HAVE YOUR GUARD UP.
AFTER ALL, YOU'D NEVER EVEN SEEN ME BEFORE.
BUT I WAS SO SURE THAT YOU'D WARM UP TO ME AFTER WE'D SPOKEN A LITTLE.
SHE'S PROBABLY RIGHT.
ANYONE WOULD ARM UP TO OMEONE AS CHARMING AS HER...

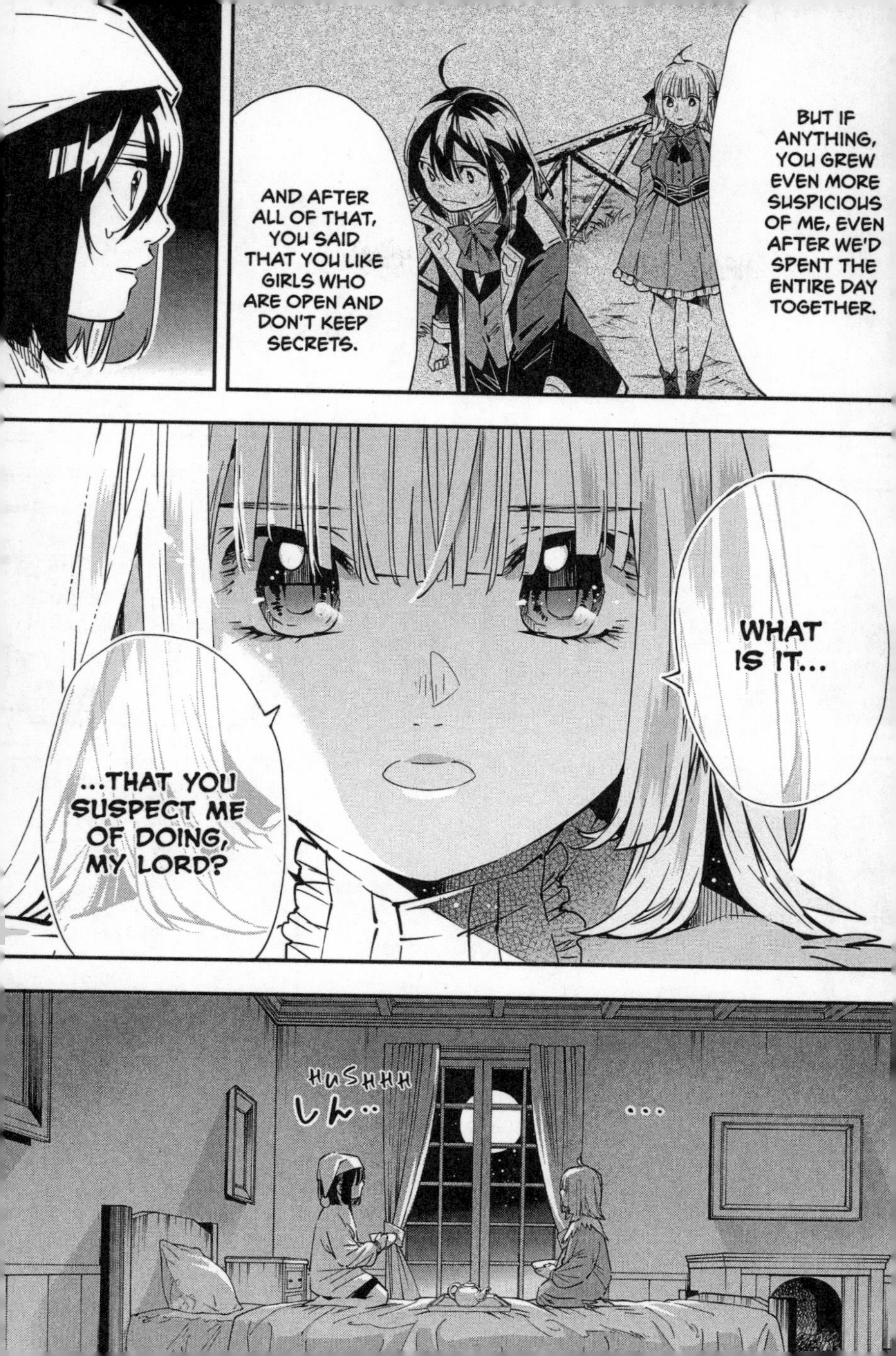
BUT IF ANYTHING, YOU GREW EVEN MORE SUSPICIOUS OF ME, EVEN AFTER WE'D SPENT THE ENTIRE DAY TOGETHER.
AND AFTER ALL OF THAT, YOU SAID THAT YOU LIKE GIRLS WHO ARE OPEN AND DON'T KEEP SECRETS.
WHAT IS IT...
...THAT YOU SUSPECT ME OF DOING, MY LORD?
...
HUSHHH
しん..

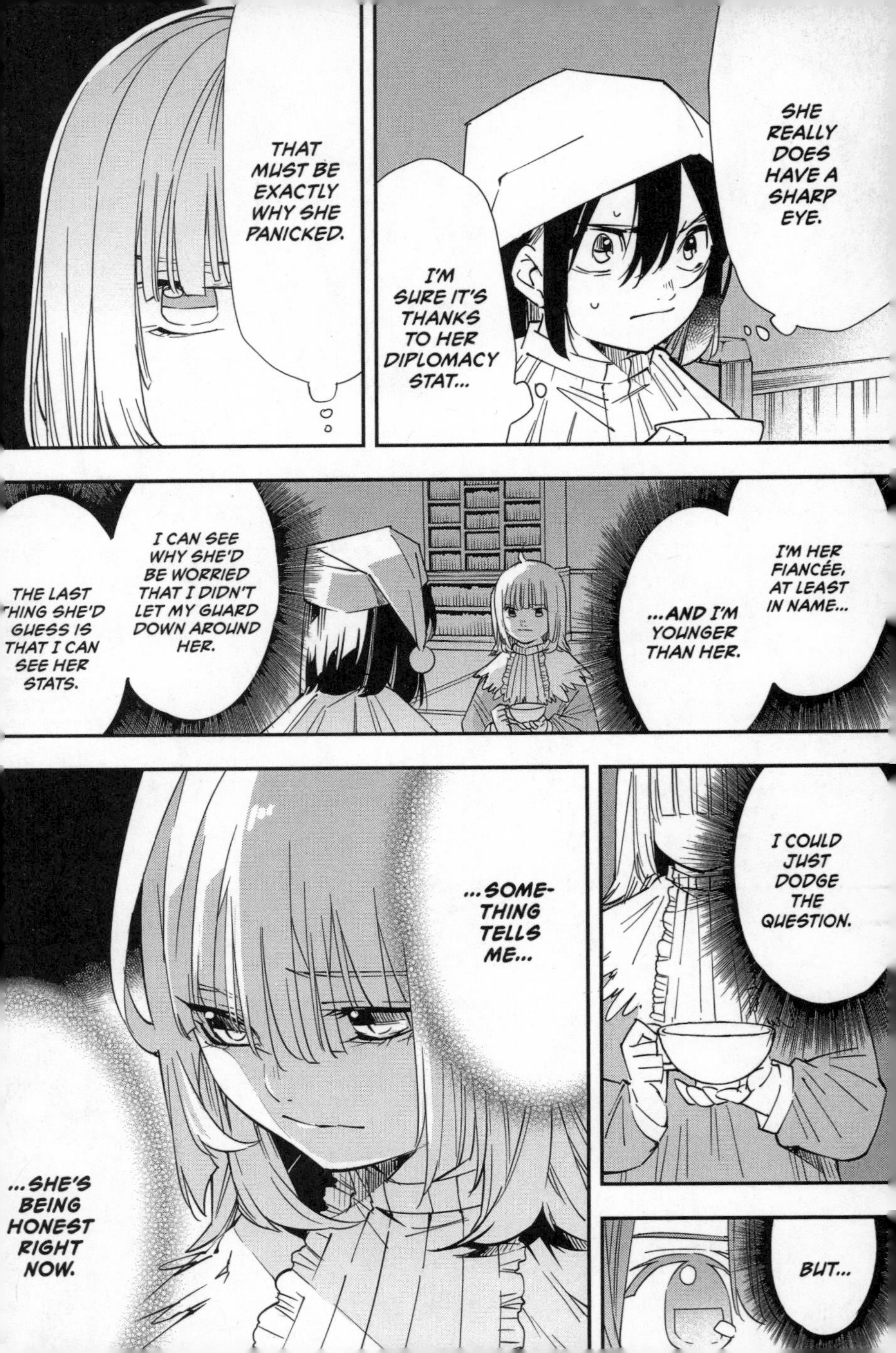
SHE REALLY DOES HAVE A SHARP EYE.
I'M SURE IT'S THANKS TO HER DIPLOMACY STAT...
THAT MUST BE EXACTLY WHY SHE PANICKED.
I'M HER FIANCÉE, AT LEAST IN NAME...
...AND I'M YOUNGER THAN HER.
I CAN SEE WHY SHE'D BE WORRIED THAT I DIDN'T LET MY GUARD DOWN AROUND HER.
THE LAST THING SHE'D GUESS IS THAT I CAN SEE HER STATS.
I COULD JUST DODGE THE QUESTION.
BUT...
...SOME-THING TELLS ME...
...SHE'S BEING HONEST RIGHT NOW.

LADY LICIA...

...NOT TO RETURN THE FAVOR.

IT WOULD BE RUD... OF ME..

...I CAN SEE PEOPLE'S ABILITIES, APTITUDES AND AMBITION..

...JUST BY LOOKING AT THEM.

I'M SORRY IF I WAS COLD TO YOU. AND I UNDERSTAND IF YOU DON'T BELIEVE ALL THAT ABOUT MY ABILITY, BUT...

I WAS WORRIED THAT THIS WAS ALL JUST AN ACT...

...THAT IT WAS PART OF SOME GRAND PLAN.

YOU HAVE A GREAT TALENT FOR DIPLOMACY... AND YOU'RE ALSO FAR MORE AMBITIOUS THAN MOST.

NO.

	5	
Intellect	45	7...
Diplomacy	77	100
Ambition	80	
Aptitude		

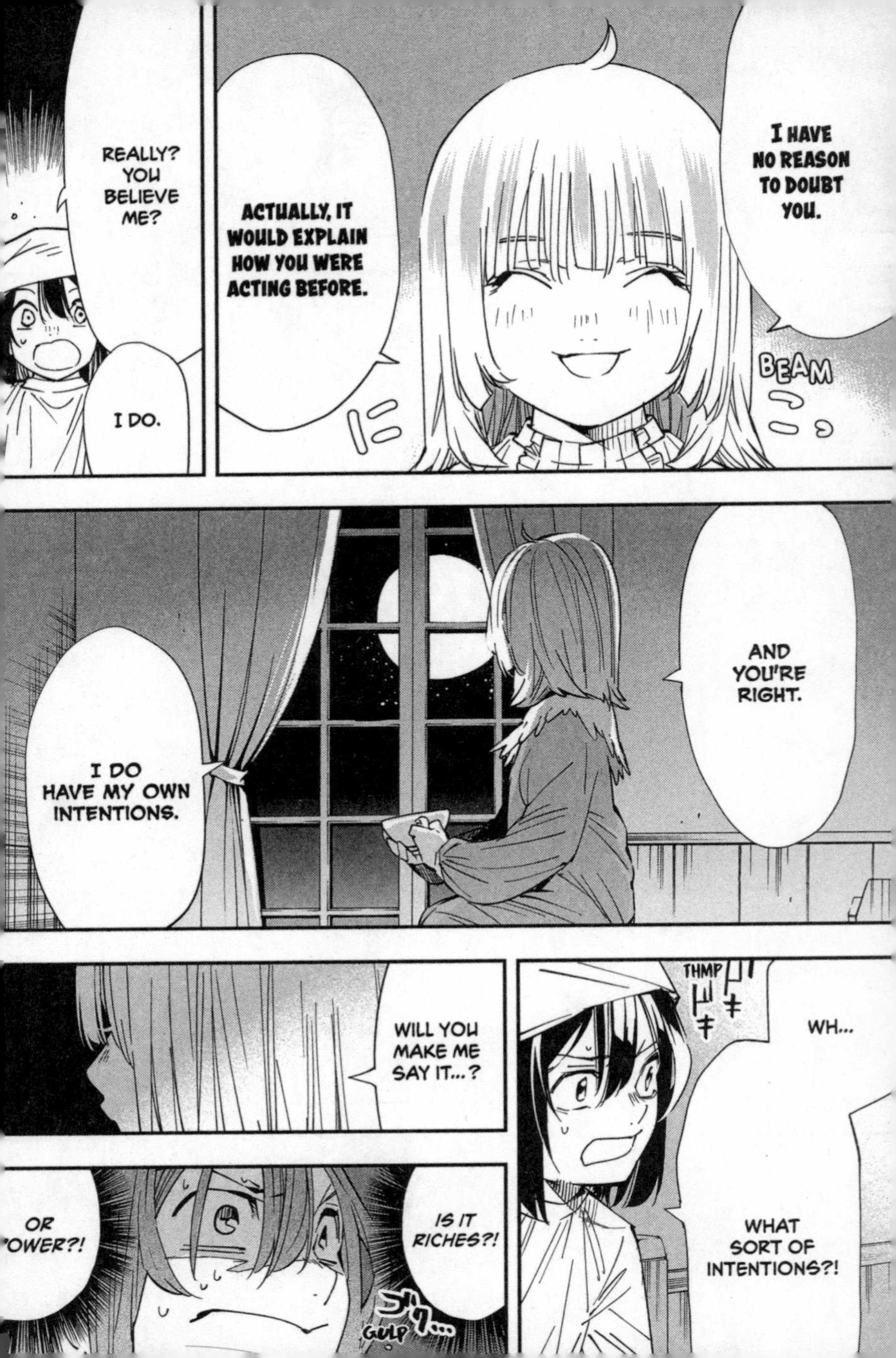
I HAVE NO REASON TO DOUBT YOU.
BEAM
ACTUALLY, IT WOULD EXPLAIN HOW YOU WERE ACTING BEFORE.
REALLY? YOU BELIEVE ME?
I DO.
AND YOU'RE RIGHT.
I DO HAVE MY OWN INTENTIONS.
THMP
WH...
WHAT SORT OF INTENTIONS?!
WILL YOU MAKE ME SAY IT...?
IS IT RICHES?!
OR
OWER?!
GULP

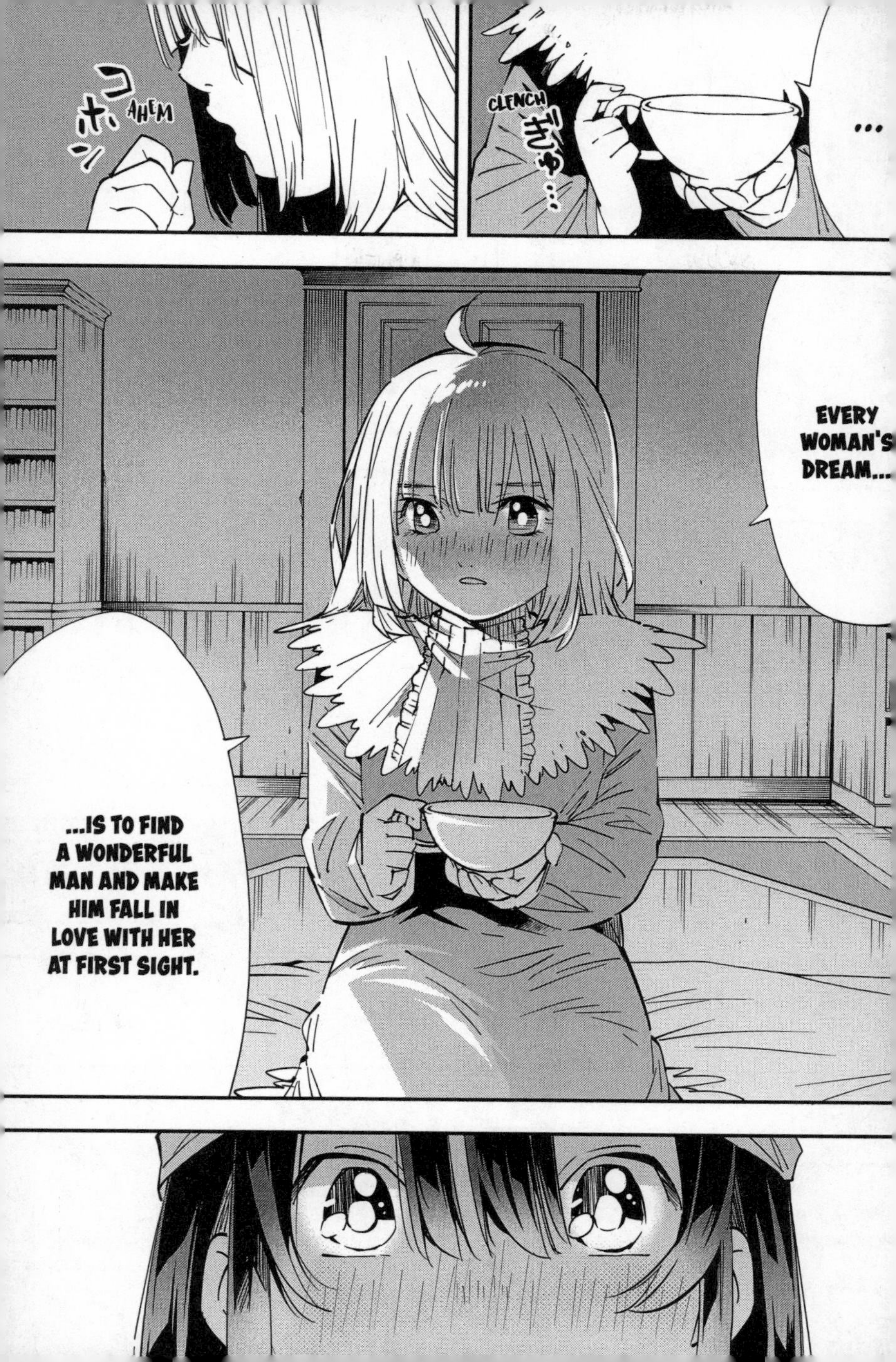
...
CLENCH
ぎゅ…
コホン
AHEM
EVERY WOMAN'S DREAM...
...IS TO FIND A WONDERFUL MAN AND MAKE HIM FALL IN LOVE WITH HER AT FIRST SIGHT.

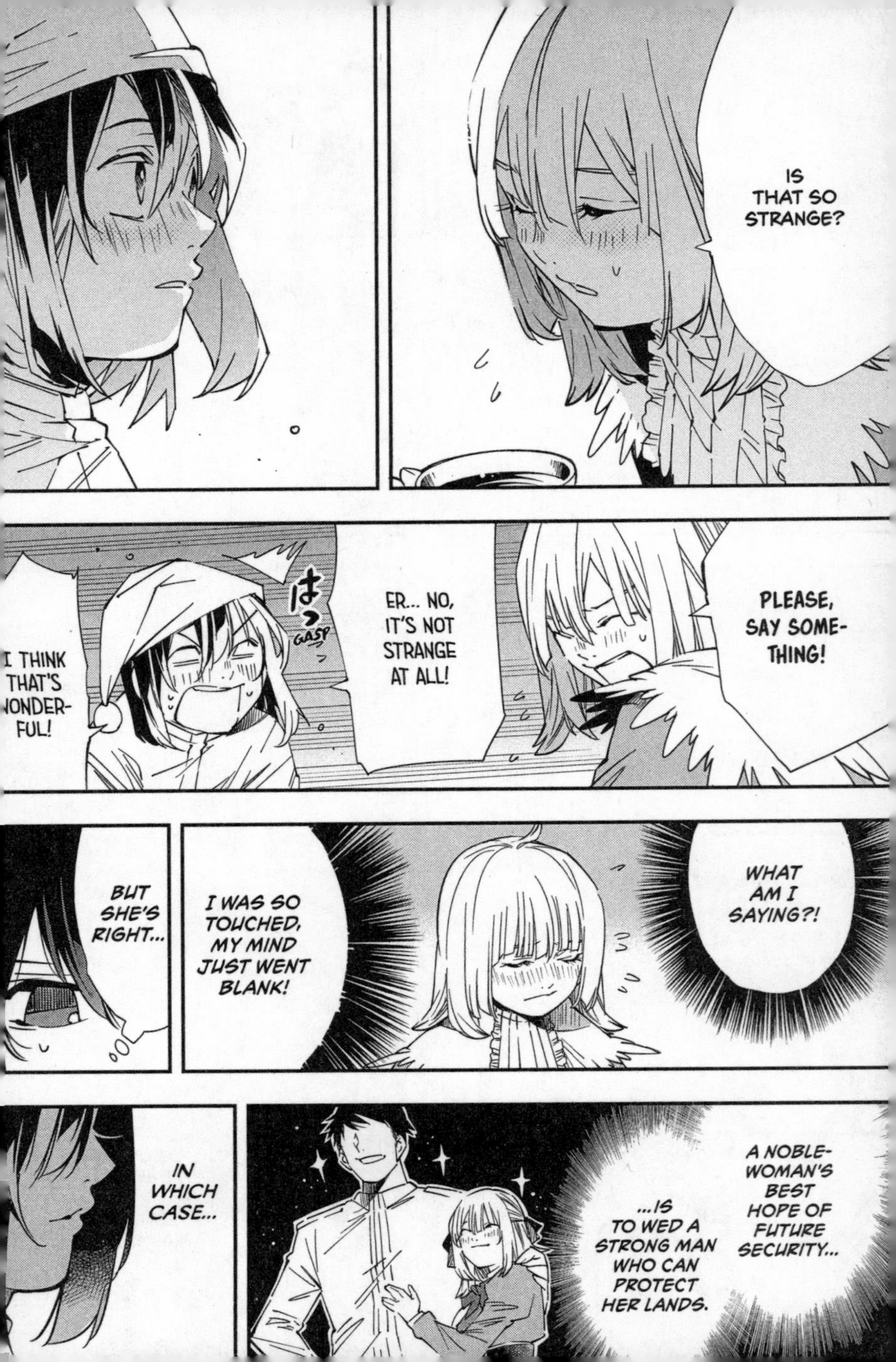
IS THAT SO STRANGE?
PLEASE, SAY SOME-THING!
ER... NO, IT'S NOT STRANGE AT ALL!
はっ GASP
I THINK THAT'S WONDER-FUL!
WHAT AM I SAYING?!
I WAS SO TOUCHED, MY MIND JUST WENT BLANK!
BUT SHE'S RIGHT...
A NOBLE-WOMAN'S BEST HOPE OF FUTURE SECURITY...
...IS TO WED A STRONG MAN WHO CAN PROTECT HER LANDS.
IN WHICH CASE...

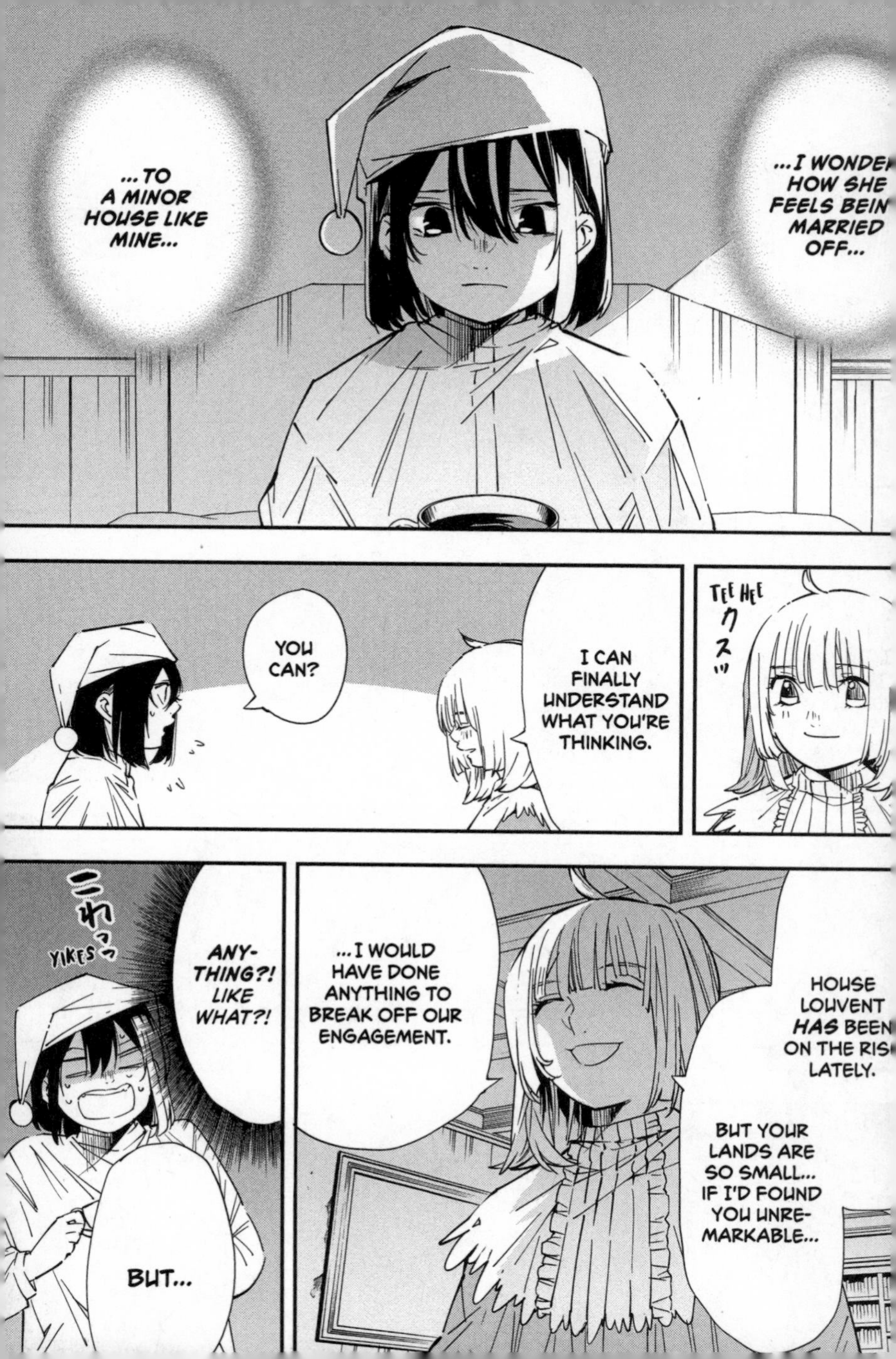
...I WONDE HOW SHE FEELS BEIN MARRIED OFF...
...TO A MINOR HOUSE LIKE MINE...
TEE HEE
クスッ
I CAN FINALLY UNDERSTAND WHAT YOU'RE THINKING.
YOU CAN?
HOUSE LOUVENT **HAS** BEEN ON THE RIS LATELY.
BUT YOUR LANDS ARE SO SMALL... IF I'D FOUND YOU UNRE-MARKABLE...
...I WOULD HAVE DONE ANYTHING TO BREAK OFF OUR ENGAGEMENT.
YIKES
これっ
ANY-THING?! LIKE WHAT?!
BUT...

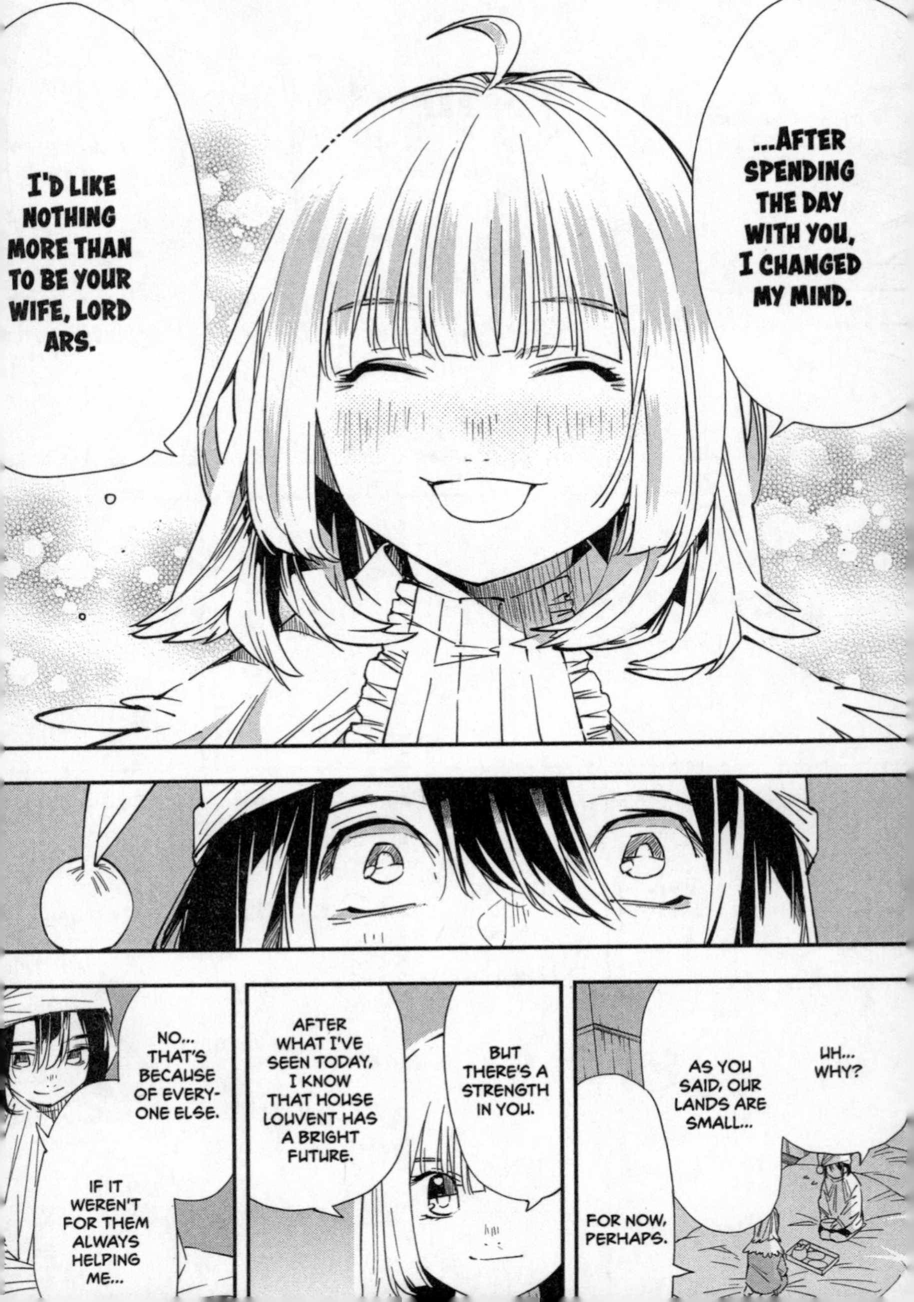
...AFTER SPENDING THE DAY WITH YOU, I CHANGED MY MIND.
I'D LIKE NOTHING MORE THAN TO BE YOUR WIFE, LORD ARS.
UH... WHY?
AS YOU SAID, OUR LANDS ARE SMALL...
FOR NOW, PERHAPS.
BUT THERE'S A STRENGTH IN YOU.
AFTER WHAT I'VE SEEN TODAY, I KNOW THAT HOUSE LOUVENT HAS A BRIGHT FUTURE.
NO... THAT'S BECAUSE OF EVERY-ONE ELSE.
IF IT WEREN'T FOR THEM ALWAYS HELPING ME...

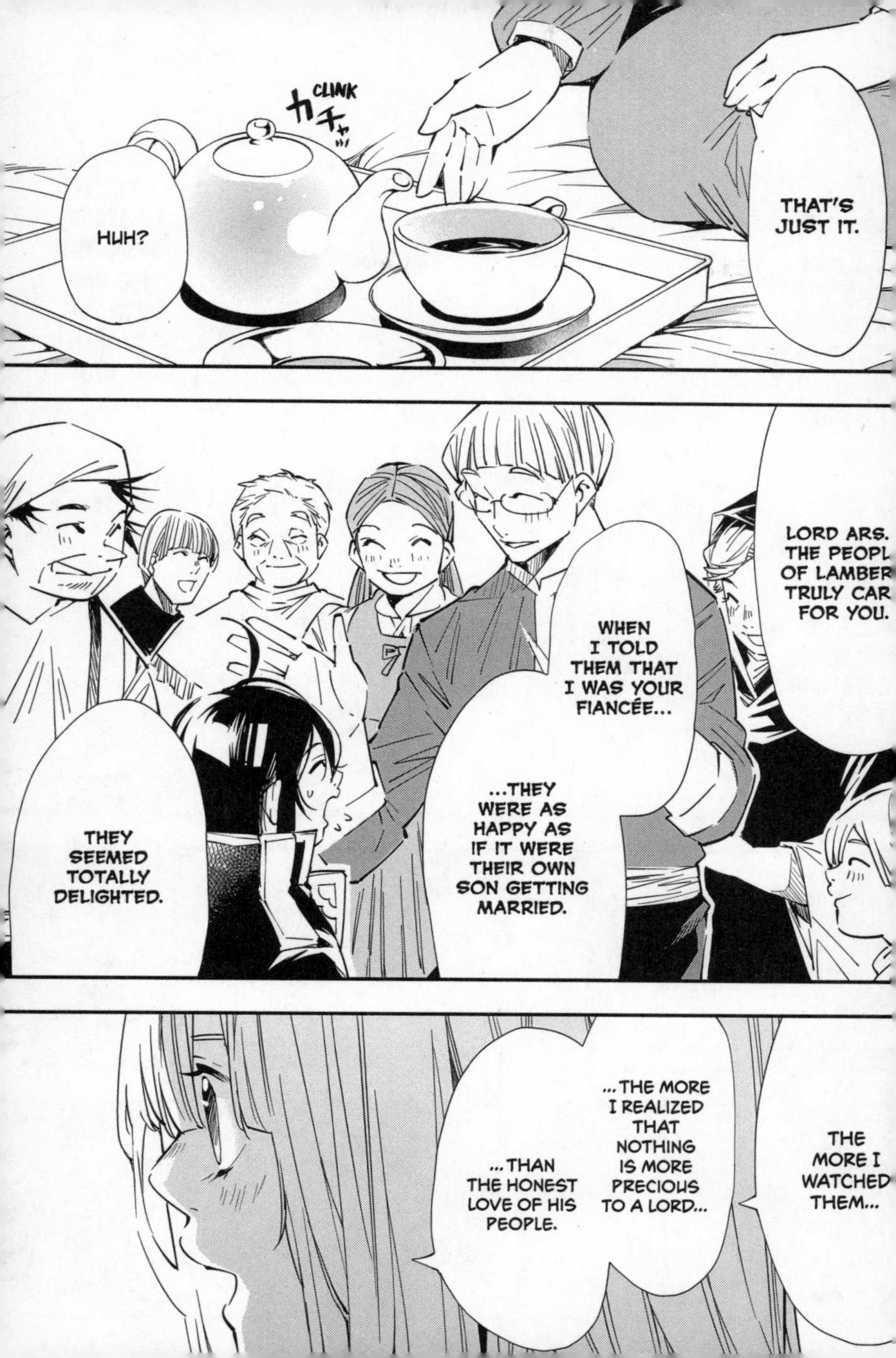
THAT'S JUST IT.
カチャッ CLINK
HUH?
LORD ARS. THE PEOPL OF LAMBER TRULY CAR FOR YOU.
WHEN I TOLD THEM THAT I WAS YOUR FIANCÉE...
...THEY WERE AS HAPPY AS IF IT WERE THEIR OWN SON GETTING MARRIED.
THEY SEEMED TOTALLY DELIGHTED.
THE MORE I WATCHED THEM...
...THE MORE I REALIZED THAT NOTHING IS MORE PRECIOUS TO A LORD...
...THAN THE HONEST LOVE OF HIS PEOPLE.

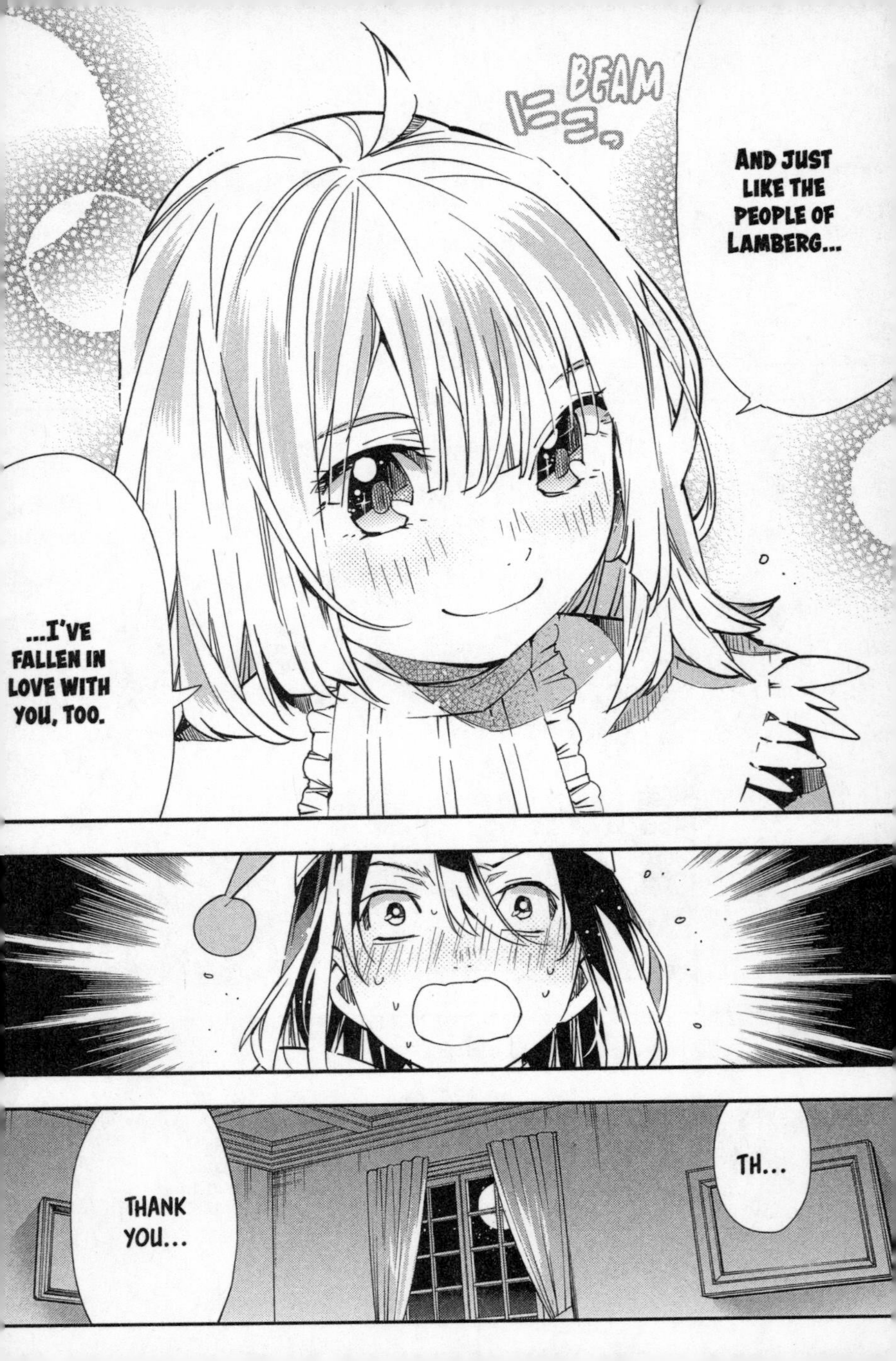
AND JUST LIKE THE PEOPLE OF LAMBERG...
BEAM
にこっ
...I'VE FALLEN IN LOVE WITH YOU, TOO.
TH...
THANK YOU...

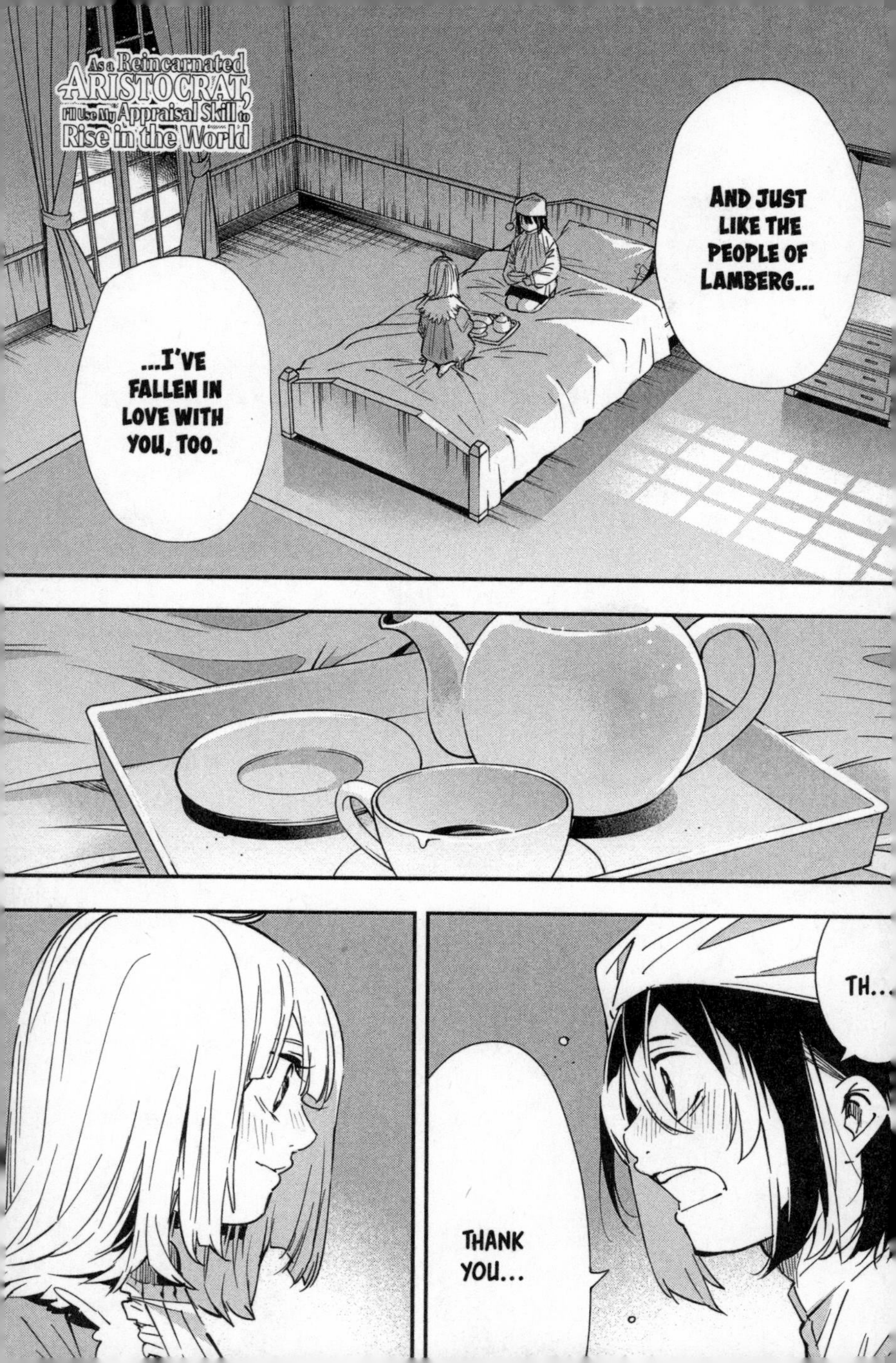
AND JUST LIKE THE PEOPLE OF LAMBERG...
As a Reincarnated ARISTOCRAT, I'll Use My Appraisal Skill to Rise in the World
...I'VE FALLEN IN LOVE WITH YOU, TOO.
TH...
THANK YOU...

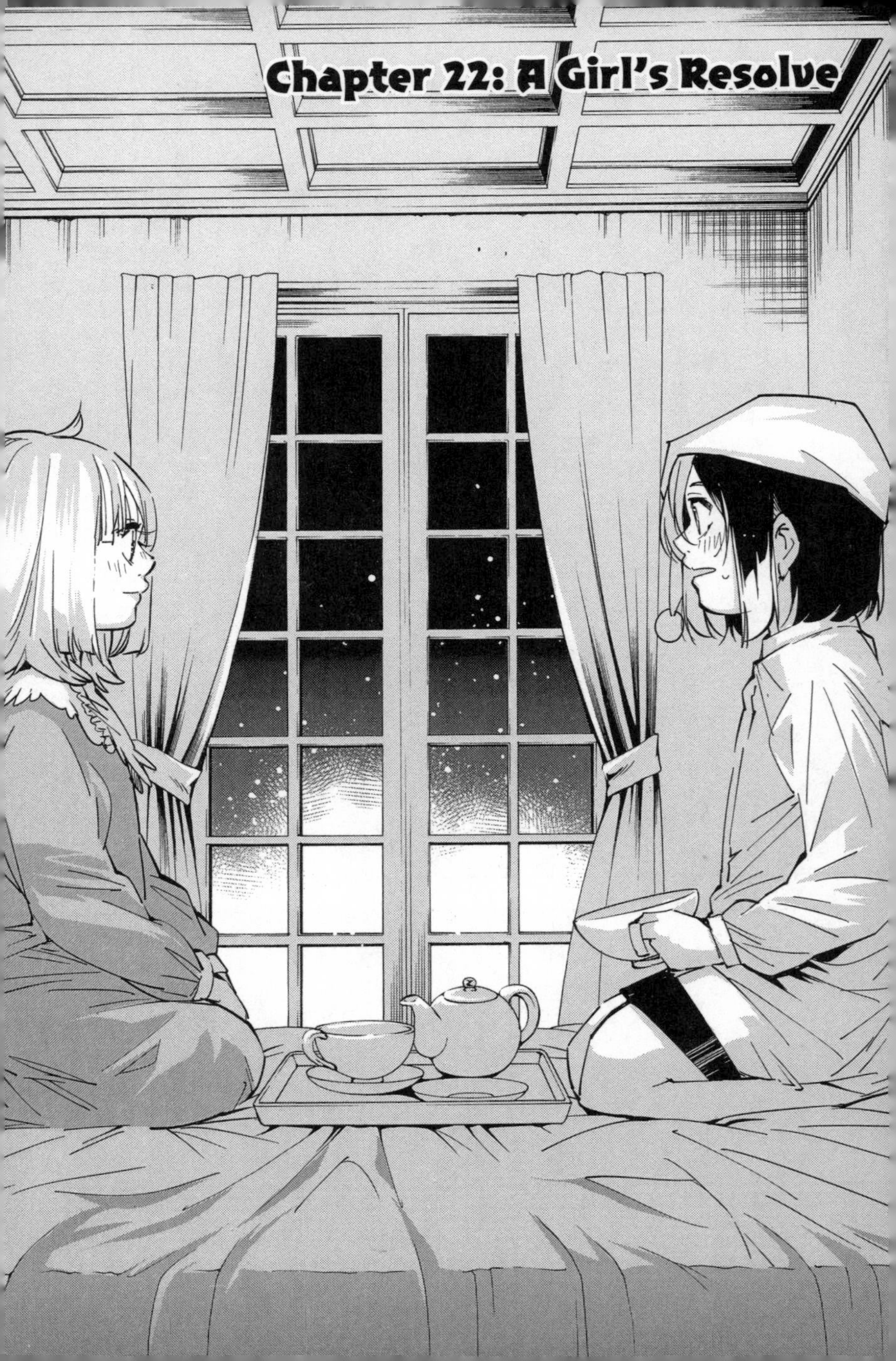
Chapter 22: A Girl's Resolve

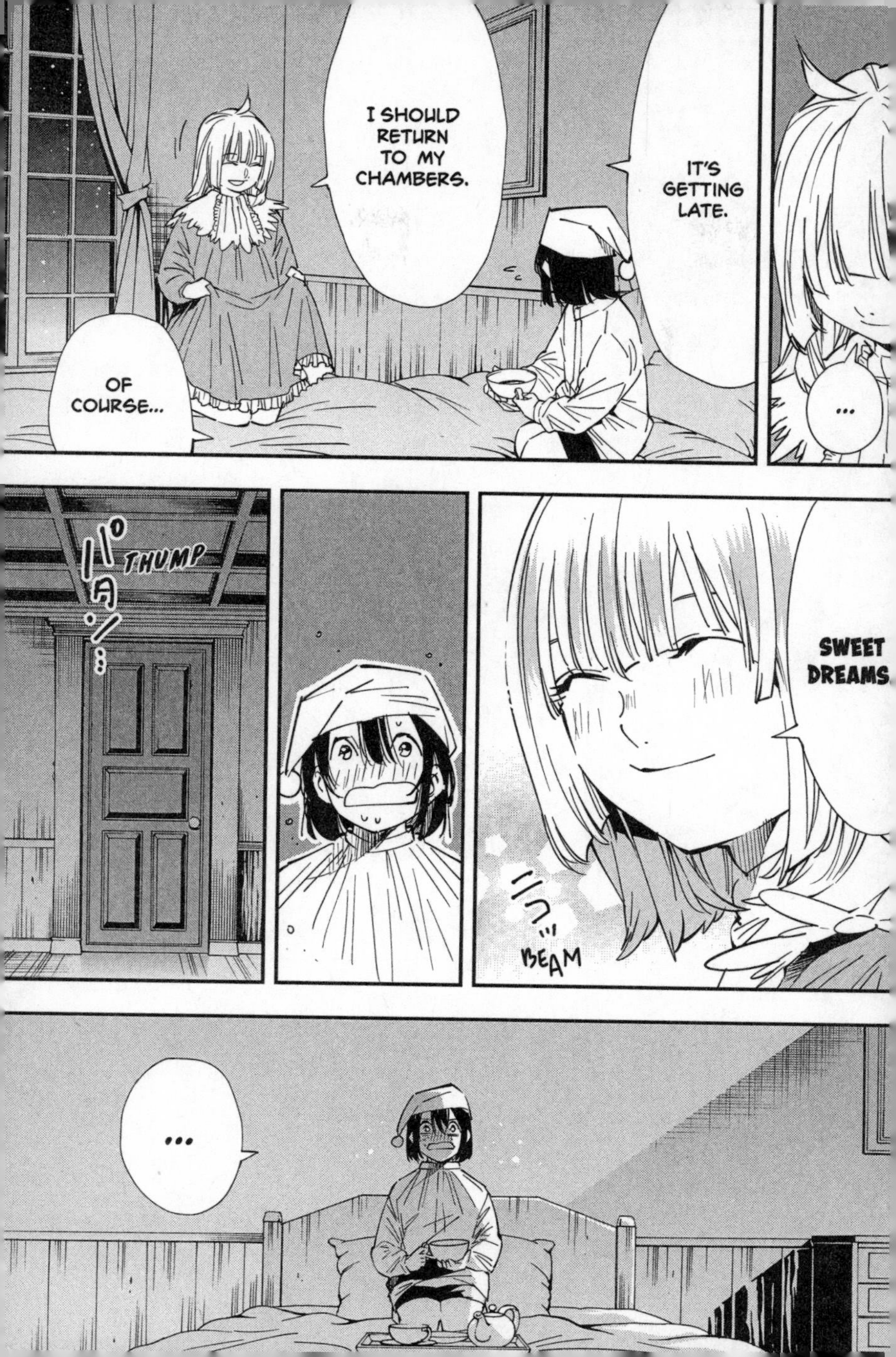
...
IT'S GETTING LATE.
I SHOULD RETURN TO MY CHAMBERS.
OF COURSE...
SWEET DREAMS
ニコッ
BEAM
パタン
THUMP
...

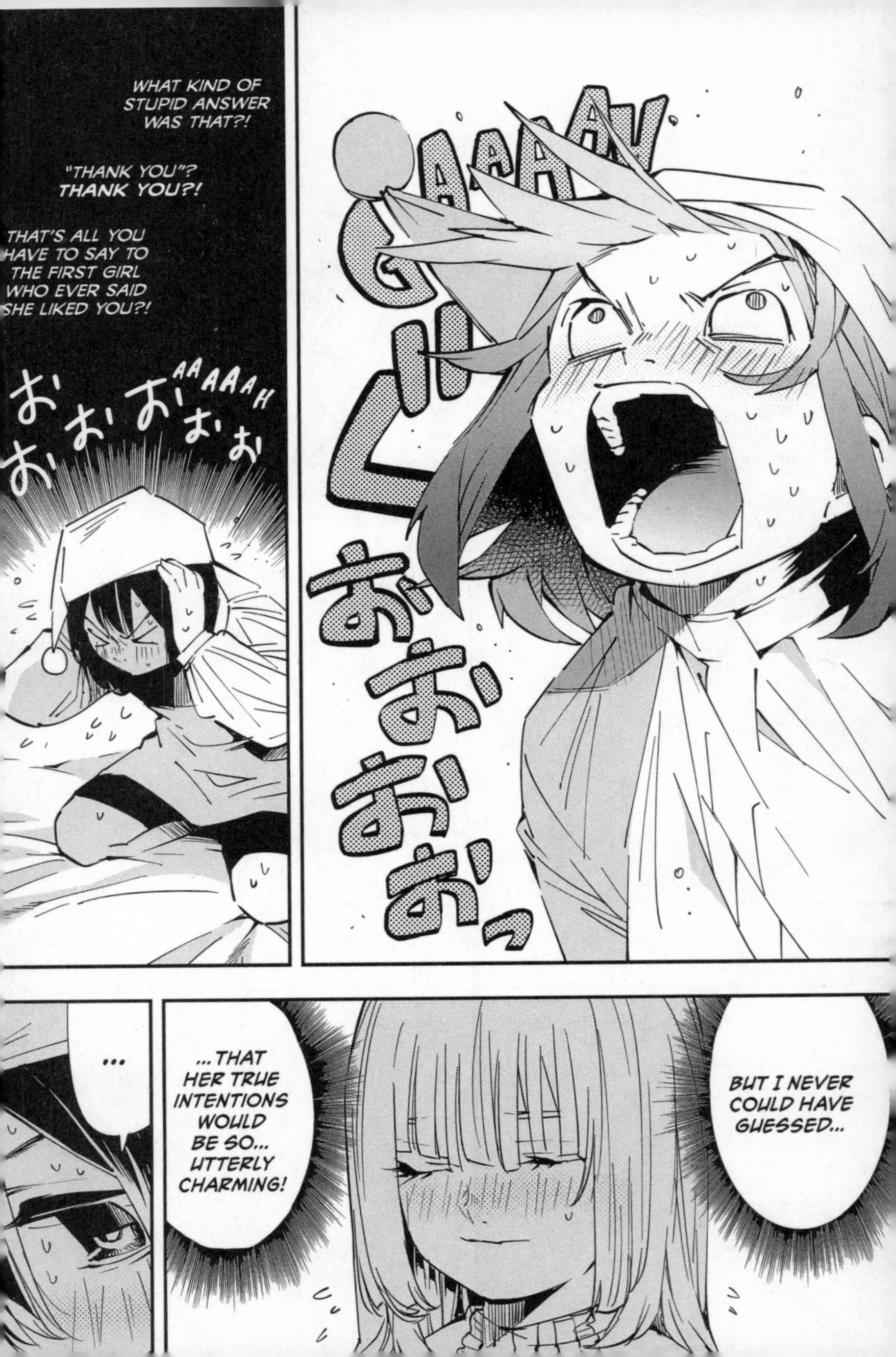

GAAAAH
お゛お゛お゛お゛っ
WHAT KIND OF STUPID ANSWER WAS THAT?!
"THANK YOU"? THANK YOU?!
THAT'S ALL YOU HAVE TO SAY TO THE FIRST GIRL WHO EVER SAID SHE LIKED YOU?!
おおおおおお
AAAAAH
BUT I NEVER COULD HAVE GUESSED...
...THAT HER TRUE INTENTIONS WOULD BE SO... UTTERLY CHARMING!
...

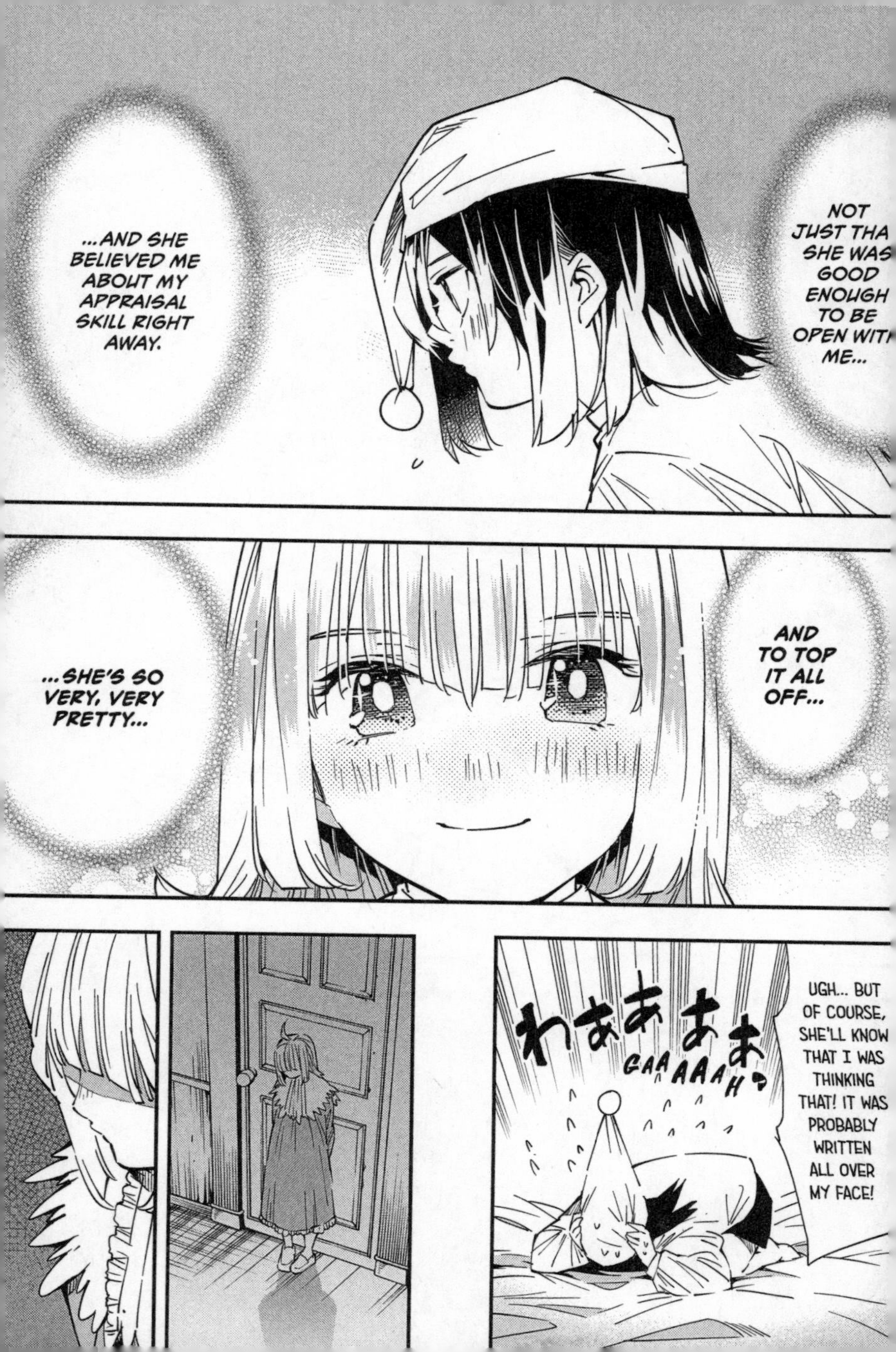
NOT JUST THA SHE WAS GOOD ENOUGH TO BE OPEN WIT ME...
...AND SHE BELIEVED ME ABOUT MY APPRAISAL SKILL RIGHT AWAY.
AND TO TOP IT ALL OFF...
...SHE'S SO VERY, VERY PRETTY...
UGH... BUT OF COURSE, SHE'LL KNOW THAT I WAS THINKING THAT! IT WAS PROBABLY WRITTEN ALL OVER MY FACE!
わぁぁぁぁ
GAAAAAH

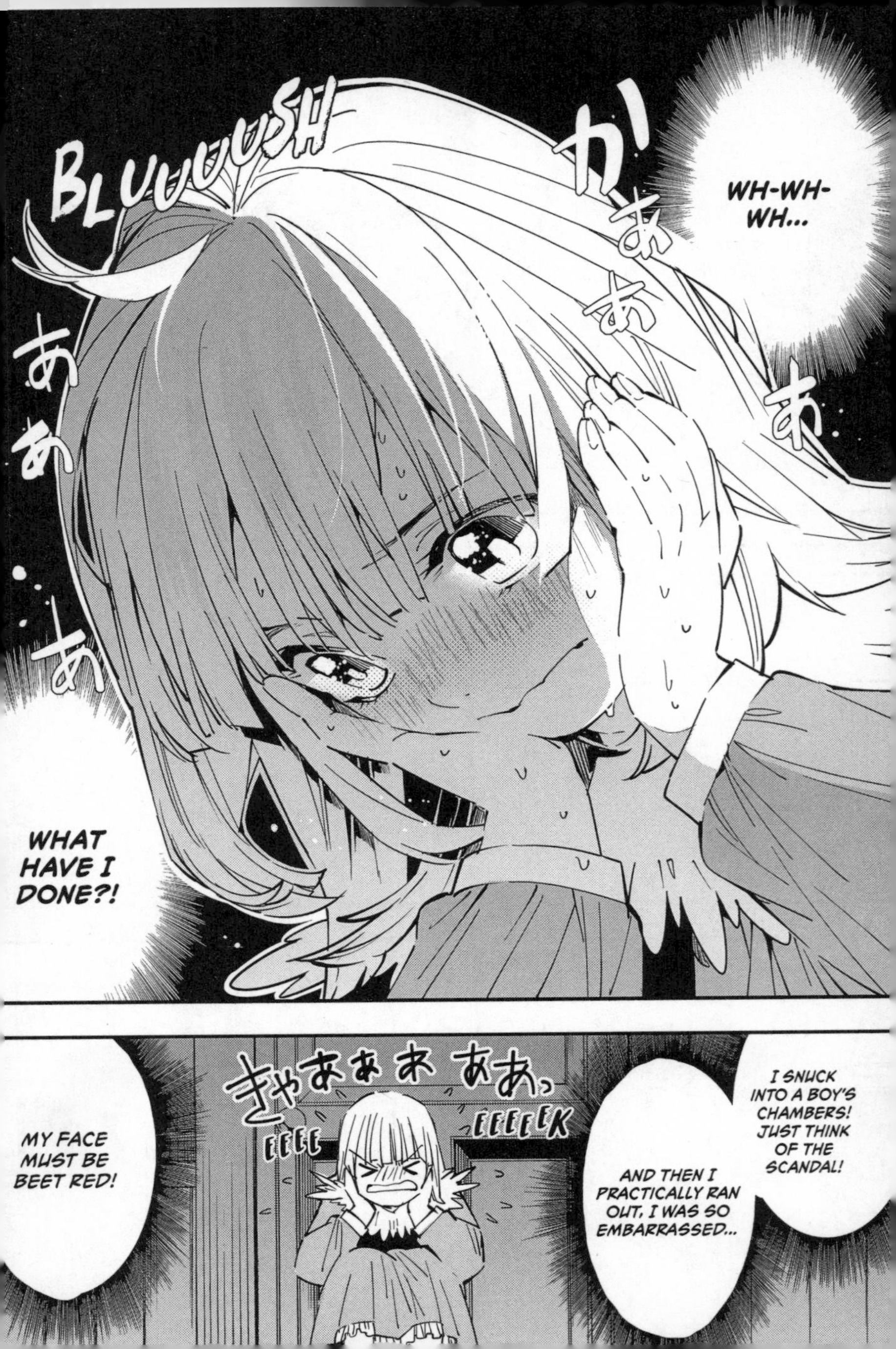
WH-WH-WH...
かあああ
BLUUUUSH
ああ…あ
WHAT HAVE I DONE?!
I SNUCK INTO A BOY'S CHAMBERS! JUST THINK OF THE SCANDAL!
AND THEN I PRACTICALLY RAN OUT, I WAS SO EMBARRASSED...
きゃあああ ああっ
EEEEEK
EEEE
MY FACE MUST BE BEET RED!

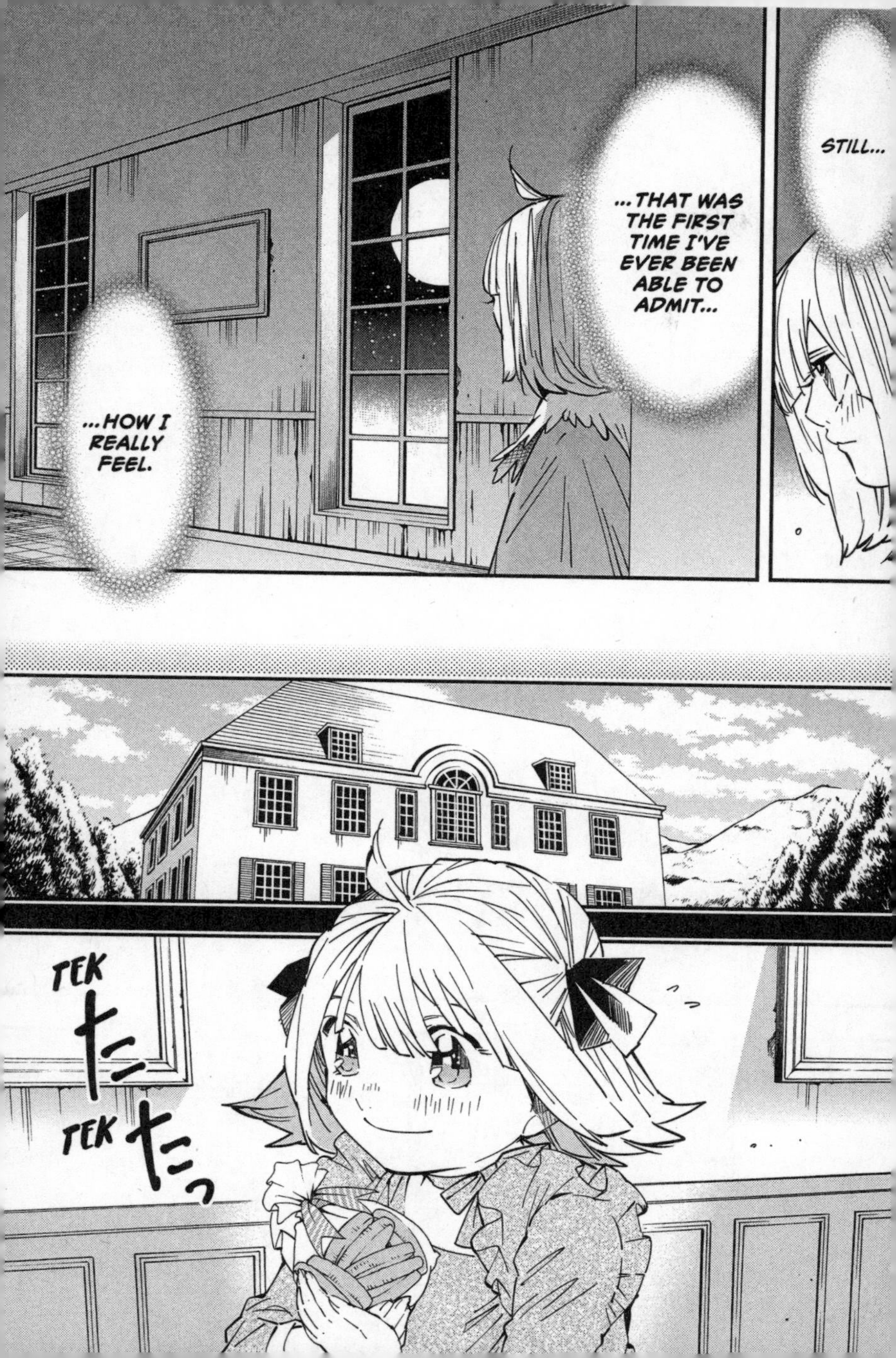
STILL...
...THAT WAS THE FIRST TIME I'VE EVER BEEN ABLE TO ADMIT...
...HOW I REALLY FEEL.
TEK たっ
TEK たっ

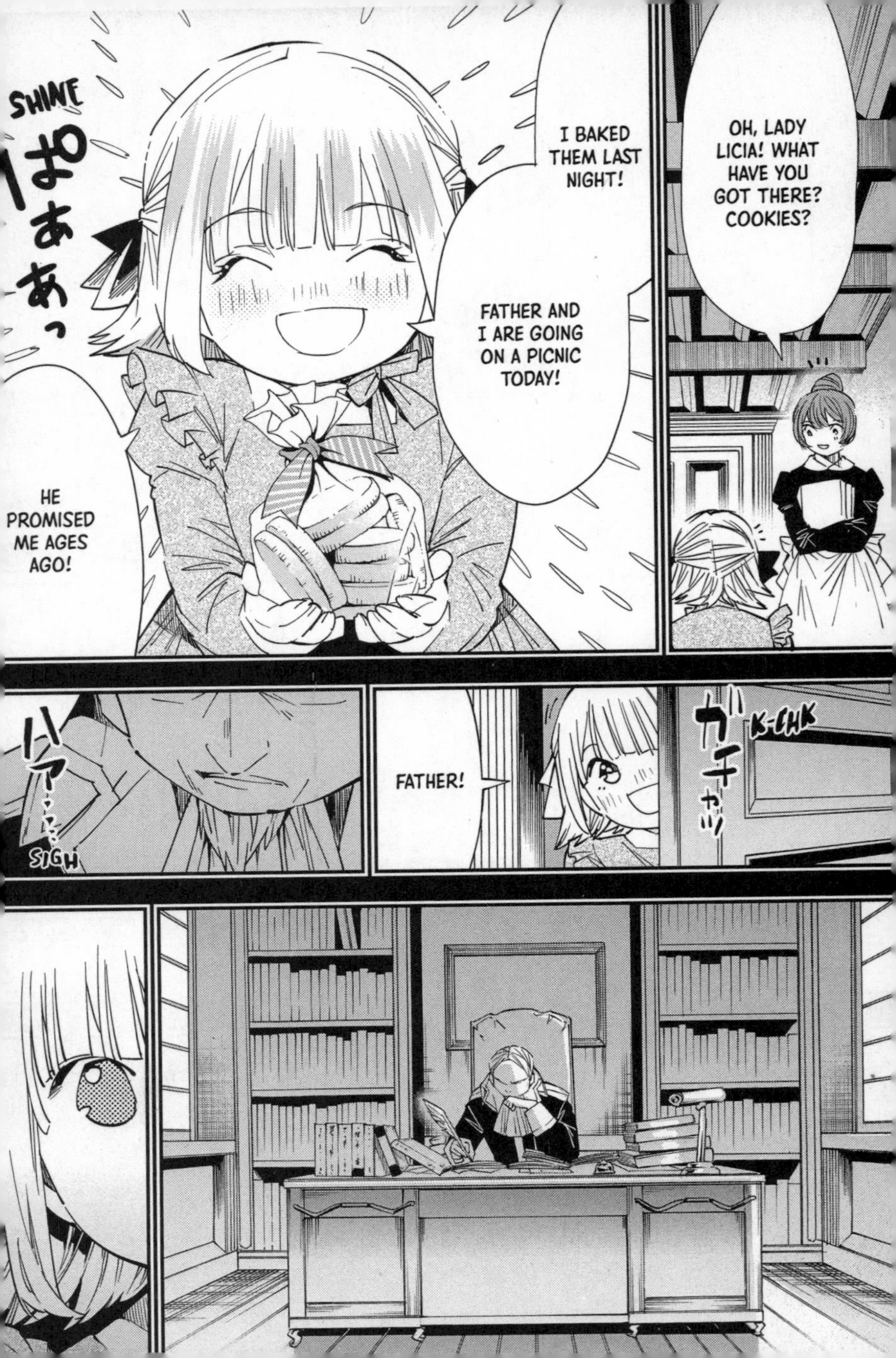
OH, LADY LICIA! WHAT HAVE YOU GOT THERE? COOKIES?
I BAKED THEM LAST NIGHT!
FATHER AND I ARE GOING ON A PICNIC TODAY!
SHINE
ぱぁあっ
HE PROMISED ME AGES AGO!
ガチャッ
K-CHK
FATHER!
ハァ…
SIGH

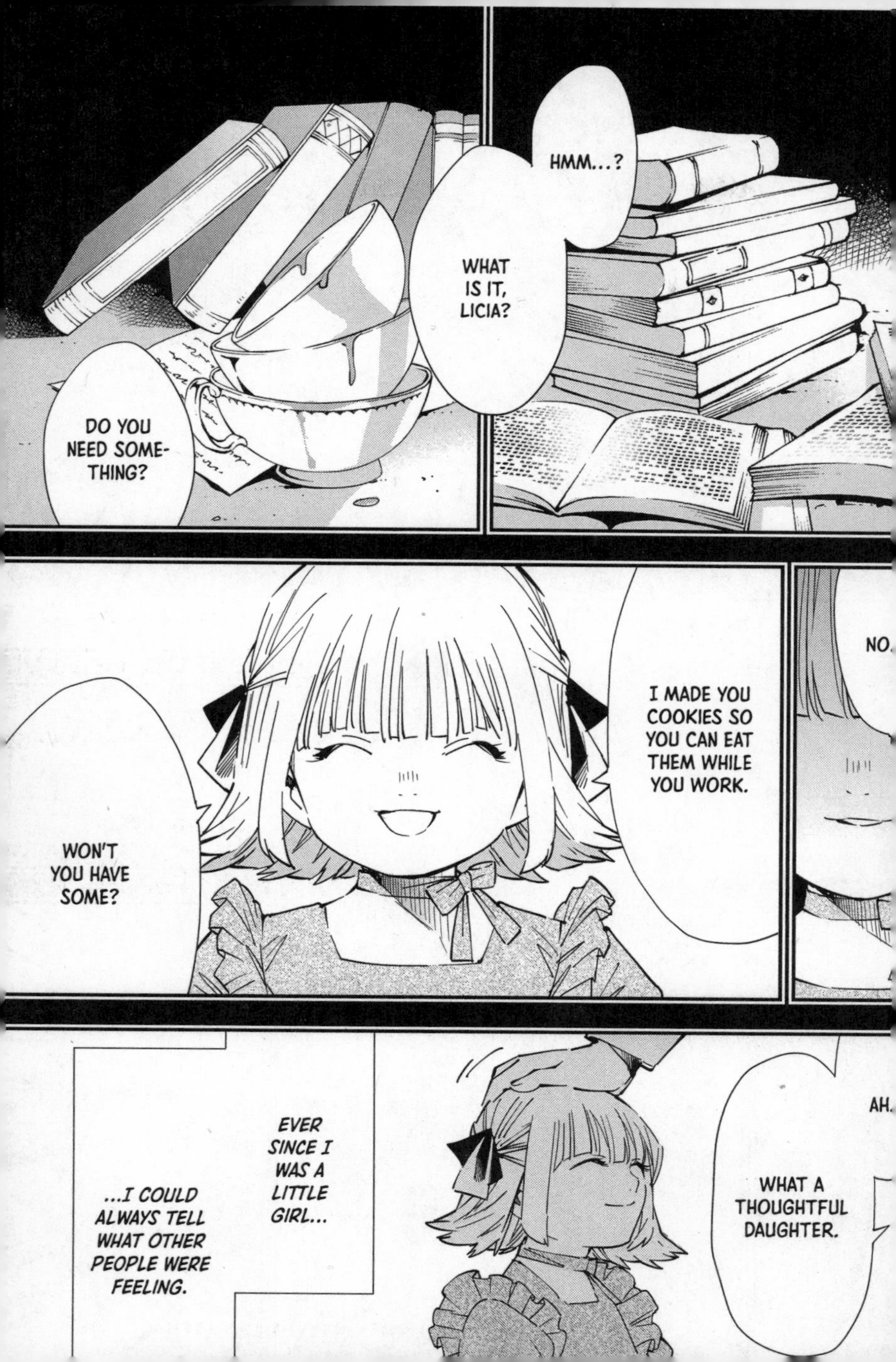
HMM...?
WHAT IS IT, LICIA?
DO YOU NEED SOMETHING?
NO.
I MADE YOU COOKIES SO YOU CAN EAT THEM WHILE YOU WORK.
WON'T YOU HAVE SOME?
AH.
WHAT A THOUGHTFUL DAUGHTER.
EVER SINCE I WAS A LITTLE GIRL...
...I COULD ALWAYS TELL WHAT OTHER PEOPLE WERE FEELING.

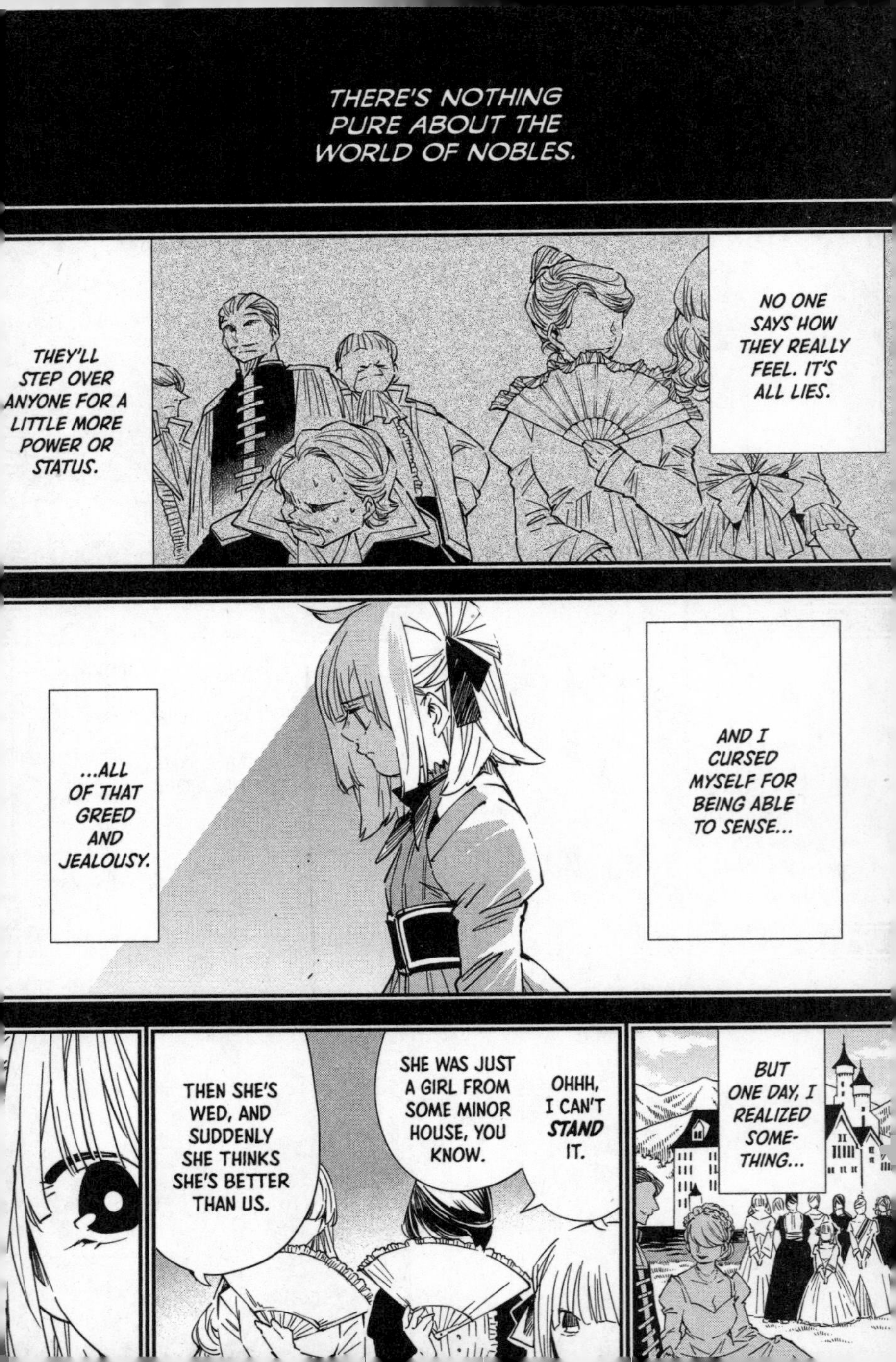
THERE'S NOTHING PURE ABOUT THE WORLD OF NOBLES.
NO ONE SAYS HOW THEY REALLY FEEL. IT'S ALL LIES.
THEY'LL STEP OVER ANYONE FOR A LITTLE MORE POWER OR STATUS.
AND I CURSED MYSELF FOR BEING ABLE TO SENSE...
...ALL OF THAT GREED AND JEALOUSY.
BUT ONE DAY, I REALIZED SOME-THING...
OHHH, I CAN'T STAND IT.
SHE WAS JUST A GIRL FROM SOME MINOR HOUSE, YOU KNOW.
THEN SHE'S WED, AND SUDDENLY SHE THINKS SHE'S BETTER THAN US.

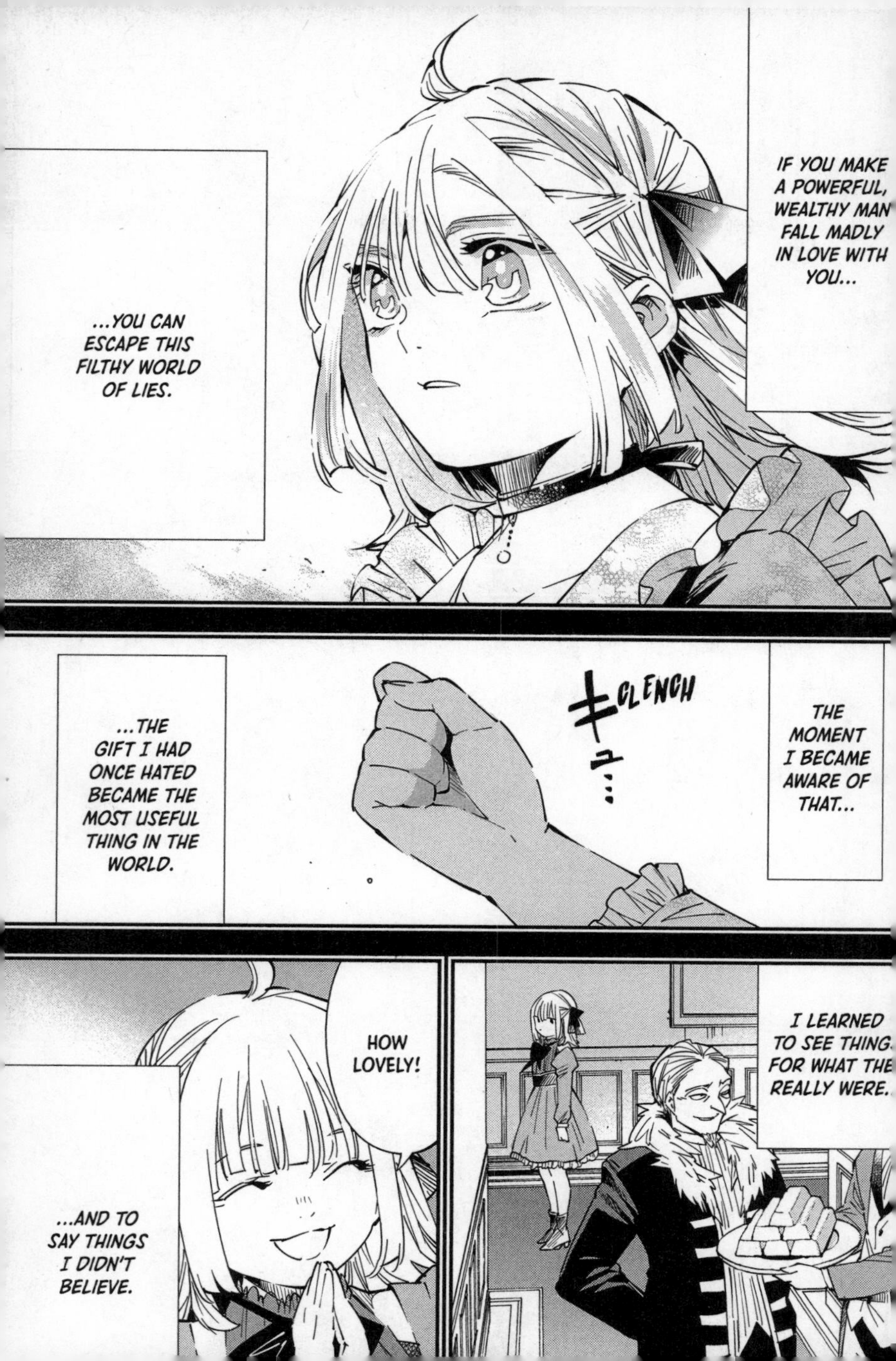
IF YOU MAKE A POWERFUL, WEALTHY MAN FALL MADLY IN LOVE WITH YOU...
...YOU CAN ESCAPE THIS FILTHY WORLD OF LIES.
THE MOMENT I BECAME AWARE OF THAT...
CLENCH
...THE GIFT I HAD ONCE HATED BECAME THE MOST USEFUL THING IN THE WORLD.
I LEARNED TO SEE THING FOR WHAT THE REALLY WERE.
HOW LOVELY!
...AND TO SAY THINGS I DIDN'T BELIEVE.

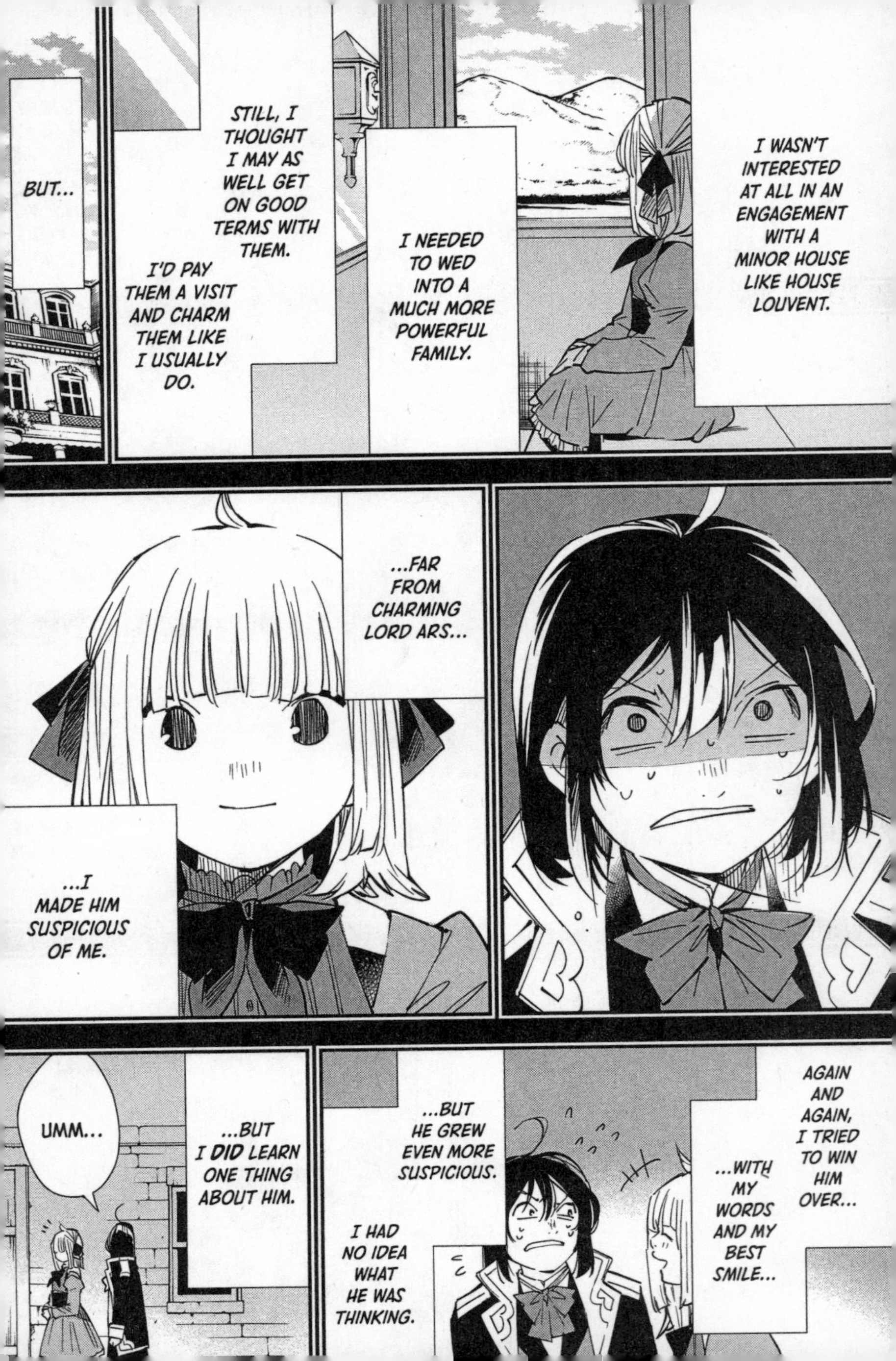
I WASN'T INTERESTED AT ALL IN AN ENGAGEMENT WITH A MINOR HOUSE LIKE HOUSE LOUVENT.
I NEEDED TO WED INTO A MUCH MORE POWERFUL FAMILY.
STILL, I THOUGHT I MAY AS WELL GET ON GOOD TERMS WITH THEM.
I'D PAY THEM A VISIT AND CHARM THEM LIKE I USUALLY DO.
BUT...
...FAR FROM CHARMING LORD ARS...
...I MADE HIM SUSPICIOUS OF ME.
AGAIN AND AGAIN, I TRIED TO WIN HIM OVER...
...WITH MY WORDS AND MY BEST SMILE...
...BUT HE GREW EVEN MORE SUSPICIOUS.
I HAD NO IDEA WHAT HE WAS THINKING.
...BUT I **DID** LEARN ONE THING ABOUT HIM.
UMM...

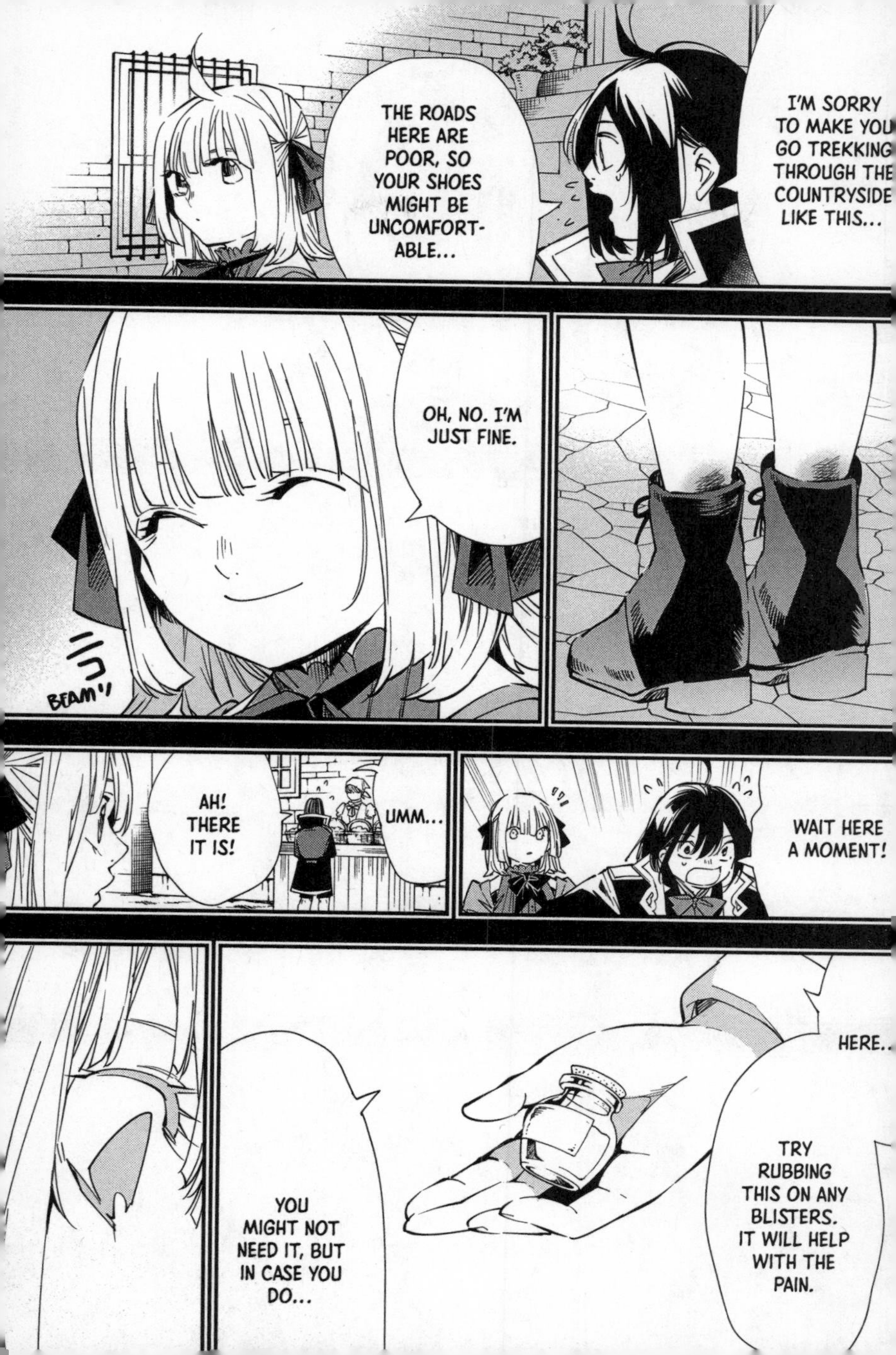
I'M SORRY TO MAKE YOU GO TREKKING THROUGH THE COUNTRYSIDE LIKE THIS...
THE ROADS HERE ARE POOR, SO YOUR SHOES MIGHT BE UNCOMFORT-ABLE...
OH, NO. I'M JUST FINE.
BEAM
WAIT HERE A MOMENT!
UMM...
AH! THERE IT IS!
HERE..
TRY RUBBING THIS ON ANY BLISTERS. IT WILL HELP WITH THE PAIN.
YOU MIGHT NOT NEED IT, BUT IN CASE YOU DO...

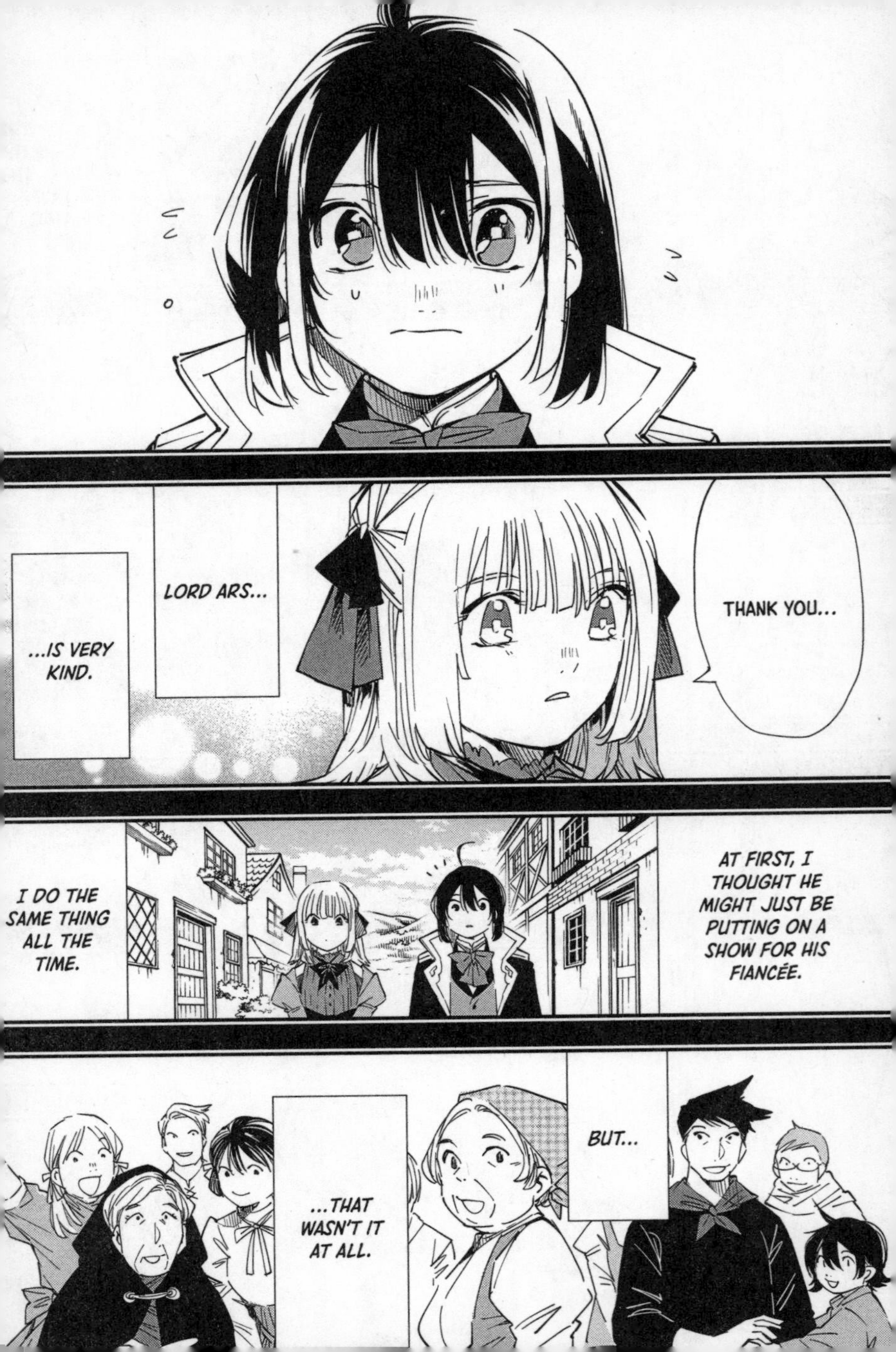
THANK YOU...
LORD ARS...
...IS VERY KIND.
AT FIRST, I THOUGHT HE MIGHT JUST BE PUTTING ON A SHOW FOR HIS FIANCÉE.
I DO THE SAME THING ALL THE TIME.
BUT...
...THAT WASN'T IT AT ALL.

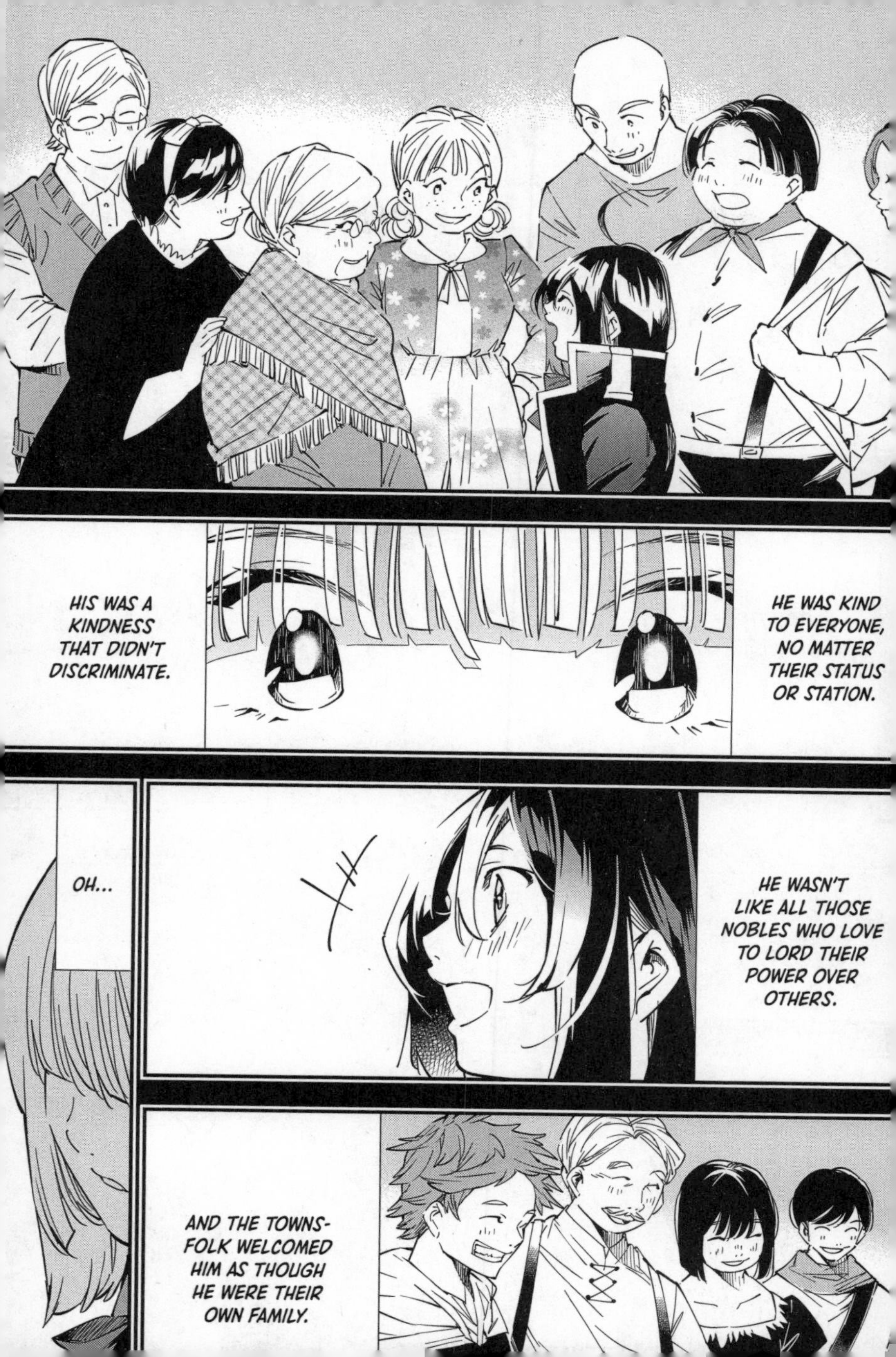
HE WAS KIND TO EVERYONE, NO MATTER THEIR STATUS OR STATION.
HIS WAS A KINDNESS THAT DIDN'T DISCRIMINATE.
HE WASN'T LIKE ALL THOSE NOBLES WHO LOVE TO LORD THEIR POWER OVER OTHERS.
AND THE TOWNS-FOLK WELCOMED HIM AS THOUGH HE WERE THEIR OWN FAMILY.
OH...

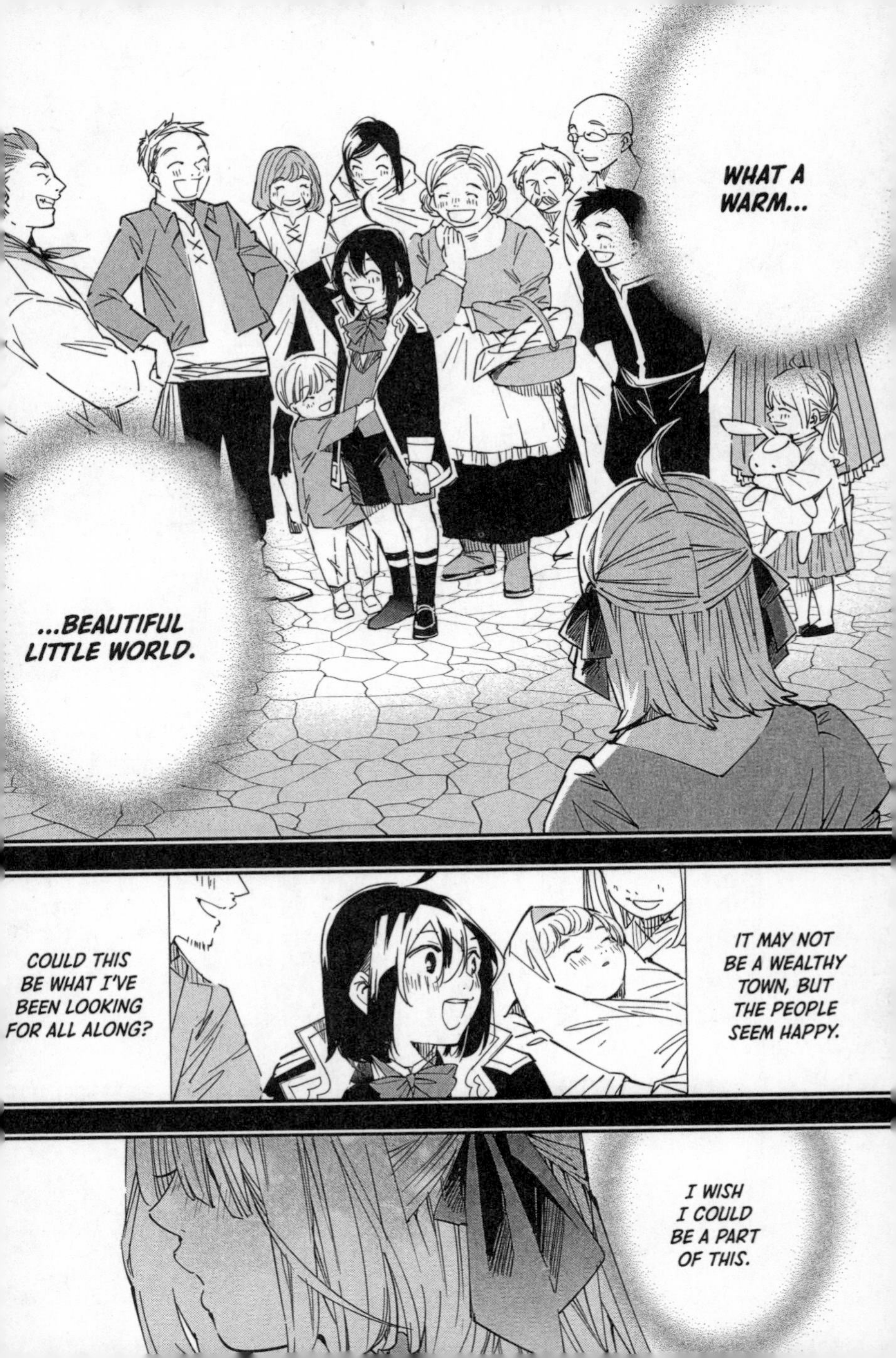
WHAT A WARM...
...BEAUTIFUL LITTLE WORLD.
IT MAY NOT BE A WEALTHY TOWN, BUT THE PEOPLE SEEM HAPPY.
COULD THIS BE WHAT I'VE BEEN LOOKING FOR ALL ALONG?
I WISH I COULD BE A PART OF THIS.

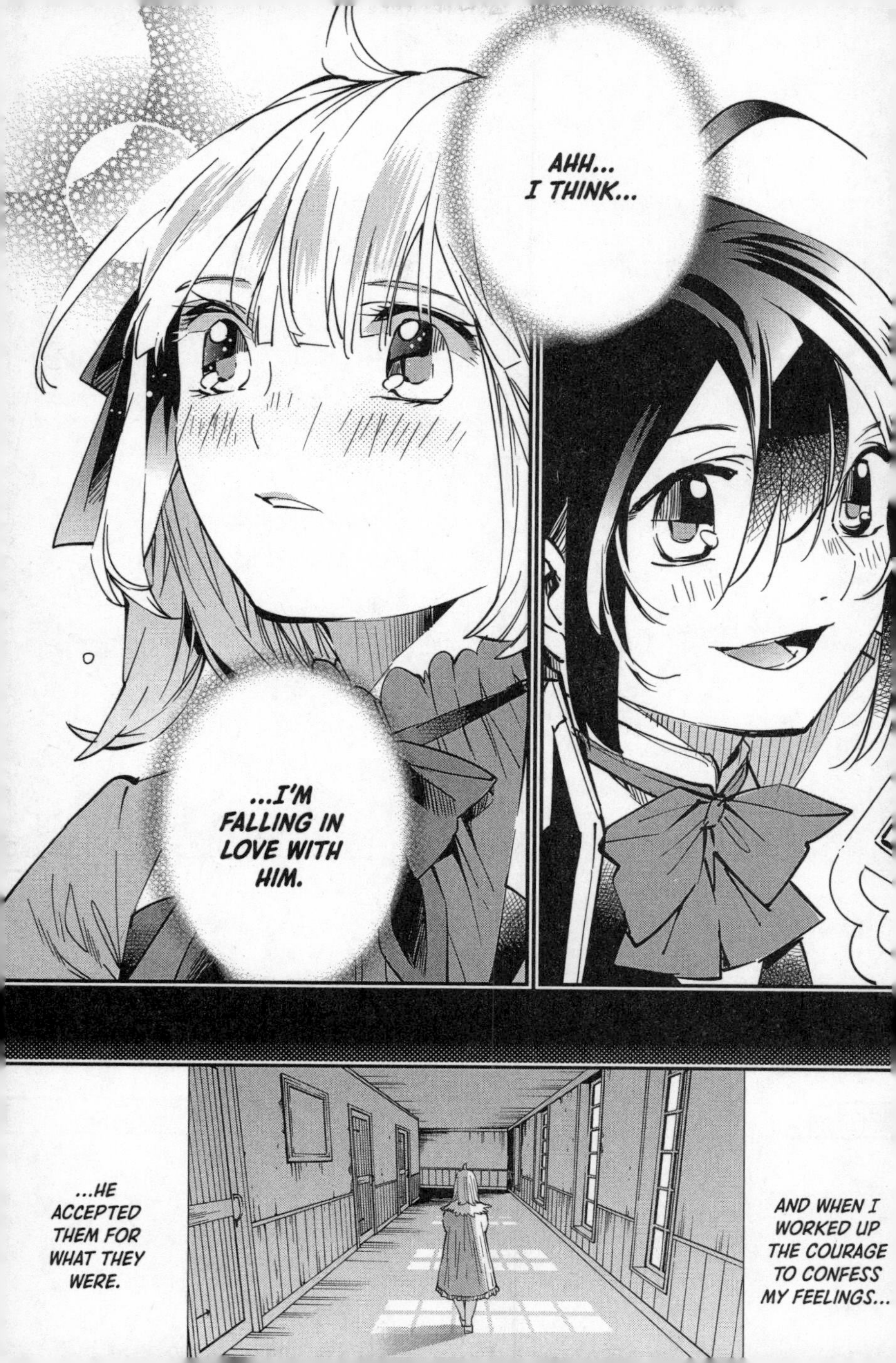
AHH... I THINK...
...I'M FALLING IN LOVE WITH HIM.
AND WHEN I WORKED UP THE COURAGE TO CONFESS MY FEELINGS...
...HE ACCEPTED THEM FOR WHAT THEY WERE.

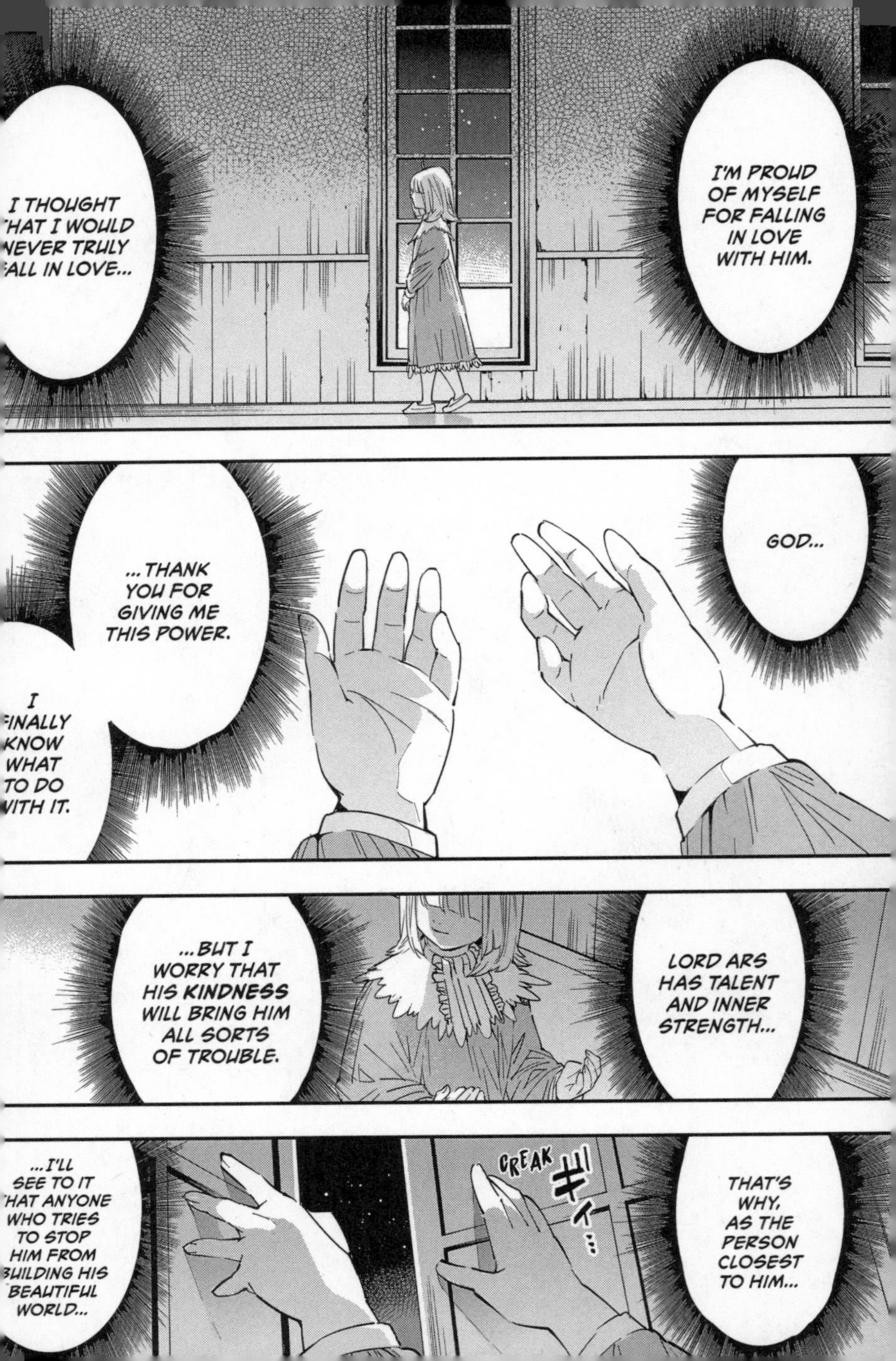
I'M PROUD OF MYSELF FOR FALLING IN LOVE WITH HIM.
I THOUGHT HAT I WOULD NEVER TRULY ALL IN LOVE...
GOD...
...THANK YOU FOR GIVING ME THIS POWER.
I INALLY KNOW WHAT TO DO ITH IT.
LORD ARS HAS TALENT AND INNER STRENGTH...
...BUT I WORRY THAT HIS KINDNESS WILL BRING HIM ALL SORTS OF TROUBLE.
THAT'S WHY, AS THE PERSON CLOSEST TO HIM...
CREAK
ギィ…
...I'LL SEE TO IT HAT ANYONE WHO TRIES TO STOP HIM FROM UILDING HIS BEAUTIFUL WORLD...

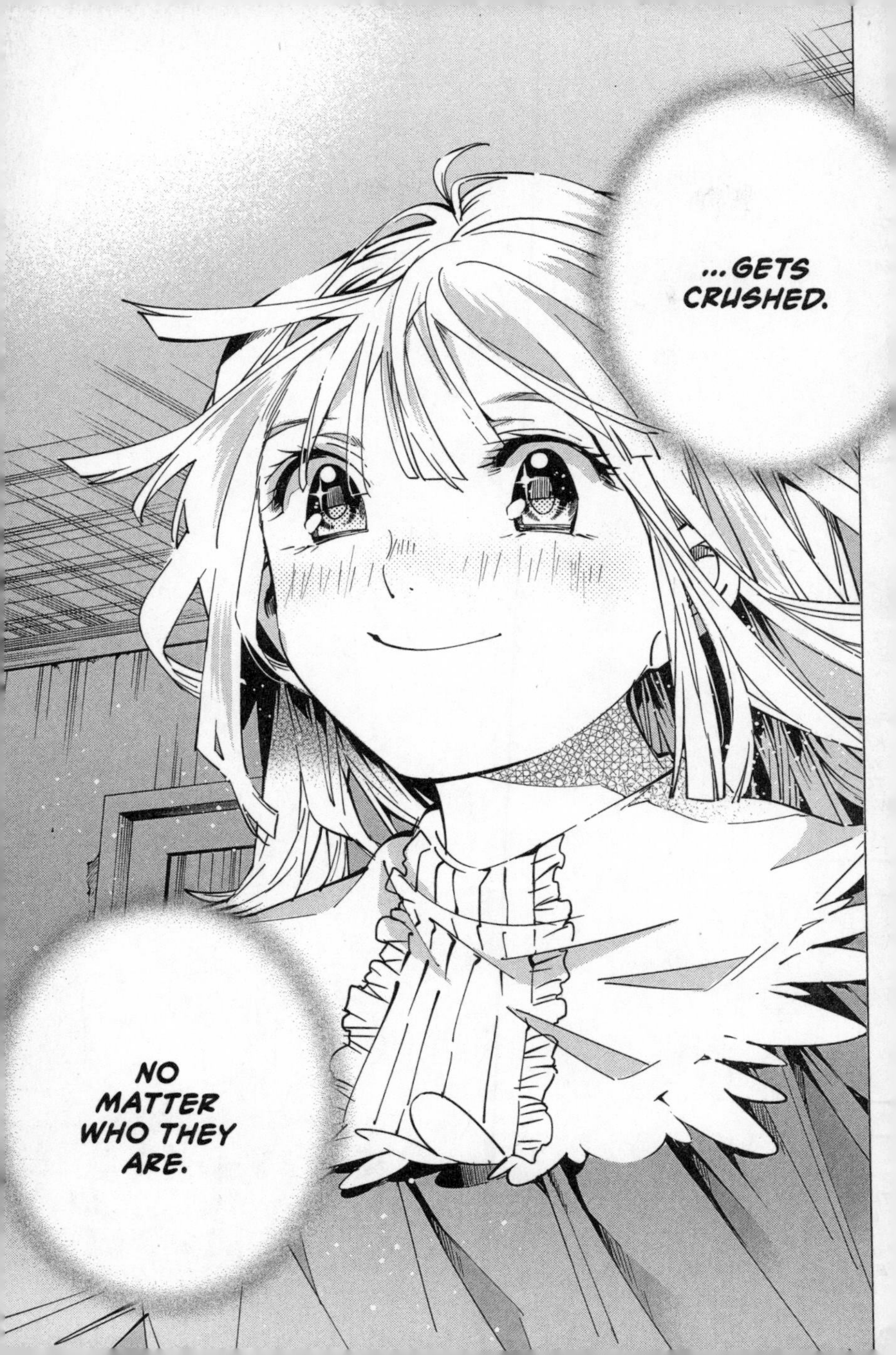
...GETS CRUSHED.
NO MATTER WHO THEY ARE.

As a Reincarnated
ARISTOCRAT,
I'll Use My Appraisal Skill to
Rise in the World

Chapter 23: The Changing Times

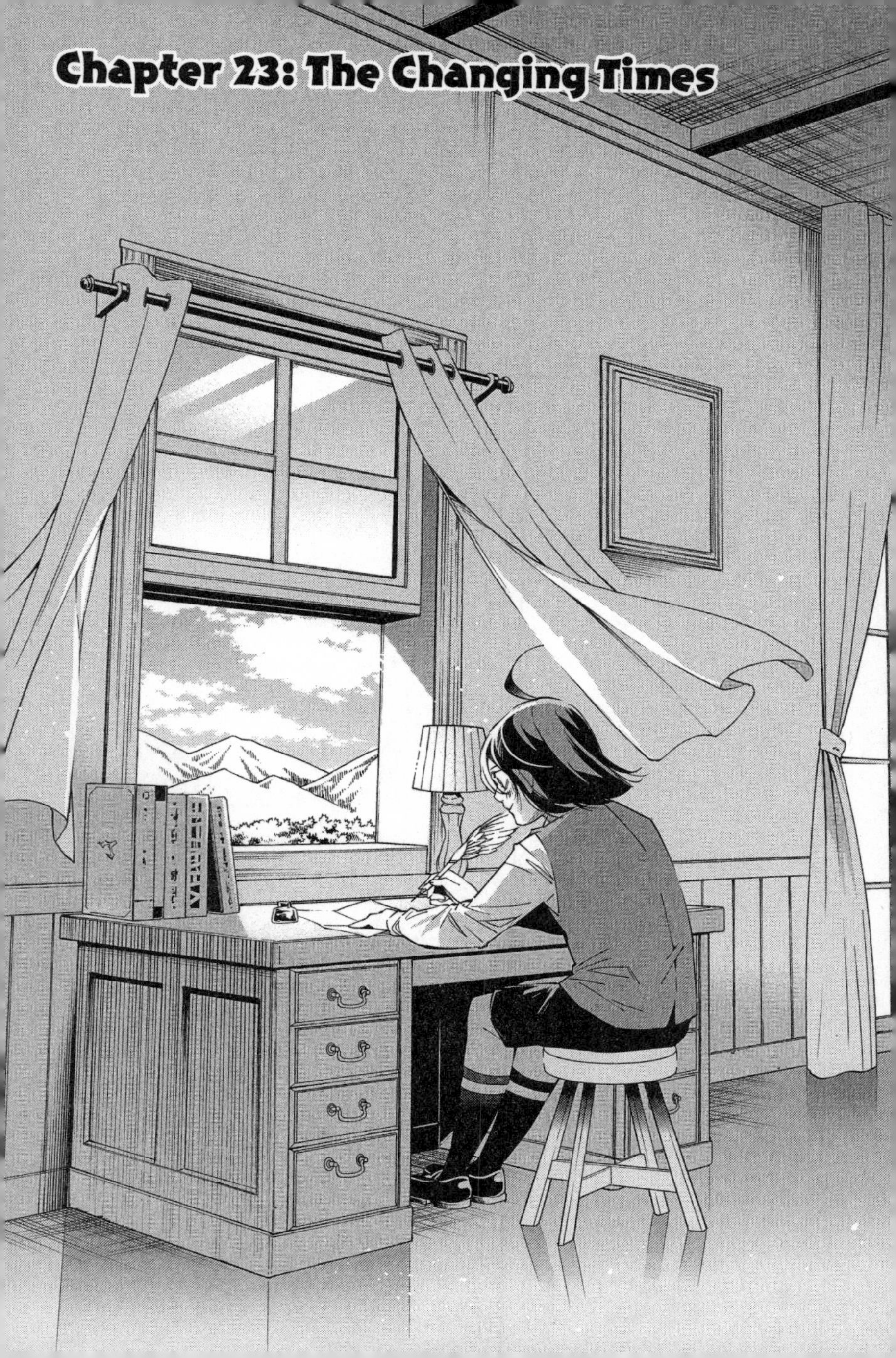

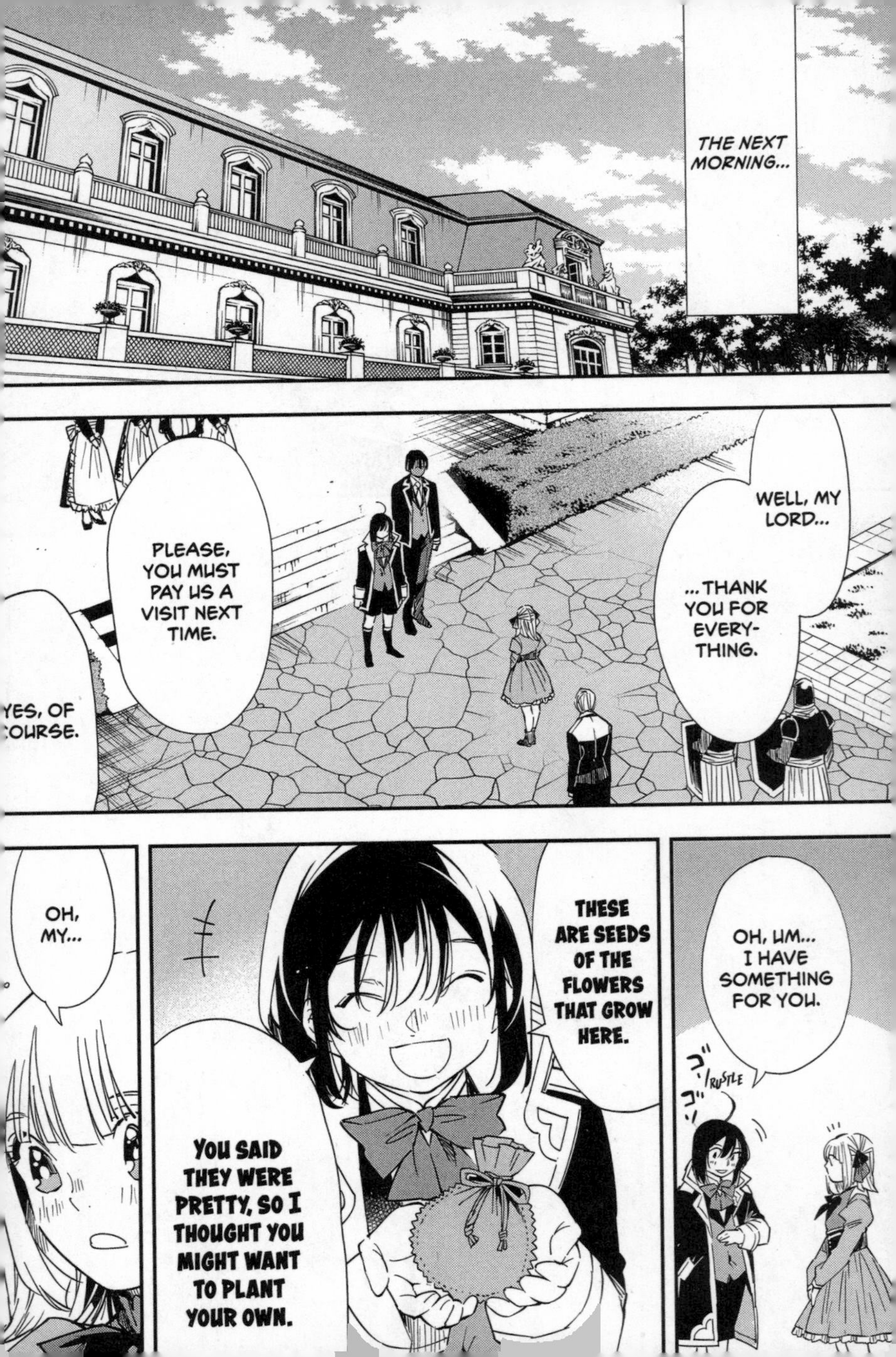
THE NEXT MORNING...
WELL, MY LORD...
...THANK YOU FOR EVERY-THING.
PLEASE, YOU MUST PAY US A VISIT NEXT TIME.
YES, OF COURSE.
OH, UM... I HAVE SOMETHING FOR YOU.
RUSTLE
THESE ARE SEEDS OF THE FLOWERS THAT GROW HERE.
YOU SAID THEY WERE PRETTY, SO I THOUGHT YOU MIGHT WANT TO PLANT YOUR OWN.
OH, MY...

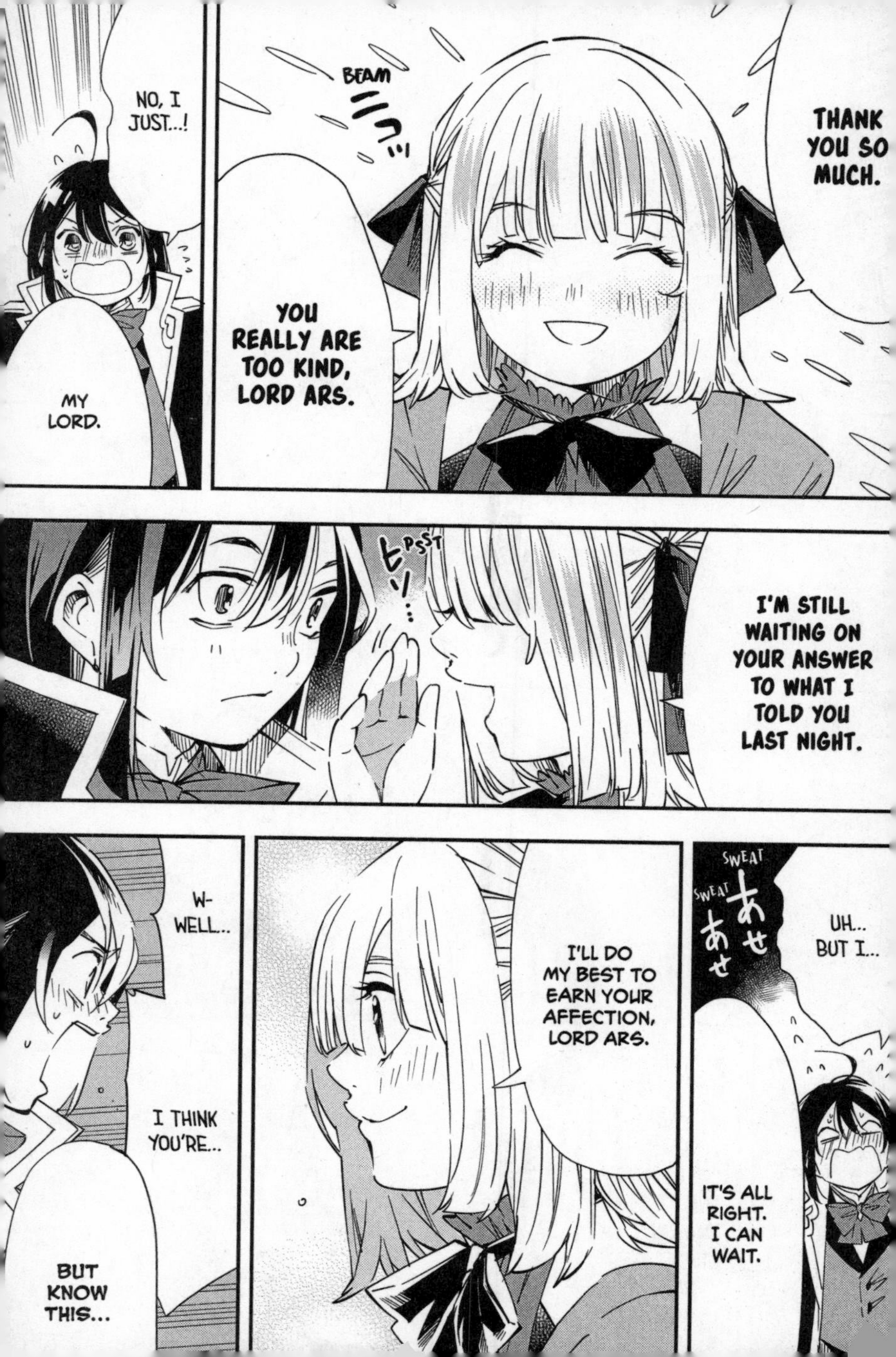
THANK YOU SO MUCH.
BEAM
ニコッ
YOU REALLY ARE TOO KIND, LORD ARS.
NO, I JUST...!
MY LORD.
ヒソ…
PSST
I'M STILL WAITING ON YOUR ANSWER TO WHAT I TOLD YOU LAST NIGHT.
SWEAT
SWEAT
あせあせ
UH... BUT I...
IT'S ALL RIGHT. I CAN WAIT.
I'LL DO MY BEST TO EARN YOUR AFFECTION, LORD ARS.
W-WELL...
I THINK YOU'RE...
BUT KNOW THIS...

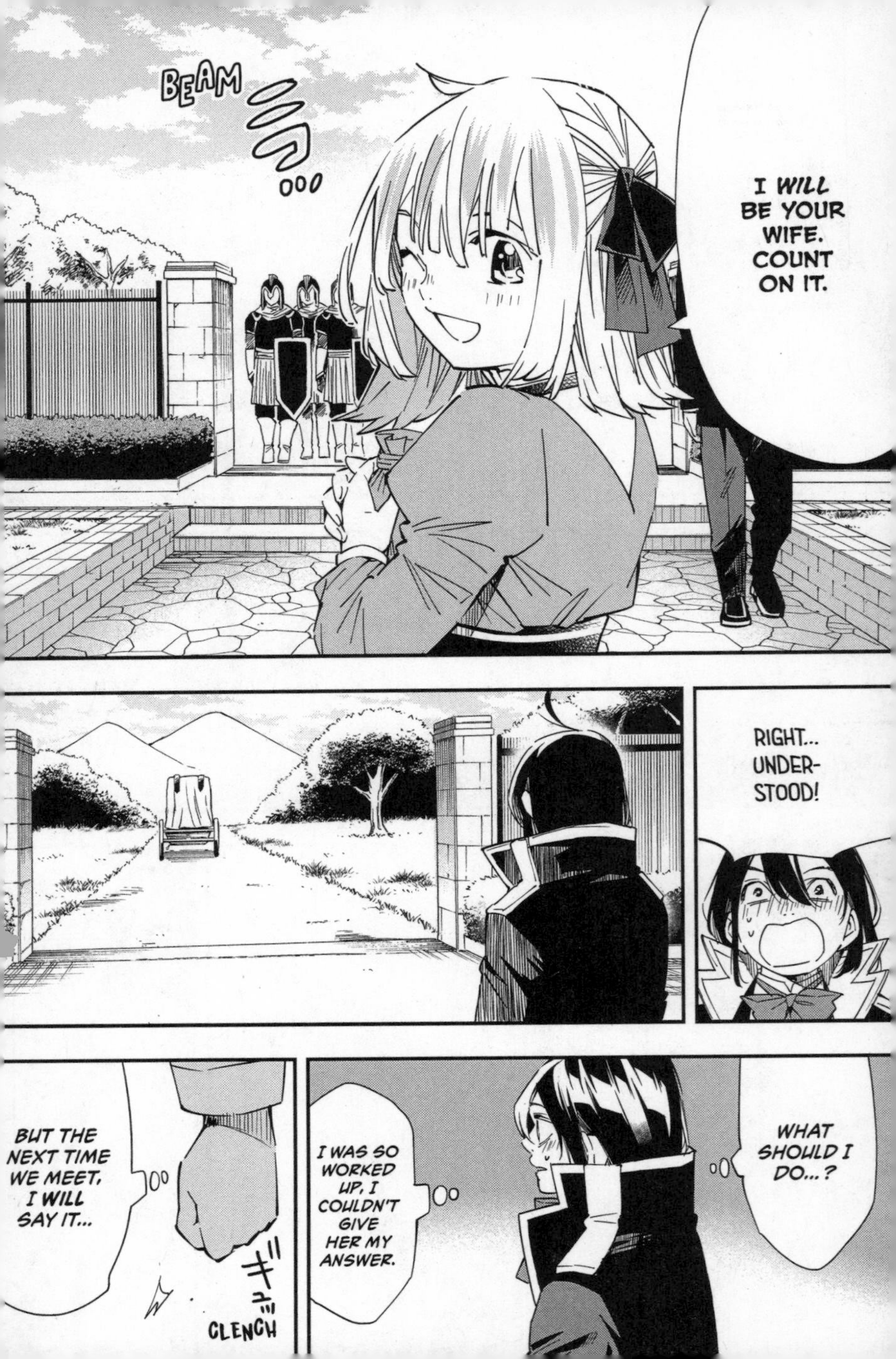
I WILL BE YOUR WIFE. COUNT ON IT.
BEAM
OOO
RIGHT... UNDER-STOOD!
WHAT SHOULD I DO...?
I WAS SO WORKED UP, I COULDN'T GIVE HER MY ANSWER.
BUT THE NEXT TIME WE MEET, I WILL SAY IT...
CLENCH

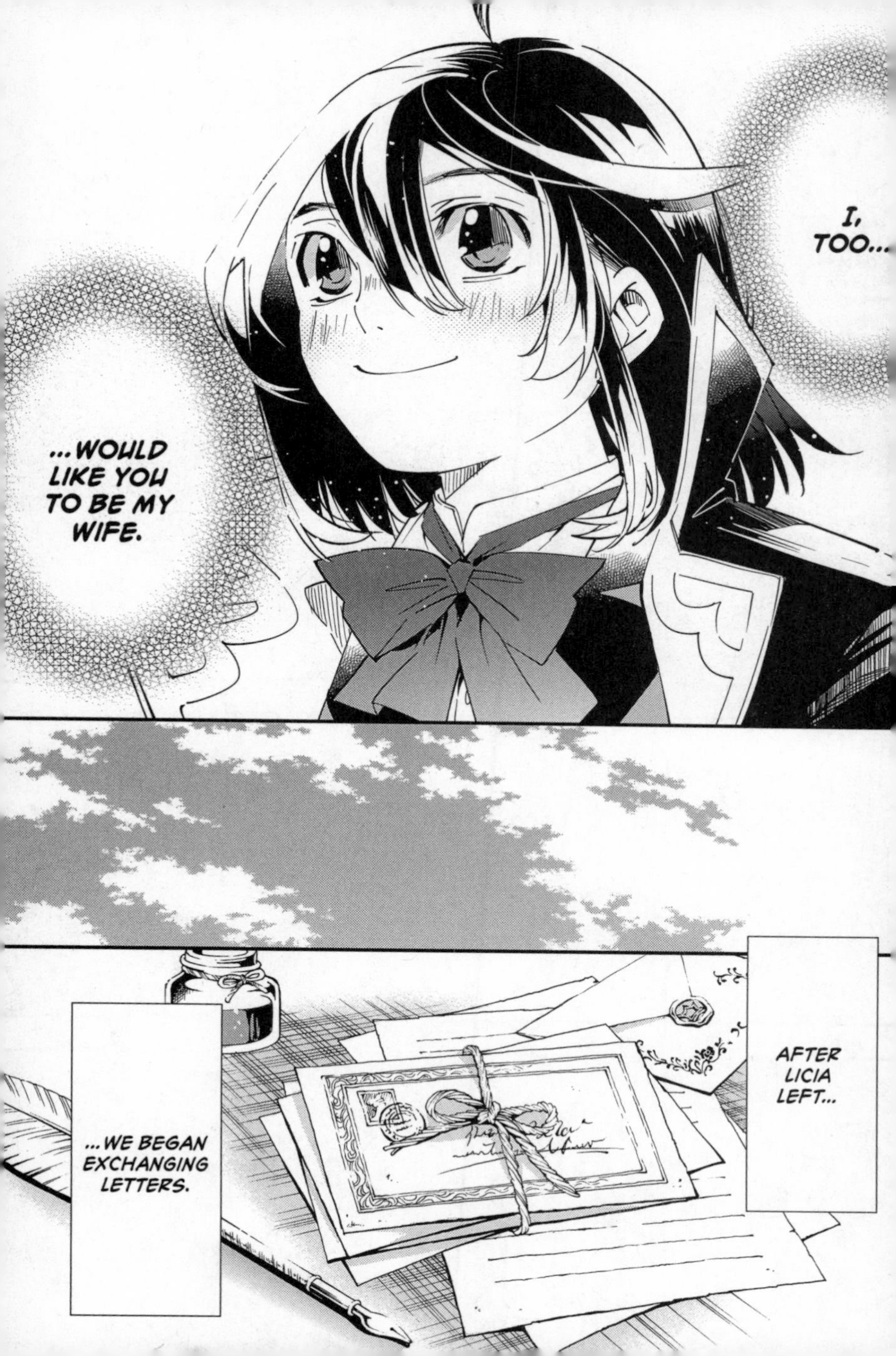
I, TOO...
...WOULD LIKE YOU TO BE MY WIFE.
AFTER LICIA LEFT...
...WE BEGAN EXCHANGING LETTERS.

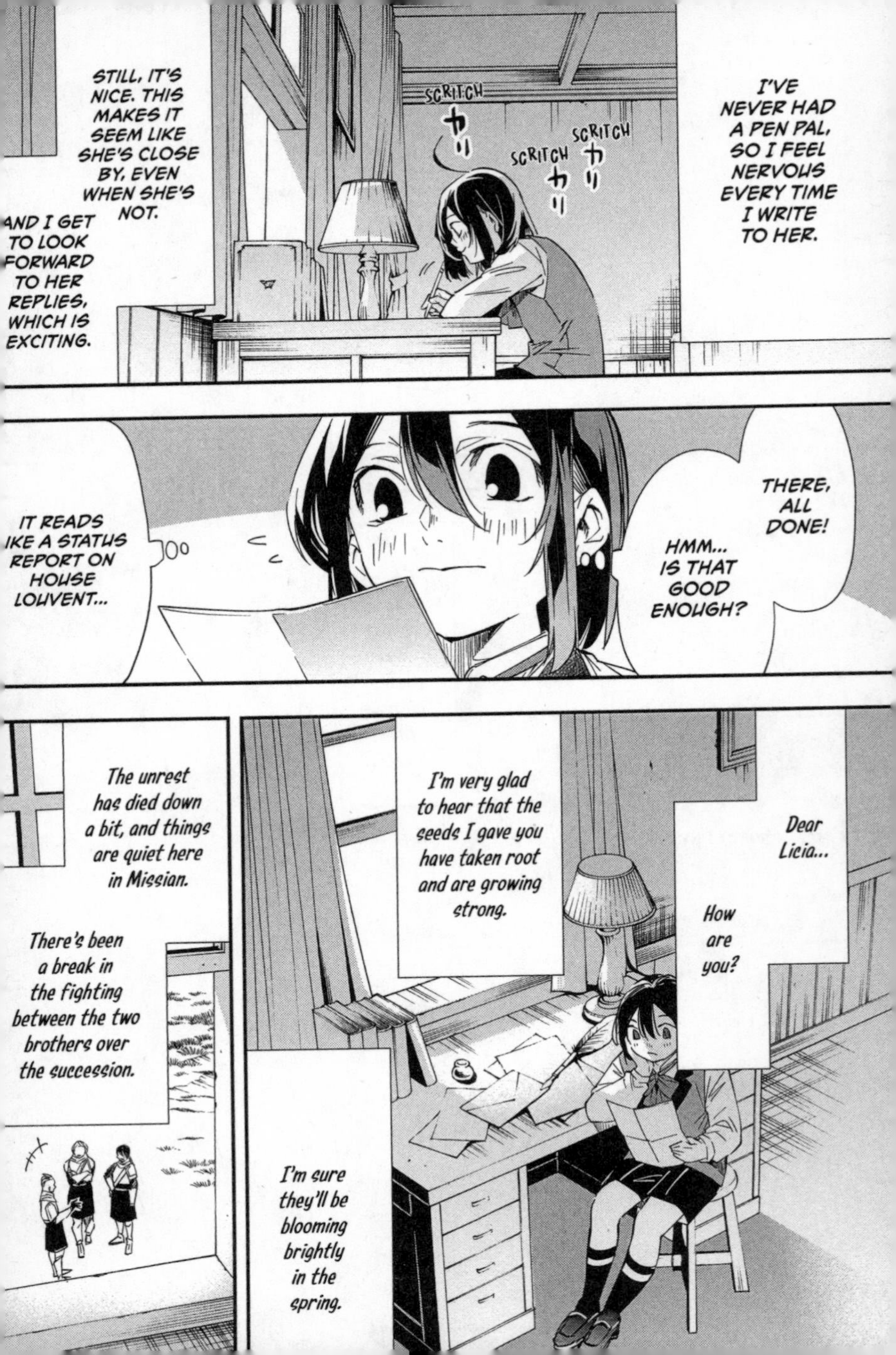
I'VE NEVER HAD A PEN PAL, SO I FEEL NERVOUS EVERY TIME I WRITE TO HER.
SCRITCH
SCRITCH
SCRITCH
STILL, IT'S NICE. THIS MAKES IT SEEM LIKE SHE'S CLOSE BY, EVEN WHEN SHE'S NOT.
AND I GET TO LOOK FORWARD TO HER REPLIES, WHICH IS EXCITING.
THERE, ALL DONE!
HMM... IS THAT GOOD ENOUGH?
IT READS IKE A STATUS REPORT ON HOUSE LOUVENT...
Dear Licia...
How are you?
I'm very glad to hear that the seeds I gave you have taken root and are growing strong.
I'm sure they'll be blooming brightly in the spring.
The unrest has died down a bit, and things are quiet here in Missian.
There's been a break in the fighting between the two brothers over the succession.

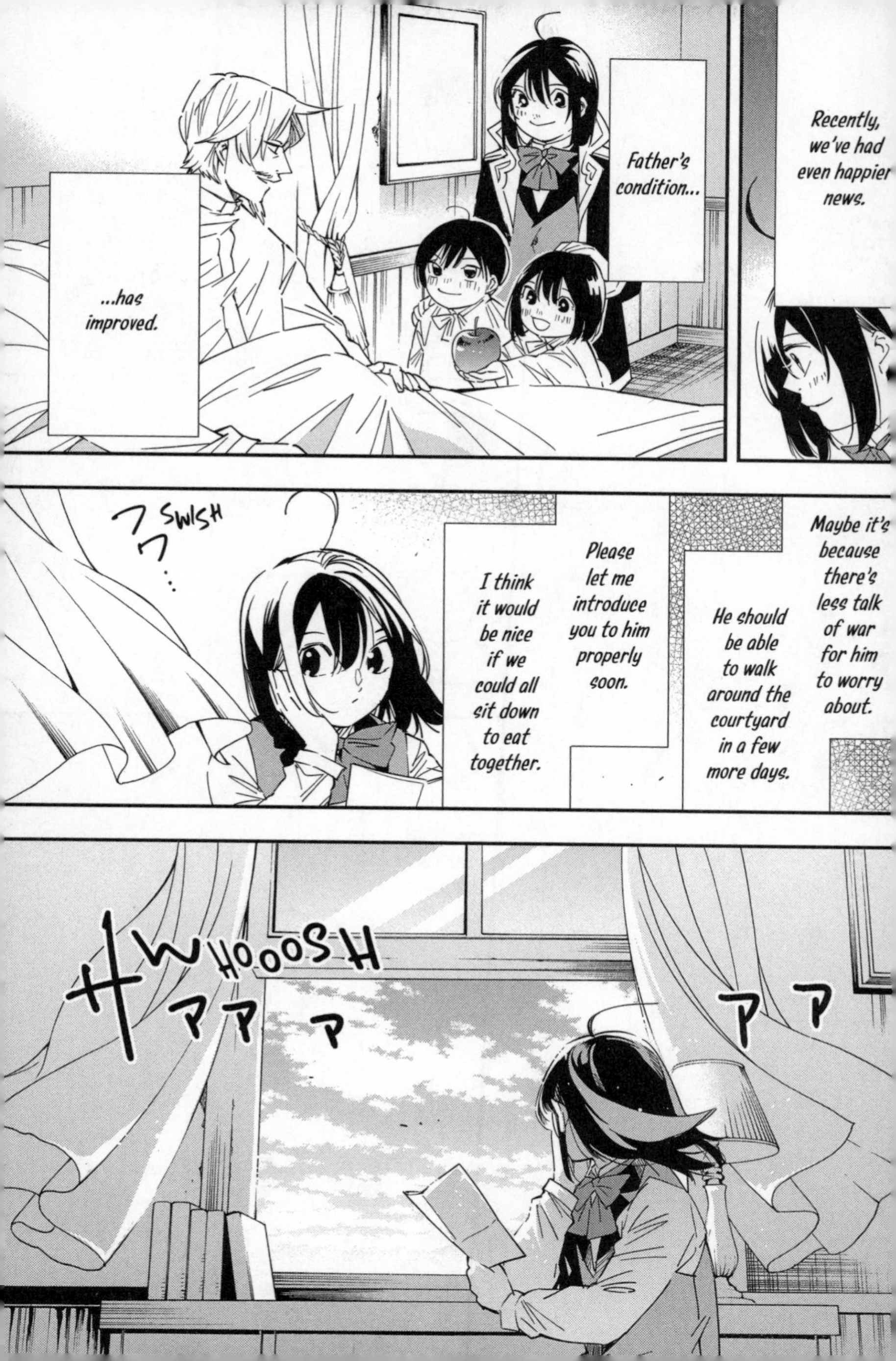
Recently, we've had even happier news.
Father's condition...
...has improved.
Maybe it's because there's less talk of war for him to worry about.
He should be able to walk around the courtyard in a few more days.
Please let me introduce you to him properly soon.
I think it would be nice if we could all sit down to eat together.
SWISH
WHOOOSH

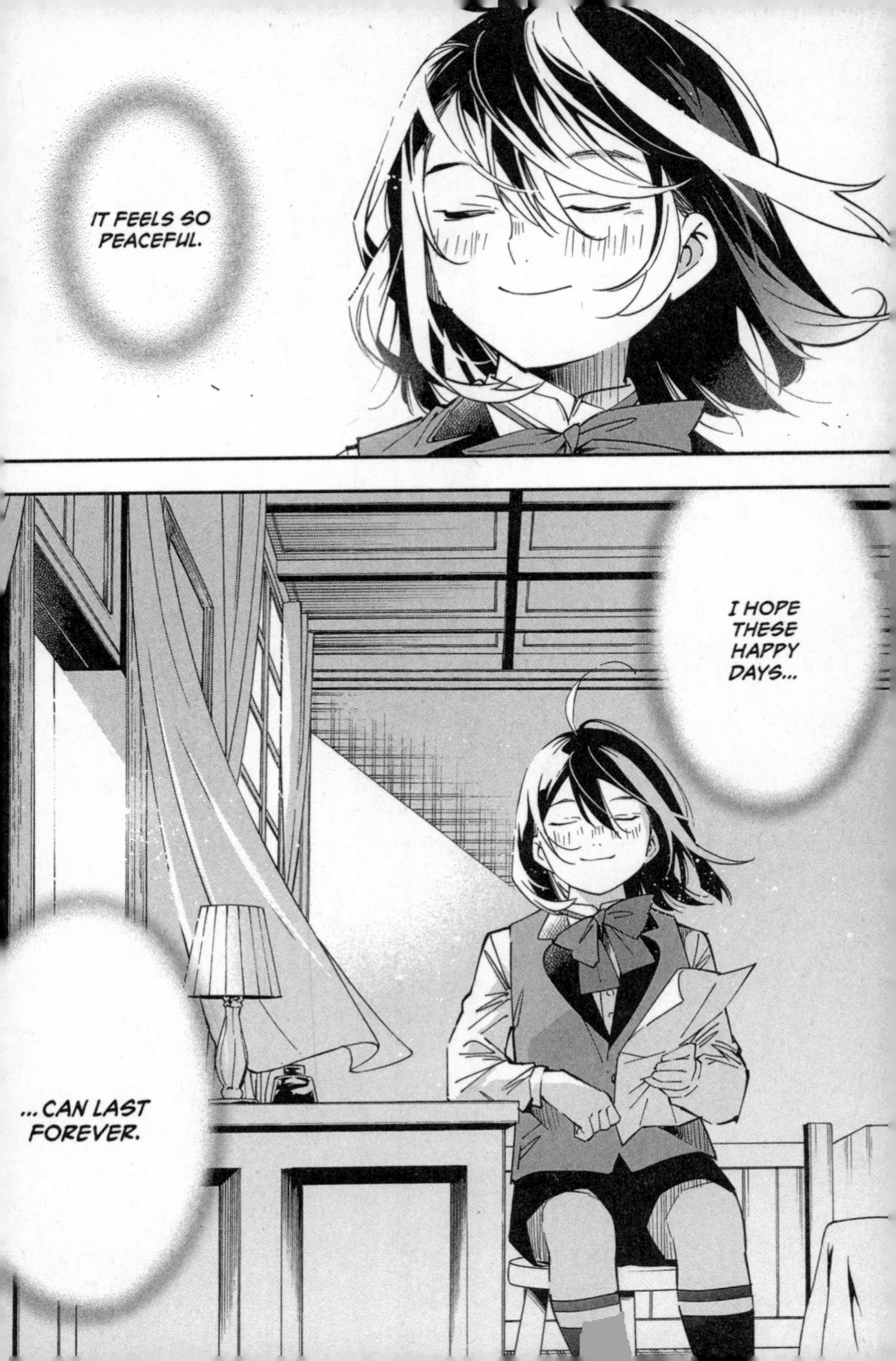
IT FEELS SO PEACEFUL.
I HOPE THESE HAPPY DAYS...
...CAN LAST FOREVER.

ONE AND A
HALF YEARS
LATER...

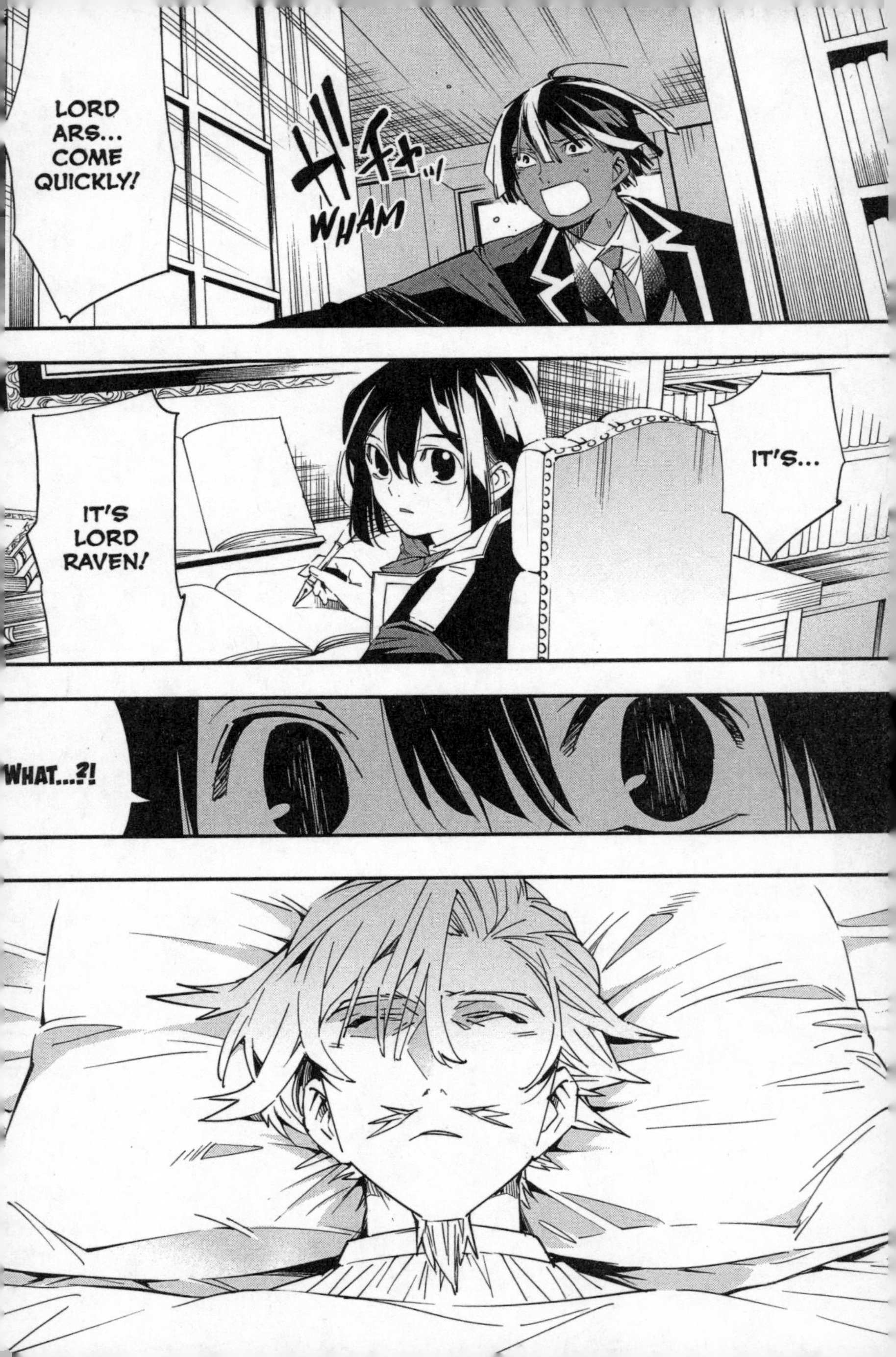
ガチャッ
WHAM
LORD ARS... COME QUICKLY!
IT'S...
IT'S LORD RAVEN!
WHAT...?!

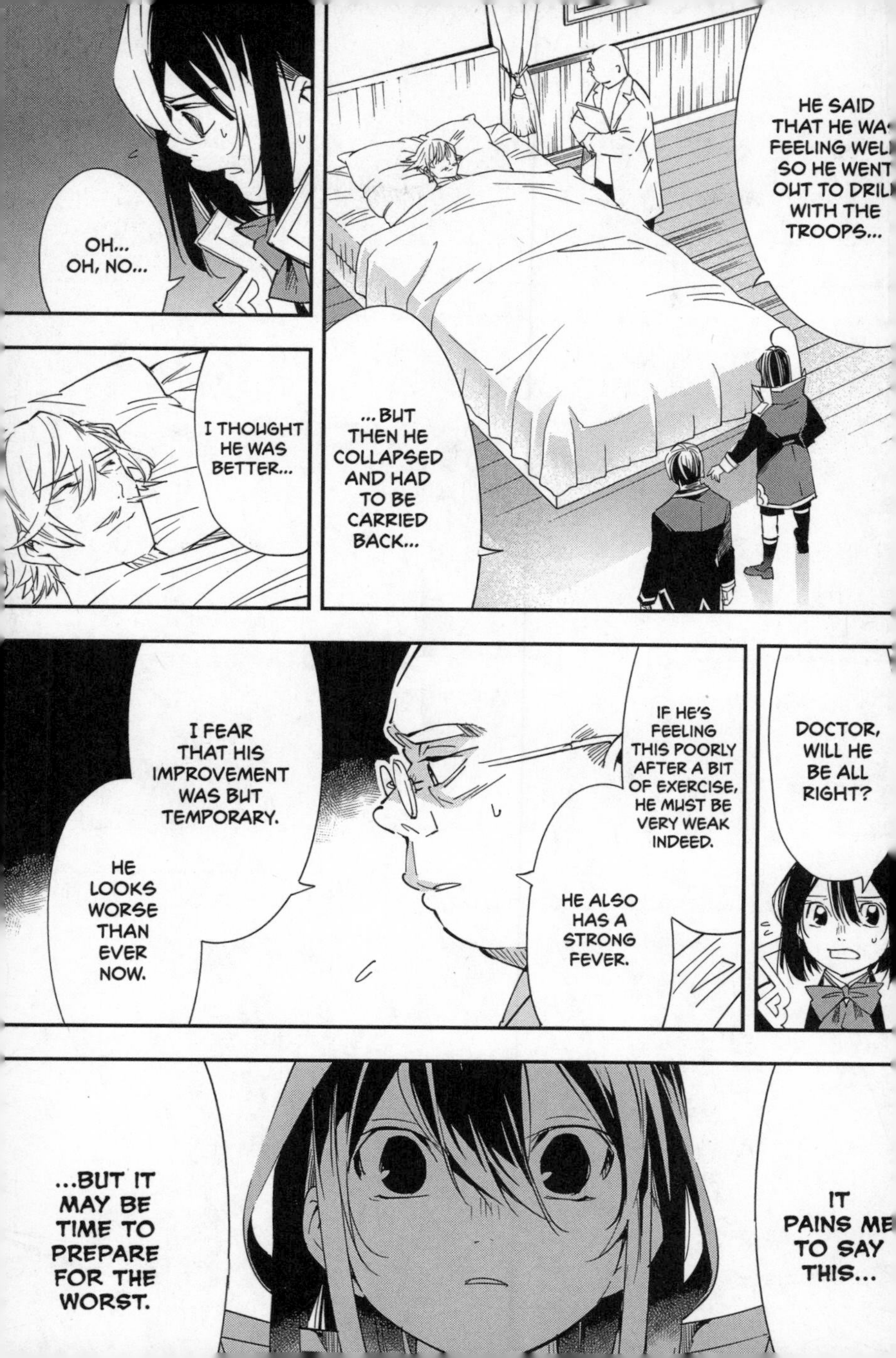
HE SAID THAT HE WA FEELING WEL SO HE WENT OUT TO DRIL WITH THE TROOPS...
...BUT THEN HE COLLAPSED AND HAD TO BE CARRIED BACK...
OH... OH, NO...
I THOUGHT HE WAS BETTER...
DOCTOR, WILL HE BE ALL RIGHT?
IF HE'S FEELING THIS POORLY AFTER A BIT OF EXERCISE, HE MUST BE VERY WEAK INDEED.
HE ALSO HAS A STRONG FEVER.
I FEAR THAT HIS IMPROVEMENT WAS BUT TEMPORARY.
HE LOOKS WORSE THAN EVER NOW.
IT PAINS ME TO SAY THIS...
...BUT IT MAY BE TIME TO PREPARE FOR THE WORST.

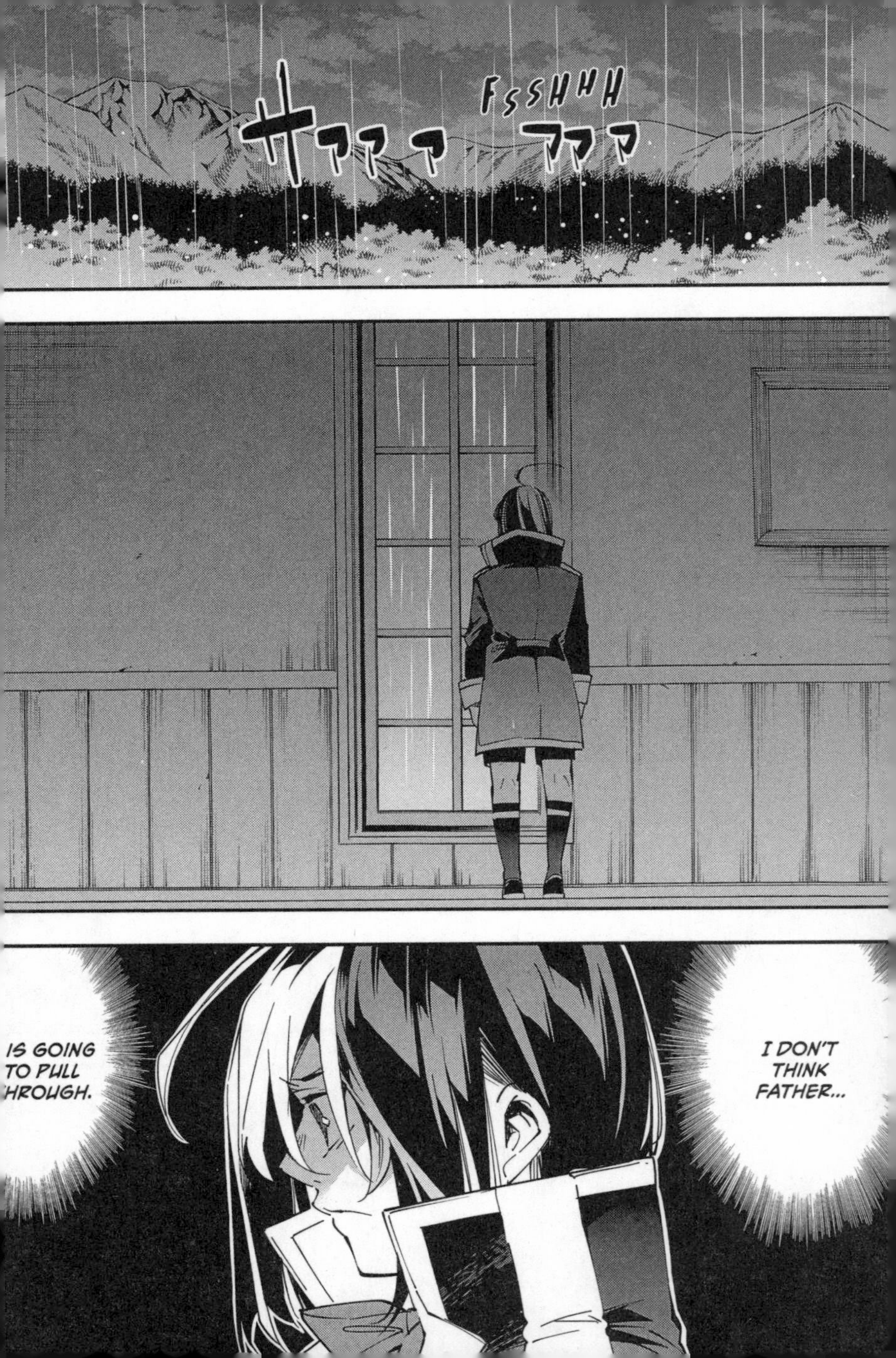
FSSHHH
I DON'T THINK FATHER...
IS GOING TO PULL THROUGH.

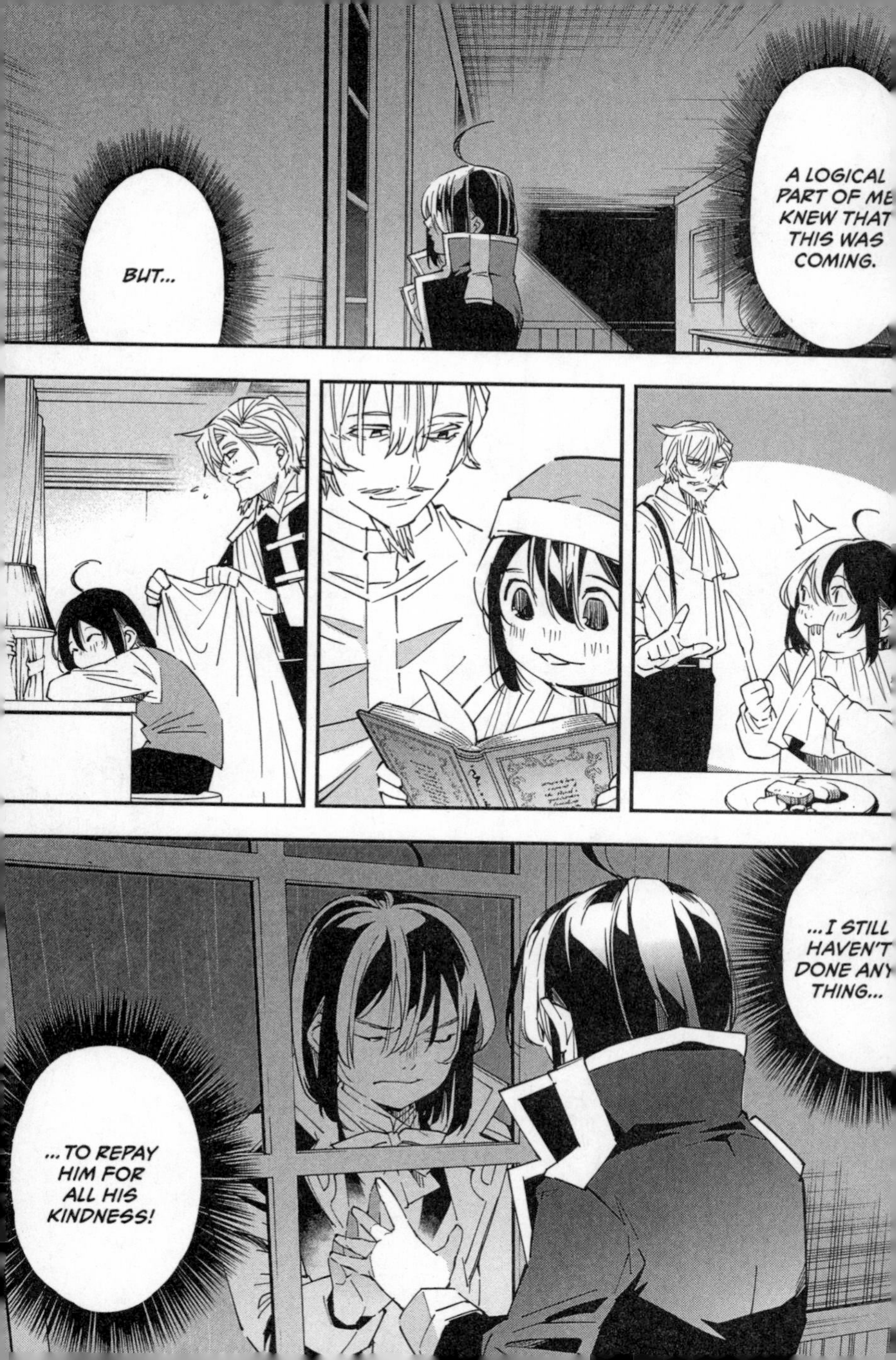
A LOGICAL PART OF ME KNEW THAT THIS WAS COMING.
BUT...
...I STILL HAVEN'T DONE ANYTHING...
...TO REPAY HIM FOR ALL HIS KINDNESS!

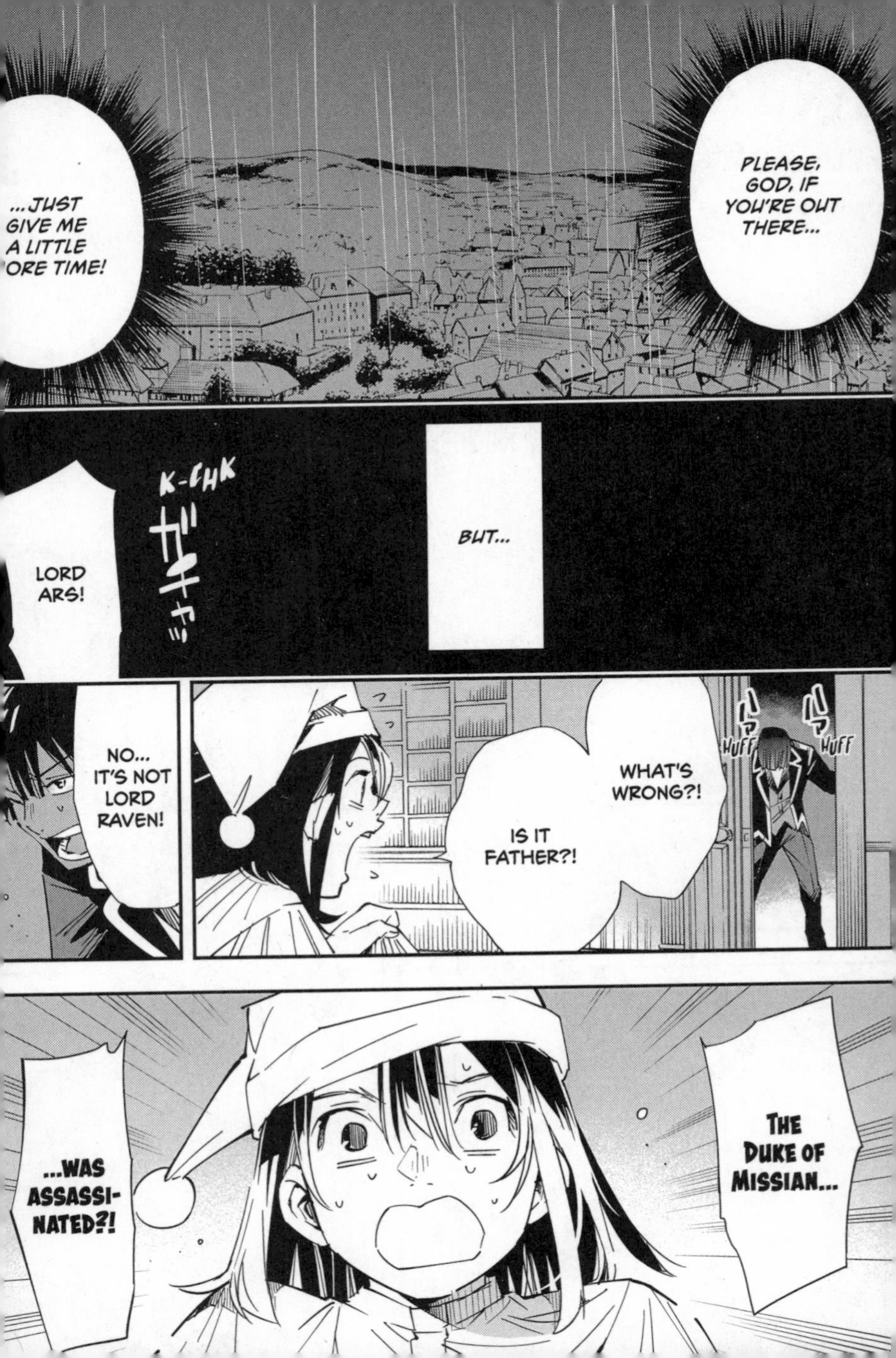
PLEASE, GOD, IF YOU'RE OUT THERE...
...JUST GIVE ME A LITTLE ORE TIME!
BUT...
K-CHK
ガチャッ
LORD ARS!
HUFF HUFF
WHAT'S WRONG?!
IS IT FATHER?!
NO... IT'S NOT LORD RAVEN!
THE DUKE OF MISSIAN...
...WAS ASSASSI-NATED?!

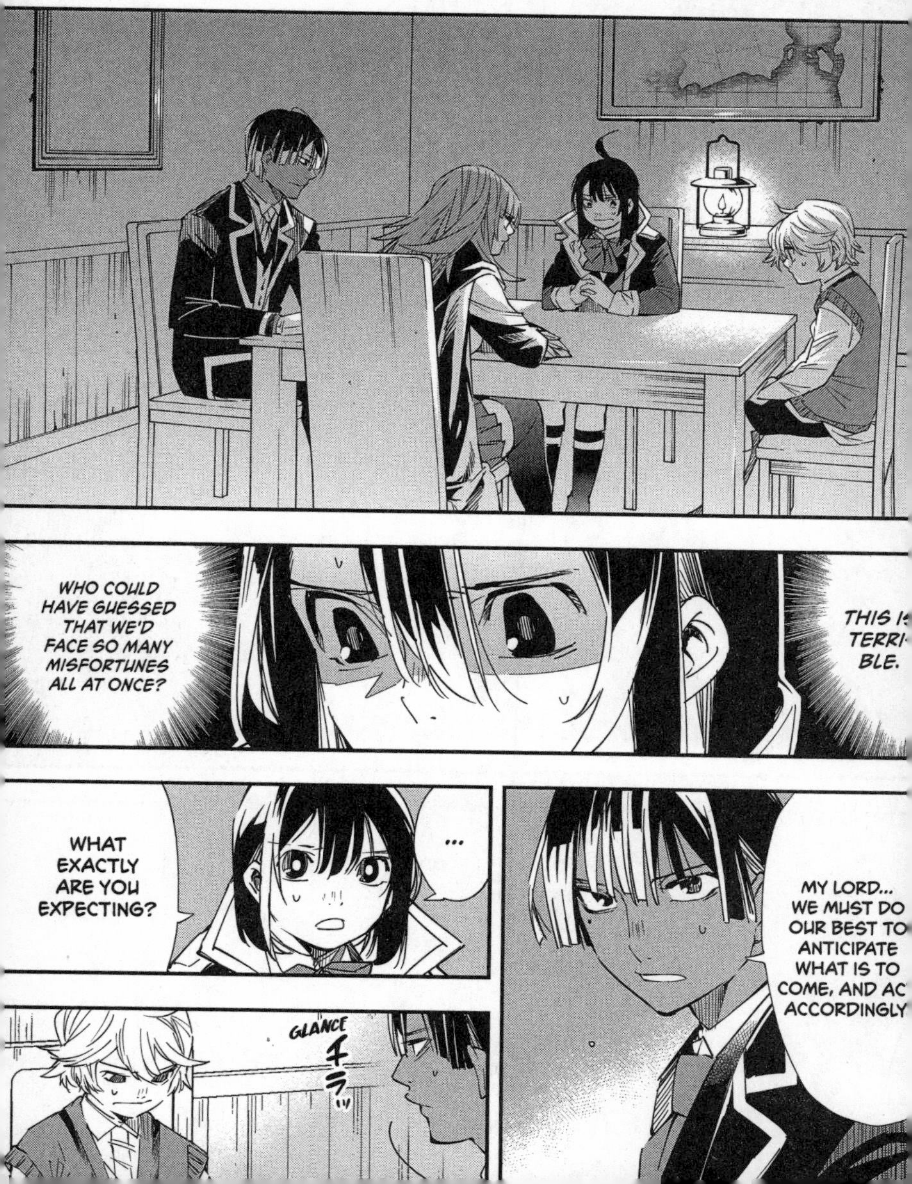
THIS IS TERRI-BLE.
WHO COULD HAVE GUESSED THAT WE'D FACE SO MANY MISFORTUNES ALL AT ONCE?
MY LORD... WE MUST DO OUR BEST TO ANTICIPATE WHAT IS TO COME, AND ACT ACCORDINGLY
...
WHAT EXACTLY ARE YOU EXPECTING?
GLANCE
チラッ

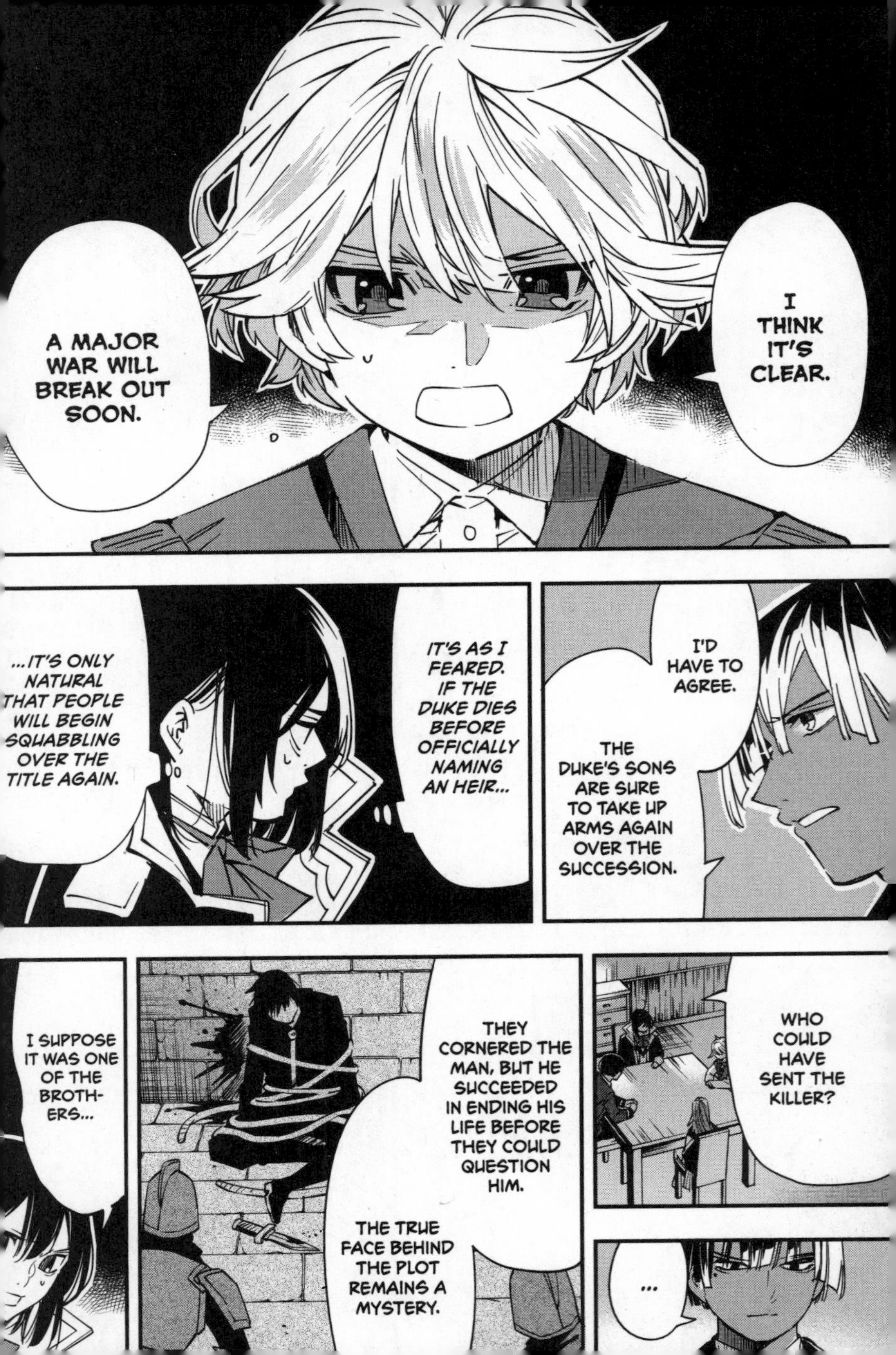
I THINK IT'S CLEAR.
A MAJOR WAR WILL BREAK OUT SOON.
I'D HAVE TO AGREE.
THE DUKE'S SONS ARE SURE TO TAKE UP ARMS AGAIN OVER THE SUCCESSION.
IT'S AS I FEARED. IF THE DUKE DIES BEFORE OFFICIALLY NAMING AN HEIR...
...IT'S ONLY NATURAL THAT PEOPLE WILL BEGIN SQUABBLING OVER THE TITLE AGAIN.
WHO COULD HAVE SENT THE KILLER?
...
THEY CORNERED THE MAN, BUT HE SUCCEEDED IN ENDING HIS LIFE BEFORE THEY COULD QUESTION HIM.
THE TRUE FACE BEHIND THE PLOT REMAINS A MYSTERY.
I SUPPOSE IT WAS ONE OF THE BROTHERS...

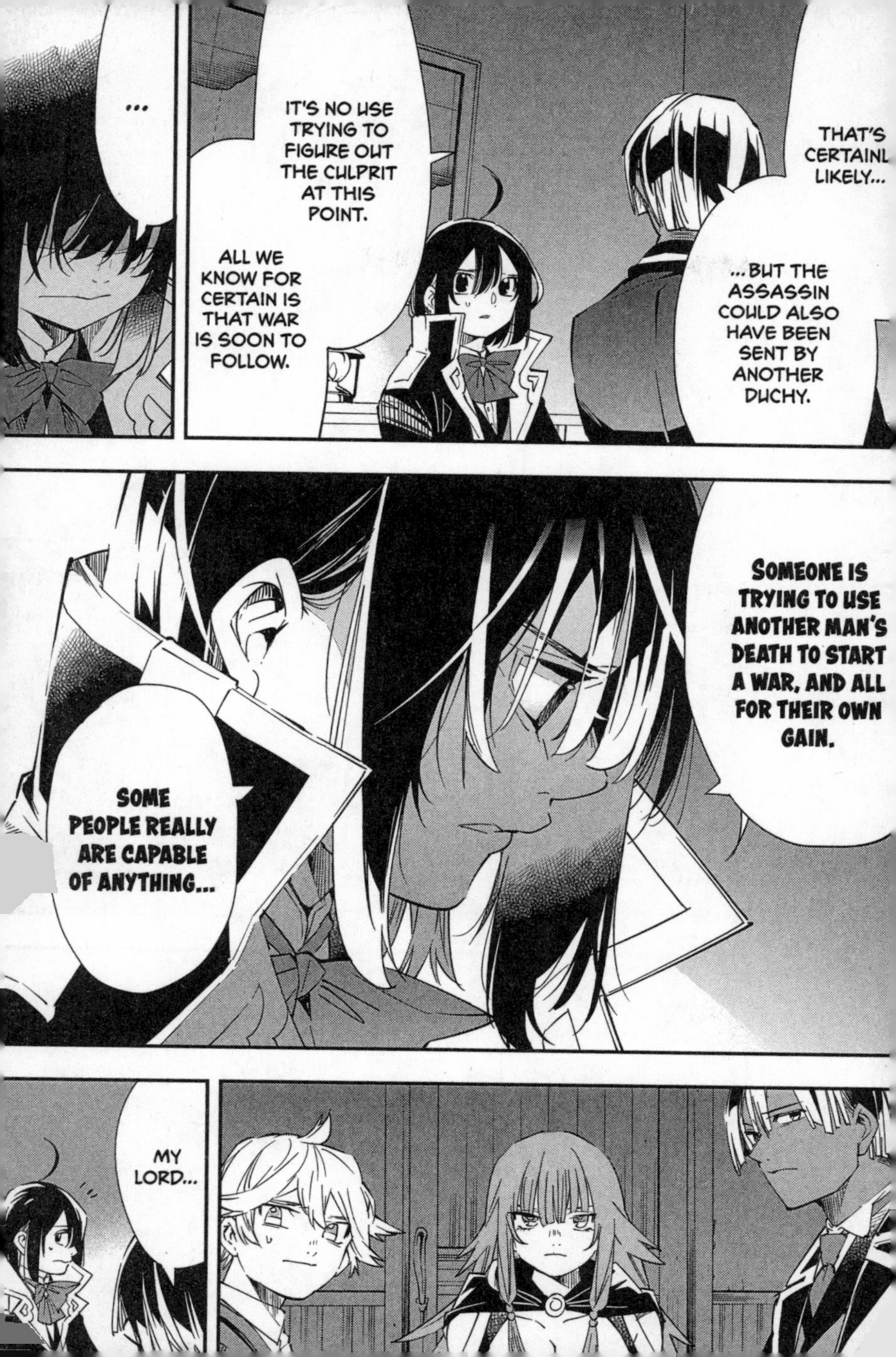
THAT'S CERTAINL LIKELY...
...BUT THE ASSASSIN COULD ALSO HAVE BEEN SENT BY ANOTHER DUCHY.
IT'S NO USE TRYING TO FIGURE OUT THE CULPRIT AT THIS POINT.
ALL WE KNOW FOR CERTAIN IS THAT WAR IS SOON TO FOLLOW.
...
SOMEONE IS TRYING TO USE ANOTHER MAN'S DEATH TO START A WAR, AND ALL FOR THEIR OWN GAIN.
SOME PEOPLE REALLY ARE CAPABLE OF ANYTHING...
MY LORD...

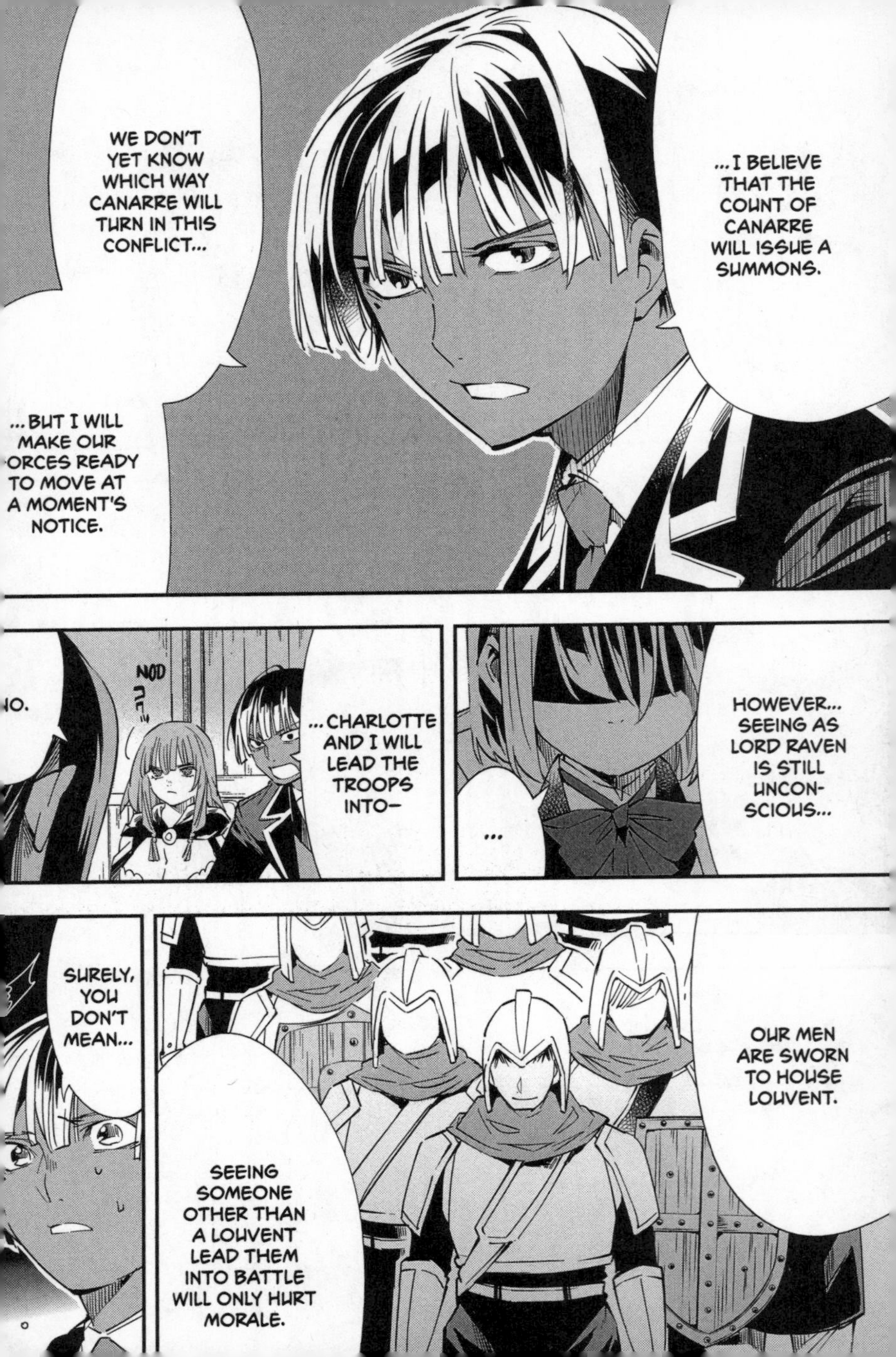
...I BELIEVE THAT THE COUNT OF CANARRE WILL ISSUE A SUMMONS.
WE DON'T YET KNOW WHICH WAY CANARRE WILL TURN IN THIS CONFLICT...
...BUT I WILL MAKE OUR ORCES READY TO MOVE AT A MOMENT'S NOTICE.
HOWEVER... SEEING AS LORD RAVEN IS STILL UNCON-SCIOUS...
...
...CHARLOTTE AND I WILL LEAD THE TROOPS INTO—
NOD
IO.
OUR MEN ARE SWORN TO HOUSE LOUVENT.
SEEING SOMEONE OTHER THAN A LOUVENT LEAD THEM INTO BATTLE WILL ONLY HURT MORALE.
SURELY, YOU DON'T MEAN...

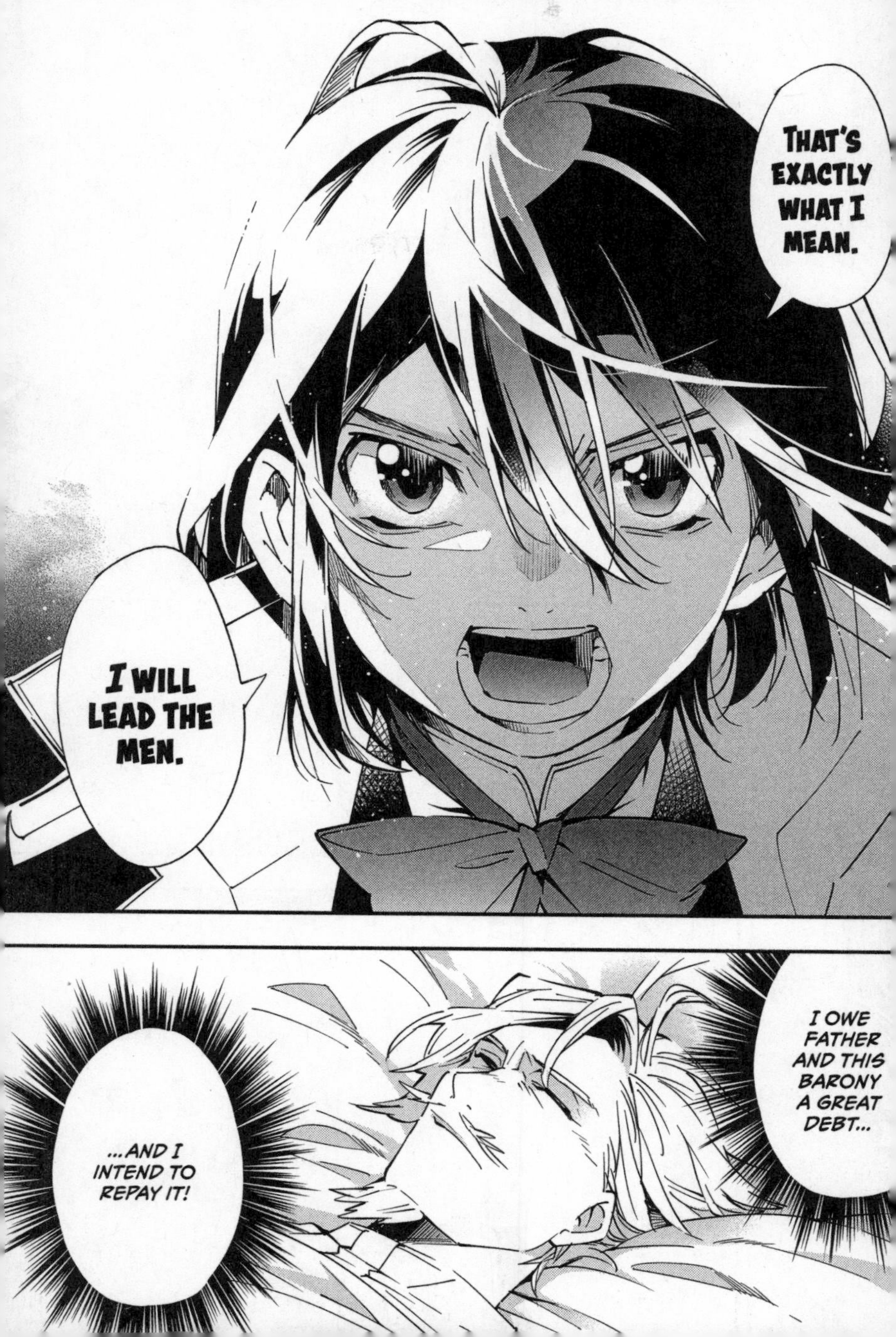
THAT'S EXACTLY WHAT I MEAN.
I WILL LEAD THE MEN.
I OWE FATHER AND THIS BARONY A GREAT DEBT...
...AND I INTEND TO REPAY IT!

As a Reincarnated ARISTOCRAT, I'll Use My Appraisal Skill to Rise in the World

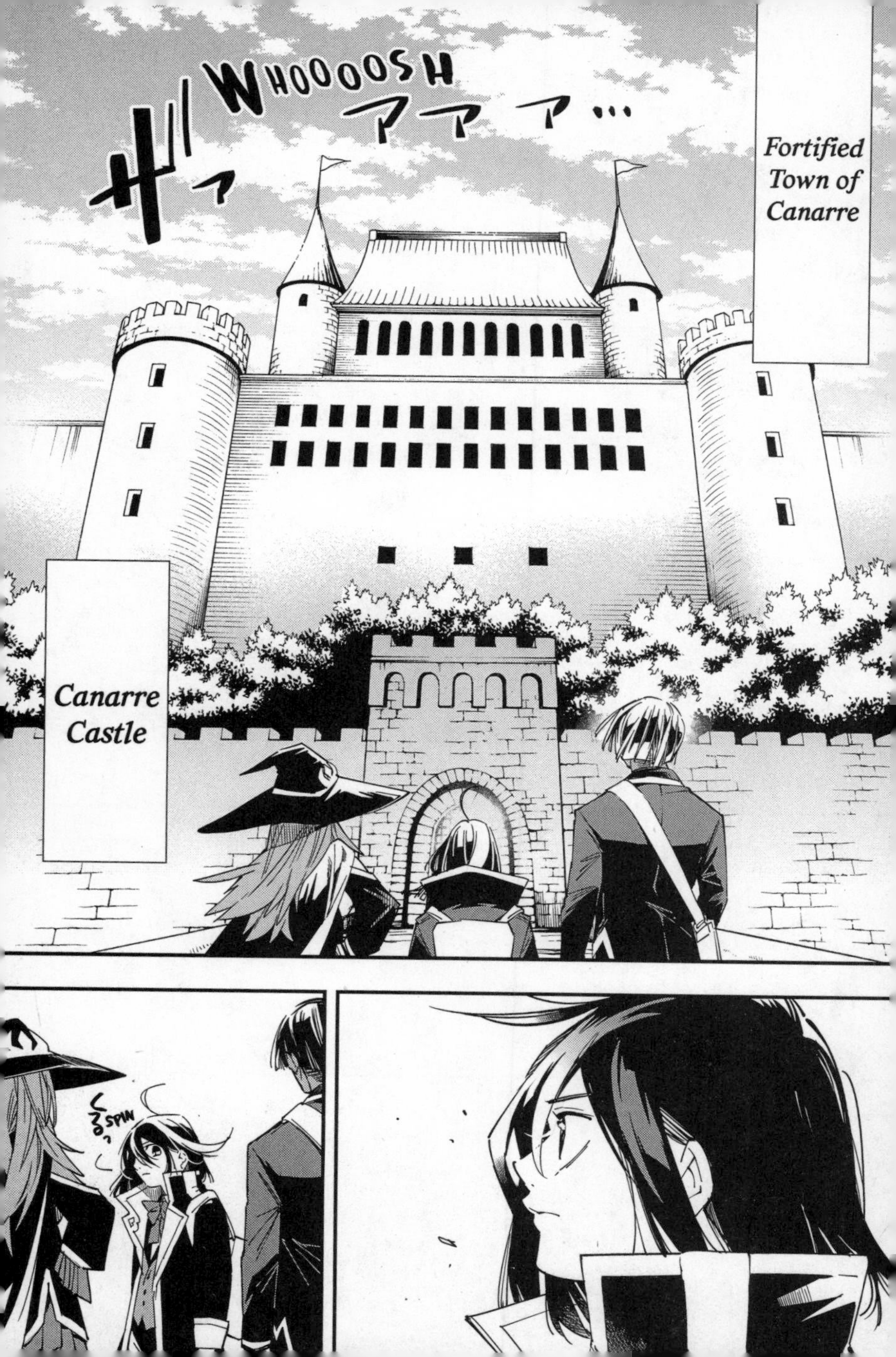

Fortified Town of Canarre
WHOOOOSH
ザァアアア…
Canarre Castle
SPIN

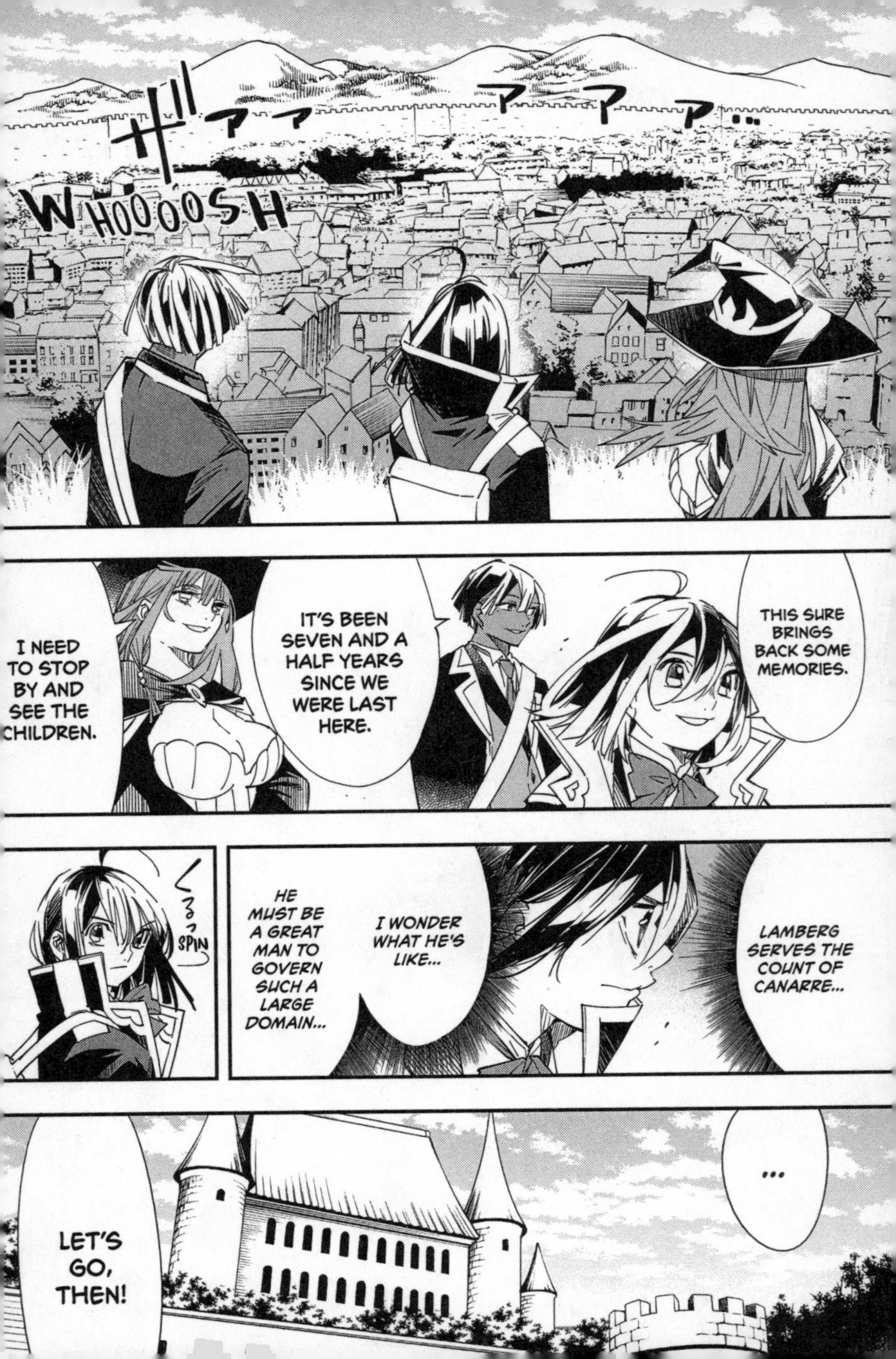

ザァァァァァ…
WHOOOOSH
THIS SURE BRINGS BACK SOME MEMORIES.
IT'S BEEN SEVEN AND A HALF YEARS SINCE WE WERE LAST HERE.
I NEED TO STOP BY AND SEE THE CHILDREN.
LAMBERG SERVES THE COUNT OF CANARRE...
I WONDER WHAT HE'S LIKE...
HE MUST BE A GREAT MAN TO GOVERN SUCH A LARGE DOMAIN...
くるっ
SPIN
...
LET'S GO, THEN!

Chapter 24: War Council, pt. 1

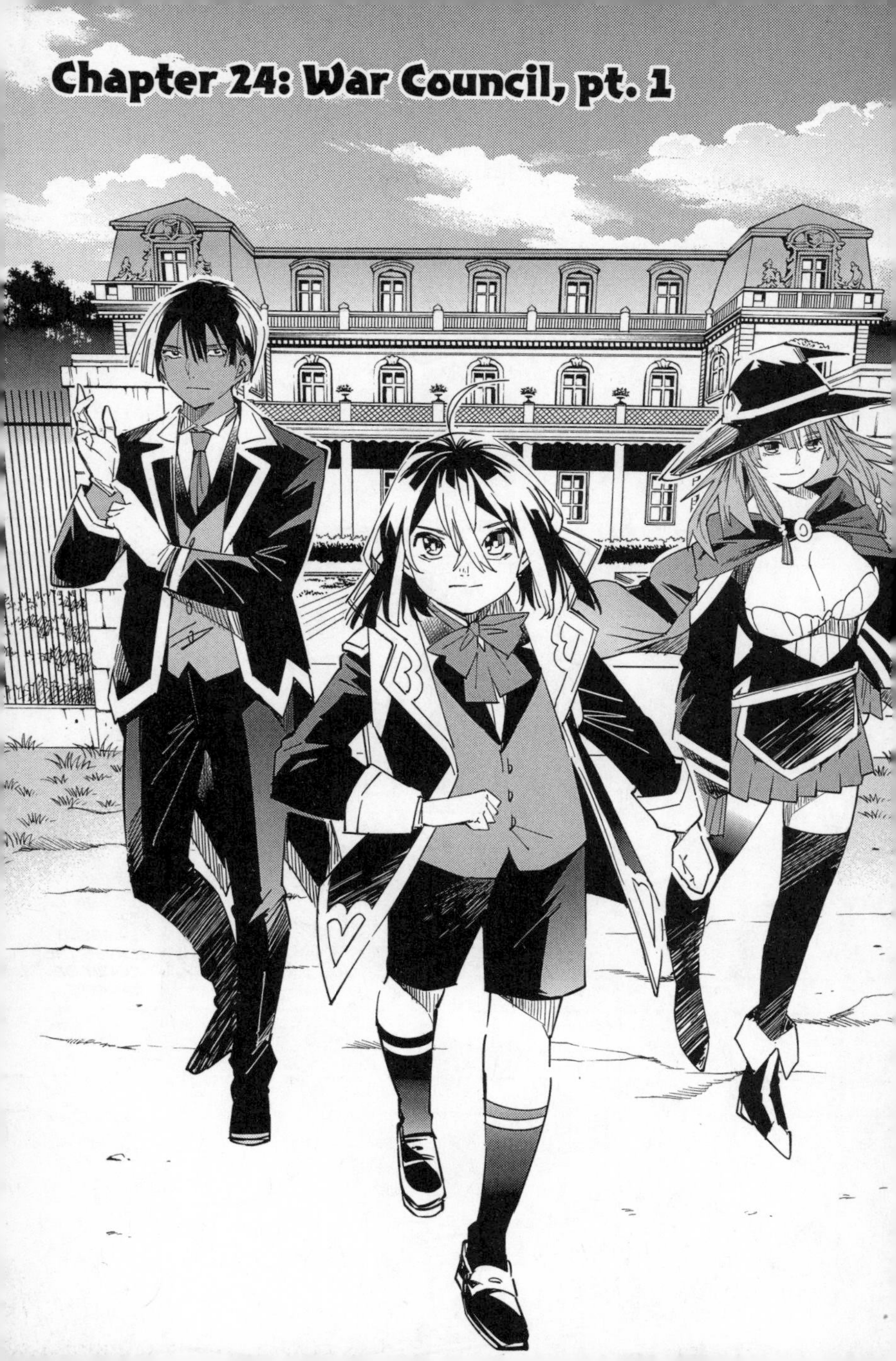

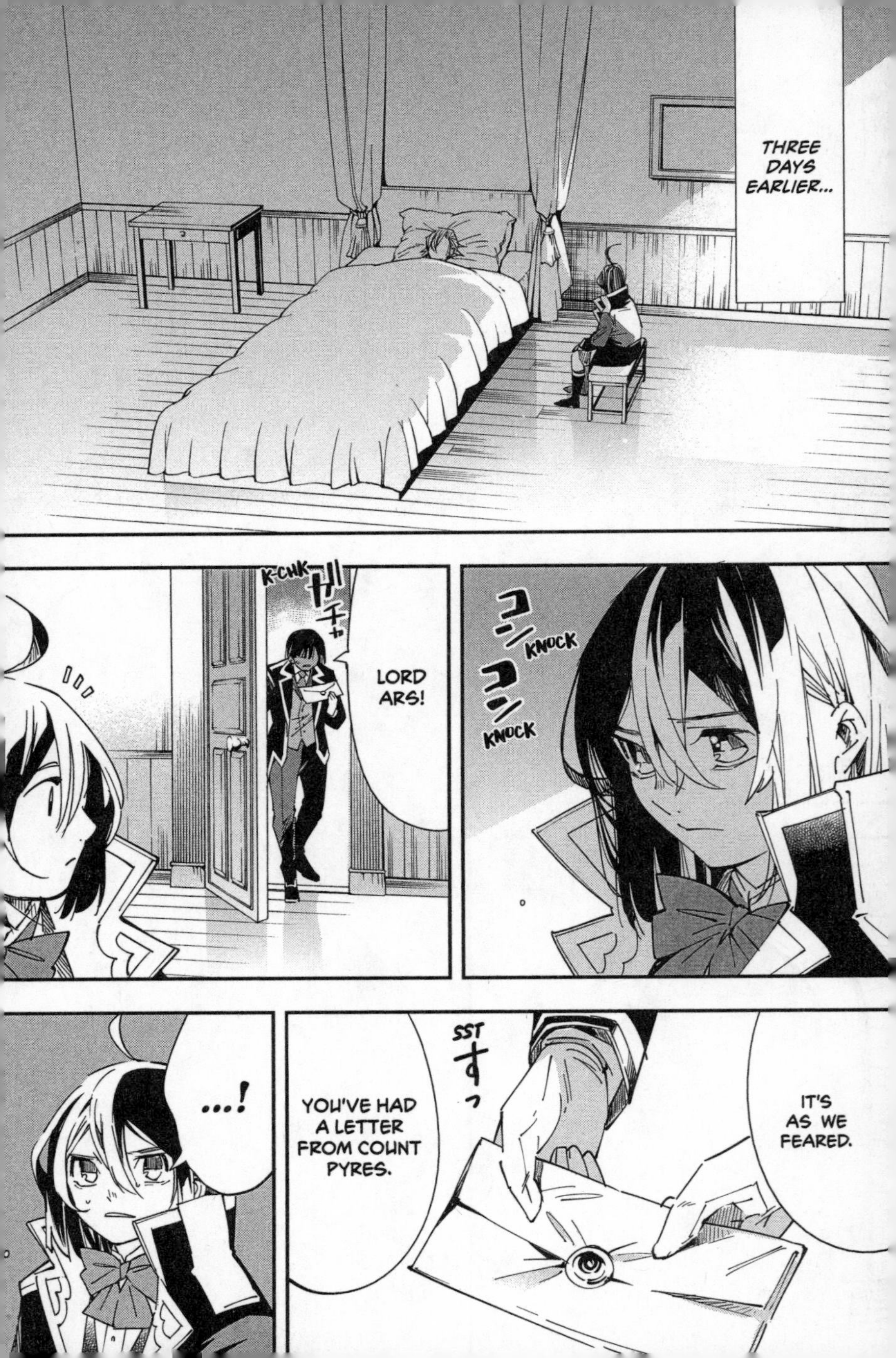
THREE DAYS EARLIER...
コン KNOCK
コン KNOCK
K-CHK ガチャ
LORD ARS!
IT'S AS WE FEARED.
SST すっ
YOU'VE HAD A LETTER FROM COUNT PYRES.
...!

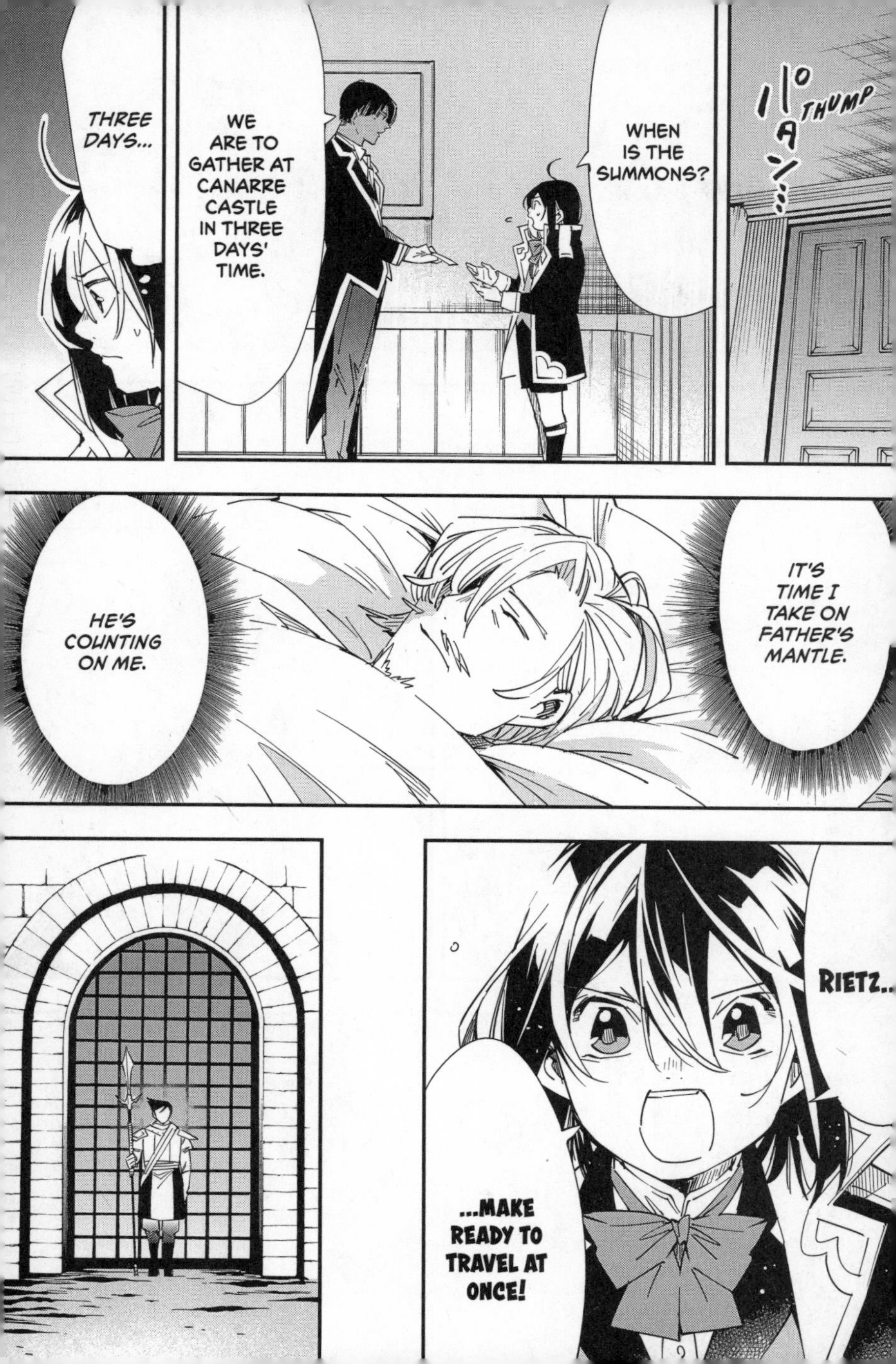

パン…
THUMP
WHEN IS THE SUMMONS?
WE ARE TO GATHER AT CANARRE CASTLE IN THREE DAYS' TIME.
THREE DAYS...
IT'S TIME I TAKE ON FATHER'S MANTLE.
HE'S COUNTING ON ME.
RIETZ...
...MAKE READY TO TRAVEL AT ONCE!

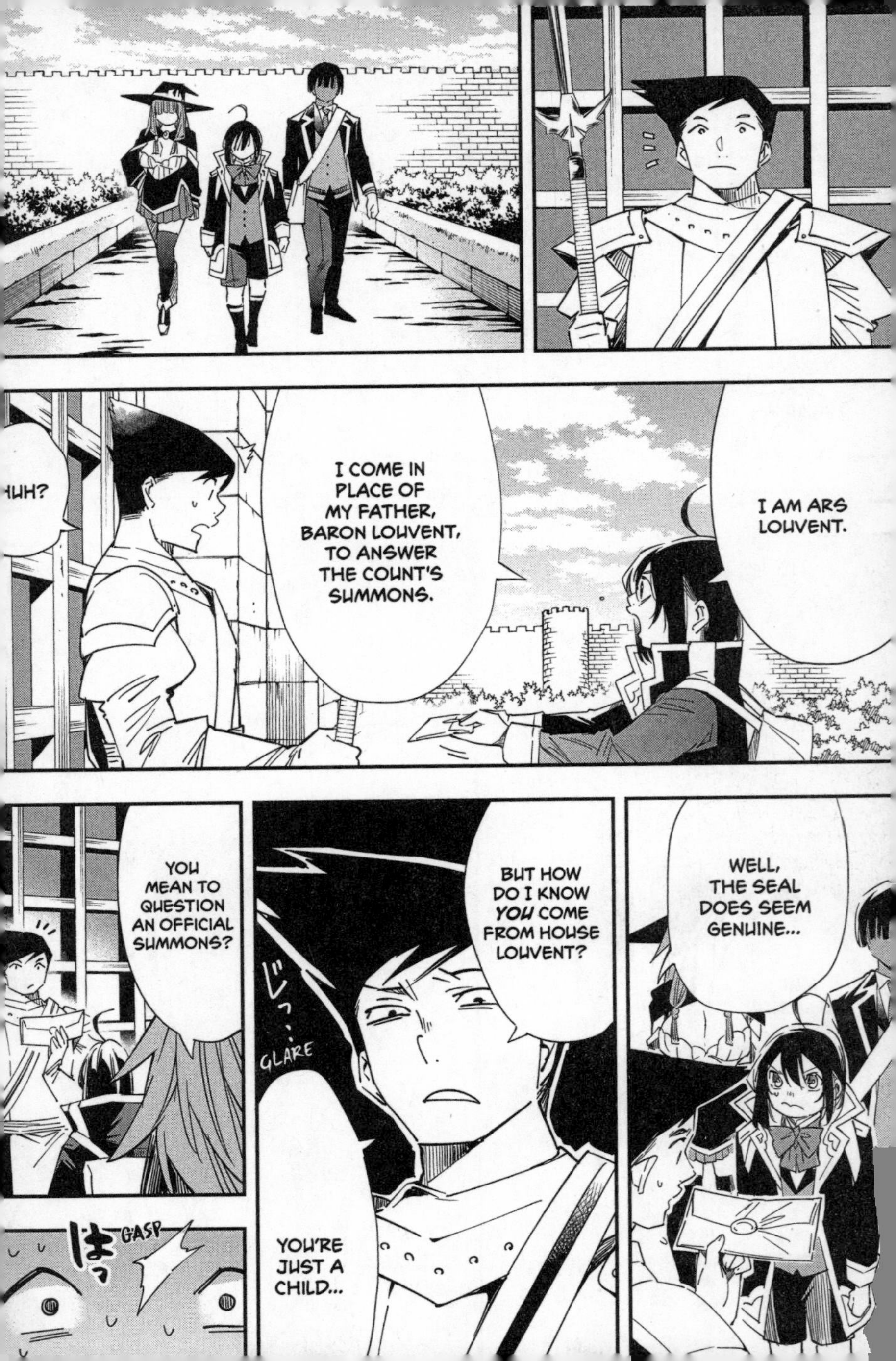
I AM ARS LOUVENT.
I COME IN PLACE OF MY FATHER, BARON LOUVENT, TO ANSWER THE COUNT'S SUMMONS.
HUH?
WELL, THE SEAL DOES SEEM GENUINE...
BUT HOW DO I KNOW *YOU* COME FROM HOUSE LOUVENT?
じっ… GLARE
YOU'RE JUST A CHILD...
YOU MEAN TO QUESTION AN OFFICIAL SUMMONS?
はっ GASP

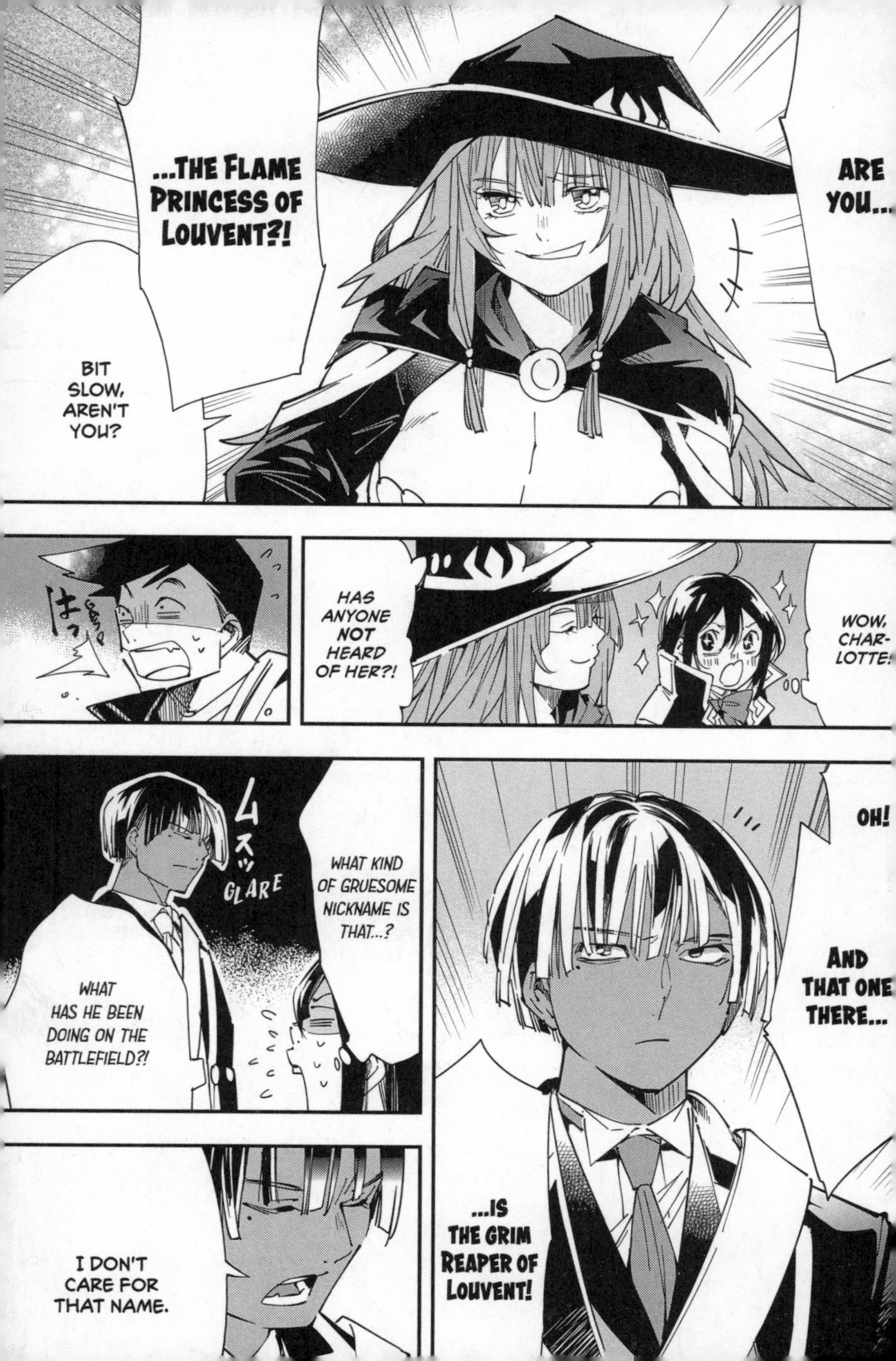
ARE YOU...
...THE FLAME PRINCESS OF LOUVENT?!
BIT SLOW, AREN'T YOU?
WOW, CHARLOTTE!
HAS ANYONE NOT HEARD OF HER?!
はっ
GASP
OH!
AND THAT ONE THERE...
...IS THE GRIM REAPER OF LOUVENT!
ムスッ
GLARE
WHAT KIND OF GRUESOME NICKNAME IS THAT...?
WHAT HAS HE BEEN DOING ON THE BATTLEFIELD?!
I DON'T CARE FOR THAT NAME.

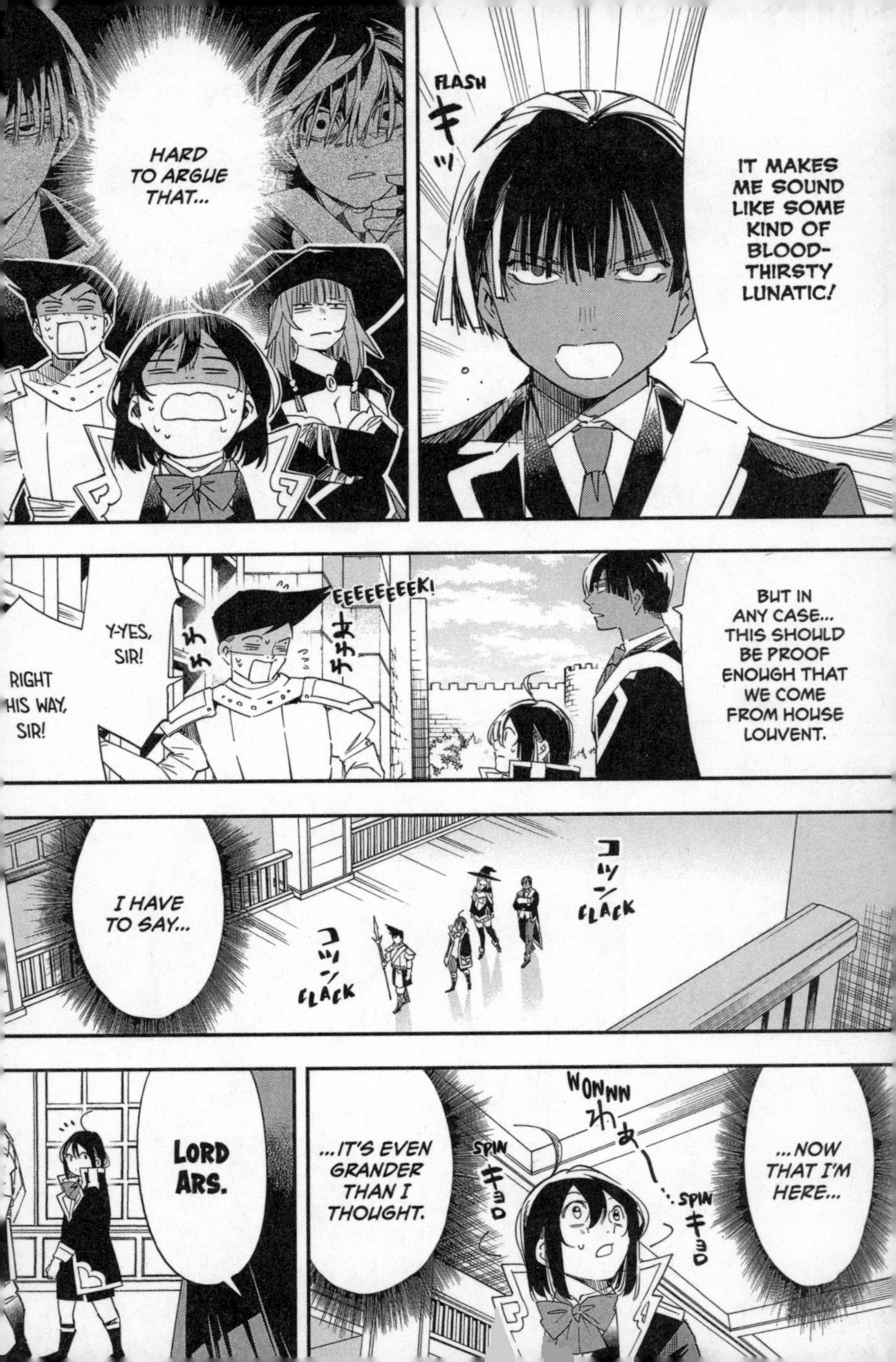
FLASH
IT MAKES ME SOUND LIKE SOME KIND OF BLOOD-THIRSTY LUNATIC!
HARD TO ARGUE THAT...
BUT IN ANY CASE... THIS SHOULD BE PROOF ENOUGH THAT WE COME FROM HOUSE LOUVENT.
EEEEEEEEK!
Y-YES, SIR!
RIGHT HIS WAY, SIR!
CLACK
CLACK
I HAVE TO SAY...
...NOW THAT I'M HERE...
WONNN
SPIN
SPIN
...IT'S EVEN GRANDER THAN I THOUGHT.
LORD ARS.

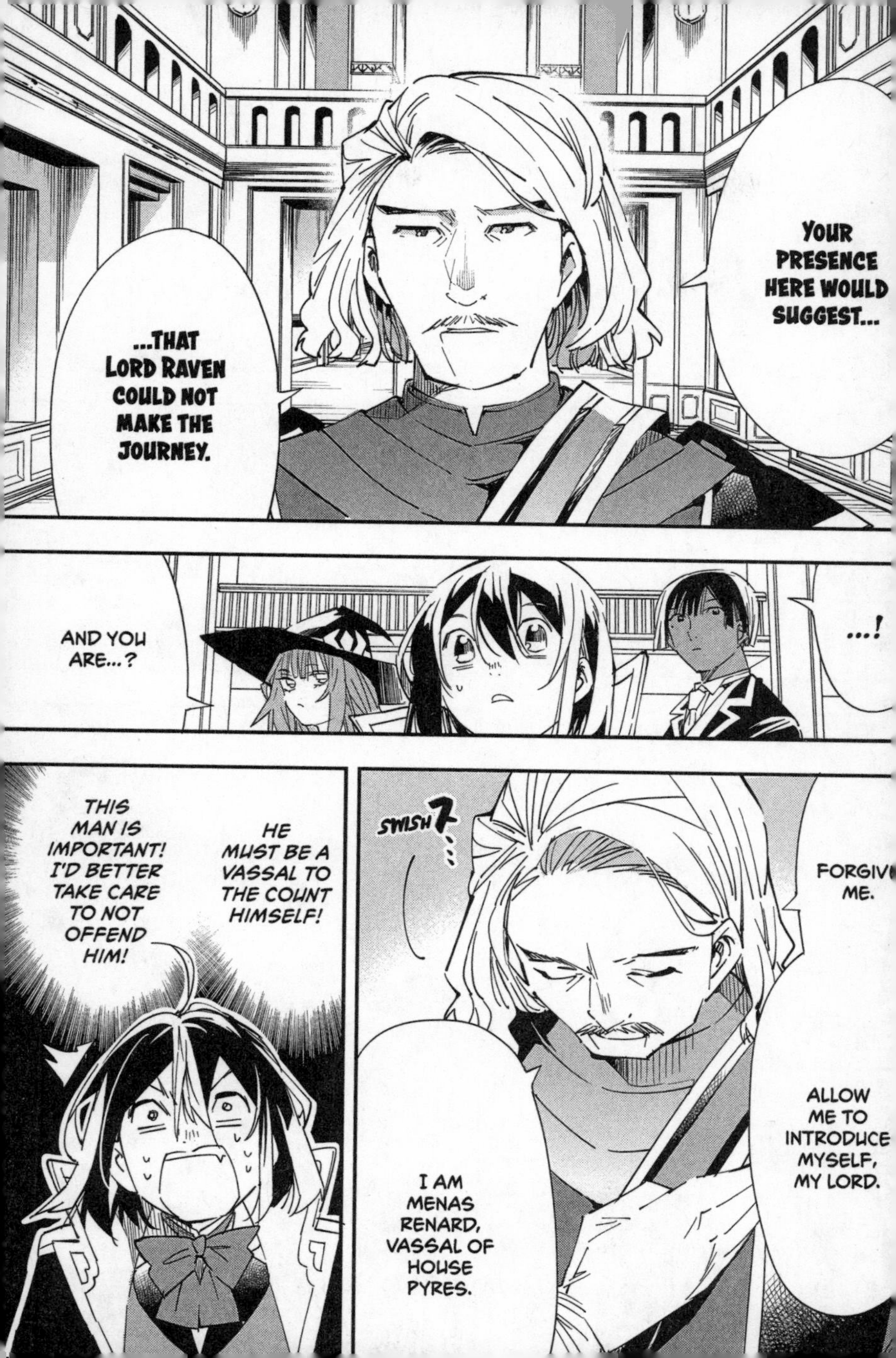
YOUR PRESENCE HERE WOULD SUGGEST...
...THAT LORD RAVEN COULD NOT MAKE THE JOURNEY.
...!
AND YOU ARE...?
FORGIV ME.
SWISH
ALLOW ME TO INTRODUCE MYSELF, MY LORD.
I AM MENAS RENARD, VASSAL OF HOUSE PYRES.
HE MUST BE A VASSAL TO THE COUNT HIMSELF!
THIS MAN IS IMPORTANT! I'D BETTER TAKE CARE TO NOT OFFEND HIM!

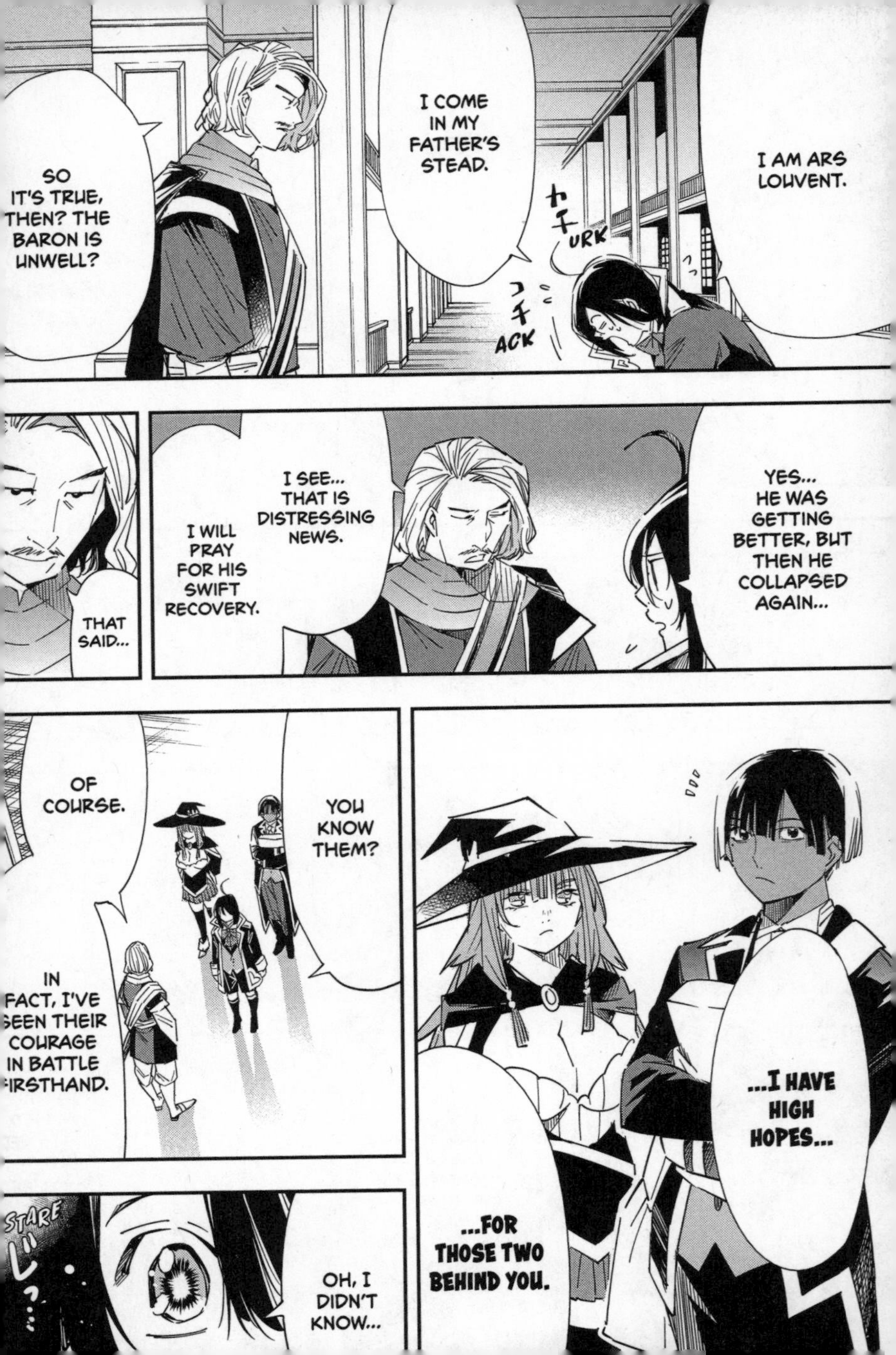
I AM ARS LOUVENT.
I COME IN MY FATHER'S STEAD.
カチ URK
コチ ACK
SO IT'S TRUE, THEN? THE BARON IS UNWELL?
YES... HE WAS GETTING BETTER, BUT THEN HE COLLAPSED AGAIN...
I SEE... THAT IS DISTRESSING NEWS.
I WILL PRAY FOR HIS SWIFT RECOVERY.
THAT SAID...
...I HAVE HIGH HOPES...
...FOR THOSE TWO BEHIND YOU.
YOU KNOW THEM?
OF COURSE.
IN FACT, I'VE SEEN THEIR COURAGE IN BATTLE FIRSTHAND.
OH, I DIDN'T KNOW...
STARE じーっ...

IT LOOKS LIKE HE'S CAPABLE IN EVERY AREA.

SIR MENAS... HIS STATS ARE ALL QUITE HIGH! JUST WHAT I'D EXPECT FROM A VASSAL OF SUCH A LARGE DOMAIN.

BUT...

Menas Renard - Age 40 ♂

Stats

	CURRENT	MAX
Command	71	71
Prowess	70	70
Intellect	75	77
Diplomacy	78	78
Ambition	25	

Aptitude

Fighter	B	Cavalier	B	Archer	A
Mage	C	Engineer	B	Armorer	D
Mariner	D	Pilot	B	Tactician	B

I'M SO GRATEFUL TO HAVE THEM AS MY VASSALS...

...LOOKING AT THOSE NUMBERS ALSO MAKES ME APPRECIATE JUST HOW INCREDIBLE RIETZ AND CHARLOTTE ARE!

I CAN PROTEST ALL I WANT...

NO... YOU CAN'T!

ジャーク

YOU'LL FIND THAT CASTLE LIFE CAN BE VERY COMFORTABLE.

I MUST SAY, WE'D BE HONORED TO HAVE YOU BOTH JOIN US.

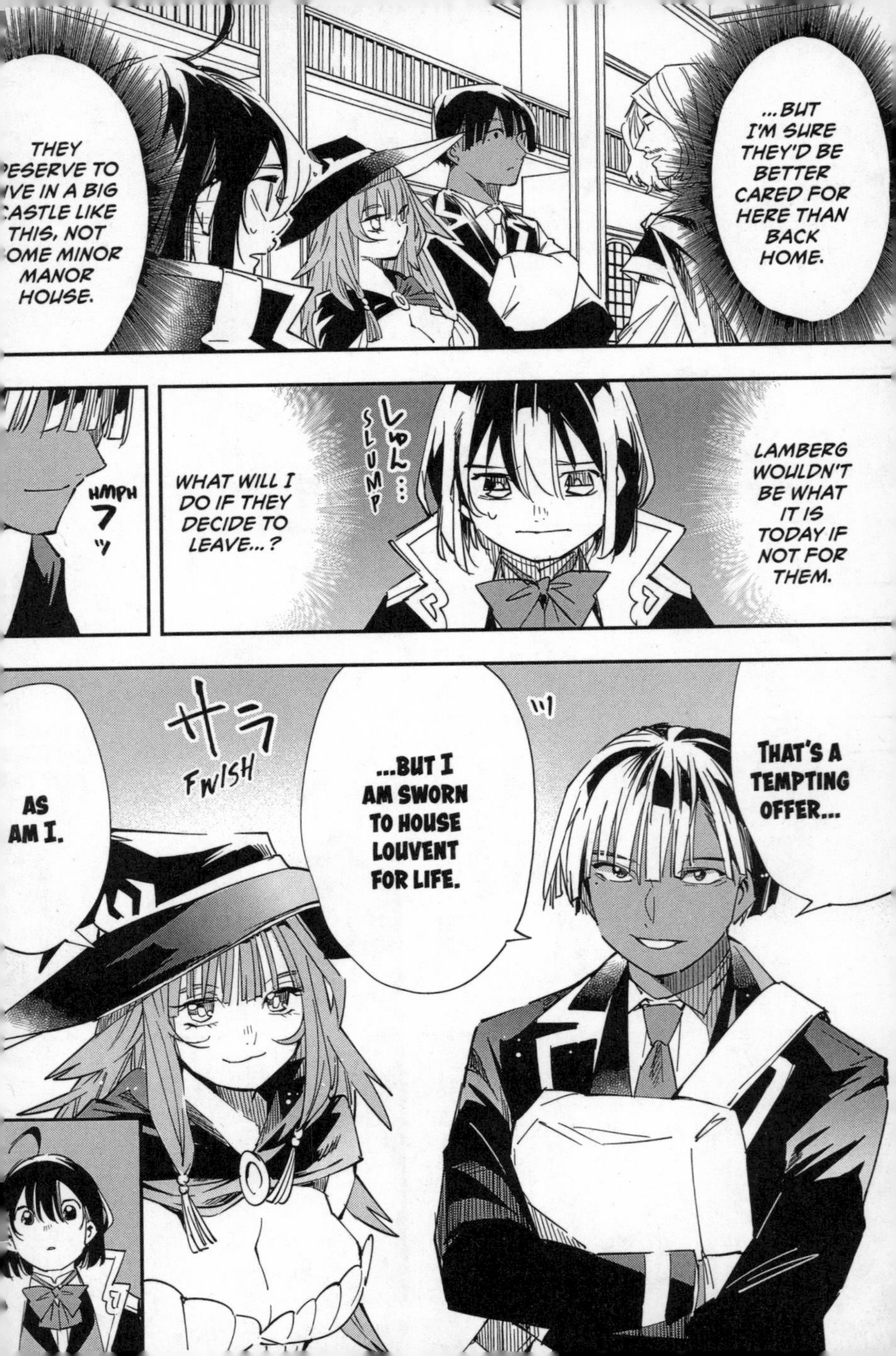
...BUT I'M SURE THEY'D BE BETTER CARED FOR HERE THAN BACK HOME.
THEY ESERVE TO IVE IN A BIG ASTLE LIKE THIS, NOT OME MINOR MANOR HOUSE.
LAMBERG WOULDN'T BE WHAT IT IS TODAY IF NOT FOR THEM.
しゅん… SLUMP
WHAT WILL I DO IF THEY DECIDE TO LEAVE...?
HMPH フッ
THAT'S A TEMPTING OFFER...
ッ
...BUT I AM SWORN TO HOUSE LOUVENT FOR LIFE.
サラ FWISH
AS AM I.

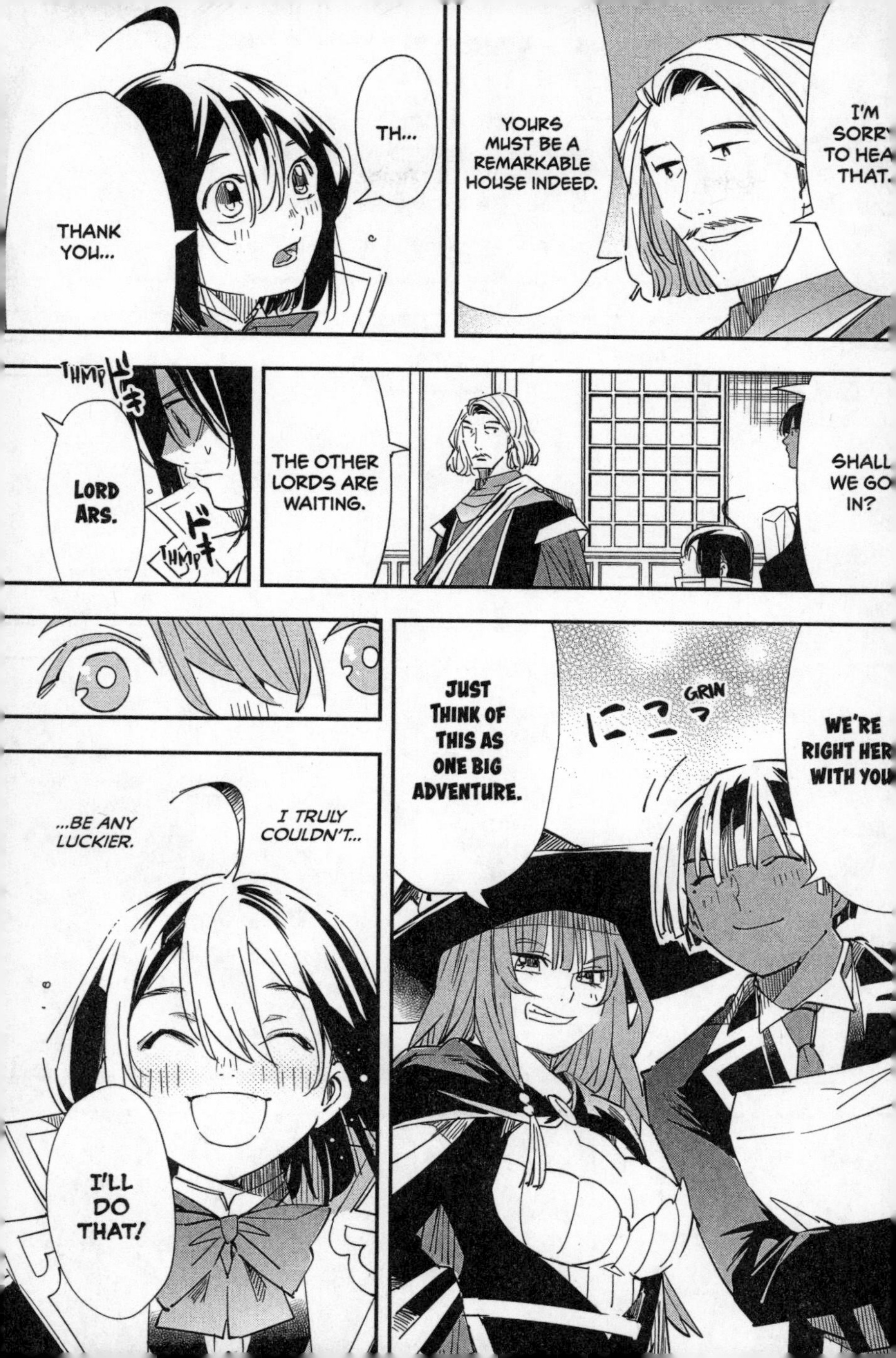
I'M SORRY TO HEA THAT.
YOURS MUST BE A REMARKABLE HOUSE INDEED.
TH...
THANK YOU...
SHALL WE GO IN?
THE OTHER LORDS ARE WAITING.
THMP
LORD ARS.
THMP
WE'RE RIGHT HER WITH YOU
GRIN
JUST THINK OF THIS AS ONE BIG ADVENTURE.
I TRULY COULDN'T...
...BE ANY LUCKIER.
I'LL DO THAT!

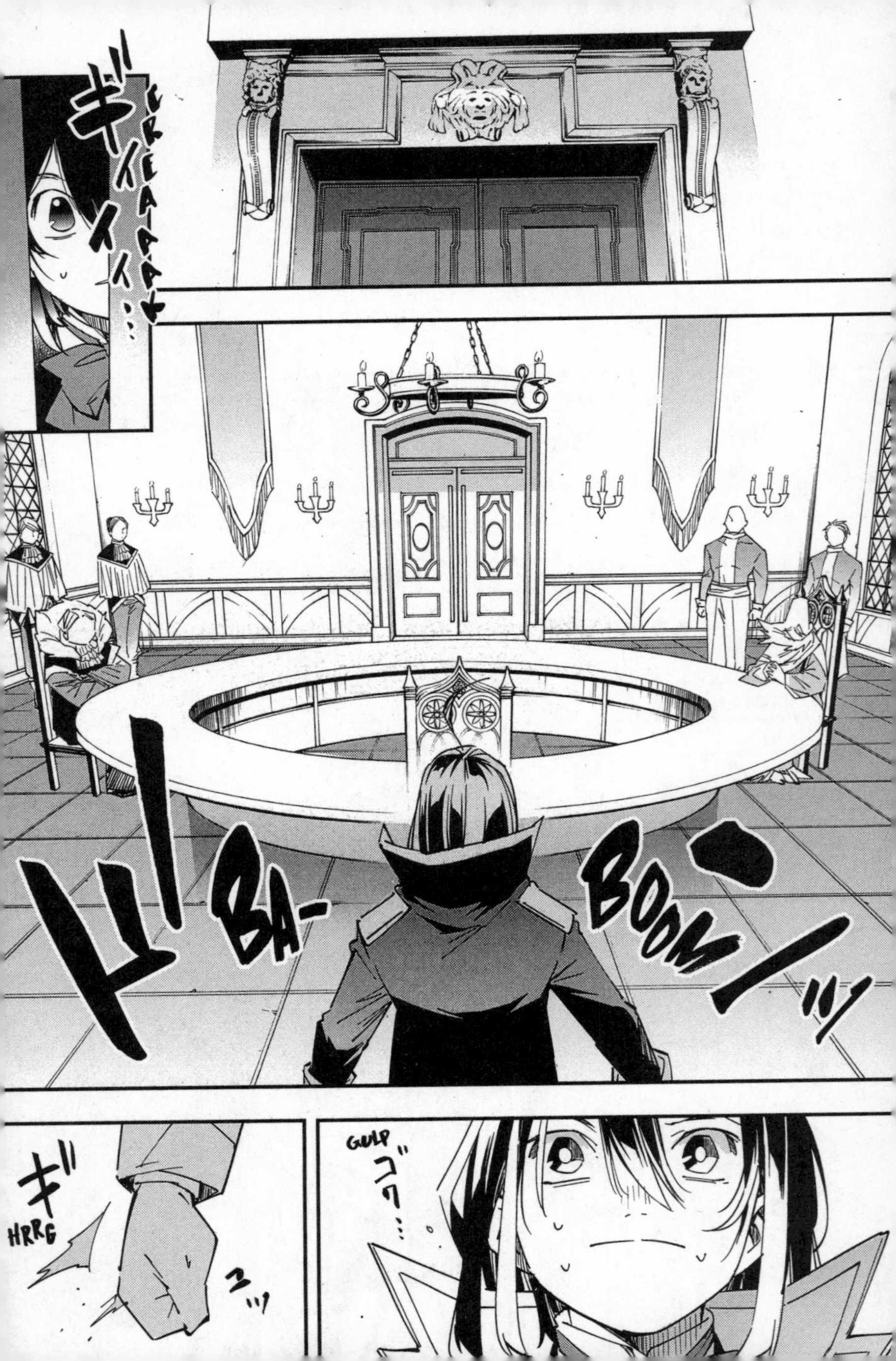
ギイイ…
CREAAAK
ドンッ
BA-BOOM
ゴク…
GULP
ギリ
HRRG
ゴッ

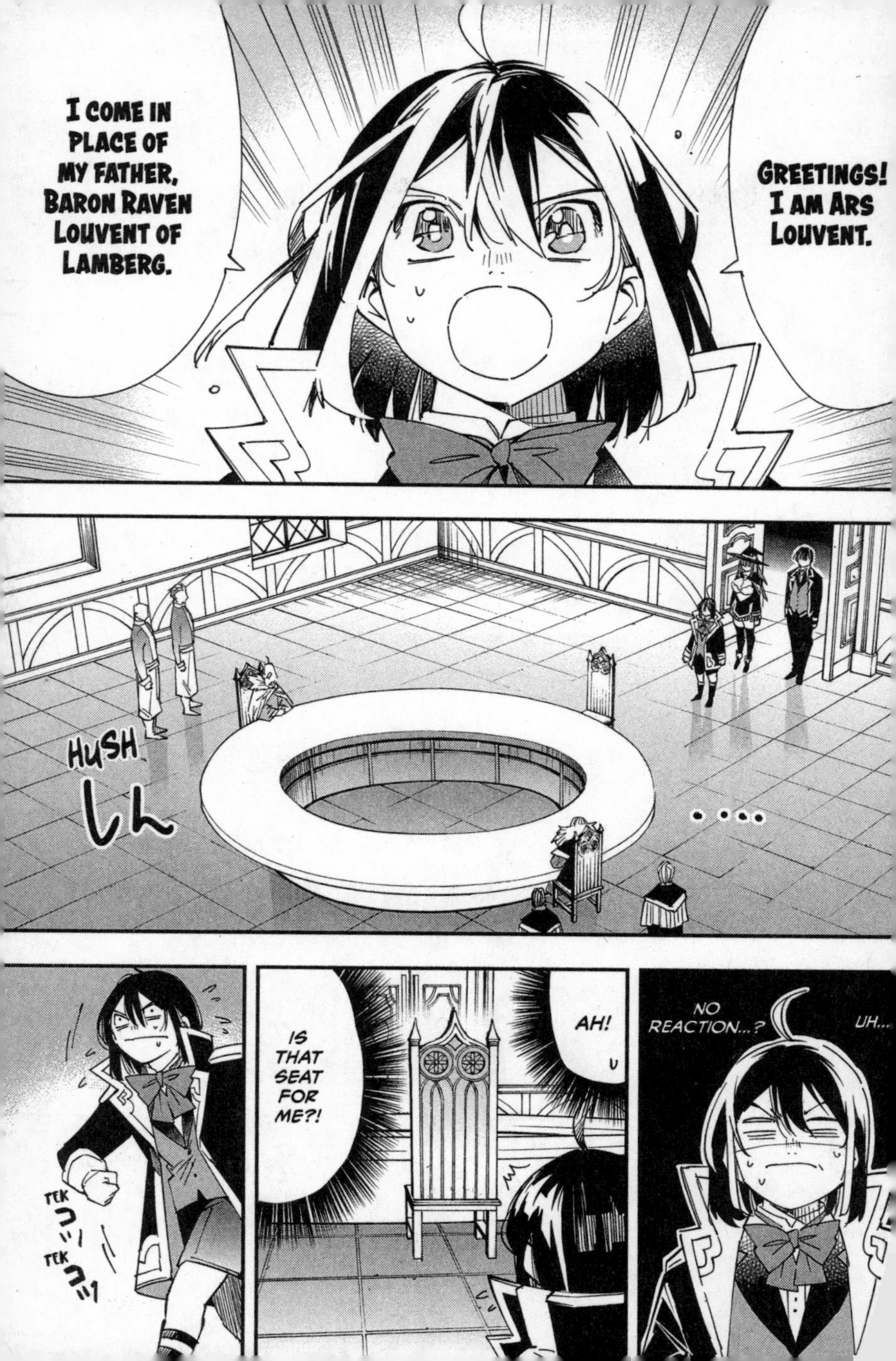
GREETINGS! I AM ARS LOUVENT.
I COME IN PLACE OF MY FATHER, BARON RAVEN LOUVENT OF LAMBERG.
....
HUSH
しん
UH...
NO REACTION...?
AH!
IS THAT SEAT FOR ME?!
TEK
コッ
TEK
コッ

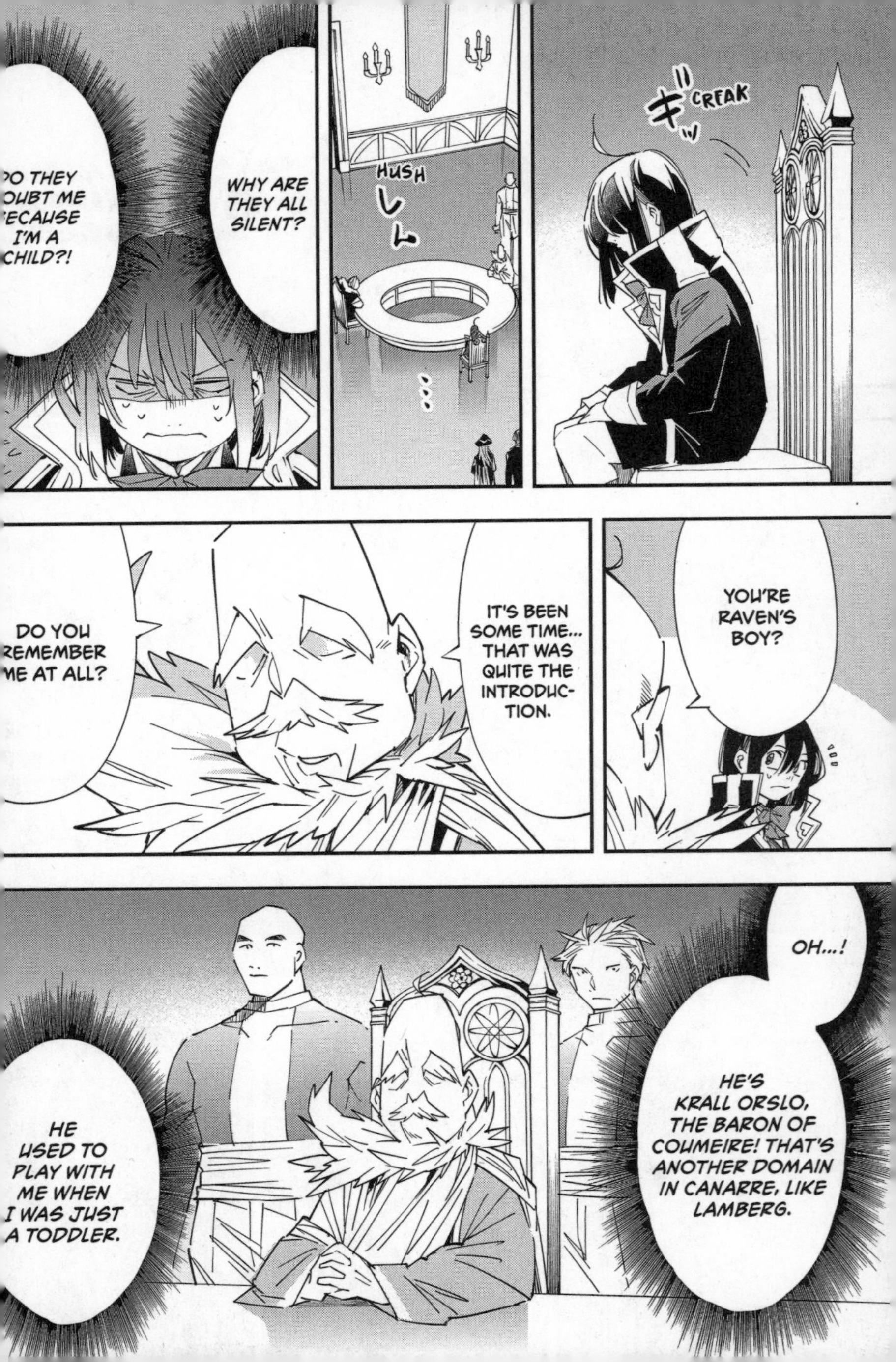
CREAK
HUSH
...
WHY ARE THEY ALL SILENT?
DO THEY DOUBT ME BECAUSE I'M A CHILD?!
YOU'RE RAVEN'S BOY?
IT'S BEEN SOME TIME... THAT WAS QUITE THE INTRODUCTION.
DO YOU REMEMBER ME AT ALL?
OH...!
HE'S KRALL ORSLO, THE BARON OF COUMEIRE! THAT'S ANOTHER DOMAIN IN CANARRE, LIKE LAMBERG.
HE USED TO PLAY WITH ME WHEN I WAS JUST A TODDLER.

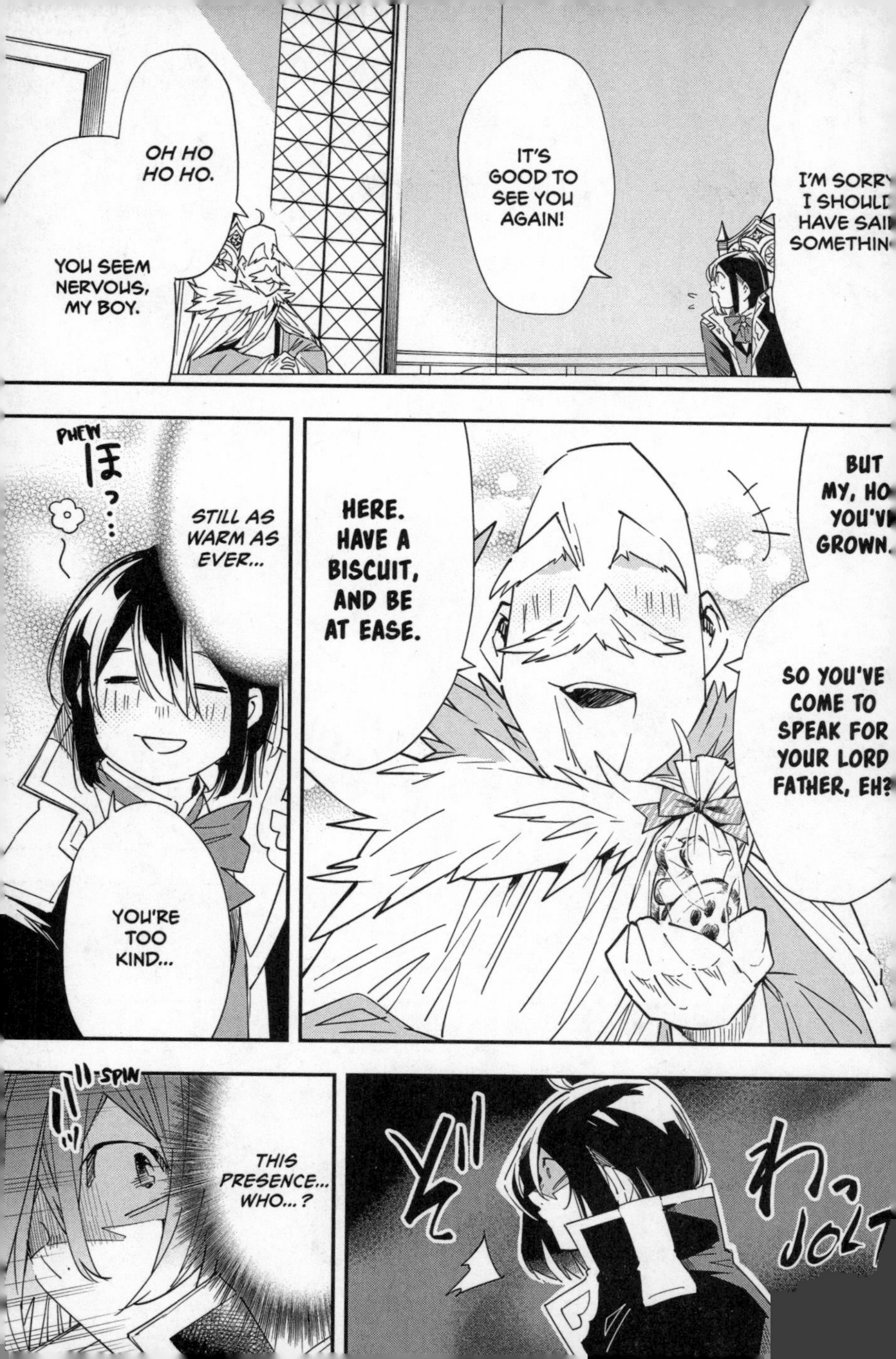
I'M SORRY I SHOULI HAVE SAI SOMETHIN
IT'S GOOD TO SEE YOU AGAIN!
OH HO HO HO.
YOU SEEM NERVOUS, MY BOY.
BUT MY, HO YOU'V GROWN.
SO YOU'VE COME TO SPEAK FOR YOUR LORD FATHER, EH?
HERE. HAVE A BISCUIT, AND BE AT EASE.
PHEW
ほっ…
STILL AS WARM AS EVER...
YOU'RE TOO KIND...
わっ
JOLT
SPIN
THIS PRESENCE... WHO...?

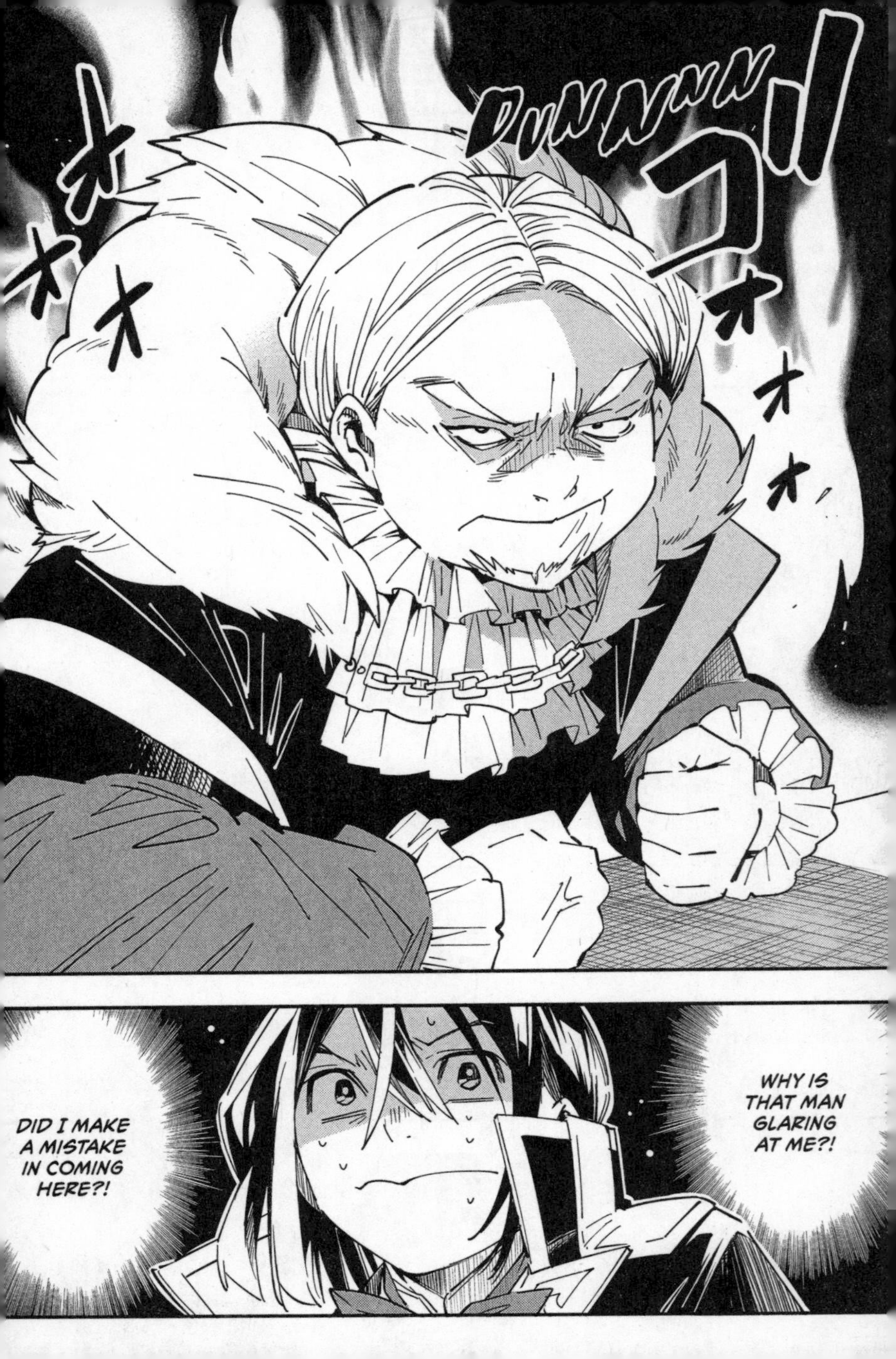
DUNNNN
ゴォォォ
ォォォ
WHY IS THAT MAN GLARING AT ME?!
DID I MAKE A MISTAKE IN COMING HERE?!

Chapter 25: War Council, pt. 2

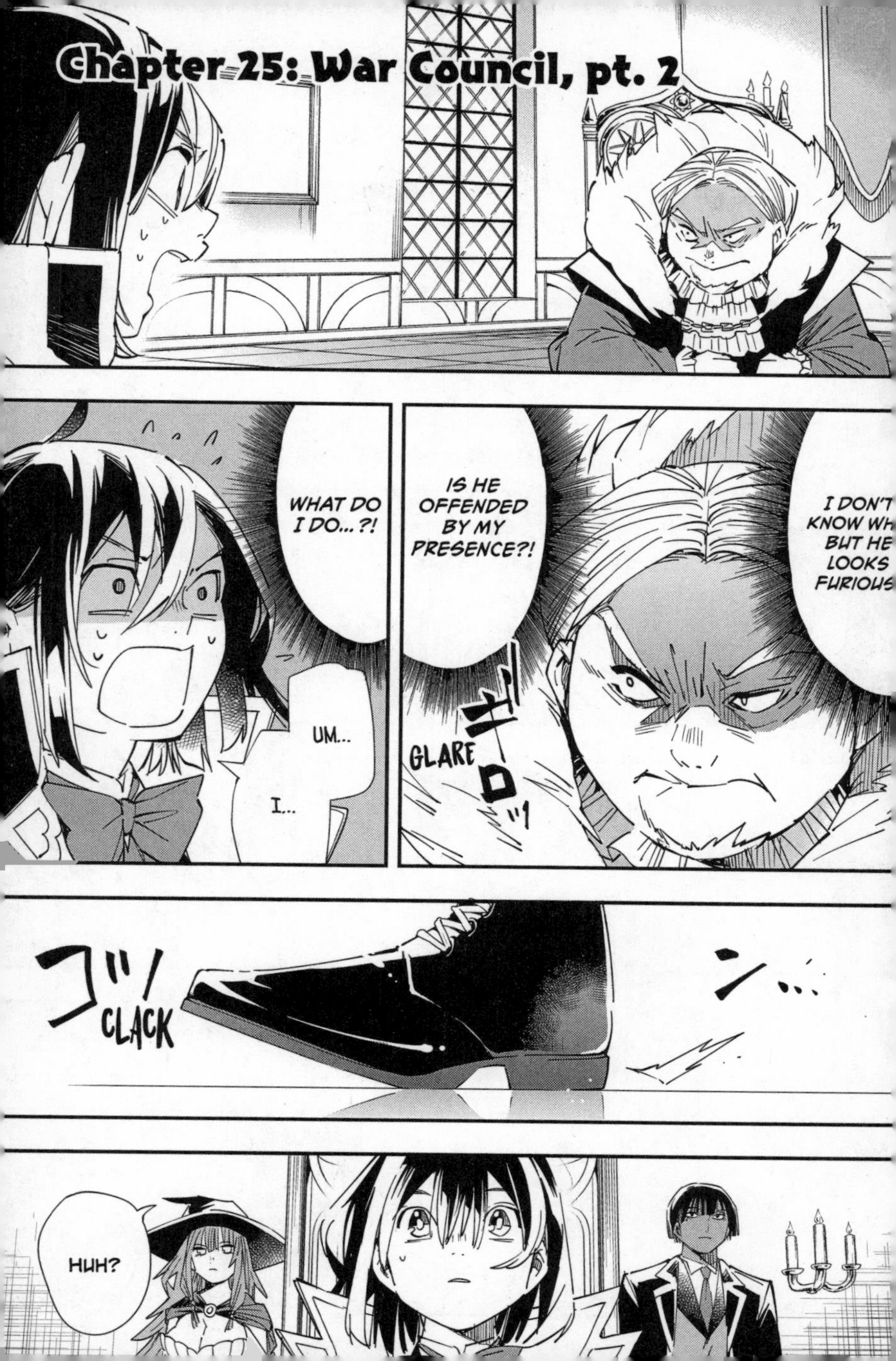
I DON'T KNOW WH
BUT HE LOOKS FURIOUS
IS HE OFFENDED BY MY PRESENCE?!
GLARE
WHAT DO I DO...?!
UM...
I...
CLACK
HUH?

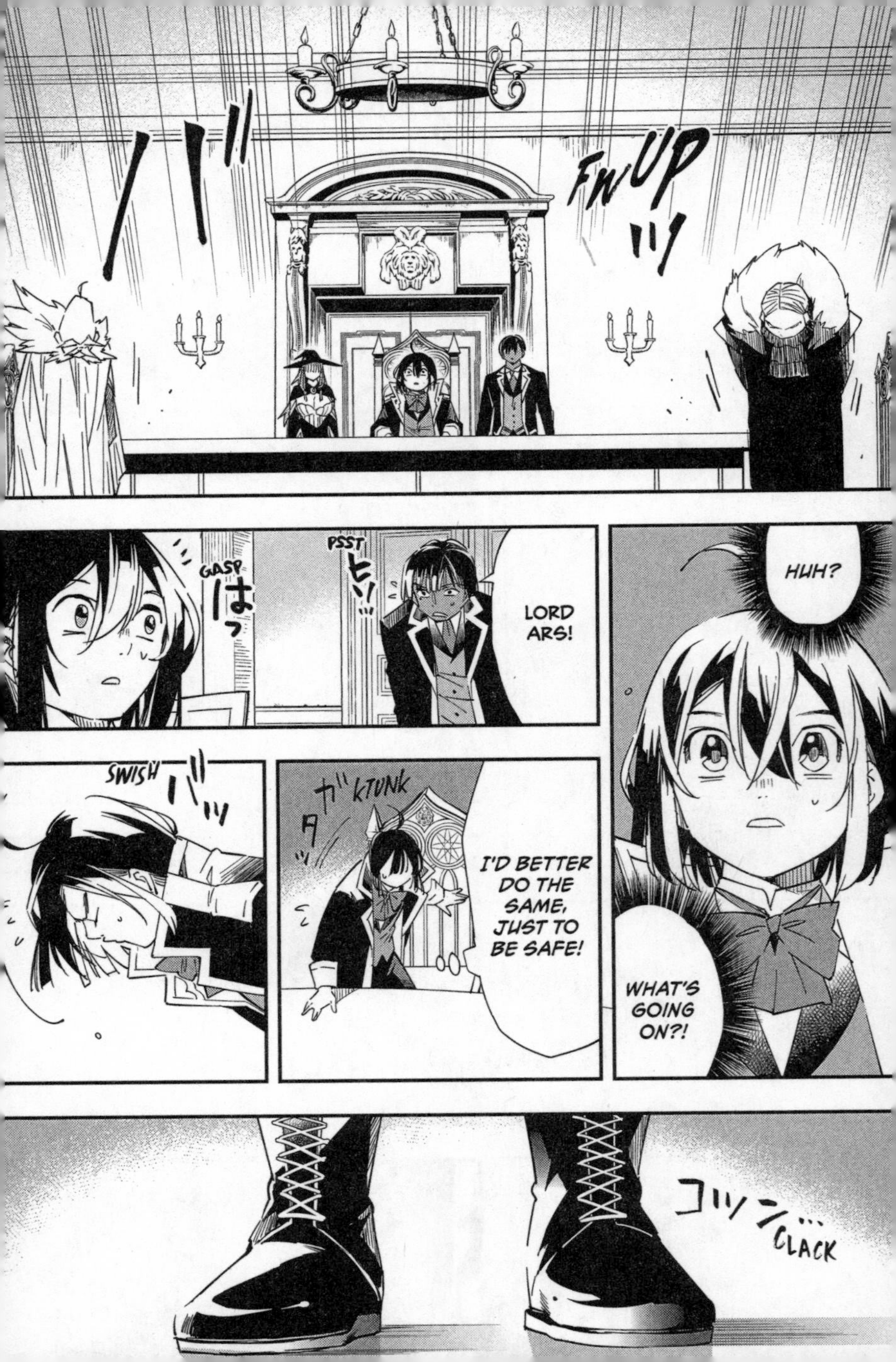
バ
FWUP
ッ
HUH?
WHAT'S GOING ON?!
PSST
ヒソッ
LORD ARS!
GASP
はっ
I'D BETTER DO THE SAME, JUST TO BE SAFE!
ガ
KTUNK
タッ
SWISH
バッ
コツン…
CLACK

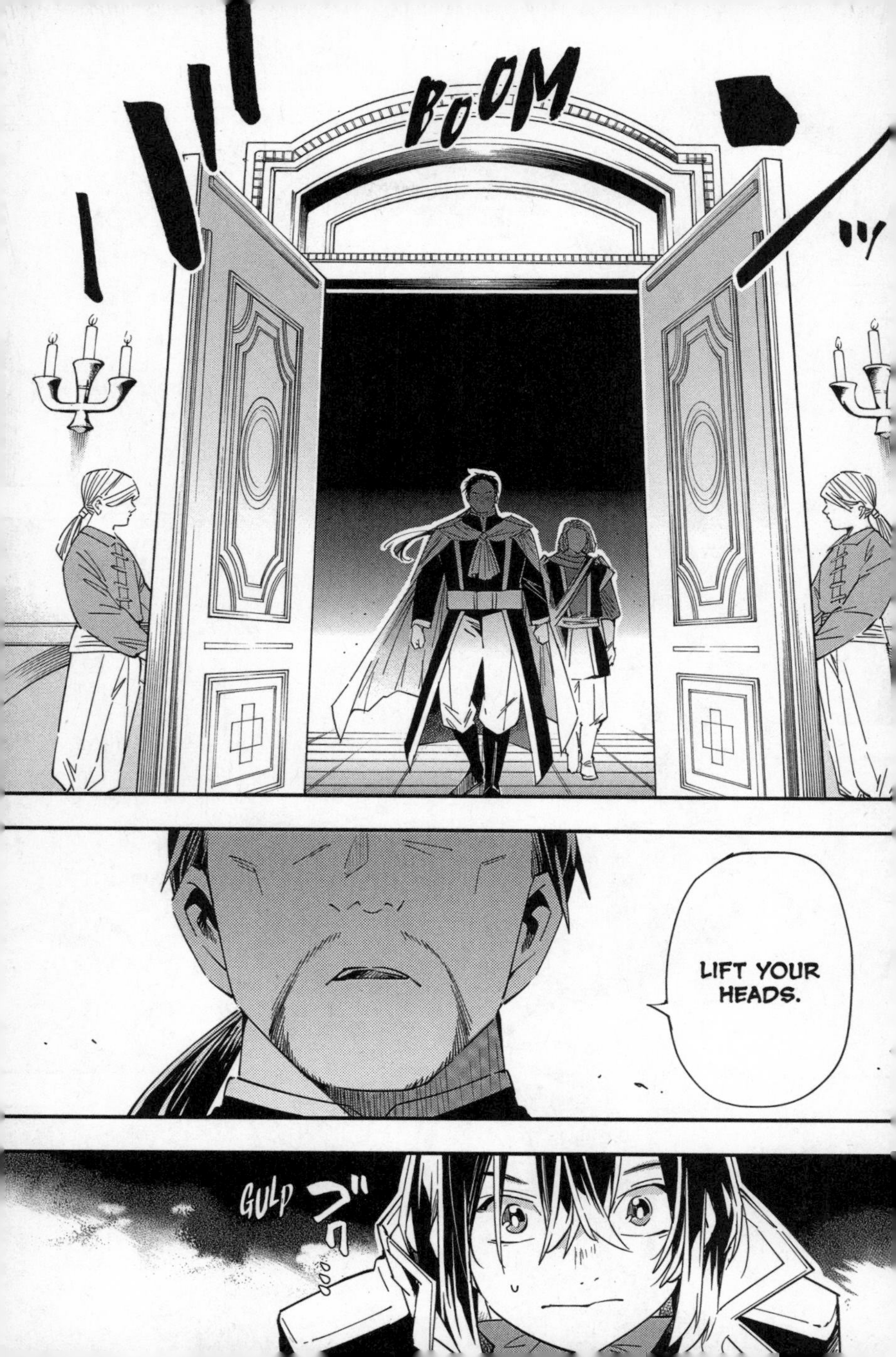
BOOM
LIFT YOUR HEADS.
GULP

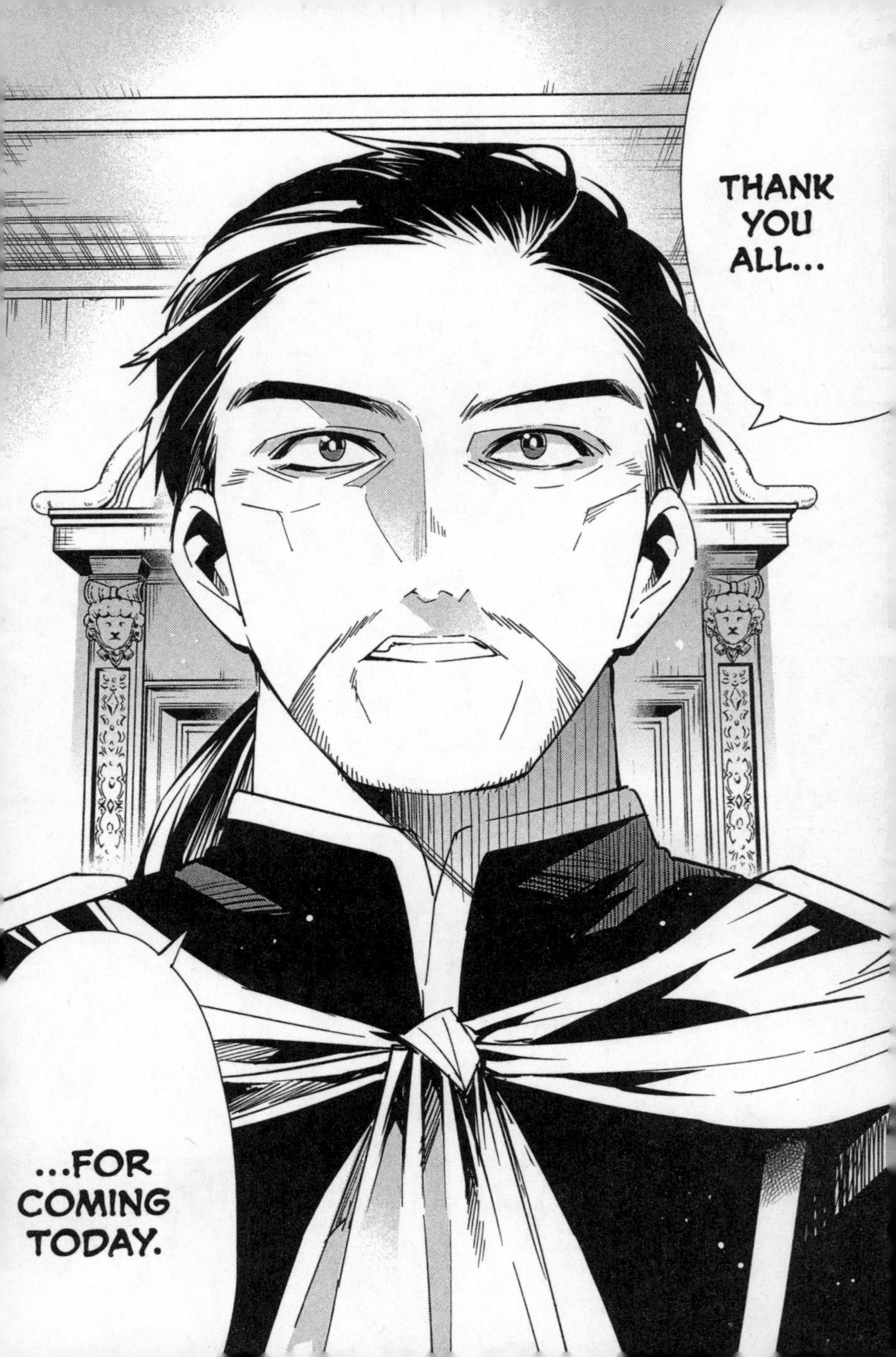
THANK YOU ALL...
...FOR COMING TODAY.

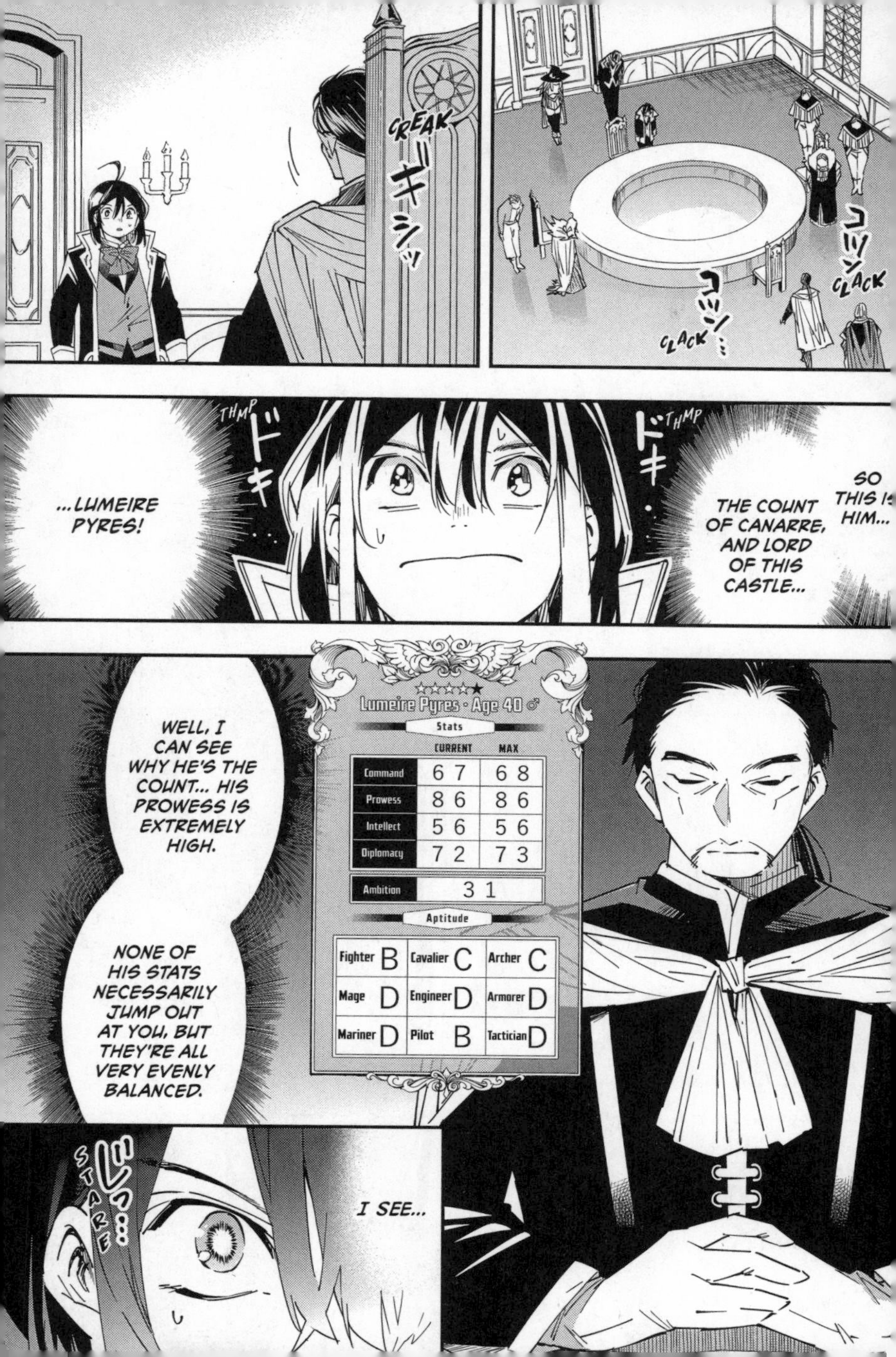

コツン CLACK
コツン… CLACK
CREAK ギギシッ
SO THIS IS HIM...
THE COUNT OF CANARRE, AND LORD OF THIS CASTLE...
ドキ THMP
ドキ THMP
...LUMEIRE PYRES!
Lumeire Pyres • Age 40 ♂
Stats
CURRENT MAX
Command 67 68
Prowess 86 86
Intellect 56 56
Diplomacy 72 73
Ambition 31
Aptitude
Fighter B Cavalier C Archer C
Mage D Engineer D Armorer D
Mariner D Pilot B Tactician D
WELL, I CAN SEE WHY HE'S THE COUNT... HIS PROWESS IS EXTREMELY HIGH.
NONE OF HIS STATS NECESSARILY JUMP OUT AT YOU, BUT THEY'RE ALL VERY EVENLY BALANCED.
じーっ… STARE
I SEE...

HAVING TWO SUCH WELL-MATCHED MEN IN CHARGE OF THE COUNTY...

...HELPS ENSURE THAT GOOD DECISIONS ARE BEING MADE.

Menas Renard - Age 40 ★★		
Stats		
	CURRENT	MAX
Command	71	71
Prowess	70	70
Intellect	75	77
Diplomacy	78	78
Ambition	25	

Aptitude					
Fighter	B	Cavalier	B	Archer	A
Mage	C	Engineer	B		
Mariner	D	Pilot	D		

Lumeire Pyres - Age 44 ★★★★★		
Stats		
	CURRENT	MAX
Command	67	68
Prowess	86	86
Intellect	56	56
Diplomacy	72	73
Ambition	31	

Aptitude					
Fighter	B	Cavalier	C	Archer	C
Mage	D	Engineer	D	Armorer	D
Mariner	D	Pilot	B	Tactician	D

NOW THAT I SEE THEM SIDE BY SIDE, THEY COMPLEMENT EACH OTHER...

MENAS IS STRONG IN AREAS WHERE COUNT PYRES IS WEAK.

ONCE AGAIN...

...I MUST APOLOGIZE FOR SUMMONING YOU ON SUCH SHORT NOTICE.

...WHAT I HAVE TO TELL YOU IS BEST SAID IN PERSON.

BUT...

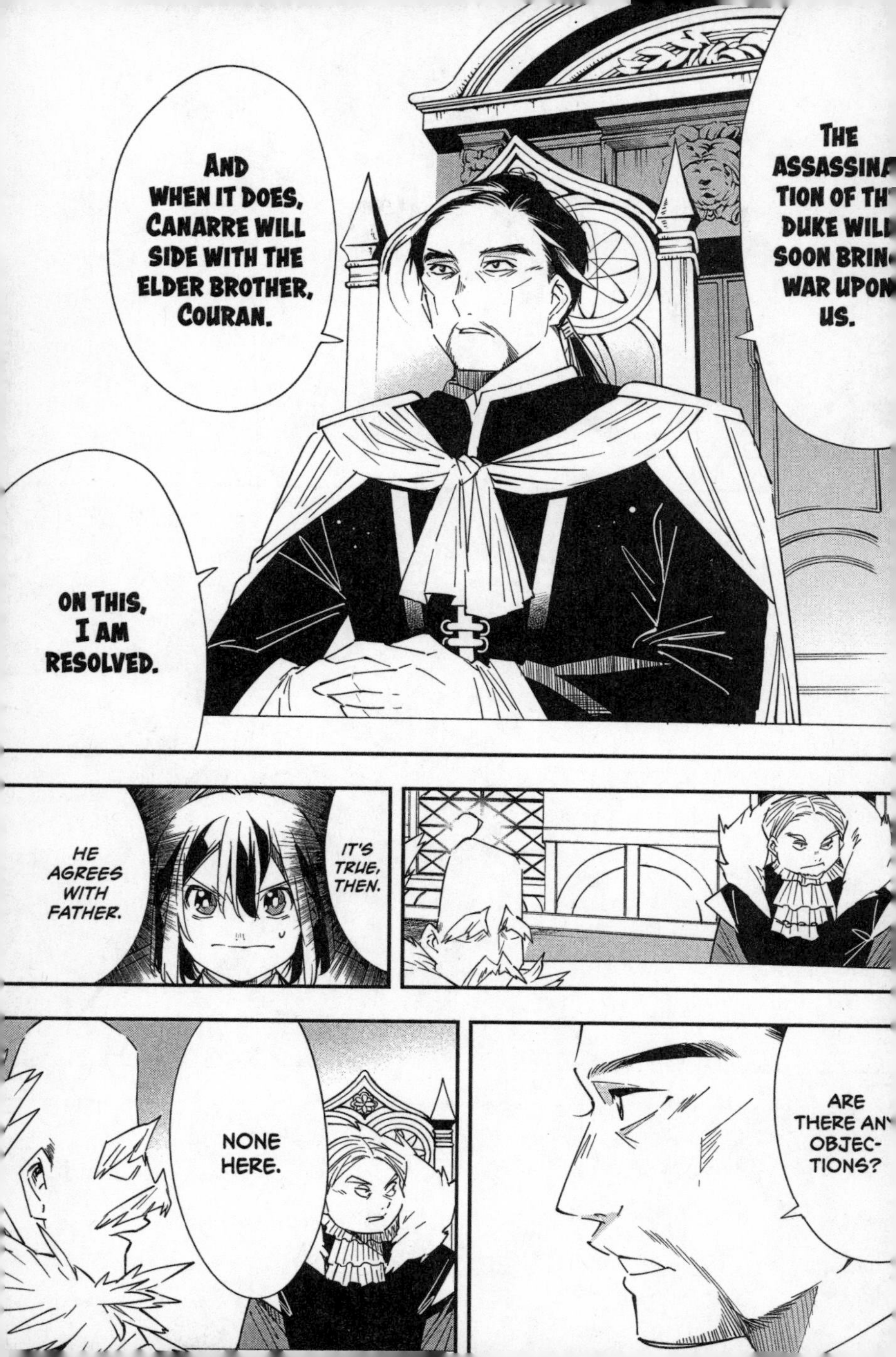
THE ASSASSINA TION OF TH DUKE WILL SOON BRIN WAR UPON US.
AND WHEN IT DOES, CANARRE WILL SIDE WITH THE ELDER BROTHER, COURAN.
ON THIS, I AM RESOLVED.
IT'S TRUE, THEN.
HE AGREES WITH FATHER.
ARE THERE AN OBJEC- TIONS?
NONE HERE.

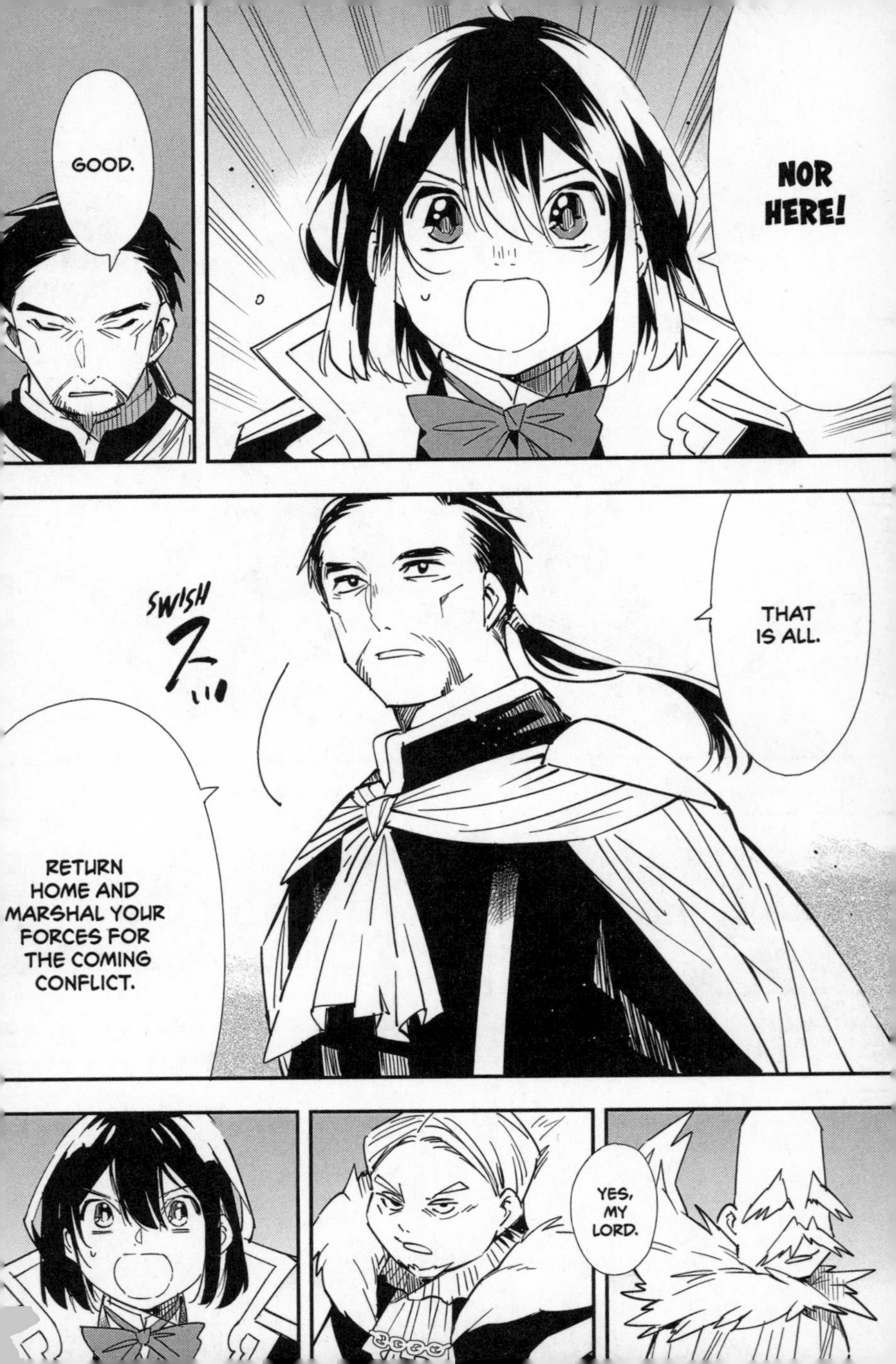
NOR HERE!
GOOD.
THAT IS ALL.
SWISH
RETURN HOME AND MARSHAL YOUR FORCES FOR THE COMING CONFLICT.
YES, MY LORD.

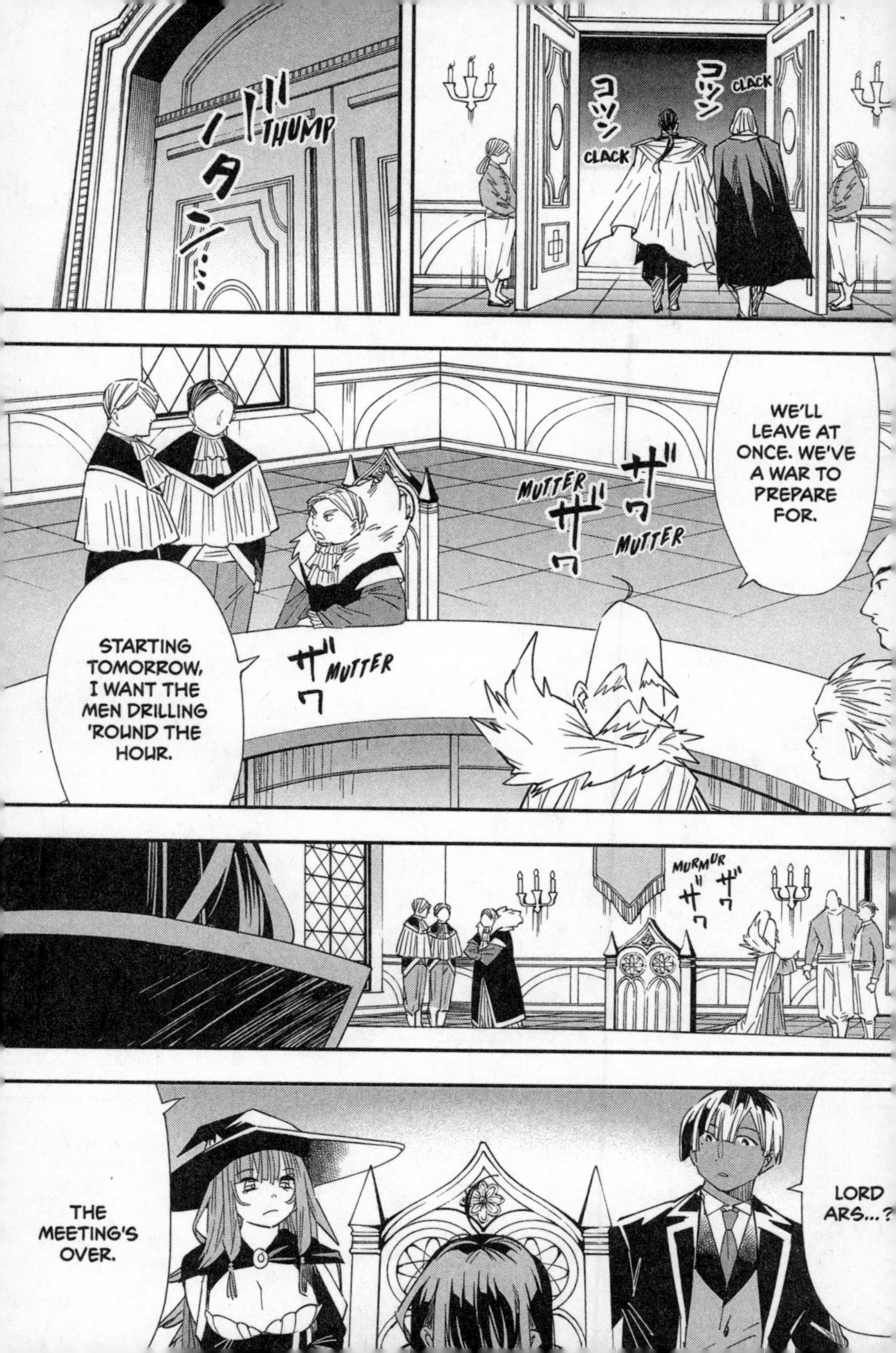

コツン
CLACK
コツン
CLACK
バタン
THUMP
WE'LL LEAVE AT ONCE. WE'VE A WAR TO PREPARE FOR.
ザワ
MUTTER
ザワ
MUTTER
STARTING TOMORROW, I WANT THE MEN DRILLING 'ROUND THE HOUR.
ザワ
MUTTER
ザワ ザワ
MURMUR
LORD ARS...?
THE MEETING'S OVER.

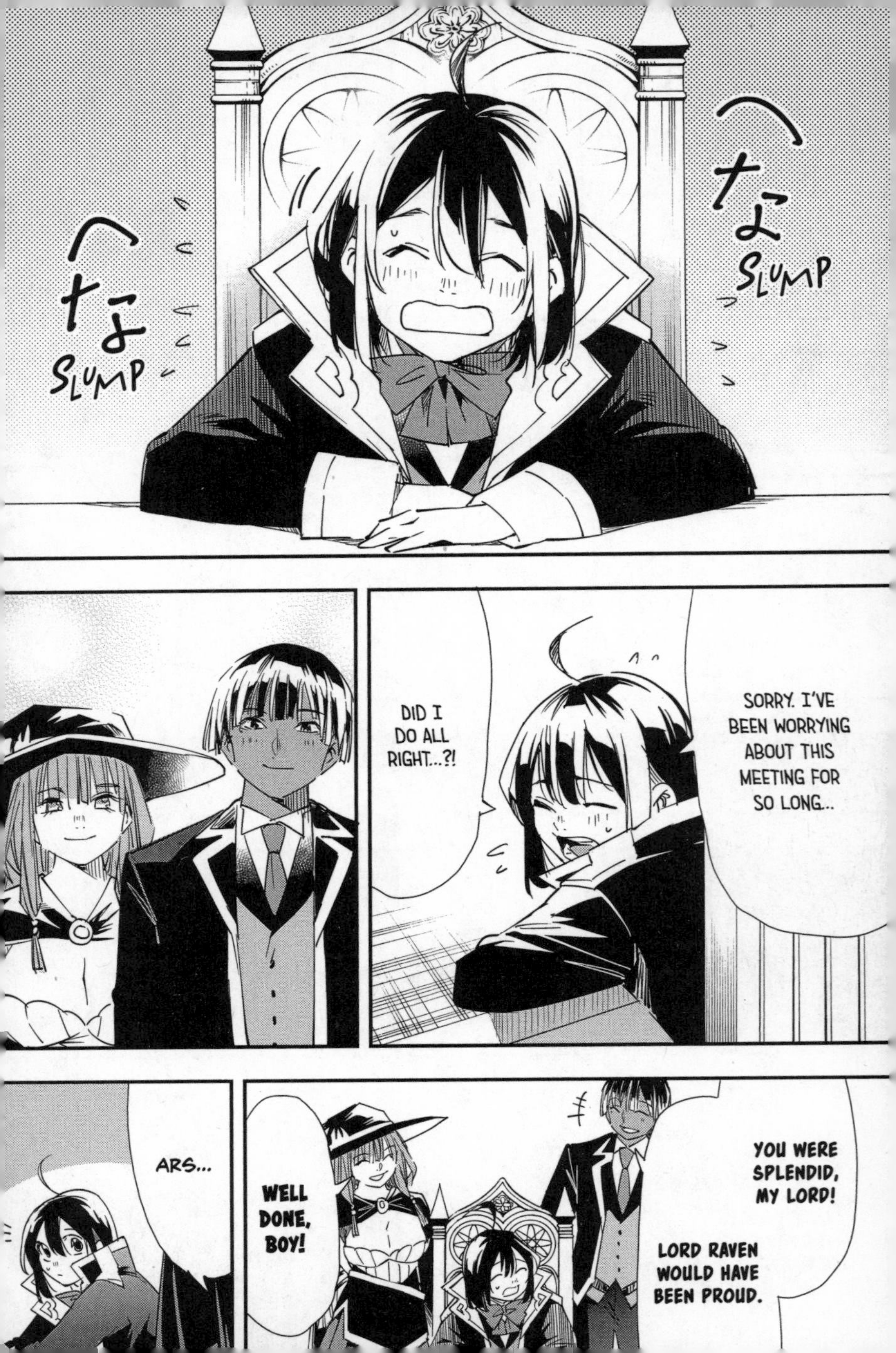
へなよ
SLUMP
へなよ
SLUMP
SORRY. I'VE BEEN WORRYING ABOUT THIS MEETING FOR SO LONG...
DID I DO ALL RIGHT...?!
YOU WERE SPLENDID, MY LORD!
LORD RAVEN WOULD HAVE BEEN PROUD.
WELL DONE, BOY!
ARS...

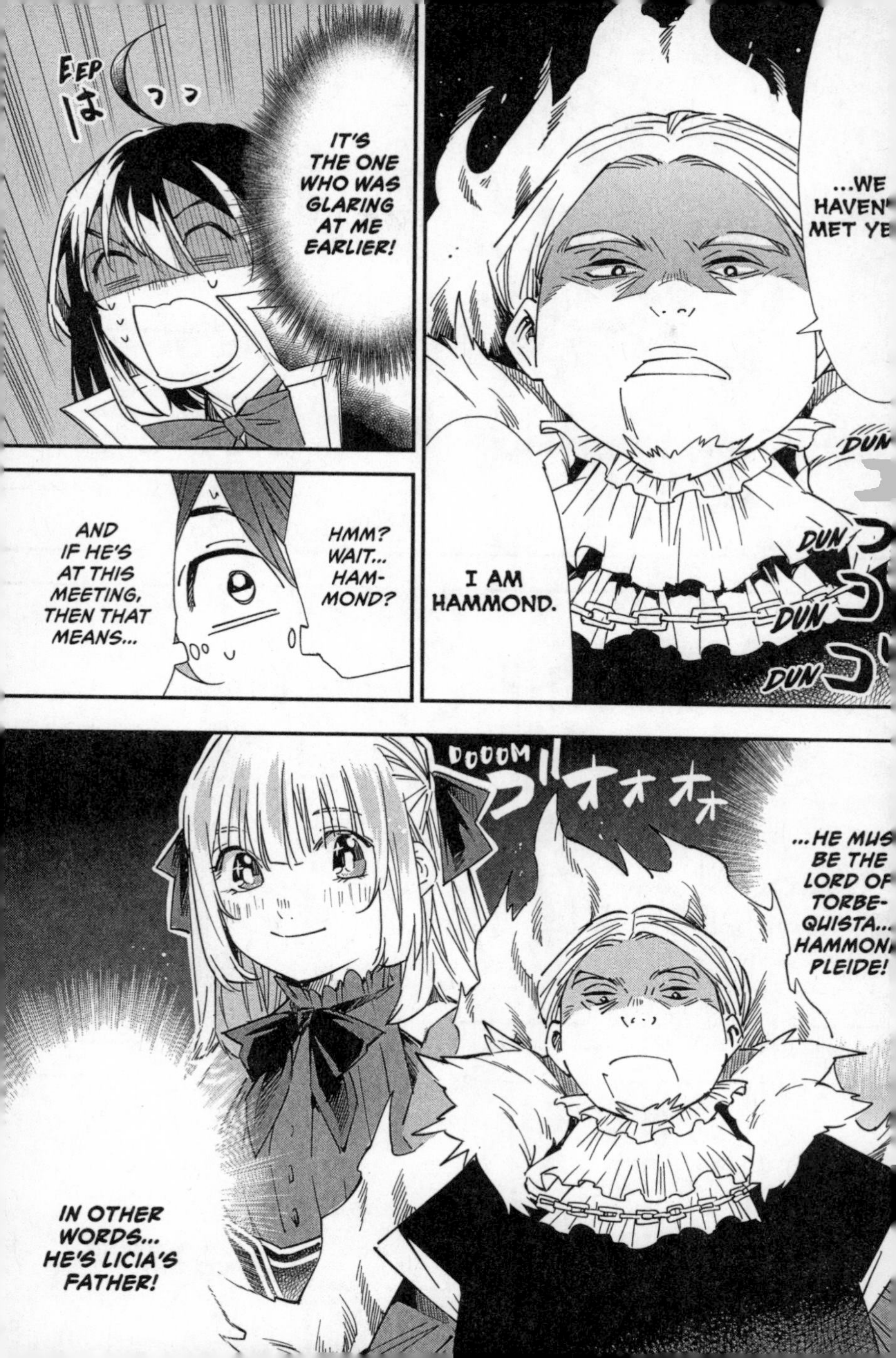
...WE HAVEN' MET YE
I AM HAMMOND.
DUN DUN DUN DUN
EEP
はっっ
IT'S THE ONE WHO WAS GLARING AT ME EARLIER!
HMM? WAIT... HAM-MOND?
AND IF HE'S AT THIS MEETING, THEN THAT MEANS...
DOOOM
ゴオオオオ
...HE MUS BE THE LORD OF TORBE-QUISTA... HAMMON PLEIDE!
IN OTHER WORDS... HE'S LICIA'S FATHER!

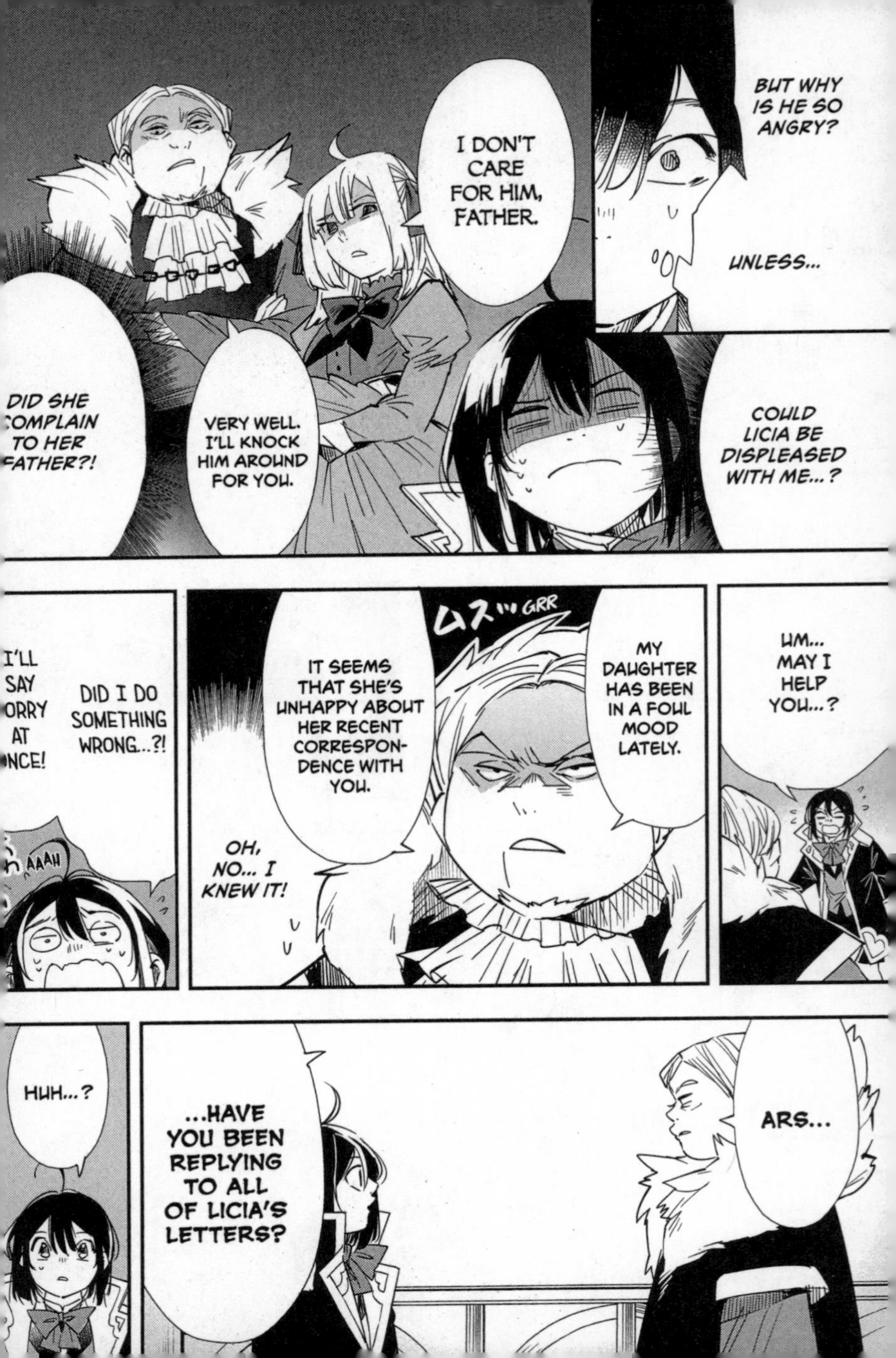
BUT WHY IS HE SO ANGRY?
UNLESS...
COULD LICIA BE DISPLEASED WITH ME...?
I DON'T CARE FOR HIM, FATHER.
VERY WELL. I'LL KNOCK HIM AROUND FOR YOU.
DID SHE OMPLAIN TO HER ATHER?!
UM... MAY I HELP YOU...?
MY DAUGHTER HAS BEEN IN A FOUL MOOD LATELY.
ムスッ GRR
IT SEEMS THAT SHE'S UNHAPPY ABOUT HER RECENT CORRESPONDENCE WITH YOU.
OH, NO... I KNEW IT!
DID I DO SOMETHING WRONG...?!
I'LL SAY ORRY AT NCE!
AAAH
ARS...
...HAVE YOU BEEN REPLYING TO ALL OF LICIA'S LETTERS?
HUH...?

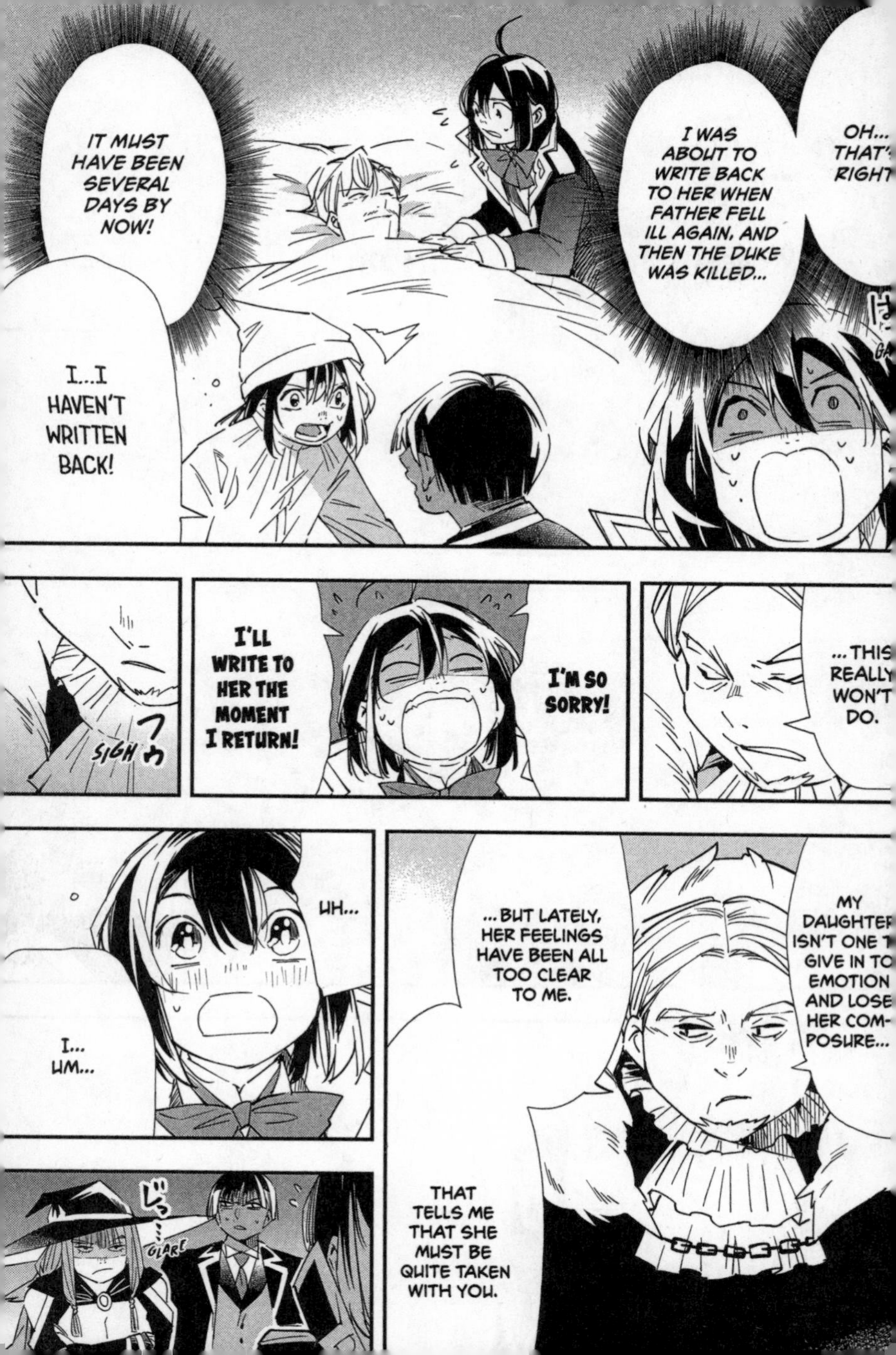
OH... THAT'S RIGHT
I WAS ABOUT TO WRITE BACK TO HER WHEN FATHER FELL ILL AGAIN, AND THEN THE DUKE WAS KILLED...
IT MUST HAVE BEEN SEVERAL DAYS BY NOW!
I...I HAVEN'T WRITTEN BACK!
...THIS REALLY WON'T DO.
I'M SO SORRY!
I'LL WRITE TO HER THE MOMENT I RETURN!
SIGH
MY DAUGHTE ISN'T ONE T GIVE IN TO EMOTION AND LOSE HER COM-POSURE...
...BUT LATELY, HER FEELINGS HAVE BEEN ALL TOO CLEAR TO ME.
THAT TELLS ME THAT SHE MUST BE QUITE TAKEN WITH YOU.
UH...
I... UM...
GLARE

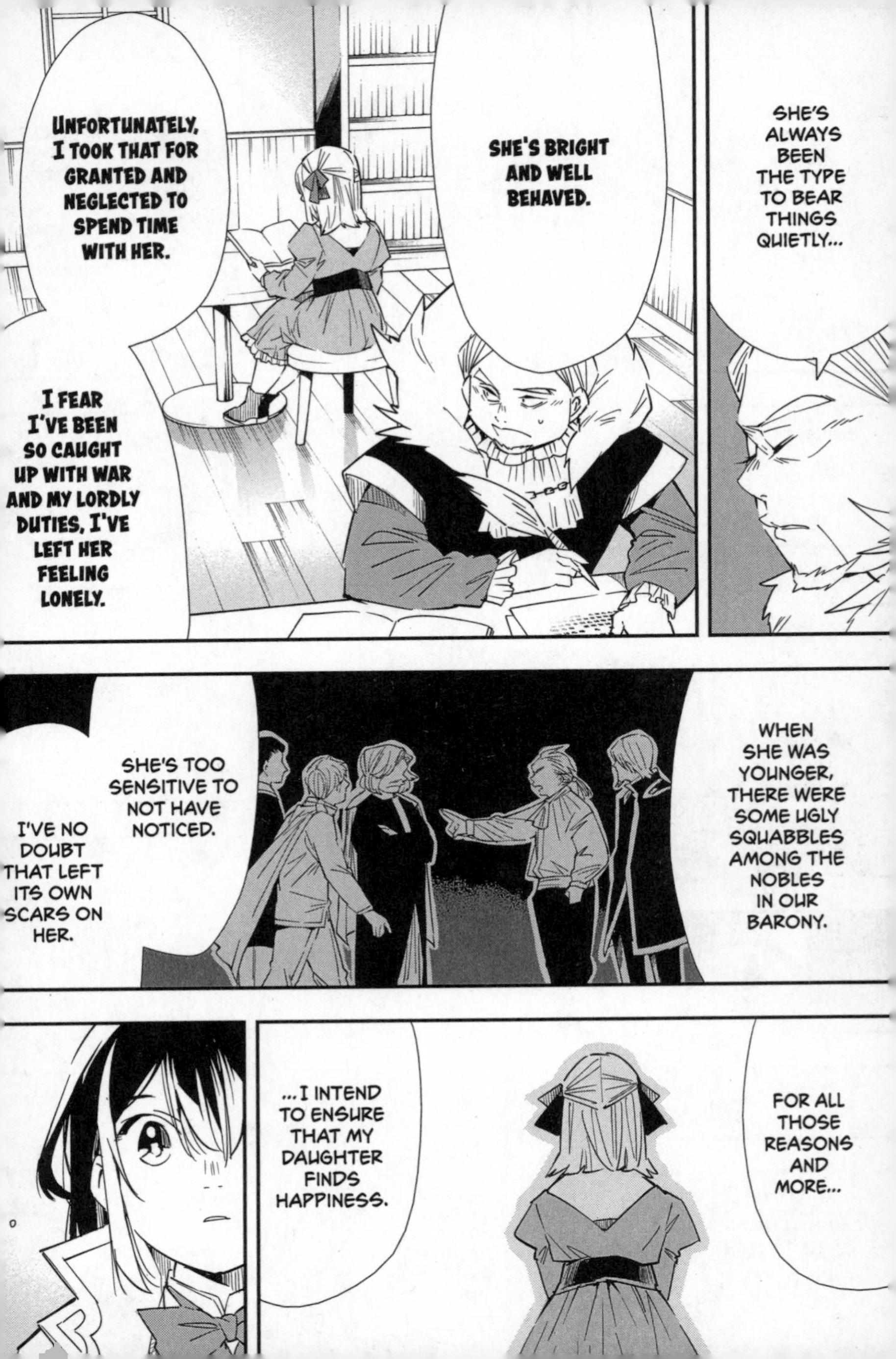
SHE'S ALWAYS BEEN THE TYPE TO BEAR THINGS QUIETLY...
SHE'S BRIGHT AND WELL BEHAVED.
UNFORTUNATELY, I TOOK THAT FOR GRANTED AND NEGLECTED TO SPEND TIME WITH HER.
I FEAR I'VE BEEN SO CAUGHT UP WITH WAR AND MY LORDLY DUTIES, I'VE LEFT HER FEELING LONELY.
WHEN SHE WAS YOUNGER, THERE WERE SOME UGLY SQUABBLES AMONG THE NOBLES IN OUR BARONY.
SHE'S TOO SENSITIVE TO NOT HAVE NOTICED.
I'VE NO DOUBT THAT LEFT ITS OWN SCARS ON HER.
FOR ALL THOSE REASONS AND MORE...
...I INTEND TO ENSURE THAT MY DAUGHTER FINDS HAPPINESS.

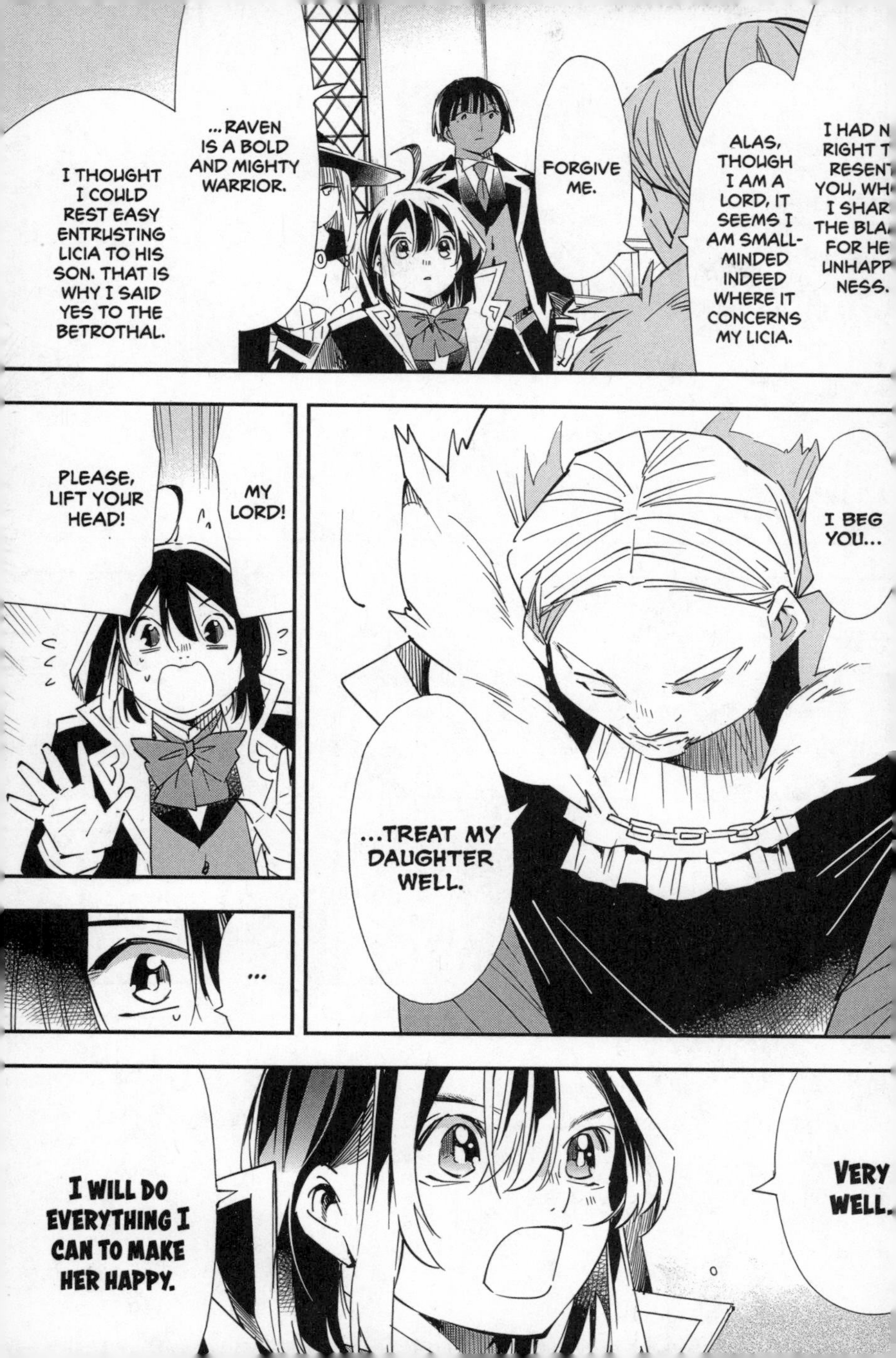
I HAD N RIGHT T RESENT YOU, WH I SHAR THE BLA FOR HE UNHAPP NESS.
ALAS, THOUGH I AM A LORD, IT SEEMS I AM SMALL-MINDED INDEED WHERE IT CONCERNS MY LICIA.
FORGIVE ME.
...RAVEN IS A BOLD AND MIGHTY WARRIOR.
I THOUGHT I COULD REST EASY ENTRUSTING LICIA TO HIS SON. THAT IS WHY I SAID YES TO THE BETROTHAL.
I BEG YOU...
...TREAT MY DAUGHTER WELL.
MY LORD!
PLEASE, LIFT YOUR HEAD!
...
VERY WELL.
I WILL DO EVERYTHING I CAN TO MAKE HER HAPPY.

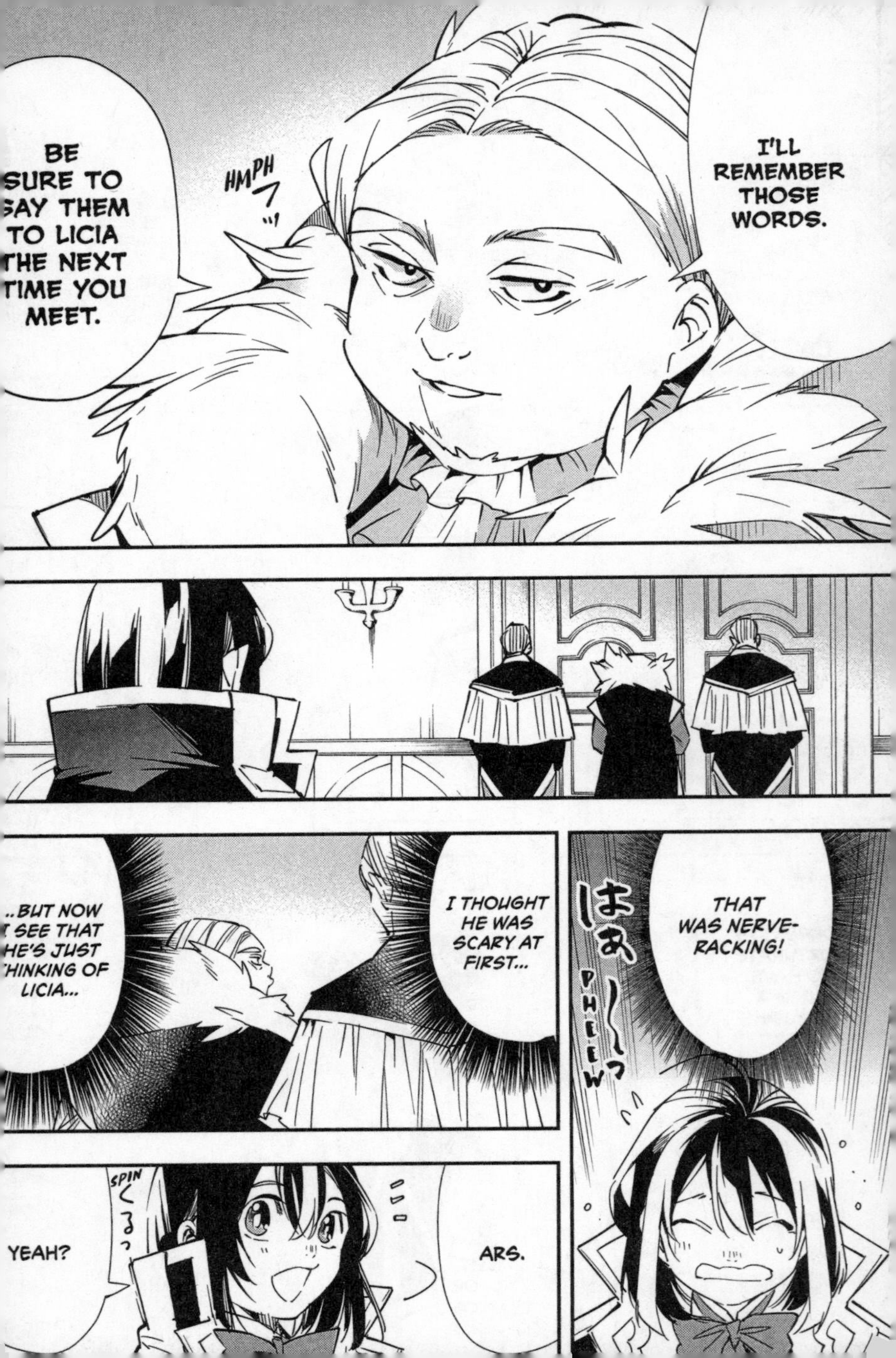
I'LL REMEMBER THOSE WORDS.
HMPH
BE SURE TO SAY THEM TO LICIA THE NEXT TIME YOU MEET.
THAT WAS NERVE-RACKING!
はあ〜しっ
PHEEEW
I THOUGHT HE WAS SCARY AT FIRST...
...BUT NOW I SEE THAT HE'S JUST THINKING OF LICIA...
ARS.
SPIN
くるっ
YEAH?

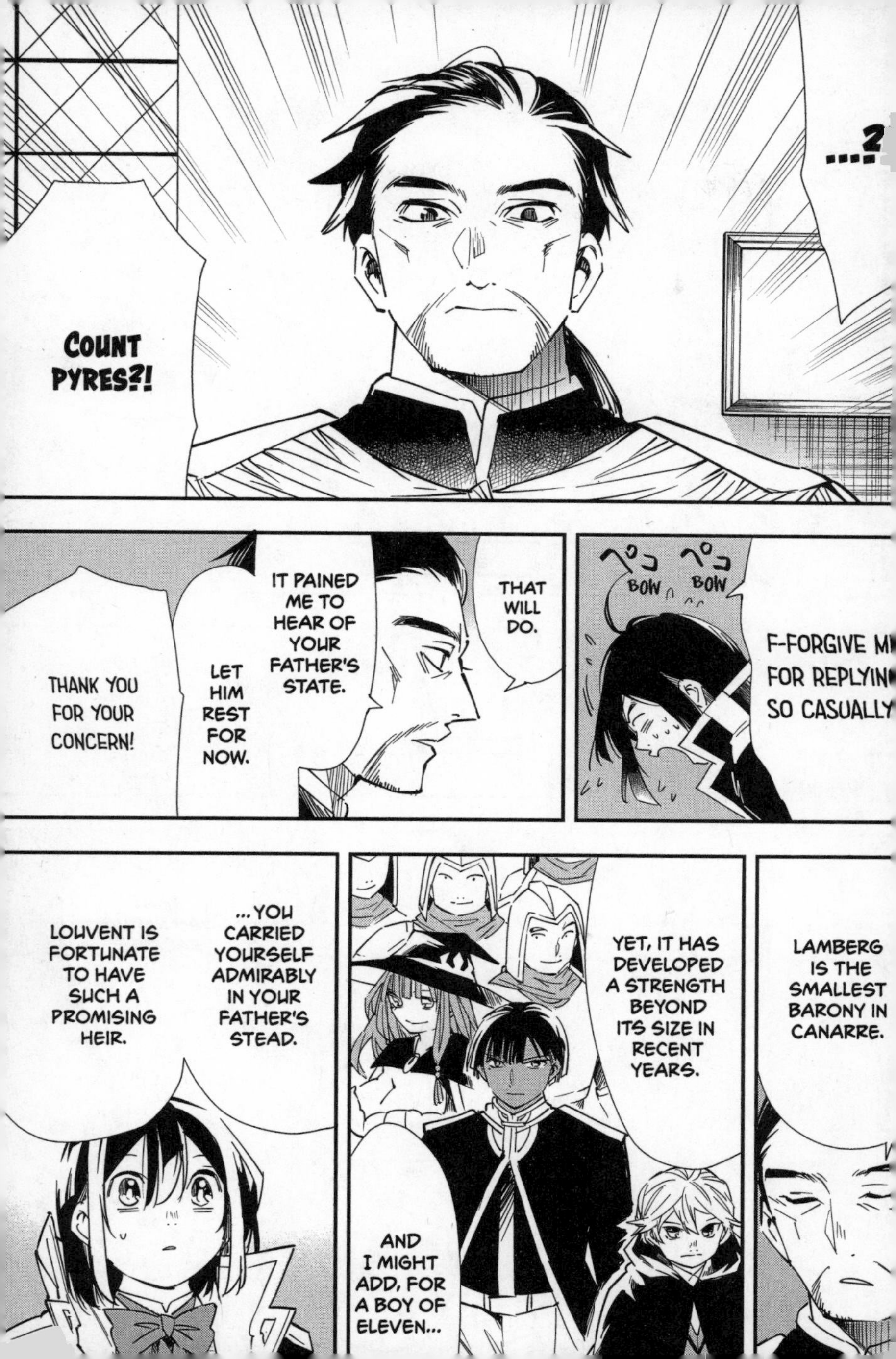
...?
COUNT PYRES?!
ペコ ペコ
BOW BOW
F-FORGIVE M
FOR REPLYIN
SO CASUALLY
THAT WILL DO.
IT PAINED ME TO HEAR OF YOUR FATHER'S STATE.
LET HIM REST FOR NOW.
THANK YOU FOR YOUR CONCERN!
LAMBERG IS THE SMALLEST BARONY IN CANARRE.
YET, IT HAS DEVELOPED A STRENGTH BEYOND ITS SIZE IN RECENT YEARS.
AND I MIGHT ADD, FOR A BOY OF ELEVEN...
...YOU CARRIED YOURSELF ADMIRABLY IN YOUR FATHER'S STEAD.
LOUVENT IS FORTUNATE TO HAVE SUCH A PROMISING HEIR.

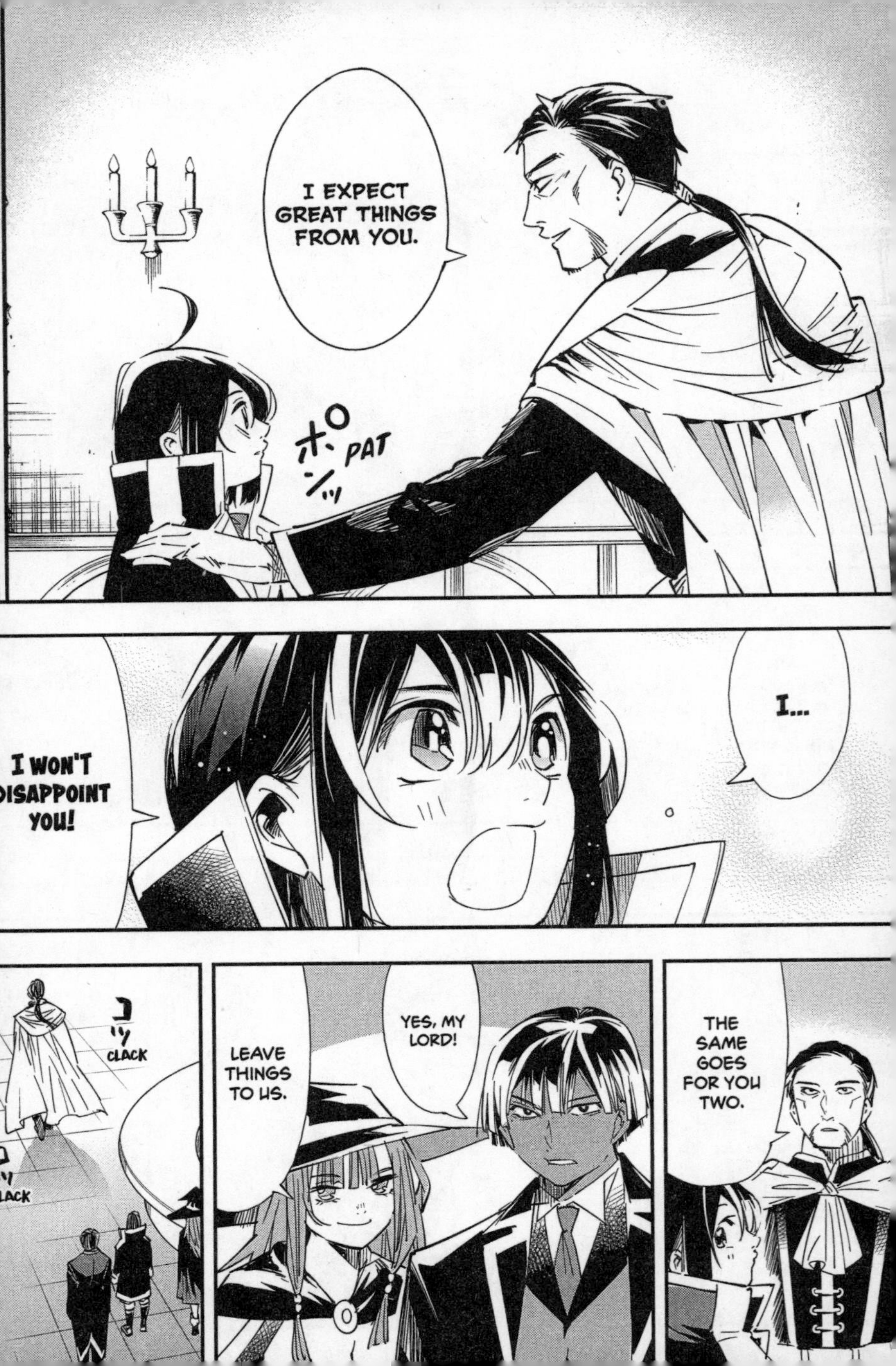
I EXPECT GREAT THINGS FROM YOU.
ポンッ PAT
I...
I WON'T DISAPPOINT YOU!
THE SAME GOES FOR YOU TWO.
YES, MY LORD!
LEAVE THINGS TO US.
コッ CLACK
LACK

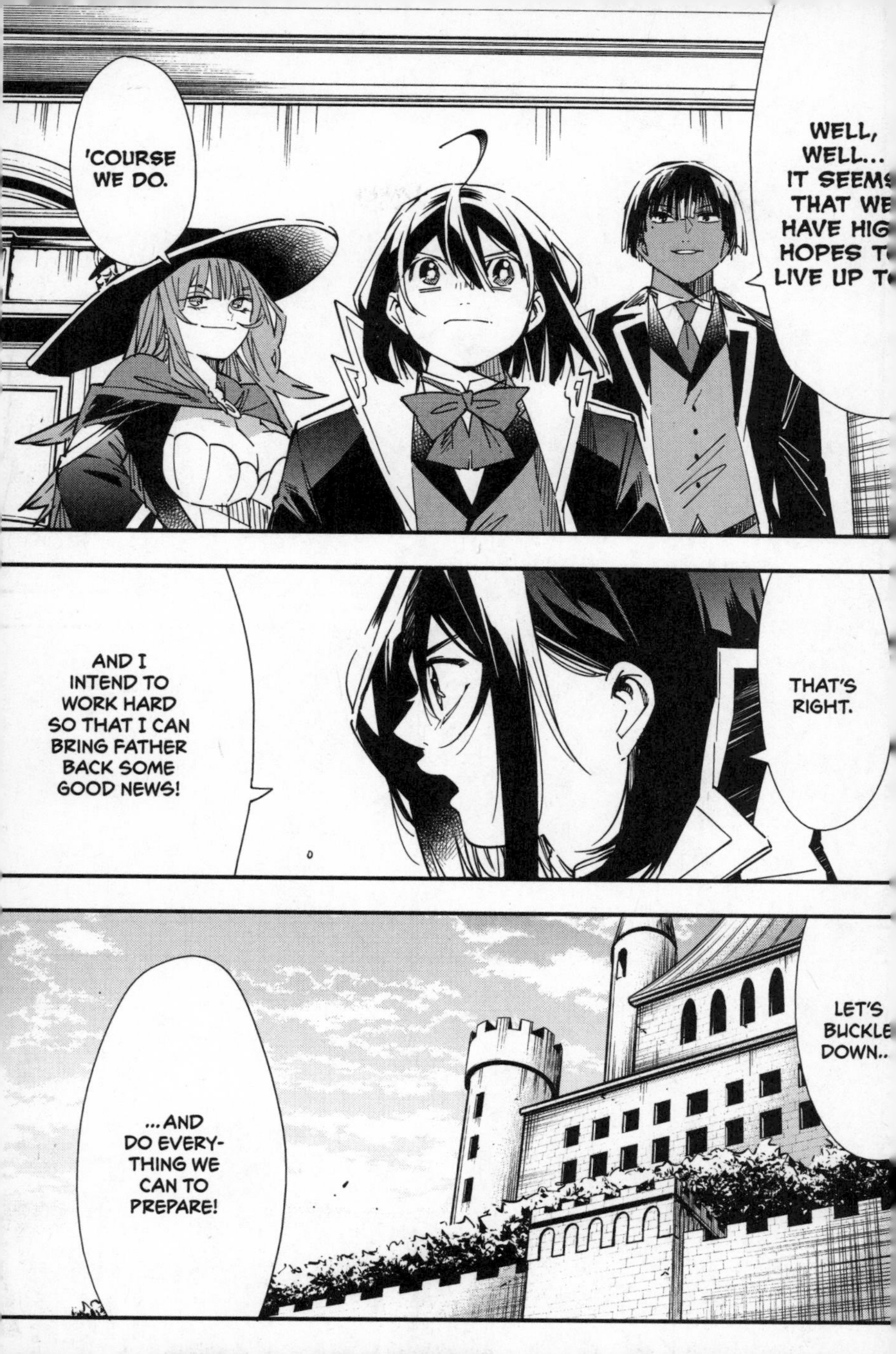
WELL, WELL... IT SEEMS THAT WE HAVE HIG HOPES T LIVE UP T
'COURSE WE DO.
THAT'S RIGHT.
AND I INTEND TO WORK HARD SO THAT I CAN BRING FATHER BACK SOME GOOD NEWS!
LET'S BUCKLE DOWN..
...AND DO EVERY-THING WE CAN TO PREPARE!

As a Reincarnated
ARISTOCRAT,
I'll Use My Appraisal Skill to
Rise in the World

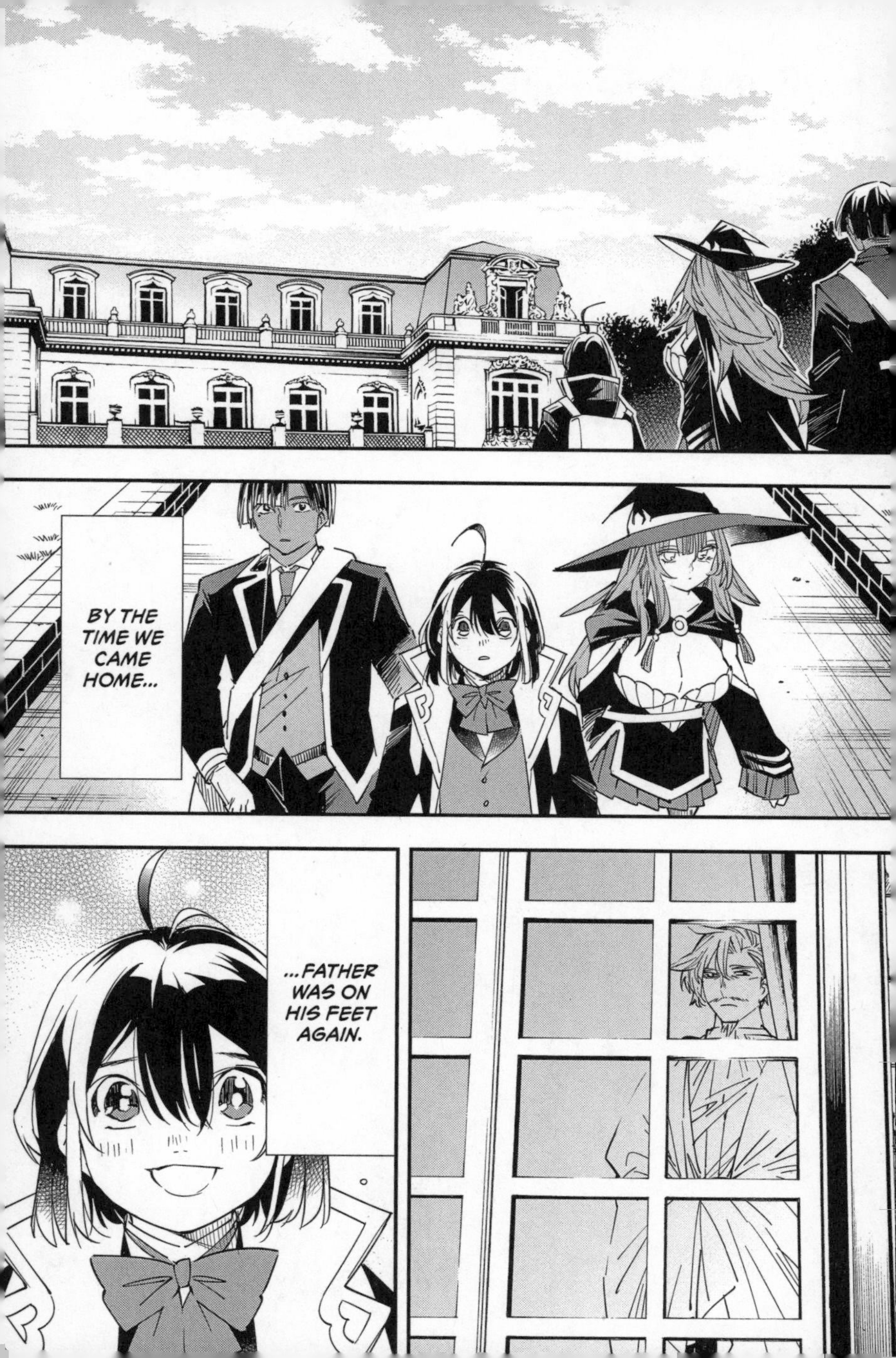
BY THE TIME WE CAME HOME...
...FATHER WAS ON HIS FEET AGAIN.

Chapter 26: To War

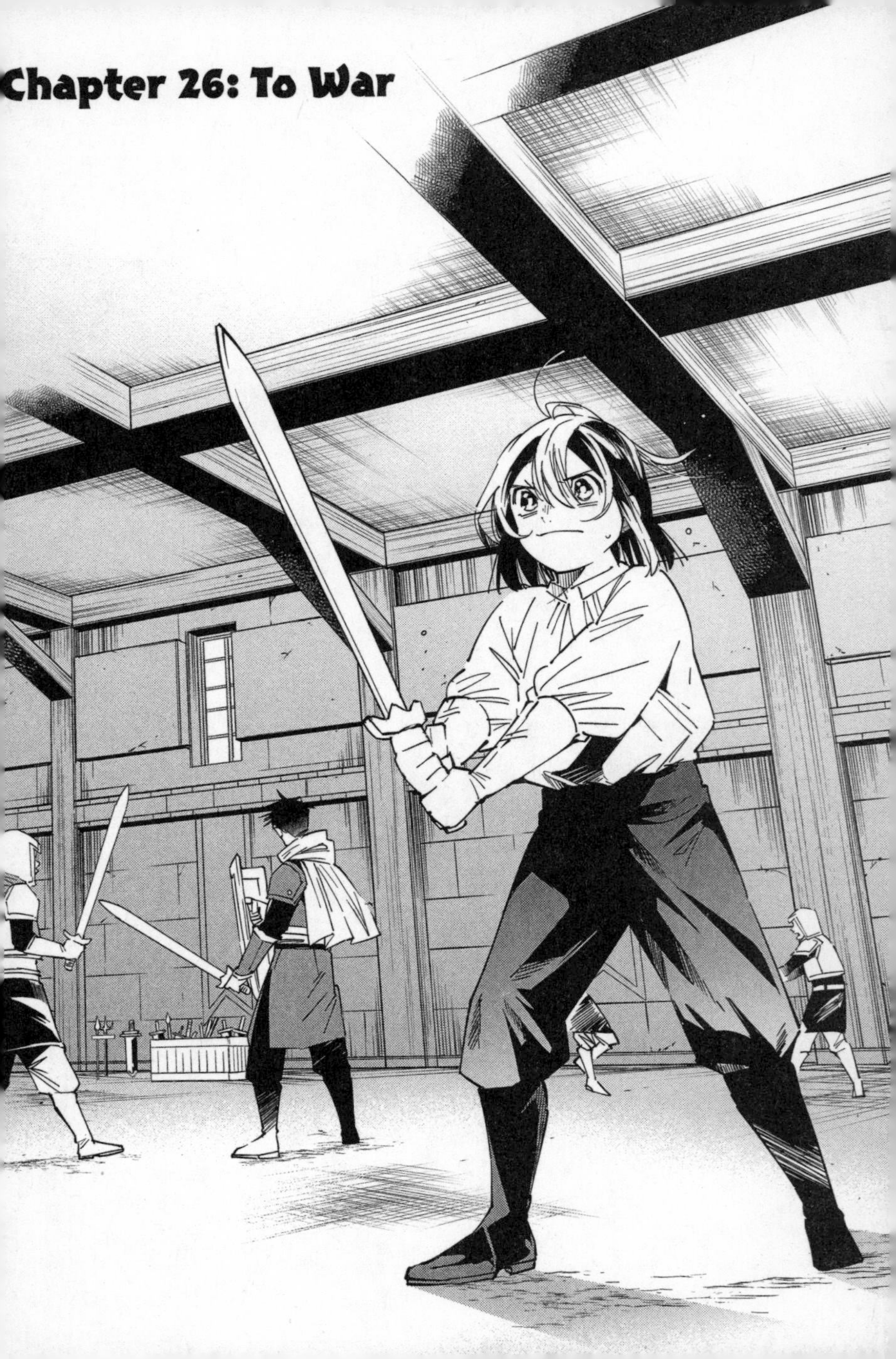

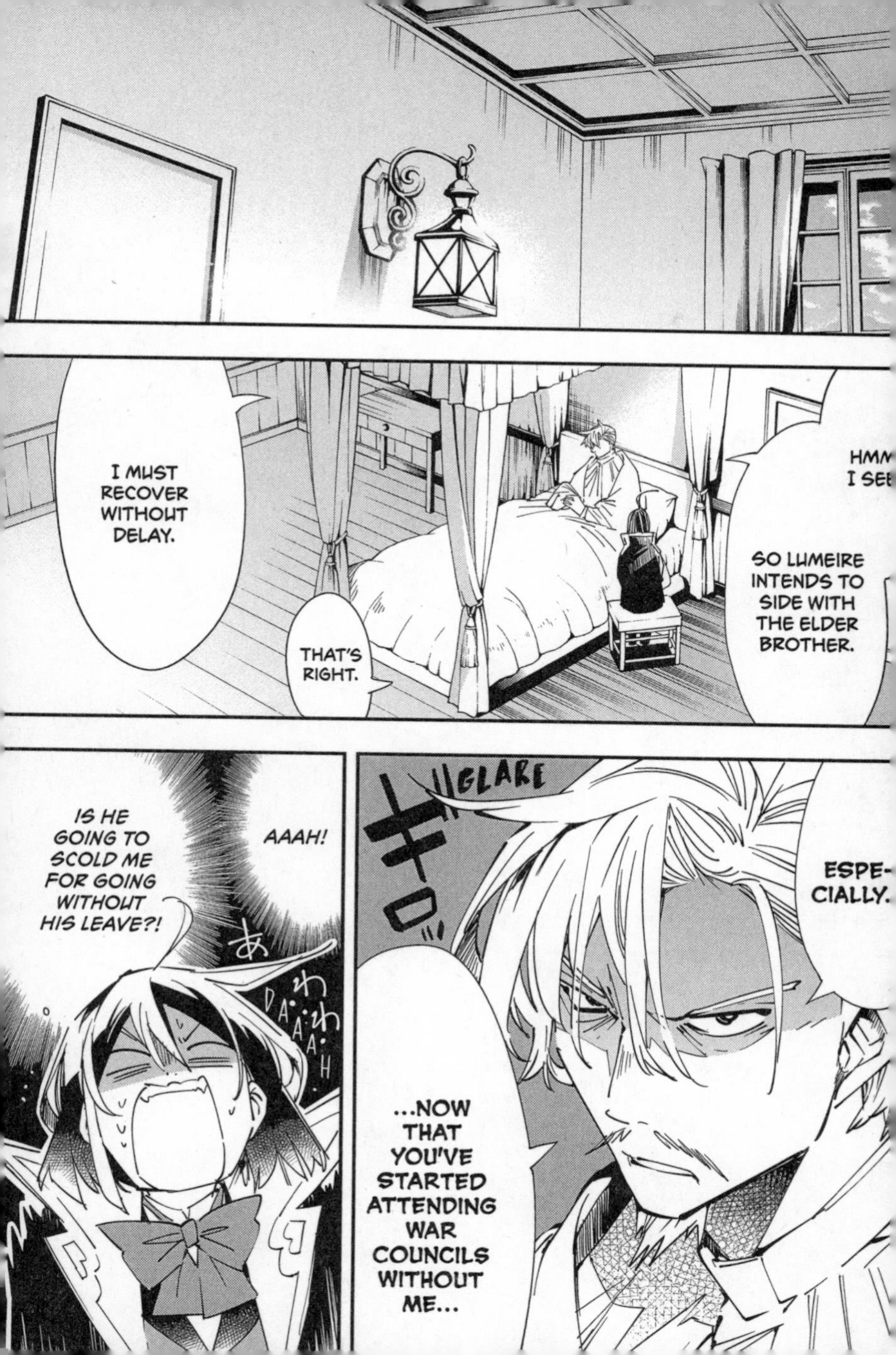
HMM
I SEE
SO LUMEIRE INTENDS TO SIDE WITH THE ELDER BROTHER.
THAT'S RIGHT.
I MUST RECOVER WITHOUT DELAY.
ESPE-
CIALLY.
GLARE
...NOW THAT YOU'VE STARTED ATTENDING WAR COUNCILS WITHOUT ME...
AAAH!
IS HE GOING TO SCOLD ME FOR GOING WITHOUT HIS LEAVE?!
DAAAAH

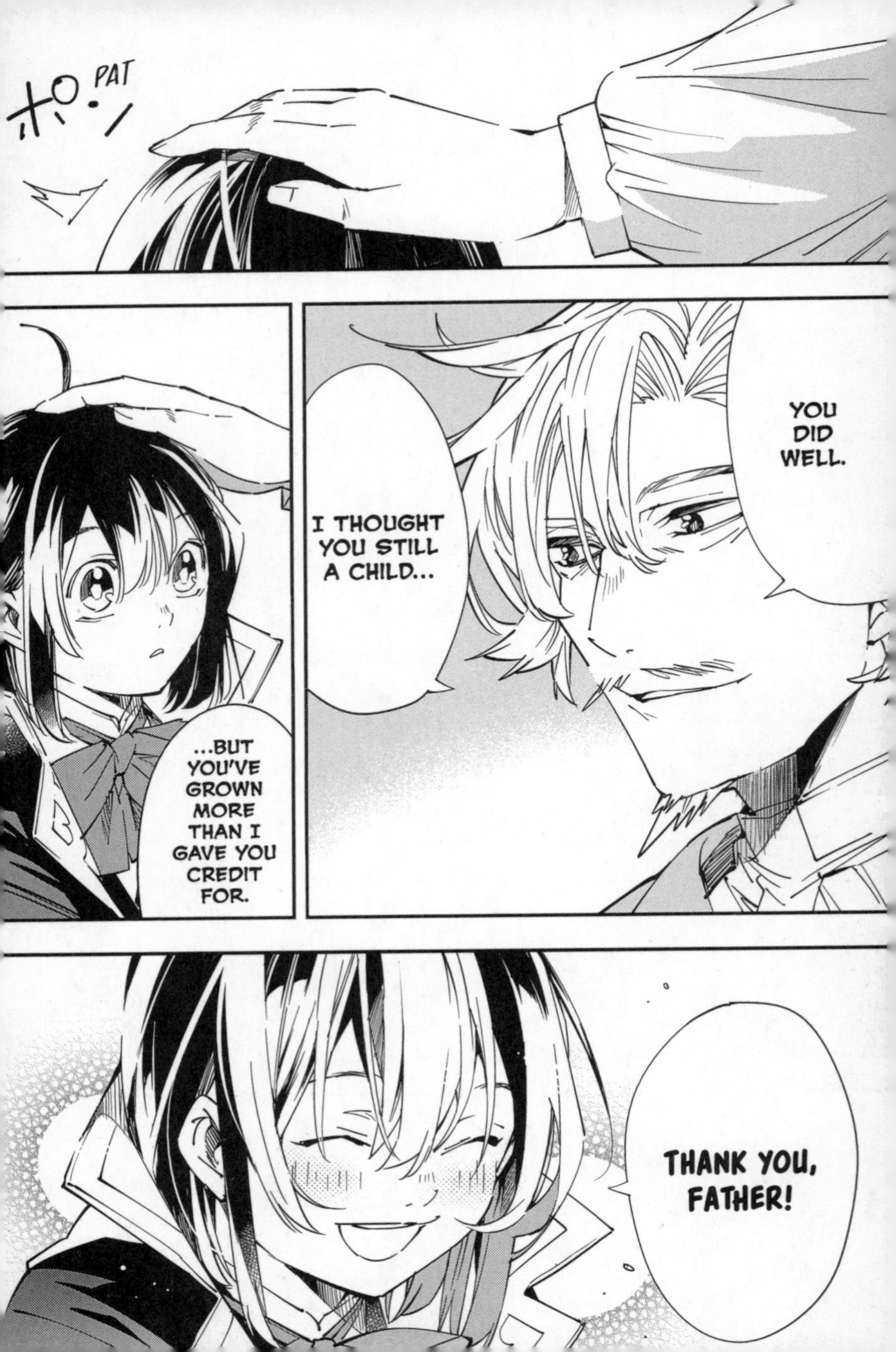
PAT
YOU DID WELL.
I THOUGHT YOU STILL A CHILD...
...BUT YOU'VE GROWN MORE THAN I GAVE YOU CREDIT FOR.
THANK YOU, FATHER!

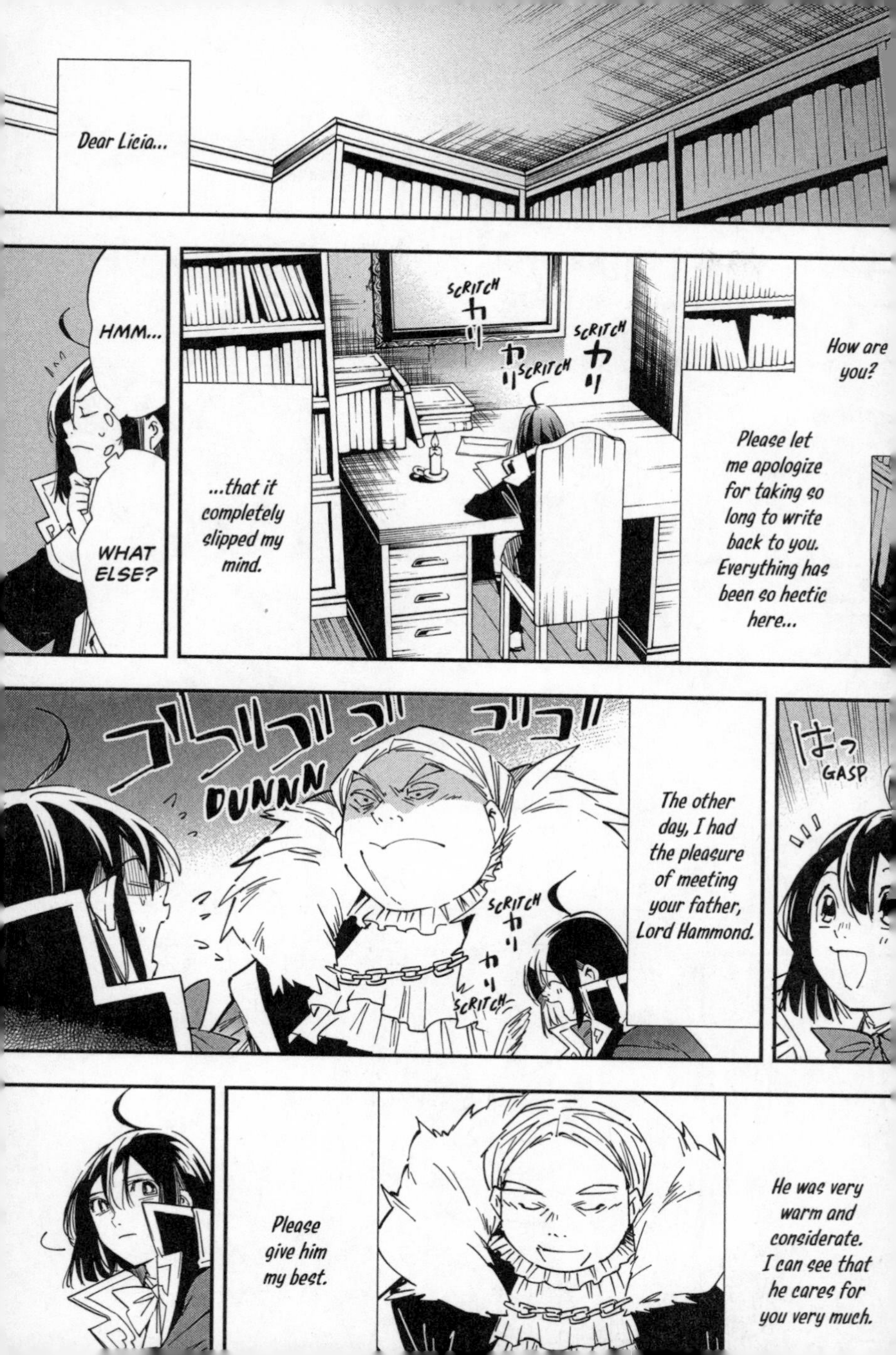
Dear Licia...
How are you?
Please let me apologize for taking so long to write back to you. Everything has been so hectic here...
SCRITCH
カリ
SCRITCH
カリ
SCRITCH
カリ
...that it completely slipped my mind.
HMM...
WHAT ELSE?
はっ
GASP
The other day, I had the pleasure of meeting your father, Lord Hammond.
DUNNN
SCRITCH
カリ
カリ
SCRITCH
He was very warm and considerate. I can see that he cares for you very much.
Please give him my best.

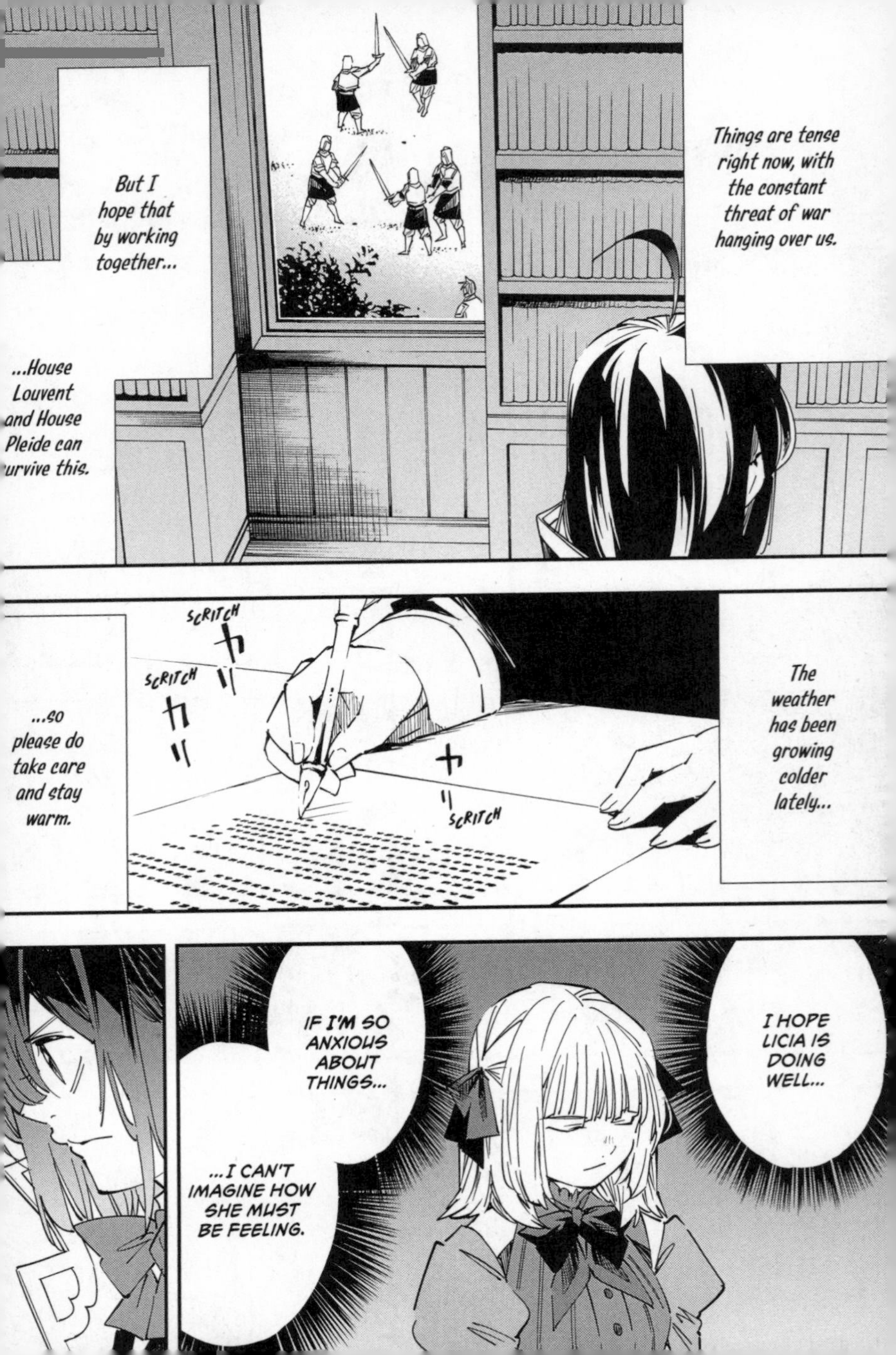
Things are tense right now, with the constant threat of war hanging over us.
But I hope that by working together...
...House Louvent and House Pleide can urvive this.
The weather has been growing colder lately...
カリ
SCRITCH
カリ
SCRITCH
カリ
SCRITCH
...so please do take care and stay warm.
I HOPE LICIA IS DOING WELL...
IF I'M SO ANXIOUS ABOUT THINGS...
...I CAN'T IMAGINE HOW SHE MUST BE FEELING.

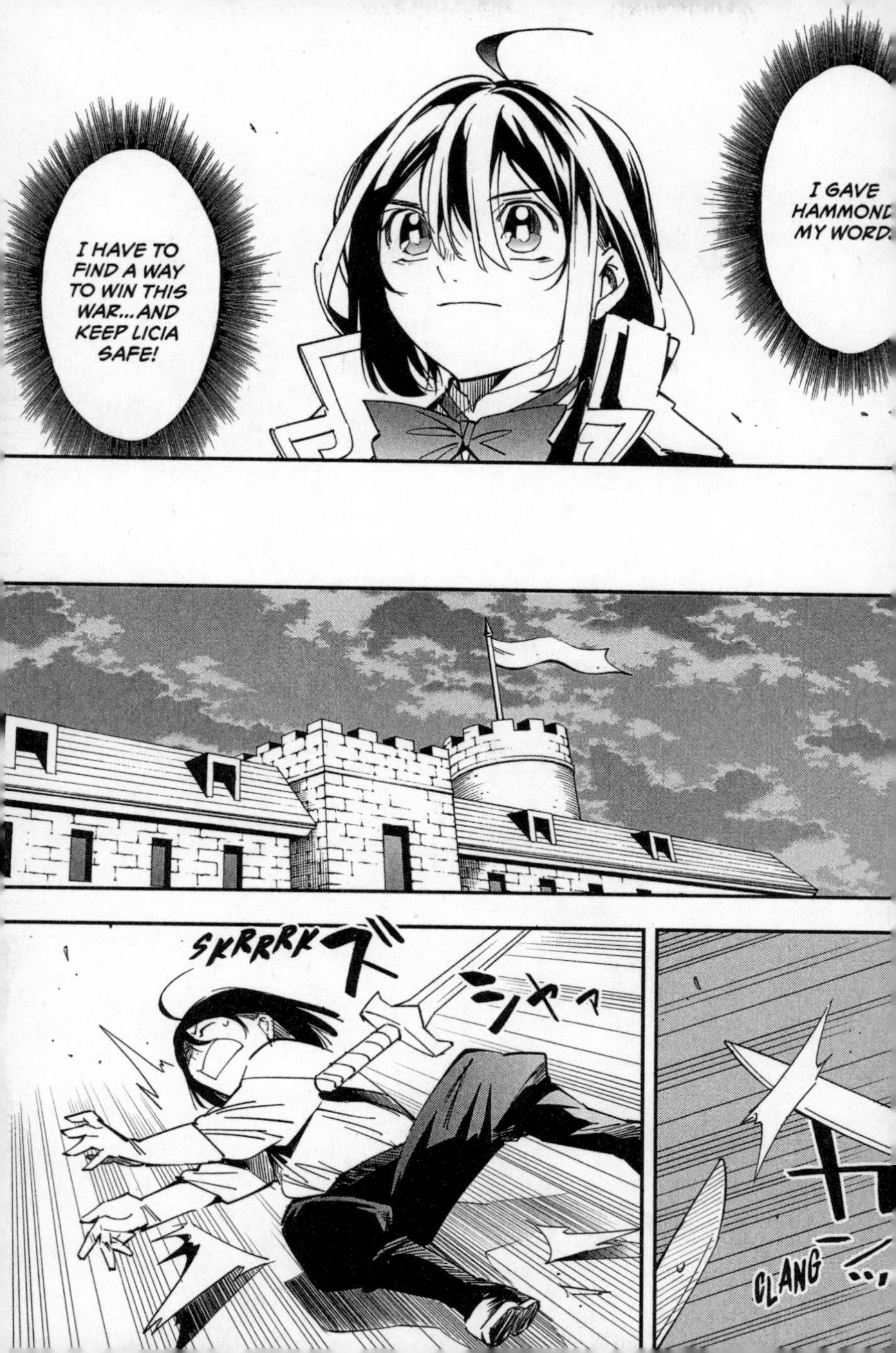
I GAVE HAMMOND MY WORD.
I HAVE TO FIND A WAY TO WIN THIS WAR...AND KEEP LICIA SAFE!
CLANG
SKRRRK

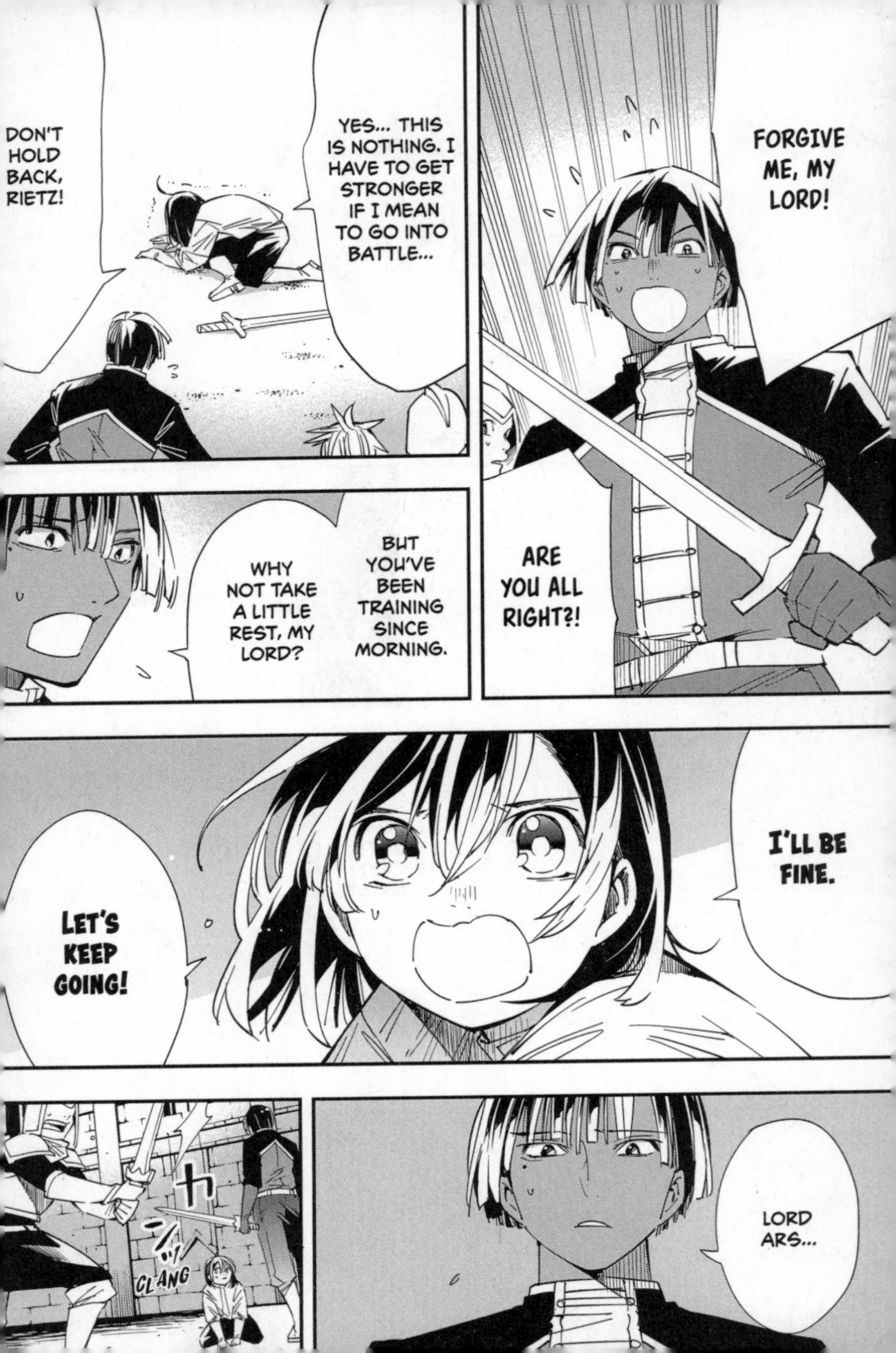

FORGIVE ME, MY LORD!
ARE YOU ALL RIGHT?!
YES... THIS IS NOTHING. I HAVE TO GET STRONGER IF I MEAN TO GO INTO BATTLE...
DON'T HOLD BACK, RIETZ!
BUT YOU'VE BEEN TRAINING SINCE MORNING.
WHY NOT TAKE A LITTLE REST, MY LORD?
I'LL BE FINE.
LET'S KEEP GOING!
LORD ARS...
CLANG

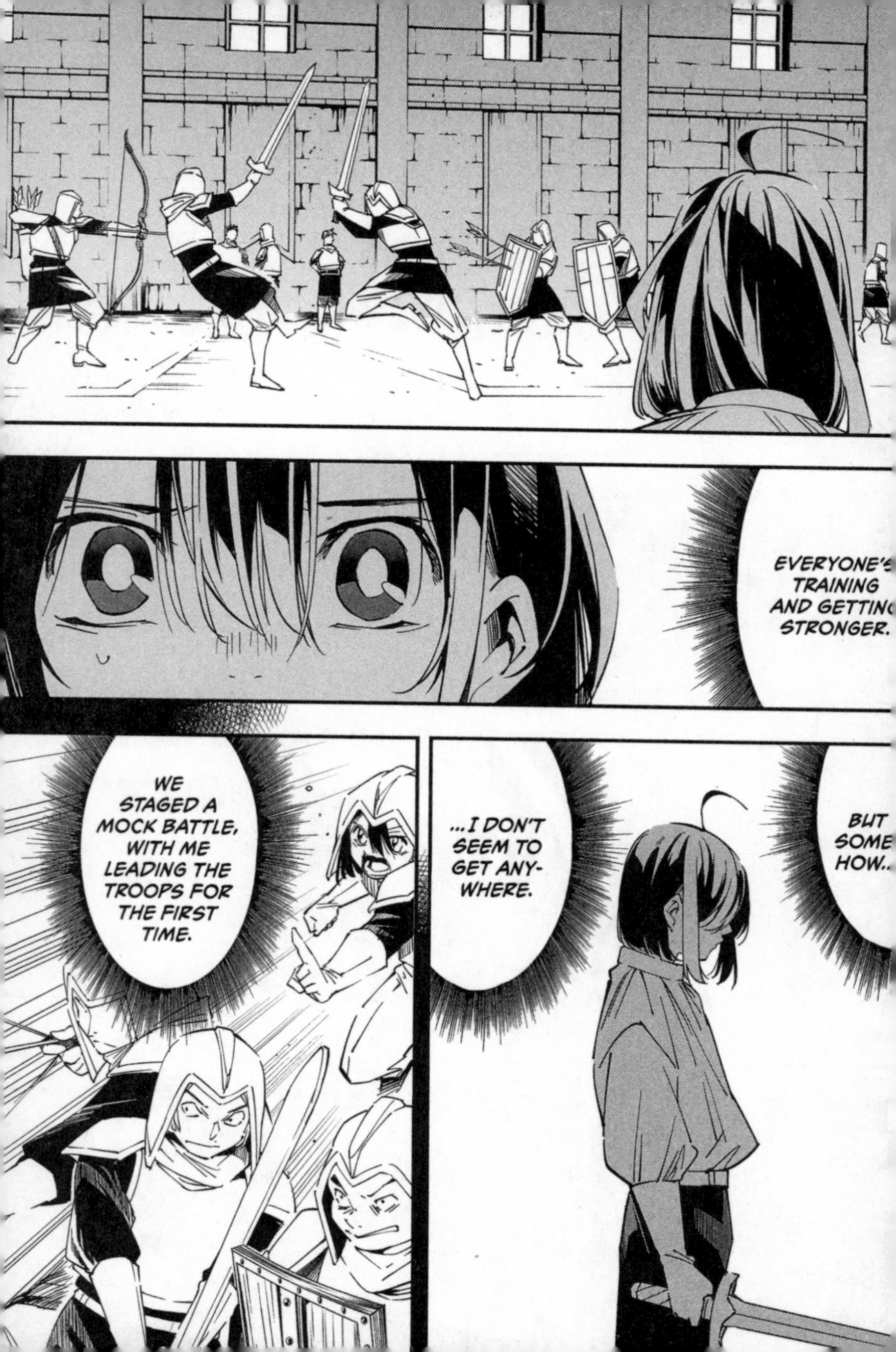
EVERYONE'S TRAINING AND GETTING STRONGER.
BUT SOMEHOW..
...I DON'T SEEM TO GET ANYWHERE.
WE STAGED A MOCK BATTLE, WITH ME LEADING THE TROOPS FOR THE FIRST TIME.

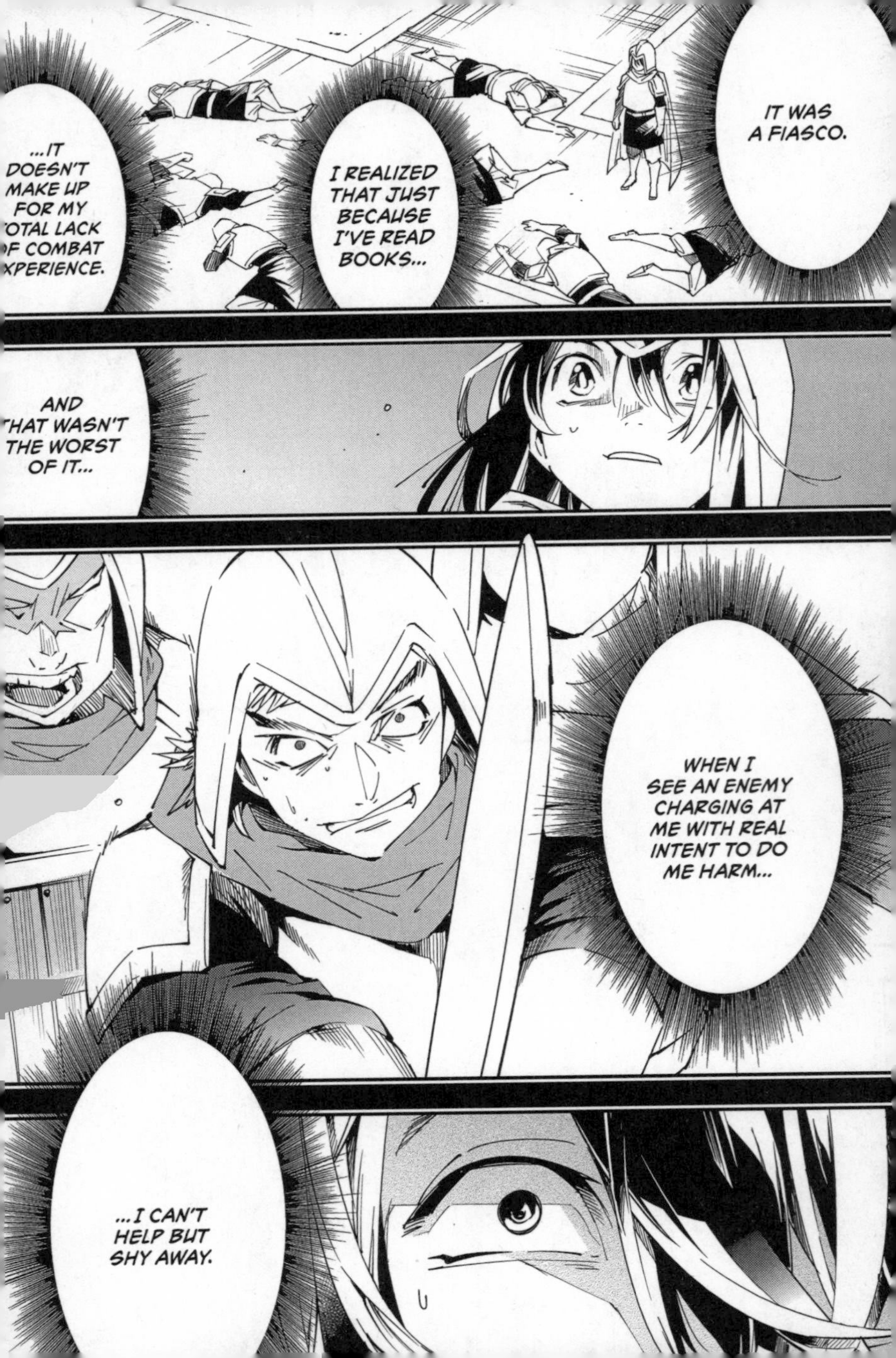
IT WAS A FIASCO.
I REALIZED THAT JUST BECAUSE I'VE READ BOOKS...
...IT DOESN'T MAKE UP FOR MY OTAL LACK F COMBAT XPERIENCE.
AND THAT WASN'T THE WORST OF IT...
WHEN I SEE AN ENEMY CHARGING AT ME WITH REAL INTENT TO DO ME HARM...
...I CAN'T HELP BUT SHY AWAY.

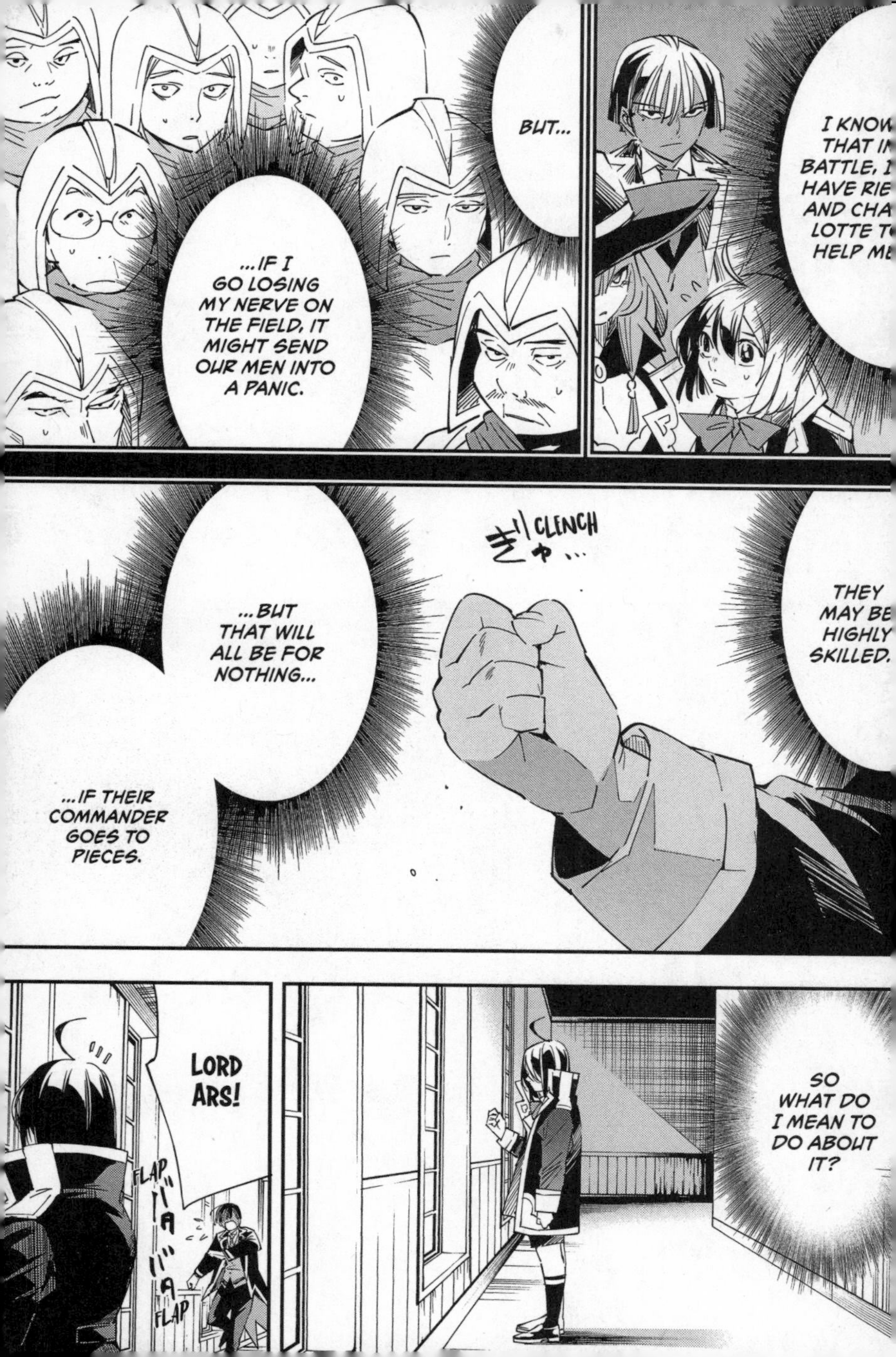

I KNOW THAT IN BATTLE, I HAVE RIE AND CHA LOTTE TO HELP ME
BUT...
...IF I GO LOSING MY NERVE ON THE FIELD, IT MIGHT SEND OUR MEN INTO A PANIC.
THEY MAY BE HIGHLY SKILLED.
ぎゅ... CLENCH
...BUT THAT WILL ALL BE FOR NOTHING...
...IF THEIR COMMANDER GOES TO PIECES.
SO WHAT DO I MEAN TO DO ABOUT IT?
LORD ARS!
バタバタ FLAP FLAP

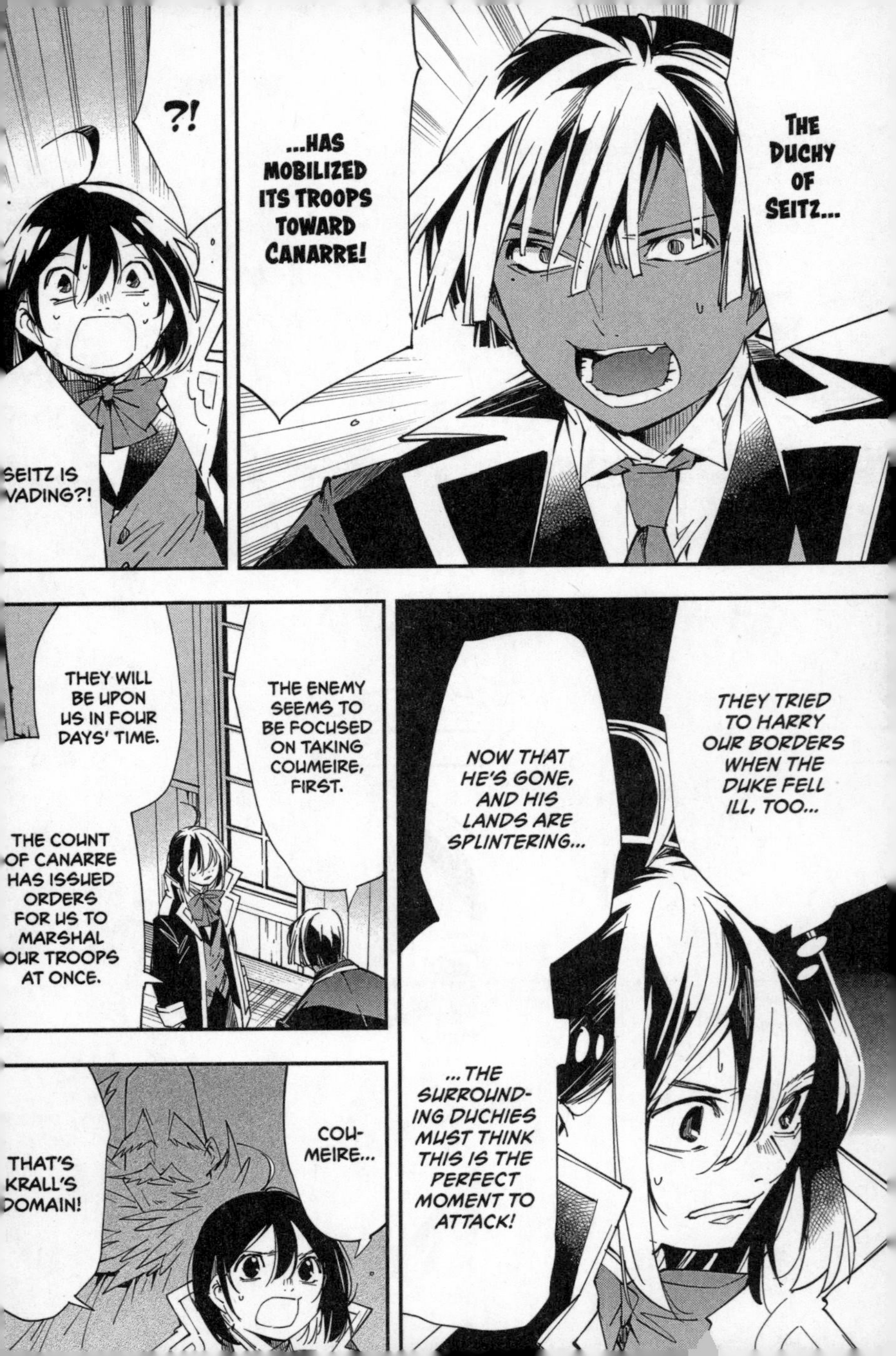
THE DUCHY OF SEITZ...
...HAS MOBILIZED ITS TROOPS TOWARD CANARRE!
?!
SEITZ IS
VADING?!
THEY TRIED TO HARRY OUR BORDERS WHEN THE DUKE FELL ILL, TOO...
NOW THAT HE'S GONE, AND HIS LANDS ARE SPLINTERING...
...THE SURROUND-ING DUCHIES MUST THINK THIS IS THE PERFECT MOMENT TO ATTACK!
THE ENEMY SEEMS TO BE FOCUSED ON TAKING COUMEIRE, FIRST.
THEY WILL BE UPON US IN FOUR DAYS' TIME.
THE COUNT OF CANARRE HAS ISSUED ORDERS FOR US TO MARSHAL OUR TROOPS AT ONCE.
COU-MEIRE...
THAT'S KRALL'S DOMAIN!

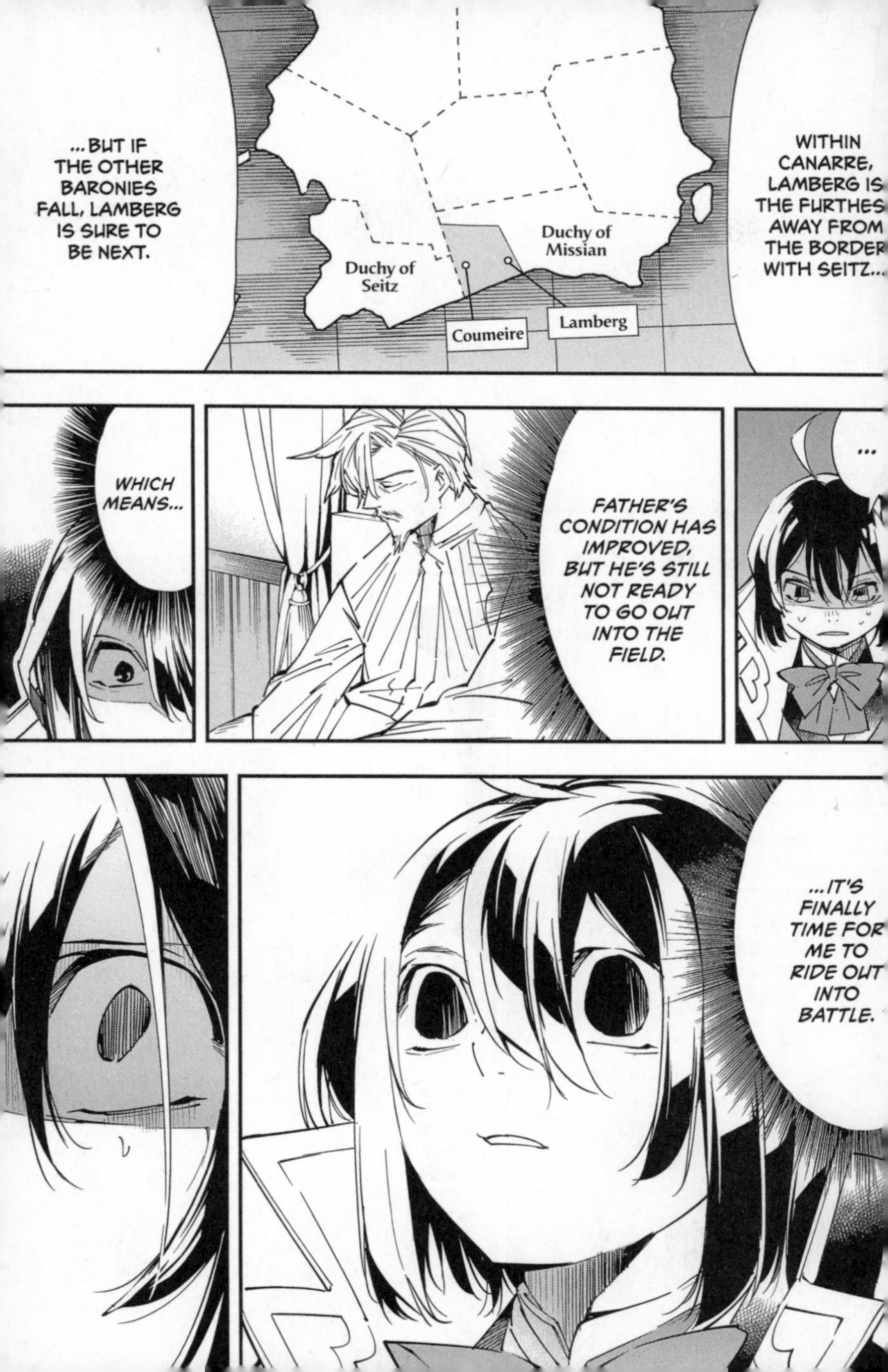

WITHIN CANARRE, LAMBERG IS THE FURTHES AWAY FROM THE BORDER WITH SEITZ...
Duchy of Missian
Lamberg
Duchy of Seitz
Coumeire
...BUT IF THE OTHER BARONIES FALL, LAMBERG IS SURE TO BE NEXT.
...
FATHER'S CONDITION HAS IMPROVED, BUT HE'S STILL NOT READY TO GO OUT INTO THE FIELD.
WHICH MEANS...
...IT'S FINALLY TIME FOR ME TO RIDE OUT INTO BATTLE.

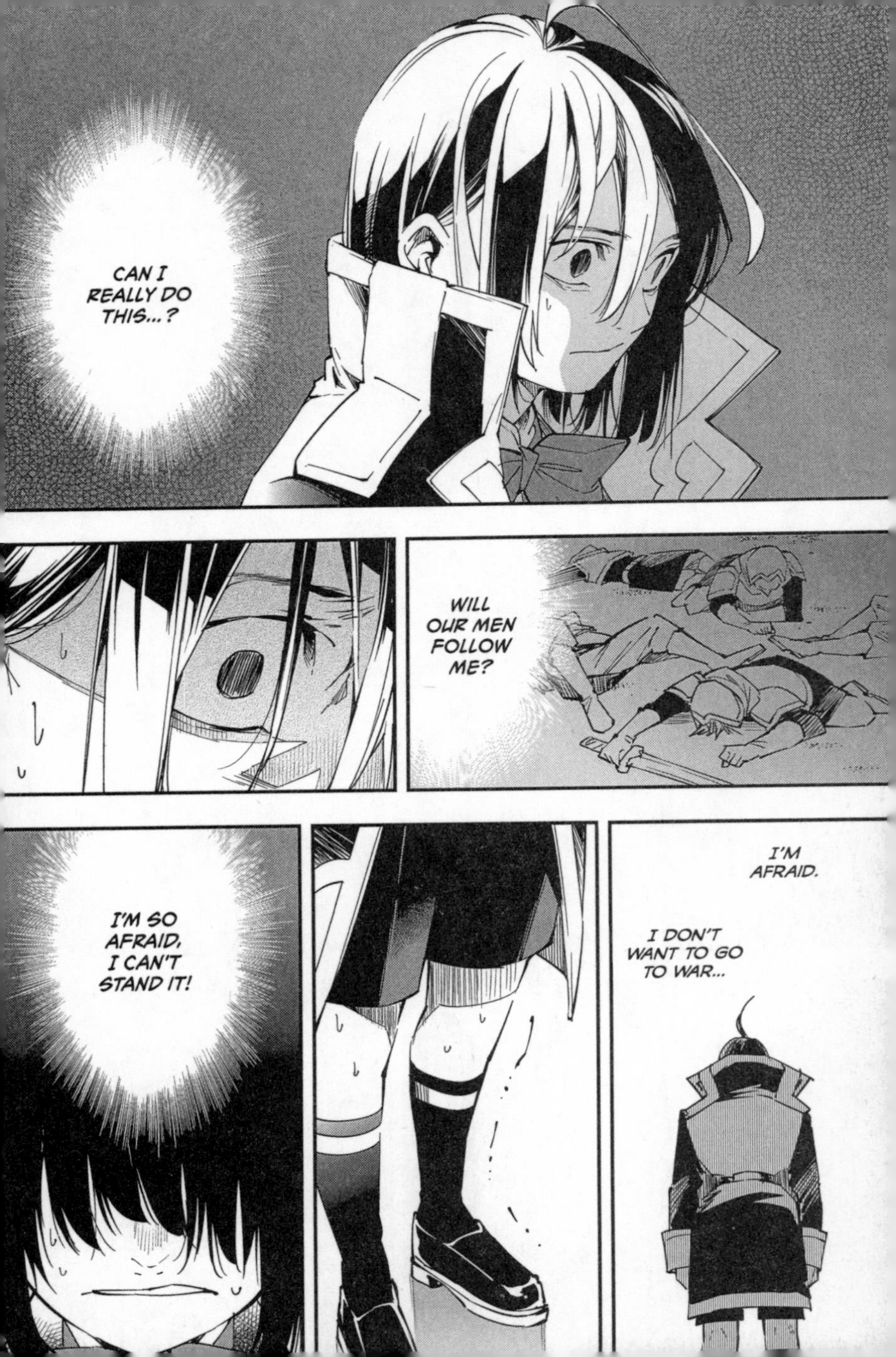
CAN I REALLY DO THIS...?
WILL OUR MEN FOLLOW ME?
I'M AFRAID.
I DON'T WANT TO GO TO WAR...
I'M SO AFRAID, I CAN'T STAND IT!

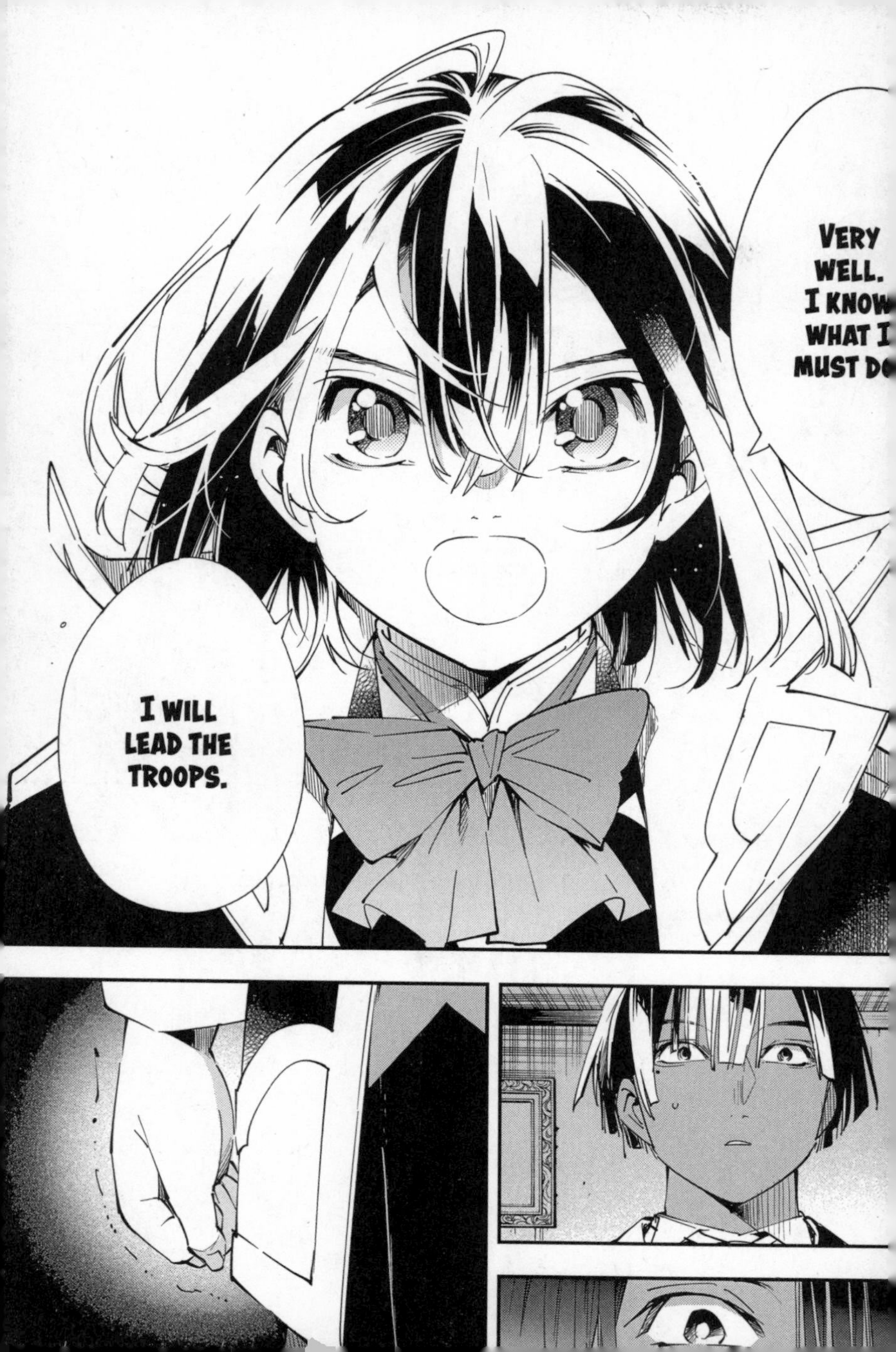
VERY WELL. I KNOW WHAT I MUST D
I WILL LEAD THE TROOPS.

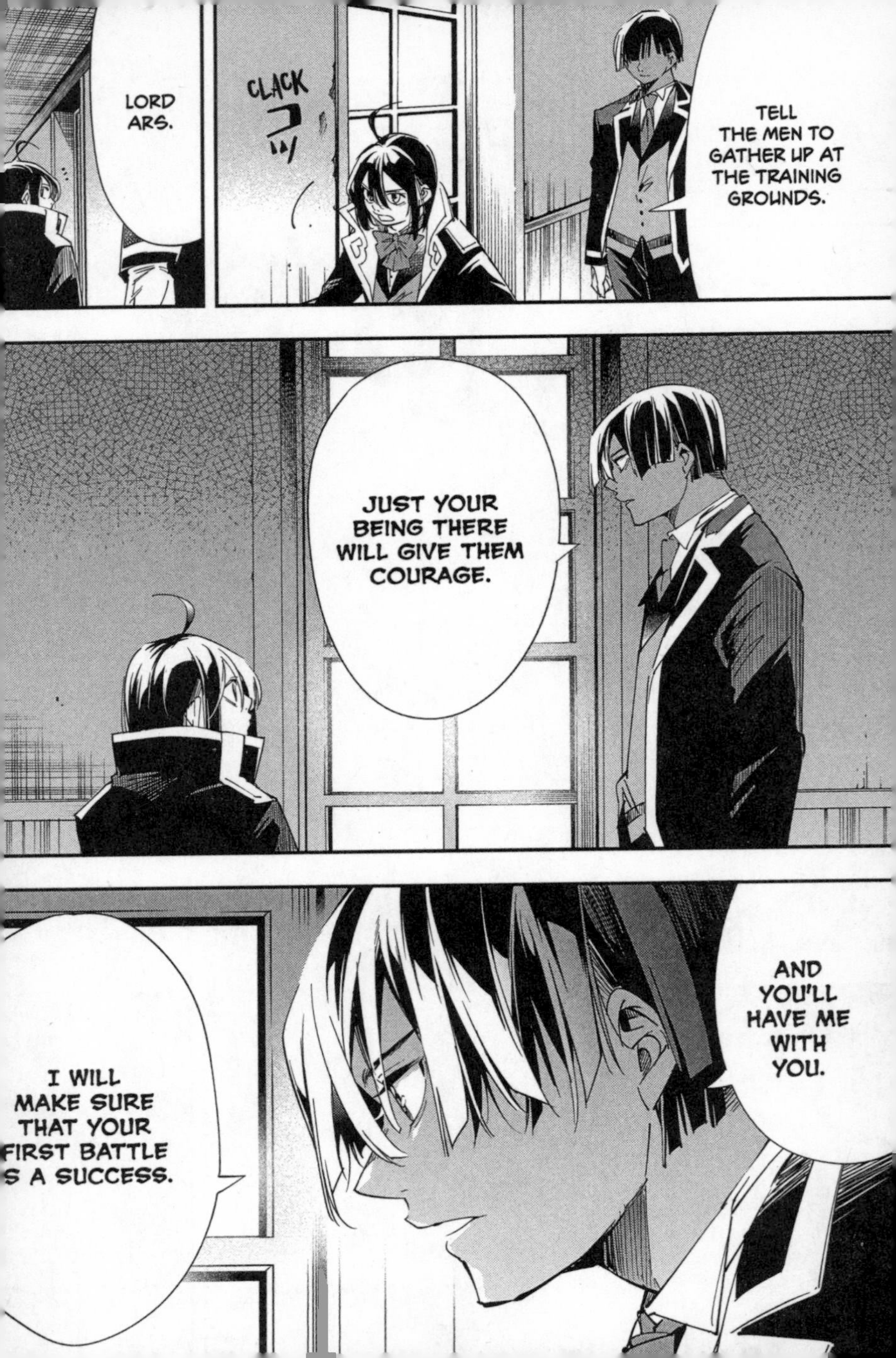
TELL THE MEN TO GATHER UP AT THE TRAINING GROUNDS.
CLACK
LORD ARS.
JUST YOUR BEING THERE WILL GIVE THEM COURAGE.
AND YOU'LL HAVE ME WITH YOU.
I WILL MAKE SURE THAT YOUR FIRST BATTLE S A SUCCESS.

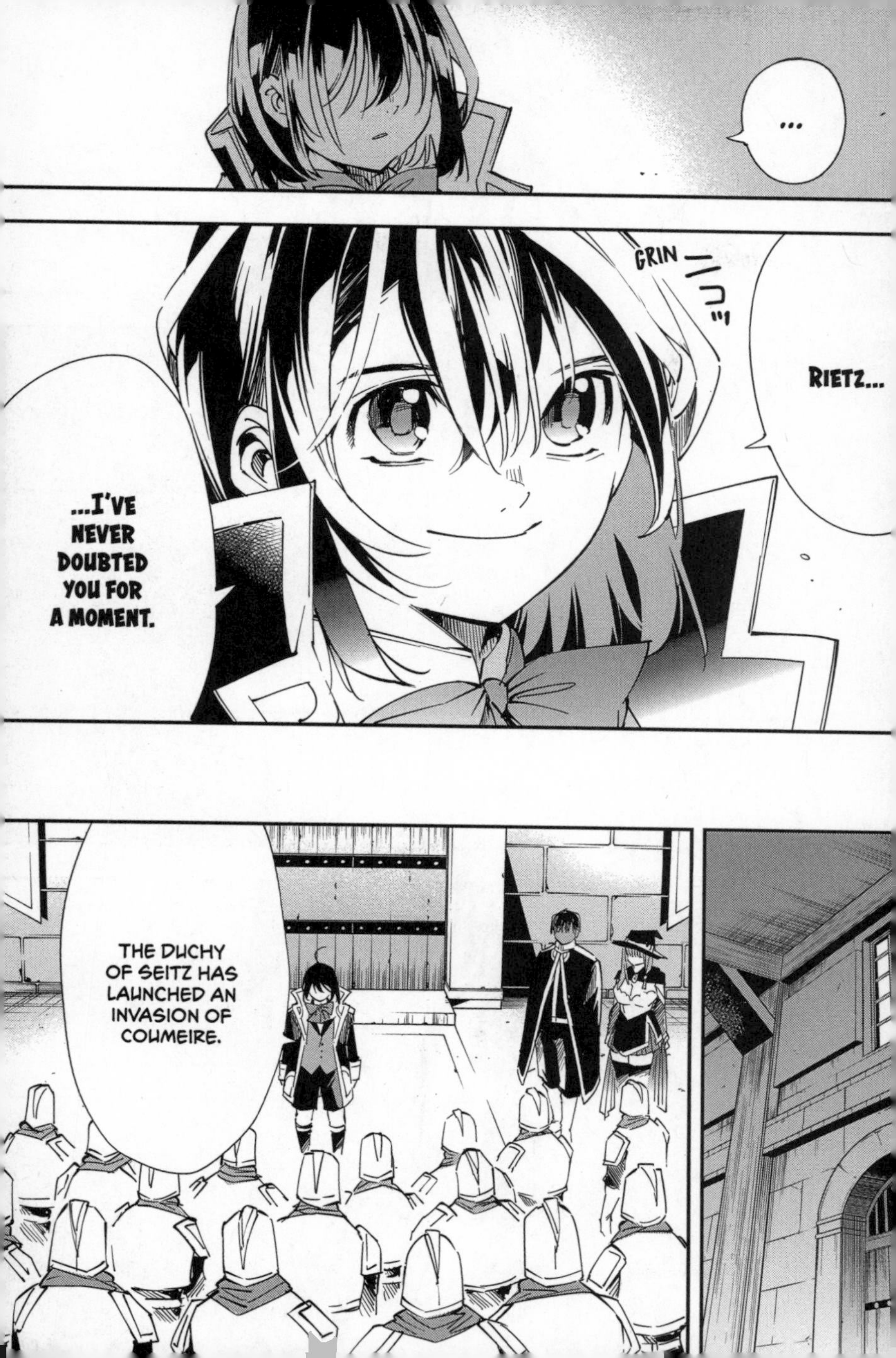
...
RIETZ...
GRIN
...I'VE NEVER DOUBTED YOU FOR A MOMENT.
THE DUCHY OF SEITZ HAS LAUNCHED AN INVASION OF COUMEIRE.

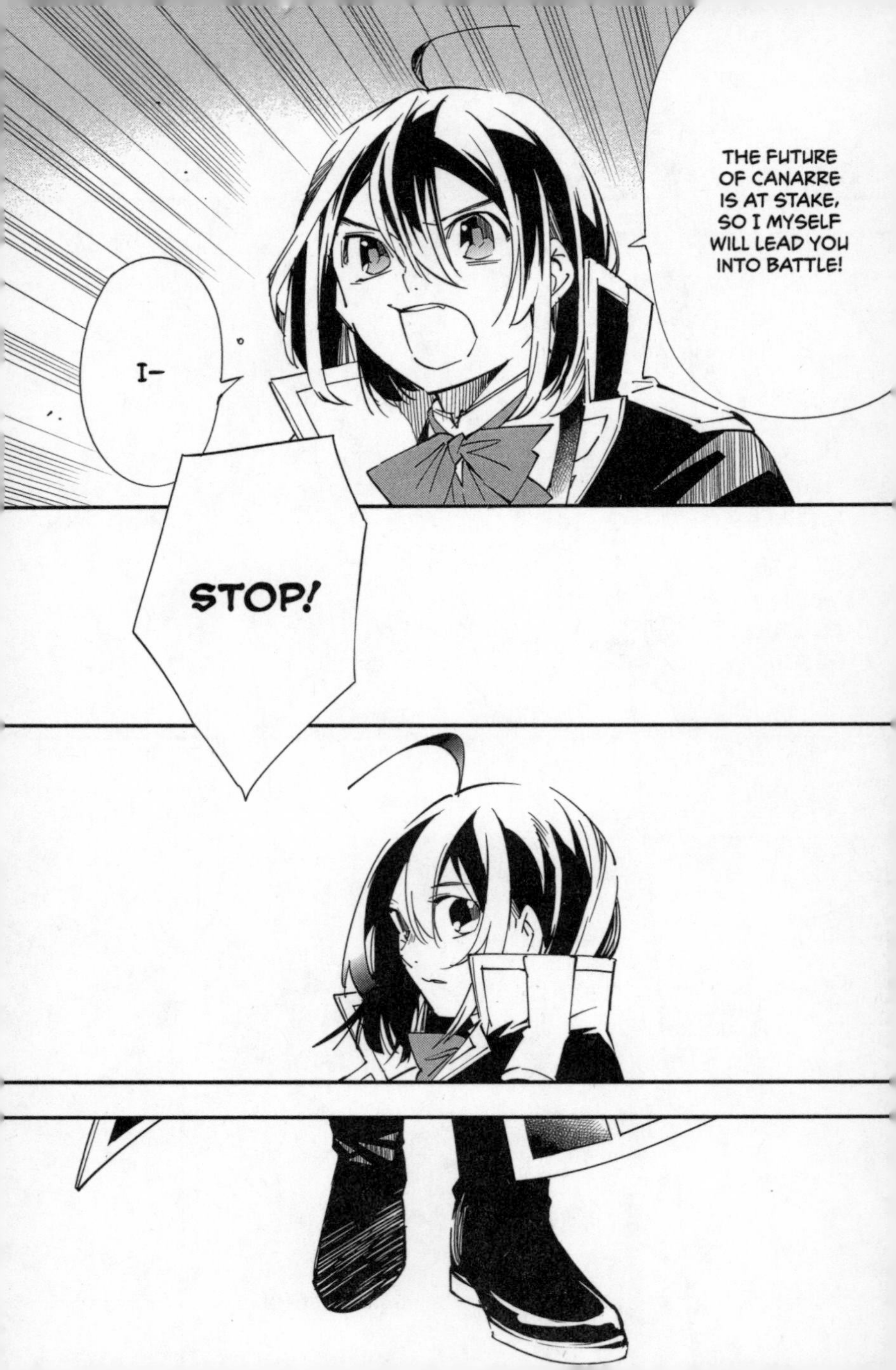
THE FUTURE OF CANARRE IS AT STAKE, SO I MYSELF WILL LEAD YOU INTO BATTLE!
I–
STOP!

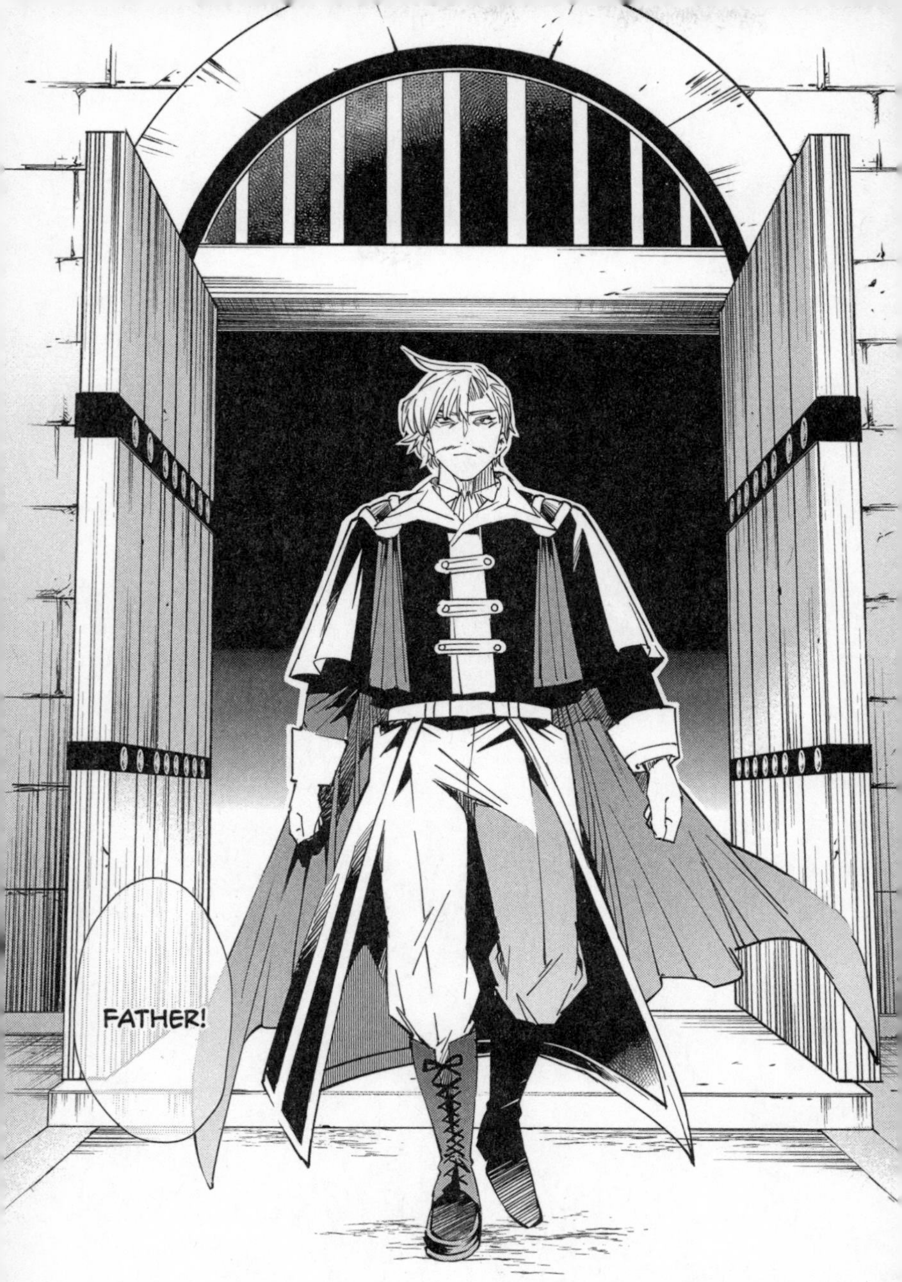
FATHER!

As a Reincarnated
ARISTOCRAT,
I'll Use My Appraisal Skill to
Rise in the World

Bonus Story

by Miraijin A

War had broken out in every corner of the Summerforth Empire. Peace became a distant memory, with local lords forced to defend themselves against deserters-turned-bandits who haunted the countryside in search of plunder. Before long, even the county of Canarre found itself beset.

A bull of a man stood amid a field of bloodied corpses. Brandishing a huge axe, he bellowed, "Ga, ha, ha, ha, ha, ha, ha! Come at me, you runts! I'll take you all at once! Let's see if you can bring down Robador the Greataxe!"

The man's rough-hewn face was covered in stubble, his crude clothing caked with grime. Everything about him screamed uncleanliness. He was, perhaps, exactly what people would picture when hearing the word "bandit." His name was Robador, and he led a group of bandits that was currently plaguing the Canarre countryside. To put it simply, the man was tough. So tough, in fact, that the soldiers sent out to exterminate the bandits now found themselves too cowed to approach him head-on. Things were truly looking bleak.

Just then, one of the soldiers strode out toward Robador. The man was young-looking, with blond hair. Though tall, he still stood a head shorter than the bandit. In his right hand he held a sword.

"Wh-who's that?" the other soldiers cried. "Come back here!" Still, the young man walked on.

Robador smirked. "What's this, boy? You mean to fight me alone? Ha, ha, ha! You've got guts, I'll give you that!"

"Nah, he's just a fool!" the bandit's men jeered. The young soldier ignored them, his confident smile never wavering.

"And you?" he asked. "Do you really mean to fight me alone? I'd come at me all at once, if I were you."

"What?" The bandit's face twisted with anger at the insolent remark. His smirk evaporated, replaced by an angry furrow across his brow.

"You must have a death wish," he sneered. "The rest of you, stay out of this! I'll cut him down myself." With that, he lifted his massive axe and brought it down in an arc.

"Too slow." The soldier nimbly avoided the blow, cutting off Robador's hand in the same motion. The bandit didn't even have time to process what had just happened. The soldier was already closing the gap and thrusting his sword into Robador's throat, pulling it away just as quickly.

"Gaah..." With a piteous wail, Robador toppled to the ground as blood gushed from his throat. In another heartbeat, he was dead.

Everything had happened so quickly that the soldiers and bandits alike could do nothing but look on, dumbfounded. Letting out a deep breath, the young soldier shouted, "That takes care of their leader! Now, see to the rest of them!"

He was not the leader of his troop; he was just one of the rank and file. Yet, seeing his tremendous display of skill, and hearing the steel in his voice, his comrades scrambled into action and charged the remaining bandits.

The bandits had just watched their leader, the man whom they had trusted above all others, defeated in the space of a breath. Such was their shock that they were unable to react to the soldiers' charge and went down one after another. The boldness of a single, nameless soldier had won the day against the brigands.

After the soldiers emerged victorious, one of them approached the mysterious young man. "Hey, that was really something. What's your name?"

"...Raven Louvent."

This feat of arms proved only the first of many for Raven Louvent, who would one day go on to become Baron Louvent.

✳✳✳

"Raven Louvent?"

Inside Canarre Castle, Count Lumeire Pyres was listening to a report from one of his advisors.

"Yes," said his advisor. "He made quick work of that ruffian, Robador, and has continued to distinguish himself ever since. They say he slew the bandit on his very first mission. His skill with the blade is startling, to say the least."

"What is his house?"

"It would appear that he comes from a family of farmers..."

"A farmer's boy, eh...? Hmm..."

It wasn't unheard of for sons of farmers to enlist in the army. Yet, most of the truly great soldiers came from wealthy families and received martial training from an early age.

Young Raven's astonishing prowess had piqued Lumeire's curiosity. "I'll admit, I'm intrigued," he said. "Canarre has never been known for the quality of its soldiers. We need all the able men we can get, and if I see that he's as skilled as people say, I may consider giving him a more important role. Can you summon him here?"

Following this meeting, Lumeire's advisor made arrangements for Raven to travel to Canarre Castle at once. It was only a few days before the count's men located Raven, who had come to live in Canarre using the earnings he'd received for his exploits in the field. Raven was eager to meet with Lumeire after hearing the details, and soon he was making his way to the castle. He came face to face with the count for the first time in the latter's chamber.

"So you're Raven," said Lumeire. "You've a good, bold look about you. How old are you?"

"Sixteen, sire."

"So young. I hear you've built yourself quite the reputation recently. Is that true?"

"Reputation? If putting down the leader of a small band of brigands is worth a reputation, then yes. I suppose I have."

Lumeire chuckled. "You think ridding the world of a man like Robador is no great feat? Some might call that impertinent. But I'd like to see if all the tales they tell about you are more than just that. What would you say to a mock duel with one of my men?

You'll use wooden swords. If you really are as strong as they say, I'll consider promoting you."

"I'll do it," Raven said at once. His eyes burned with the light of ambition.

"Ha, ha, ha. That's a bold glint in your eye. What does it mean? Do you really wish to serve me?"

"Doesn't every man dream of doing great deeds and moving up in the world? I don't wish to go to my grave with nothing to speak for but tilling the fields."

"Well, you're right about that. Show me what you can do, then. In fact... Yes... Let's see you fight Hammond, first."

The young man standing behind Lumeire gave a start, stammering, "M-me, m'lord? But I'm hardly your best soldier..."

"Why, where's the fun in starting him with the best?" the count asked lightly.

"So I'm just the opening act? Very well. If that is your wish."

Hammond came forward reluctantly to stand before Raven. Then some attendants brought each of them a wooden sword, and the two squared off. Hammond practically wilted under Raven's steely gaze. No sooner had Lumeire given them the signal than Raven burst into motion, knocking Hammond's sword out of his hands. The duel was over as quickly as it had begun.

"I see the stories were true," Lumeire nodded approvingly. "Excellent. Next!"

After that, Raven faced off against several of Lumeire's vassals, besting each of them in quick succession.

"In fact..." mused Lumeire, "I'd say the stories didn't

do you justice."

Raven appeared unfazed after the string of duels. "Is that all?" he asked cooly.

"Not quite. You'll face me, last."

"You, my lord?"

"That's right. Believe it or not, I'm a fair duelist. Seeing you fight is making me want to pick up a sword again. God knows, it's been a while." Grabbing a wooden sword, Lumeire took up a fighter's stance opposite Raven. "Feel free to attack," he said, and Raven soon obliged with a swing of his sword.

While Raven had sent all of his previous opponents' swords flying with the ferocity of his attacks, Lumeire managed to parry his initial stroke. Clearly, the man hadn't been lying about his abilities.

The duel continued. As the two traded blows, Lumeire thought to himself, "I'd say we're about evenly matched. But who knows how much stronger he could grow yet? The boy has tremendous talent."

The count couldn't help but break into a smile at his good fortune. Though Lumeire held his own against Raven for some time, his recent lack of exercise soon proved his undoing as his stamina began to flag. "I-I can't go on. I yield," Lumeire panted, dropping his sword.

"Will you take me on, then?" asked Raven, who still had energy to spare.

"Y-yes, of course. I'd be delighted to have you join us, Raven Louvent."

They shared a firm handshake. From that day on, Raven Louvent became a vassal to Count Lumeire.

Later, as Raven was preparing to depart the castle, a voice called out to him. "W-wait just a moment!"

It was Hammond, his opponent from the first duel.

"You're... Mammond, was it?" asked Raven.

"Mammond?! It's Hammond! Hammond Pleide!"

"Well? What do you need?"

"There's no need to be so cold! I happen to like a good fighter, and we're not far apart in age. So what do you say? Friends?"

Raven remained decidedly aloof, but Hammond appeared not to notice. Drawing closer, Hammond said, "I know! We should have supper together. I know a good place. We can get to know each other better over a meal."

"A good place? You're sure?"

"Yes! It'll be my treat."

"Lead the way," Raven said immediately; his stomach was growling.

The two young men talked about this and that as they ate. Though very different in temperament—Raven was reticent, where Hammond was gregarious—they were strangely well matched.

"I'm sure it can't be easy being a farmer," Hammond said, "but I have it hard, too, you know. I may be a noble, but I'm the fourth-born son. That means that unless my family is struck by some disaster, I inherit nothing. I'm not particularly talented, either, so my father expects little of me."

"Hmm."

"So tell me—how did you get so strong, Raven?"

"How? Just from fighting, I suppose. There's not much to it."

"Really, that's it?!" Hammond exclaimed; Raven made it sound so simple. "You look like someone who has great things ahead of him. I'm sure you'll go far in the world. Maybe you'll even have your own lands someday."

"That is the plan."

"There you go again, making it sound like it's the easiest thing in the world. Though truth be told, I'd like to make a name for myself, too."

"It's not as though there's no chance at all of you inheriting the title."

"It's not impossible, but it may as well be. I would inherit if my older brothers died, but unless I slip them all some poison, they're not likely to keel over dead anytime soon."

"Would you?" Raven asked pointedly. "Poison them, I mean."

"No!" cried Hammond. "They're good people, and I'd be sad to see my brothers dead. Anyhow, I don't see how I could defend our house all on my own..."

Waving this aside, Raven said, "I was only joking about the poison. But with all the fighting lately, death is always a possibility. You shouldn't be squeamish about it."

"Uh... W-well, I suppose you have a point. Say, if I inherit the family title, and you become a lord, too, why not have our children wed? I'd feel much better having you in the family."

Raven considered this for a moment. "That's an interesting thought," he said.

Hammond chuckled. "I was only joking. I've no

chance at all of inheriting. Besides, we only just met. Don't you think it's a little too soon to start making arrangements for our children?"

Hammond had laughed off the idea as though it were a wild fantasy... never guessing that a few decades later, that very thing would come to pass.

The End

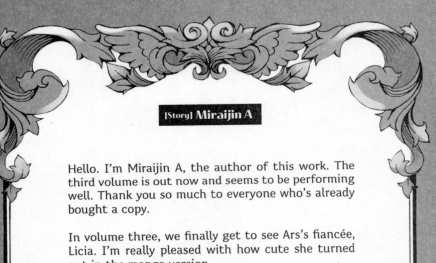

[Story] **Miraijin A**

Hello. I'm Miraijin A, the author of this work. The third volume is out now and seems to be performing well. Thank you so much to everyone who's already bought a copy.

In volume three, we finally get to see Ars's fiancée, Licia. I'm really pleased with how cute she turned out in the manga version.

I also wrote another bonus story for the back of the book. This short piece is meant to shine a spotlight on Lord Raven's past. What did you think? I've always wanted to write about it, since it doesn't get brought up much in the main narrative. If there's an opportunity to do another bonus story, I might even continue writing about Ars's father.

The narrative will undergo a big shift in volume four, becoming more of a full-scale war story. I think you'll find it even more entertaining, so I hope that you'll consider picking up the next volume.

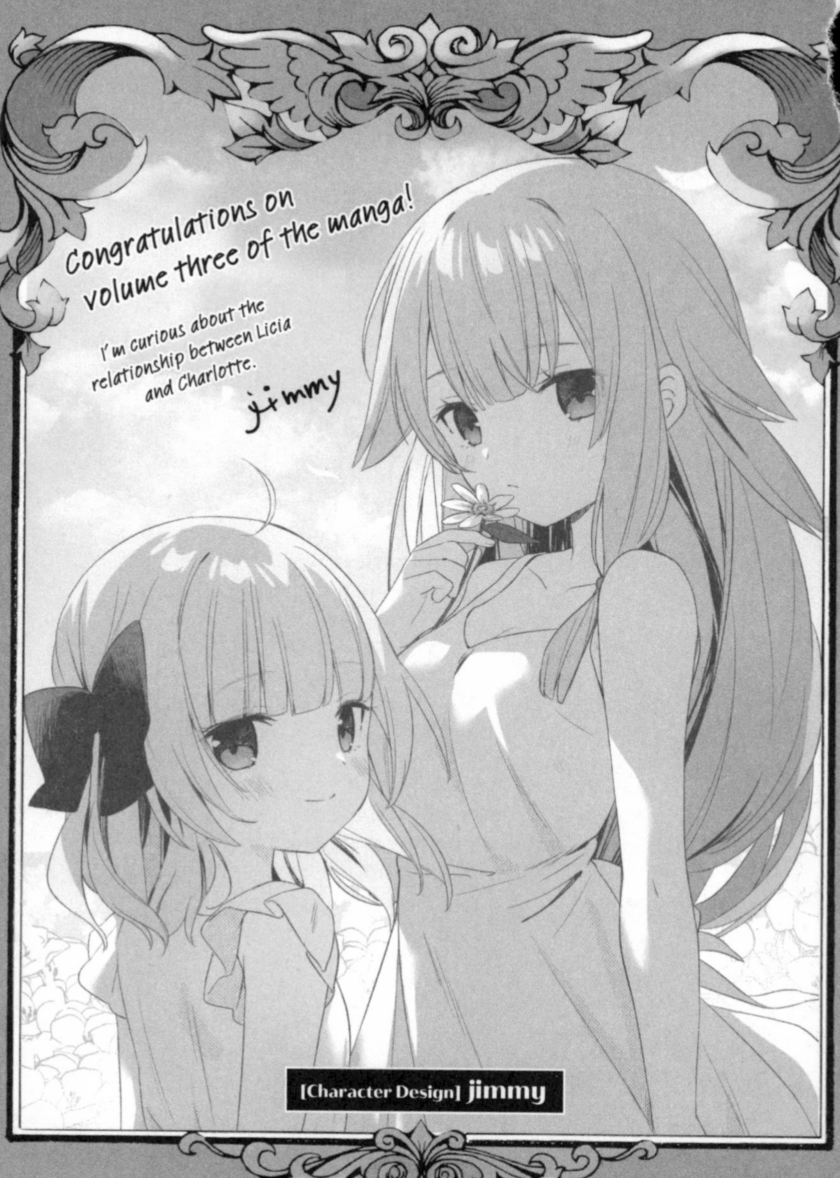
Congratulations on volume three of the manga!
I'm curious about the relationship between Licia and Charlotte.
jimmy
[Character Design] jimmy

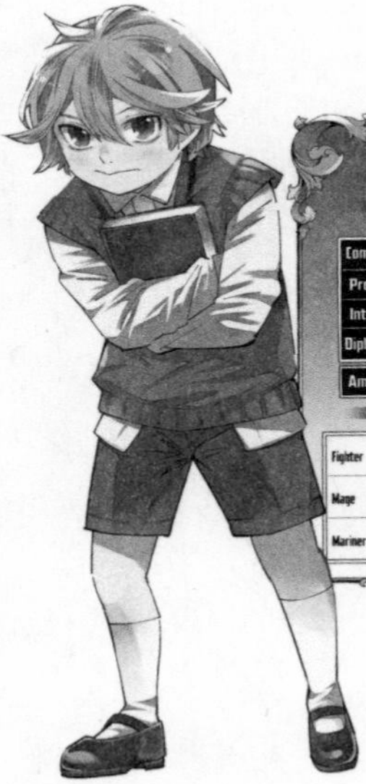

☆☆☆☆☆

Rosell Kischa - Age 8 ♂

Stats

	CURRENT	MAX
Command	40	88
Prowess	15	32
Intellect	88	109
Diplomacy	50	95
Ambition	21	

Aptitude

Fighter	D	Cavalier	D	Archer	C
Mage	C	Engineer	A	Armorer	A
Mariner	C	Pilot	A	Tactician	S

A Kodansha Trade Paperback Original

As a Reincarnated Aristocrat, I'll Use My Appraisal Skill to Rise in the World 3 copyright © 2021 Miraijin A/Natsumi Inoue/jimmy
English translation copyright © 2023 Miraijin A/Natsumi Inoue/jimmy

Published in the United States by
Kodansha USA Publishing, LLC, New York.

Publication rights for this English edition arranged through
Kodansha Ltd., Tokyo.

First published in Japan in 2021 by Kodansha Ltd., Tokyo
as *Tensei kizoku, kantei sukiru de nariagaru*, volume 3.

ISBN 978-1-64651-514-1

Printed in the United States of America.

9 8 7 6 5 4 3 2 1

Translation: Stephen Paul
Lettering: Nicole Roderick
Editing: Andres Oliver
Kodansha USA Publishing edition cover design by Pekka Luhtala

Publisher: Kiichiro Sugawara

Director of Publishing Services: Ben Applegate
Director of Publishing Operations: Dave Barrett
Publishing Services Managing Editors: Alanna Ruse, Madison Salters, with Grace Chen
Production Manager: Jocelyn O'Dowd

KODANSHA.US